A Dictionary of Mexican American Proverbs

Compiled *by* Mark Glazer

GREENWOOD PRESS
New York • Westport, Connecticut • London

Library of Congress Cataloging-in-Publication Data

Glazer, Mark.
   A dictionary of Mexican American proverbs.

   Includes indexes.
   1. Mexican American proverbs—Texas—Rio Grande
Valley—Dictionaries. I. Title.
PN6426.3.T4G5 1987   398'.9'61097644   87-23721
ISBN 0-313-25385-4 (lib. bdg. : alk. paper)

Library of Congress Catalog Card Number: 87-23721
ISBN: 0-313-25385-4

First published in 1987

Greenwood Press, Inc.
88 Post Road West, Westport, Connecticut 06881

Printed in the United States of America

∞™

The paper used in this book complies with the
Permanent Paper Standard issued by the National
Information Standards Organization (Z39.48-1984).

10 9 8 7 6 5 4 3 2 1

For my wife Diana, my mother Aimée and my son Errol,
all of whom have made my life worthwhile.

Contents

Preface

Proverbs have long held the interest of scholars and appealed
to the imagination of laymen. Collections of proverbs from
the Chicano community have been published but mainly in
nonsystematic works. This volume is an attempt at a multi-
faceted and systematic dictionary of Mexican American
proverbs. It differs from other proverb dictionaries
because it is based on currently utilized proverbs and adds
previously published materials in order to provide a compre-
hensive list. Also, it is the first annotated dictionary of
Chicano proverbs that includes contextual information and
states the frequency of male and female informants for each
proverb. It is hoped that all of this research and information provided will result in a work of interest and value
to the reader.

In preparing this volume, my work-study students helped me
in numerous ways; one of them, however, Mary Martinez,
stands out through her hard work and skill. It was through
her dedication and patience that the annotations were com-
pleted. A special thanks is also due to Janie C. Pena, who
skillfully typed the manuscript. I am, however, responsible
for the final configuration of the dictionary.

Introduction

The tapestry of American culture is a mosaic of the folklore
and folklife of diverse ethnic and cultural groups; one such
group is the Mexican American community. In spite of its
long history and fascinating culture, this community has
only recently come to national attention and become the
focus of major research. This dictionary is the result of
an effort to study Mexican American folklore and folklife
in the Lower Rio Grande Valley of Texas and is based on a
collection of proverbs from this area, to which was added
data from previously published materials. The Lower Rio
Grande Valley is a major area of Mexican American demographic and cultural concentration and is one of the richest
regions of Chicano folklore and folklife in the country.
It is made up of the Starr, Hidalgo, Cameron, and Willacy
counties. Folklore research in this area has yielded
excellent results and over the last nine years an archive
of considerable volume: over 22,215 items have been
deposited in The Rio Grande Folklore Archive at Pan American
University, Edinburg, Texas.

Of these items, 986 are proverbs; when doubles and
variants are included, the collection totals 3,485 proverbs.
Proverbs are traditional sayings with roots in oral tradi-
tion and folklore. Since they are appropriate comments on
or solutions to "common" human situations, they have often
been called "the wisdom of the folk." This, it may be
speculated, may also be why so many people dislike proverbs
in today's society, which emphasizes individuality, and in
which "common" human situations are not supposed to exist.
Such situations are, however, quite numerous in traditional
settings and of course remain so in contemporary culture.
The 986 proverbs listed in this dictionary, exclusive of
variants, suggest an equal number of common human situations
where they would apply.

The use of a proverb is a way to make a potentially
profound and culturally appropriate statement in a common
but difficult human situation. It is, however, essential
for a person to use a particular proverb in the correct

context. If not, the user of the proverb might commit a
potentially serious and possibly embarrassing faux pas. For
example, if someone's lover is going away for a short time,
it would be correct to say, "Love at a distance makes the
heart grow fonder." On the other hand, if someone receives
a "Dear John" letter, this proverb would not be appropriate
at all. Perhaps a more appropriate proverb to use in this
instance would be the Spanish, "Amor de lejos amor de pendejos" (Love at a distance is love for fools).

In determining what is considered a proverb, it is not
sufficient, however, for a saying, or dicho in Spanish, to
be used in an appropriate setting: to be recognized as a
proverb, the saying has to be a fixed form, always using the
same set of words and structure, and conforming to a culture's repretory of common but difficult human situations.
If not in fixed form, it will not be recognized as a proverb
and therefore will not have the desired impact. For example,
in English one says, "Business is business," and in an
appropriate context its meaning is obvious. On the other
hand, if one said, "Business is the market" instead of
"Business is business," this would not be the use of a
proverb. The proverb is in fixed form and therefore recog-
nizable as such, while the other statement is a personal
statement and not proverbial.

As one of the major genres of oral folklore, proverbs
have been studied in detail in many parts of the world,
though very little scholarly work has been done exclusively
on Mexican American proverb collections since Aurelio M.
Espinoza's pioneering work of 1913 (see Bibliography). The
publication of this first annotated dictionary of Chicano
proverbs is then especially significant. To achieve our
research goals the following methods and approaches were
utilized in the preparation of the dictionary.
A. Approaches: The dictionary is based on a collection of
3,485 items, 986 of which are proverbs and the remaining
2,499 being duplicates and/or variants of these proverbs.
The collection was developed on the basis of a survey
utilizing a collection form (see Appendices). The form of
entry includes the following information: the proverb in
its original Spanish form(s), an English translation or
interpretation, contextual information, and demographic data
on the informant of the proverb. The entries in the dictionary include the proverbs collated from the collection
form plus annotations from published sources, which complete
each entry.
B. Method and Presentation of Data: Based on the proverbs
obtained through the collection forms and previously published materials, the dictionary includes specific information for each of the 986 proverbs. Every proverb is listed
alphabetically in Spanish by the underlined key word,
usually the first noun or verb in the proverb, and assigned
an entry code consisting of a number and a letter. Where
there are variants, the most common is given as the entry.
Each variant is listed and assigned an entry code consisting
of the entry number and succeeding alphabetical letter. For
example, on page 4, entries 11(A) and 12(A) have no variants,

while entry 13 offers five forms of the proverb: 13(A),
13(B), 13(C), 13(D), and 13(E). An English translation or
interpretation of every proverb is provided and a represen-
tative example from the contextual information/informants'
comments is given. The number of times the proverb was
reported is stated, as is the number of male and female informants who reported the proverb and its variants. Finally,
previously published similar proverbs are noted with their
sources and annotated with reference to the Rio Grande collection; variant forms are given.

Published sources are noted by author and page number.
Full citations may be found in the "Bibliography and Key
to Annotations" immediately following this introduction.
The locations from which proverbs were collected in the
published sources are provided in the "List of Locations
for Annotated Materials" directly after the bibliography.

Data that would have been difficult and somewhat irre-
levant to include in individual entries are summarized in
a series of tables in the appendix section following the
proverb entries. Tables for the following items pertaining
to the informants are included: country of birth, languages
spoken, ethnic group, sex, age, source from whom informant
heard the proverb, informant's occupation, date proverb was
first heard, and place collected. The subject index, in
both Spanish and English versions, supplements the key-word
entry system by providing the reader with topical access to
the proverbs. Recognizing that most readers are unlikely
to be seeking a proverb with the initial key word in mind,
we have prepared the index based on content analysis. We
hope it will prove useful for locating proverbs.
C. Analysis of Data: On the basis of the data, the following can be said about the informants from the Lower Rio
Grande Valley who supplied the proverbs.

About 62% of the informants were born in the United
States and considered themselves Mexican American, while 27%
considered themselves Mexican. Most of the latter by defi-
nition, however, also were Mexican Americans. Sixty-five
percent of the informants were bilingual in English and
Spanish, while 30% spoke only Spanish and 2% only English.

Of the 95% of the informants of whom gender information
was gathered, it is interesting to note that 65% were female
while 30% were male. Of the female informants, 36% were
between 21 and 50 years of age, which signifies that the
use or at least knowledge of proverbs is very active among
Mexican American women. This compares with 17% of the males
of the same age group. Therefore, the proverb seems to be
a predominantly female form of folklore within the Chicano
community. This statement is strengthened by the fact that
24% of the informants had heard the proverbs from their
mothers, while only about 15% had heard them from their
fathers.

The two most common occupations of our informants were
housewife (28.3%) and student (25.3%); after these, the most
common categories were clerical (7.7%), professional (6.85%),
and craftsmen (6.0%).

It is curious that the years most proverbs were heard
by our informants for the first time were 1950, 1960, 1970,

and 1979. Edinburg, McAllen, Pharr, Mission, Harlingen,
Weslaco, and Mercedes, Texas, were the cities and towns
where proverbs were most commonly collected. Some proverbs,
as expected, were more often reported than others.
    An analysis of the 3,485 proverbs collected in this
survey of the Mexican American community of the Lower Rio
Grande Valley of Texas revealed that 20.02%, approximately
one-fifth of the total collection is made up of only 16
proverbs. This represents a total of 698 occurrences,
counting doubles and variants. These proverbs can be
grouped around the following three categories: (A) social
issues, (B) making a living, and (C) getting in trouble:
A. Social Issues:

1. [No. 30] Amor de lejos, amor de pendejos : Love at a
    distance is love for fools (42 occurrences).
2. [No. 662] Ojos que no ven, corazón que no siente :
    Eyes that do not see, heart that does not feel (54
    occurrences, 1.54%).
3. [No. 695] De tal palo tal astilla : From such a stick
    such a splinter (56 occurrences, 1.60%).
4. [No. 702] Panza llena, corazón contento : Belly full,
    heart content (36 occurrences, 1.03%).
5. [No. 800] Dime con quien andas y te dire quien eres :
    Tell me with who you walk and I will tell you who you
    are (91 occurrences, 2.61%).
6. [No. 864] El sordo no oye pero compone : The deaf does
    not hear but he composes (41 occurrences, 1.17%).
7. [No. 940] Más vale solo que mal acompañado : It is
    better alone than in bad company (33 occurrences,
    0.91%).
Considering doubles and variants, these 7 proverbs were
reported 353 times, accounting for 10.13% of the collection
and indicating the importance of social issues in the Mexican
American community.
    Also, the single most common proverb (No. 5 above)
stresses the importance of appropriate company as does No.
seven, and these two make up roughly 3.5% or roughly 122 of
all the proverbs collected.
B. Making a Living:

8. [No. 320] El que madruga, Dios le ayuda : He who early
    rises will be helped by God (38 occurrences, 1.09%).
9. [No. 324] El que mucho abarca, poco aprieta : He who
    embraces a lot, squeezes less (47 occurrences, 1.34%).
10. [No. 565] No dejes para mañana lo que puedes hacer hoy
    : Don't leave for tomorrow what you can do today (37
    occurrences, 1.06%).
11. (No. 606] El muerto al poso y el vivo al negocio : The
    dead to the grave and the live to his business (29
    occurrences, 0.83%).
12. [No. 686] Más vale un pájaro en la mano que cien volando
    : Better to have one bird in the hand than one-hundred
    flying (50 occurrences, 1.43%).
    With variants, these proverbs total 201 proverbs or
5.76% of the collection. Interestingly, the most common

proverbs here stress the importance of not going overboard
as one approaches a task (see Nos. 9 and 12 above). These
two proverbs account for 2.77% of the total collection or
approximately 96 proverbs.
C. Getting in Trouble:

13. [No. 89] En boca cerrada no entran moscas : No fly will
    get in a closed mouth (31 occurrences, 0.88%).
14. [No. 131] Camaron que se duerme se lo lleva la co-
    rriente : Shrimp that sleeps will be taken by a current
    (40 occurrences, 1.14%).
15. [No. 337] El que no habla, Dios no lo ayuda : He who
    doesn't talk, God doesn't hear (39 occurrences, 1.11%).
16. [No. 941] Mas vale tarde que nunca : It is better late
    than never (34 occurrences, 0.97%).
    With variants, the total for the proverbs above is 144
or 4.13% of the total collection. The emphasis here is on
keeping àlert, with No. 14 representing 1.14% of the total
collection. In summary, the most prevalent proverbs concern issues which are "common" human situations, and the 16
proverbs above seem to be the most often mentioned in the
Mexican American community.

Bibliography
and Key to Annotations

Adame, Ramon. Dichos Mexicanos. El Paso, Texas: Southwest Training Institute, Inc., 1980.

Alcala Venceslada, Antonio. Vocabulario Andaluz. Madrid: Real Academia Española, 1951.

Aranda, Charles. Dichos: Proverbs and Sayings From the Spanish. Santa Fe, New Mexico: The Sunstone Press, 1977.

Armas, Daniel. Diccionario de la Expresión Popular Guatemateca. Guatamala City: (Tip Naccional), 1971.

Arora, Shirley L. Proverbial Comparisons and Related Expressions in Spanish. Los Angeles, California: Folklore Studies (29) University of California Press, 1977.

Ballesteros, Octavio A. Mexican Proverbs: The Philosophy, Wisdom and Humor of a People. Burnet, Texas: Eakin Press, 1979.

Benavides Sumpter, Magdalena, ed. Discovering Folklore Through Community Resources. Austin: Dissemination and Assessment Center for Bilingual Education, 1978.

Caballero, Ramon. Diccionario de Modismos de la Lengua Castellana. Buenos Aires: Libreria de Ateneo, 1947.

"California Spanish Proverbs and Adages." Western Folklore (3), 1944: 121-23.

Campa, Arthur L. Sayings and Riddles in New Mexico. Albuquerque, University of New Mexico, 1937.

Bibliography

Cerda, Gilberto, Berta Cabaza and Julieta Farias. Vocabu-
    lario Español de Texas. 2 ed. Austin and London:
    University of Texas Press, 1970.

Cobos, Ruben. Southwestern Spanish Proverbs-Refranes
    Españoles Del Sudoeste. Cerillos, New Mexico: San
    Marcos Press, 1973.

Conde, Manuel. Dichos Ciertos...y Ciertos Dichos. Mexico,
    D.F.: B. Costa-Amic, 1971.

Correas, Gonzalo. Vocabulario de Refranes y Frases Prover-
    biales. (1627), ed. 1. Combet. Bordeaux 1967.

Covarrubias Horozco, Sebastian de. Tesoro de la Lengua
    Castellana O Española segun la Impresión de 1611, con
    las Adiciones de Benito Renegio Hoydens Publicadas en
    la de 1674. Ed. Martin de Riquer. Barcelona: S.A.
    Horta, 1943.

Chavez, Tibo J. New Mexican Folklore of the Rio Abajo.
    Portales, New Mexico: Bishop Printing Co., 1972.

De Barros, Alonso. Refranero Español. 7th Edition.
    Madrid: Ediciones Ibericas, 1968.

Espinosa, Aurelio M. "New Mexican Spanish Folklore Parts
    IV and V." Journal of American Folklore, XXVI (1913),
    97-123.

Espinosa, Francisco De. Refranero (1527-1547). Ed. Eleanor
    S. O'Kane (Boletin de la Real Academia Española, Anejo
    18). Madrid 1967.

Galvan, Roberto A. and Richard Teschner. El Diccionario del
    Español Chicano. Silver Spring, Maryland: Institute
    of Modern Languages, (1977): 124-35.

Gamiz, E. Colección de Refranes, Proverbios y Otros Expre-
    siones Que Se Usan En El Estado De Durango. In:
    Investigaciones Linguisticas 4 (1937): 73-94.

Glazer, Mark, Ph.D. Flour From Another Sack and Other Pro-
    verbs, Folk Belief, Tales, Riddles and Recipes. Edin-
    burg, Texas: Pan American University Printshop, 1982.

Jaramillo Lodoño, Agustin. Testamento del Paisa. 3rd
    Edition. Medillin: Bedout, 1962: 359-429.

Lea, Aurora Lucero-White. Literary Folklore of the Hispanic
    Southwest. San Antonio, Texas: Naylor Company, 1953.

Lucero-White, Aurora. "The Folklore of New Mexico. Volume
    1 (1941)" in Hispano Cultura of New Mexico. ed. Carlos
    E. Cortez. New York: Arno Press (1976): 33-36.

MacArthur, Mildred Yorba. California Spanish Proverbs. San
     Francisco: Colt Press, 1944.

Maldonado, Felipe C. R. Refranero Clasico Español y Otros
     Dichos Populares. Madrid: Taurus Ediciones. 1960
     and 1966.

Martinez Press, Jose. Dichos Dicharachos y Refranes Mexi-
     canos. Mexico D.F.: Editores Mexicanos Unidos, S.A.
     1977.

Molera, Frances M. "California Spanish Proverbs." Western
     Folklore (6) (1947): 65-67.

Paredes, Americo. "Dichos" Mexican American Authors. ed.
     Americo Paredes and Raymund Paredes. Boston: Houghton
     Mifflin, 1977: 27-34.

Perez, Soledad. "Mexican Folklore from Austin, Texas" in
     The Healer of Los Olmos and Other Mexican Folklore.
     (Texas Folklore Society Publications 25) ed. William
     Hudson. Dallas: Southern Methodist University Press,
     1951: 118-25.

Robe, Stanley ed. Antologia del Saber Popular: A Selection
     from Various Genres of Mexican Folklore Across Borders.
     Los Angeles: University of California, Los Angeles,
     Chicano Studies Center, 1971.

Rodriguez Marin, Francisco. Doce Mil Seiscientos Refranes
     Mas. Madrid. 1930.

Rodriguez Marin, Francisco. Mas de Veintiun Mil Refranes
     Castellanos No Contenidos en la Copiosa Colección Del
     Maestro Gonzalo Correas. Madrid. 1926.

Rubio, Darío. Refranes, Proverbios y Dichos y Dicharachos
     Mexicanos. Mexico, D.F.: A.P. Marquez. 1940.

Santamaria, Francisco Jr. Diccionario General de America-
     nismos . 3 Vols. Mexico, D.F.: Pedro Robledo, 1942.

Sbarbi, J.M. Gran Diccionario de Refranes de la Lengua
     Española. Buenos Aires: 1943.

Vasquez, Lobardo Keno Dr., María Enriqueta Vasquez. Region-
     al Dictionary of Chicano Slang. Austin, Texas: Jenkins
     Book Publishing Company, Inc., 1975.

Velasco Valdes, Miguel. Refranero Popular Mexicano. 7th
     Edition. Mexico, D.F.: B. Costa-Amic, 1978.

Villafuerta, C. Voces y Costumbres de Catamarca. Vols. 1
     and 2. Buenos Aires. 1961.

Bibliography

Wesley, Howard D. "Ranchero Sayings of the Border." Puro
    Mexicano. ed. J. Frank Dobie. Dallas, Texas: South-
    ern Methodist University Press. 1935.

Yañez, Agustin. Las Tierras Flacas. 3rd Edition. Mexico,
    D.F.: Joaquin Mortiz, 1968.

The references in the annotations are by the author's
last name. If there is more than one book by the same
author, it is by name and date. In cases where two authors
have the same last names, initials are used to differentiate
them.

List of Locations
for Annotated Materials

List of Locations

Rubio	Mexico
Santamaria	Mexico
Sbarbi	Spain
Vasquez	Texas
Velasco	Mexico
Villafuerte	Spain
Wesley	Texas
Yañez	Mexico

A Dictionary
of Mexican American
Proverbs

1 (A). De favor te <u>abrazan</u> y quieres que te aprieten.

<u>Translation or Interpretation</u>: You are not content with the fact that I am hugging you. Now you want me to squeeze you.

<u>Context</u>: A friend of ours went out with a boy she had just met. He wanted to take her to a movie on the first date, but she wanted to go to a dance so they did. He said to us that being the first date she had been hugged, but she wanted a kiss also. (Four occurrences. Informants: two female, two male).

<u>Sources and Annotations</u>: Adame, p. 23, De milagro te abrazan y quieres que te besen; p. 27, De milagro te abrazan y quieres que te besen. Cobos, p. 28, same as A. Conde, p. 102, De caridad lo abrazan..., p. 172, same as A. Robe, p. 69, De favor la abrazan y quiere que la besen. Rubio, p. 104, same as A.

2 (A). El <u>agraviado</u> con dulces palabras ha de ser aplacado.

<u>Translation or Interpretation</u>: A soft answer driveth away wrath.

<u>Context</u>: Sometimes if a person is angry and is answered by a calm person (his anger will disappear). (One occurrence. Informant: female).

<u>Sources and Annotations</u>: Correas, p. 85, same as A.

3 (A). <u>Agua</u> que no has de beber déjala correr.

<u>Translation or Interpretation</u>: Water that you won't drink, let it run.

<u>Context</u>: There was a greedy lady (who) always wanted more food or material things than she could eat or have. This proverb was said (about) her, meaning that if she can't use the food or material someone else can, so let them. (24 occurrences. Informants: 20 female, three male, one not stated).

<u>Sources and Annotations</u>: Adame, p. 8, same as A; p. 10, same as A. Aranda, p. 1, same as A. Armas, p. 408, same as A. Ballesteros, p. 19, same as A. Cerda, p. 247, same as A. Cobos, p. 10, same as A. Conde, p. 24, same as A. De Barros, p. 69, same as A. Gamiz, p. 78, same as A. Glazer, p. 41, same as A. Jaramillo, p. 361, same as A. Lea, p. 233, same as A. Lucero-White, p. 33, same as A. Rodriguez-Marin (1926), p. 352, same as A. Rubio, p. 18, No debe moverse el agua cuando no se ha de beber. Santamaria, p. 55, same as A. Yanez, p. 52, No debe moverse el agua cuando no se ha de beber.

4 (A). De esa <u>agua</u> no bebo yo.

<u>Translation or Interpretation</u>: I don't drink that water, or type of. It is applicable to whatever the sayer suggests.

<u>Context</u>: Book reference. Someone could be at a party ob-staining from drinking "spiked" punch. (One occurrence. Informant: anonymous).

<u>Sources and Annotations</u>: Caballero, p. 400, De esta agua no bebere. Covarrubias, p. 213, Nadie diga de esta agua no bebere. De Barros, p. 307, Nadie diga de esta agua no bebere. Espino-sa, F., p. 114, Nadien diga en este mundo. De esta agua no bebere, por revuelta que la vea le puede apretar la sed. Jara-millo, p. 407, Nadie diga: d'esta agua no bebere. Maldonado, p. 156, Nadie diga de esta agua no bebere. Nadie no diga ..., No diga nadie... Rodriguez-Marin (1926), p. 317, Nadie diga "De esta agua no bebere" ni "De este pan no comere".

5 (A). Esta como <u>agua</u> para chocolate.
5 (B). Estoy como <u>agua</u> para chocolate.

<u>Translation or Interpretation</u>: To be like boiling water (as) for chocolate.

<u>Context</u>: M. V.'s mother would always tell her this when she would get mad. Meaning that she was boiling hot and this was like hot water ready for chocolate. (Four occurrences. In-formants: three female, one male).

<u>Sources and Annotations</u>: Arora, p. 43, same as A. Cerda, p. 248, Estar como agua para chocolate. Conde, p. 175, same as A. Martínez, p. 60, Como aguita pa' chocolate. Rubio, p. 233, Estar como agua para chocolate. Santamaria, p. 55, Como agua para chocolate. Velasco, p. 34, Como agua para choco-late. Wesley, p. 213, Como agua para chocolate. Yanez, p. 57, El agua esta para el chocolate.

6 (A). Lo del <u>agua</u> (al) agua.

<u>Translation or Interpretation</u>: From water to water.

<u>Context</u>: If you find something and then lose it, it's because it didn't belong to you in the first place. (Six occurrences. Informants: six female).

<u>Sources and Annotations</u>: Ballesteros, p. 10, same as A. Cerda, p. 247, same as A. Cobos, p. 73, Lo del agua, al agua. Conde, p. 232, Lo del agua, al agua. Martinez, p. 164, same as A. Rubio, p. 293, same as A. Velasco, p. 96, Lo de agua, al agua.

7 (A). Ni en la primera <u>agua</u> se cose.

<u>Translation or Interpretation</u>: (Not even) in the first water will it cook. This means that something is too old to cook or ripen.

<u>Context</u>: Informant told me a lady was talking to someone else about a man and she used this saying. This happened recently. (One occurrence. Informant: female).

<u>Sources and Annotations</u>: None.

8 (A). No da <u>agua</u> ni para el gallo de la pasión.

<u>Translation or Interpretation</u>: This proverb means that a person is so stingy that he would not even give a small amount of water to (the) rooster that crows on Easter.

<u>Context</u>: Informant said that she had a friend who needed fifty cents. This girl asked another girl if she could have the fifty cents since she had more than enough at the time. The girl replied "no." Proverb was mentioned then. (One occurrence. Informant: Female).

<u>Sources and Annotations</u>: Cerda, p. 248, No le da agua ni al gallo de la pasión. Conde, p. 292, No le da agua ni al gallo de la pasión. Santamaria, p. 55, No darle agua ni al gallo de la pasión.

9 (A). No le muevas al <u>agua</u> que el rio esta inundado.

<u>Translation or Interpretation</u>: Don't move the water, the river is already flooding.

<u>Context</u>: Possibly in trying to get a point across about leaving matters as is. (One occurrence. Informant: female).

<u>Sources and Annotations</u>: Arranda, p. 23, No revuelvas el agua.

10 (A). Nunca andes en contra de la corriente porque te ahogas.
10 (B). No hay que caminar contra la corriente del <u>agua</u>.

<u>Translation or Interpretation</u>: Never (go) against the current because you will drown.

<u>Context</u>: Informant heard it in a conversation between a group of friends. They were talking in general about so many rules that society has set. One of them said the proverb, meaning that if you go against society you are somehow pinpointed. (Two occurrences. Informant: one female, one male).

<u>Sources and Annotations</u>: None.

11 (A). Nunca debes decir "De esa _agua_ no bebere."

Translation or Interpretation'.' You should never say "I'll never drink from that water."

Context" Meaning you should never say I'll never do that because that is exactly what you will do. (One occurrence. Informant: female).

Sources and Annotations: Caballero, p. 807, Nadie diga de esta agua no bebere; p. 824, No digas de esta agua no bebere; p. 860, Nunca digas de esta agua no bebere. Correas, p. 34, Aunque mas turbia la vea, no dire, de esta agua no bebere. De Barrios, p. 322, No diga nadie de esta agua no bebere. Lea, p. 236, Nadie diga- de esta agua no bebere. Maldonado, p. 59, No diga nadie de esta agua no bebere; p. 61, Por turbia que este, no digas de esta agua no bebere. Sbardi, p. 42, Nadie diga: De esta agua no bebere por muy turbia que este.

12 (A). Si no _aguantas_ no jueges.

Translation or Interpretation: If you can't stand the heat, get out of the kitchen.

Context: None. (One occurrence. Informant: male).

Sources and Annotations: None.

13 (A). Dos _agujas_ no se pican.
13 (B). Dicen que dos _agujas_ no se pican.
13 (C). Dicen que dos _agujas_ no se hacen nada.
13 (D). _Aguja_ con _aguja_ no se puede hacer nada.
13 (D). Dos _agujas_ no pueden hacerse nada.

Translation or Interpretation: Two needles cannot prick each other.

Context: This is when two people have the same temperament and they cannot get along because at least one of them has to give in, and if neither does, then things just won't work out. (Six occurrences. Informants: four female, two male).

Sources and Annotations: Aranda, p. 9, same as A. Balles-teros, p. 45, Dos agujas no se hacen nada. Cobos, p. 35, Dos agujas no se hacen nada. Espinoza, A., p. 104, Dos agujas no se hacen nada; Dos alesnas no se pican. Gamez, p. 94, Dos alesnas no se pican. Rodriguez-Marin (1926), p. 140, Dos espinas no se pican.

14 (A). Muerto el _ahijado_ se acabo el compadrazgo.

Translation or Interpretation: Dead the godson, the friend-ship ends.

Context: When a husband or wife dies the living member no longer relates to the dead party's relatives in this case. (One occurrence. Informant: female).

Sources and Annotations: Cerda, p. 249, Se acabo el ahijado, se acabo el compadrazgo. Cobos, p. 109, Se murio el ahijado, se acabo el compadrazgo. Gamiz, p. 90, Se acabo el ahijado y se acabo el compadrazgo. Perez, p. 185, Muerto el ahijado, se acabo el compadrazgo. Rodriguez-Marin (12600Refranes), p. 212, Muerto el ahijado se acabo el compadrazgo. Sbarbi, p. 45, Muriose el ahijado, acabase el padrinazgo. Velasco, p. 105, Muerto el ahijado acabo el compadrazgo.

15 (A). En el ajeno cae la desgracia.
15 (B). En lo ajeno cae lo malo.

Translation or Interpretation: In what belongs to others harm will fall.

Context: I once had a friend and her parents never liked for her to use other people's things. One day she was sent by her neighbor to buy something from the store, and was told she could use the car. It happened that when she was coming back she had an accident in her neighbor's car, and her father told her the saying later. (Two occurrences. Informants: female).

Sources and Annotations: Cobos, p. 55, En lo ajeno siempre cae la desgracia. Rubio, p. 218, same as A.

16 (A). Algo es algo, peor es nada, y algo vale más que nada.
16 (B). Algo es algo.
16 (C). Vale más algo que nada.

Translation or Interpretation: Something is something, nothing is worse, and something is worth more than nothing.

Context: What this means is that when you find yourself with very few of something you wanted a lot of, you should be glad to have a little and not any at all. (Three occurrences. Informants: two female, one male).

Sources and Annotations: Ballesteros, p. 30, Más vale algo que nada. Caballero, p. 90, same as B. Cobos, p. 79, Más vale algo que nada; p. 118, same as C. Conde, p. 403, same as C. Espinosa, A., p. 111, same as C; p. 113, same as C. Espinosa, F., p. 41, Más vale algo que nada. Galvan, p. 130, Más vale algo que nada. Galvan, p. 131, Más vale algo que nada. Gamiz, p. 76, same as C. Maldonado, p. 150, Más vale algo que nada. 0 ... que no nada. Rodriguez-Marin (1930), p. 16, Algo es algo y comia hielo. Santamaria, p. 81, Más vale algo que nada. Sbardi, p. 55, Más vale algo que nada. Villafuerte, p. 38, same as B.

17 (A). Tener el <u>alma</u> bien puesta.

Translation or Interpretation: To have a very strong soul. To have courage.

Context: An uncle was describing my father, who I have never met, and my uncle said "Tenia el alma bien puesta." (One occurrence. Informant: female).

Sources and Annotations: Caballero, p. 1053, same as A. Sbarbi, p. 59, same as A.

18 (A). Un <u>alma</u> sola ni canta ni llora.

Translation or Interpretation: A solitary soul neither sings nor cries.

Context: If there is a person that is always alone, never goes out, and always quiet he or she is always sad (and) has no reason to sing or cry about what goes around the world. He or she has no feelings nor anybody because nobody cared for him or her to understand those feelings. (One occurrence. Informant: female).

Sources and Annotations: Maldonado, p. 31, same as A. Sbarbi, p. 60, same as A.

19 (A). Antes que resuelvas nada, consúltalo con la <u>almohada</u>.
19 (B). Consultar con la <u>almohada</u>.

Translation or Interpretation: Before making an important decision, sleep on it -- consult the pillow.

Context: My parents are in the process of buying a house. The real estate agent suggested that my father "consultar la almohada" before deciding on it. (Two occurrences. Informants: one female, one male).

Sources and Annotations: Armas, p. 233, same as B. Caballero, p. 393, same as B. Conde, p. 203, La almohada es buen conse- jera. Correas, p. 70, Aconsejarse con la almohada, p. 81, El almohada es buen consejero, que despasio de el consejo; o que pensando da el consejo; p. 181, La almohada es buen consejero. Covarrubias, p. 100, Consultar un negocio con el almohada. Espinosa, F., p. 42, El consejo del almohada es mejor de todos. Maldonado, p. 151, La almohada es buen consejo. Rodriguez- Marin (1930), p. 322, Tomar consejo con el almohada, cosa acertada. Rodriguez-Marez (1926), p. 35, same as A. Sbarbi, p. 60, same as B.

20 (A). <u>Almuerza</u> mucho, come mas, cena poco y viviras.

<u>Translation or Interpretation</u>: Eat a lot for breakfast, more at lunch, a little at dinner, and you will live.

<u>Context</u>: My informant says he heard it years ago from his father. He is originally from Robstown, Texas. The context which he used it is that we were talking about health and a-bout how obesity can affect one's health when suddenly he said this. One can use it when warning others to take care of their health. It can also be used when someone is eating excessively at a late hour. This proverb would best be well said to rela-tives or very close friends, but not recommended for strangers since they may not like you getting into their business and might be offended. This proverb can be said to anyone if the context is appropriate. (One occurrence. Informant: male).

<u>Sources and Annotations</u>: Maldonado, p. 91, Bebe poco y come asaz, duerme en alto y viviras; p. 103, Come poco y cena mas, duerme en alto y viviras.

21 (A). El mas <u>amigo</u> es traidor y el más verdadero miente.

<u>Translation or Interpretation</u>: The best friend is a traitor and the most truthful lies.

<u>Context</u>: This proverb was told to me by my father who learned it from his father many years ago in Brownsville, Texas, where he was born and raised. It means that your best friend will betray you and the man that seems so sincere and truthful will lie to you, so beware. (Four occurrences. Informants: Two female, two male).

<u>Sources and Annotations</u>: Cobos, p. 39, same as A. Conde, p. 136, same as A. Espinosa, A., p. 107, same as A; p. 113, No has más amigo que Dios esto es claro y evidente, que el mas amigo es traidor y el más verdadero miente. Martinez, p. 107, El mas amigo es traidor y el mas veridico miente. Velasco, p. 63, El mas amigo es traidor y el mas veridico miente.

22 (A). El mejor <u>amigo</u> del hombre es el perro.

<u>Translation or Interpretation</u>: Man's best friend is his dog.

<u>Context</u>: You cannot trust a friend to be there when you need him, but your dog will always be there. (One occurrence. Informant: female).

<u>Sources and Annotations</u>: Rodriguez-Marin (1930), p. 275, ¿Quien es tu amigo? mi perro. Rodriguez-Marin (1926), p. 162, El mejor amigo - un perro. Sbarbi, p. 67, El mejor amigo, un perro.

23 (A). Un <u>amigo</u> en apuro es <u>amigo</u> seguro.

<u>Translation or Interpretation</u>: A friend in need is a friend indeed.

<u>Context</u>: Sometime ago a friend of mine wrecked his car, this eventually complicated his life. For an entire week he visited me everyday until he asked if he could borrow my car seeing I was coming to school and didn't need a car in the morning. Of course I said "no" because it would eventually complicate my wife's working schedule. "But aren't we friends," he commented. "Sure I'm your friend, but not when you're in need. Visit me sometime when you are free of problems, maybe we'll go out and have a few beers." (One occurrence. Informant: male).

<u>Sources and Annotations</u>: Cobos, p. 13, Amigo en adversidad, amigo de verdad. Lucero-White, p. 34, El amigo en la adversidad es amigo en realidad.

24 (A). <u>Amigos</u> que pelean por un pedazo de pan de centeño, o
         el hambre es grande o el amor es pequeño.

<u>Translation or Interpretation</u>: When friends quarrel over a crust of rye bread, either the hunger is great or the friendship is small.

<u>Context</u>: If two friends are fighting or trying to buy land even if they know they are fighting with each other. Their friendship is too small or their ambition is too great. (One occurrence. Informant: female).

<u>Sources and Annotations</u>: Correas, p. 76, same as A.

25 (A). Entre dos <u>amigos</u> un notario y dos testigos.

<u>Translation or Interpretation</u>: Two friends should do business through a notary and with (two witnesses).

<u>Context</u>: If two friends are making a deal or even borrowing money they should do it through a notary and with each as a witness because many forget to pay. Like they say in friendship, if you borrow from somebody, you say to that person, "write it on ice." (One occurrence. Informant: female).

<u>Sources and Annotations</u>: Cobos, p. 56, Entre amigo y amigo un fiscal y dos testigos. Rodriguez-Marin (1926), p. 195, Entre amigos, un notario y dos testigos y entre hermanos cuatro testigos y dos notarios. Sbarbi, p. 69, same as A.

26 (A). <u>Amistad</u> con todos, confianza con pocos.

<u>Translation or Interpretation</u>: Be friendly with everyone, but trust only a few.

<u>Context</u>: Juan has many acquaintances, however, he only has a few friends that he can trust with his personal confidences. There are few he can rely on when the going gets rough. (Three occurrences. Informants: two female, one male).

<u>Sources and Annotations</u>: Conde, p. 41, same as A. Rodriguez-Marin (1926), p. 31, same as A.

27 (A). <u>Amistad</u> que siempre dice dame, más que <u>amistad</u> parece hambre.

<u>Translation or Interpretation</u>: A friendship that is always asking for something you can do without.

<u>Context</u>: Mr. I. uses this proverb because usually his so (called) friends are not what you really call friends. They usually want something, or a favor done by him. (One occurrence. Informant: male).

<u>Sources and Annotations</u>: Conde, p. 41, same as A. Lucero-White, p. 31, same as A.

28 (A). La <u>amistad</u> vale más que el dinero.

<u>Translation or Interpretation</u>: Friendship is worth more than what money can buy.

<u>Context</u>: A friend was trying to make friends and going about it by buying the other person things that he wanted until the mother told him that "la amistad vale mas que el dinero." (One occurrence. Informant: anonymous).

<u>Sources and Annotations</u>: Cobos, p. 101, Primero es la amistad que el dinero. Rodriguez-Marin (1926), p. 31, A quien no tiene amigos, pobre les digo. Rubio II, p. 108, primero es la amistad que el dinero.

29 (A). <u>Amor</u> con <u>amor</u> se paga.
29 (B). <u>Amor</u> con <u>amor</u> se paga, lo demás son vanas palabras.

<u>Translation or Interpretation</u>: Love is repaid with love.

<u>Context</u>: My sister says she uses this all the time when my brother-in-law has been out on a drinking spree and then tries to get forgiveness by telling her how much he loves her, and that she should understand that his actions do not reflect his feelings. (Six occurrences. Informants: five female, one male).

Sources and Annotations: Adame, p. 8, same as A; p. 12, same as A. Alcala, p. 43, same as A. Aranda, p. 3, same as A. Armas, p. 408, same as A. Ballesteros, p. 1, same as A. Caballero, p. 114, same as A. Cobos, p. 13, same as A. Conde, p. 42, Amor con amor se paga, y lo demas con dinero. De Barros, p. 95, same as A; p. 140, Con amor se paga amor y con tales otras las buenas obras. Galvan, p. 124, same as A; p. 132, same as A. Lea, p. 233, same as A. Lucero-White, p. 33, same as A. Maldonado, p. 85, same as A; p. 107, Con amor se paga amor y con tales obras las buenas obras. Rodriguez-Marin (1930), p. 23, Amor con amor se paga y con buenas palabras. Rodriguez-Marin (1926), p. 31, Amor con amor se paga, lo demas son vanas palabras. Sbarbi, p. 71, same as A.

30 (A). Amor de lejos, amor de pendejos.
30 (B). Amor de lejos es para los pendejos.
30 (C). Amores lejos son señas de pendejos.
30 (D). Amor de lejos, vida de pendejos.
30 (E). Amor lejano es para los estupidos.

Translation or Interpretation: Love from afar is love for fools.

Context: The boyfriend of my sister joined the army. When he left he insisted that she should not go out with no one but to wait from him until he was through. Well, he got married in Germany because he got a girl pregnant, while my sister did not go out with anyone because she was waiting for him. My grandmother told her the above proverb. (42 occurrences. Informants: 25 female, 17 male).

Sources and Annotations: Adame, p. 8, Amor de lejos, amor de tontos; p. 12, Amor de lejos, amor de tontos. Ballesteros, p. 20, Amor de lejos, amor de tontos. Cerda, p. 250, same as A. Cobos, p. 13, Amor de lejos, amor pa los pendejos; p. 35, Amor de lejos, amor pa los pendejos. Galvan, p. 124, same as A; p. 131, same as A. Glazer, p. 42, same as A. Martínez, p. 31, Amor de lejos es de pendejos. Robe, p. 63, same as A. Rubio, p. 45, same as A. Vasquez, p. 89, same as A. Velasco, p. 19, Amor de lejos es de pendejos.

31 (A). Amor de urraca.

Translation or Interpretation: The love of a blackbird.

Context: According to my informant, my uncle, this proverb has been passed down from generation to generation. He said that it applied to all new born babies. Naturally, the paternal affection parents have for their babies implies that they are beautiful in every way. Since no one would say an unkind word against the child this has been assumed. Yet most babies aren't especially pretty at all, except, of course, to their parents. (One occurrence. Informant: male).

Sources and Annotations: None.

32 (A). <u>Amor</u> que no es atrevido nunca logra sino olvido.

<u>Translation or Interpretation</u>: Love that is not bold will only accomplish being forgotten.

<u>Context</u>: My sister says that when she was going to come to the U.S. she was torn by a dilemma because she had a boyfriend in Mexico (whom) she loved very much. She waited and hoped that he would do something to detain her, like propose marriage, but the fellow never took that step. Ever since, when she remembers him, she uses this <u>dicho</u> as a reference. (One occurrence. Informant: female).

<u>Sources and Annotations</u>: Conde, p. 43, Amor que no es atrevido, lo que logra es el olvido. Rodriguez-Marin (1930), p. 24, Amor que no se atreve, llámalo nieve.

32 (A). <u>Amor</u> y olvido nace de descuido.

<u>Translation or Interpretation</u>: It means that you cannot take love for granted or you will lose it.

<u>Context</u>: The informant said she heard it from a girlfriend. Her girlfriend said her mother had told her this when the girl remarked that so-and-so was not calling anymore the way he usually did. (Nine occurrences. Informants: eight female, one male).

<u>Sources and Annotations</u>: Rubio, p. 25, Amor viejo, ni te olvido ni te dejo.

33 (A). Con <u>amor</u> y aguardiente nada se siente.

<u>Translation or Interpretation</u>: With love and brandy nothing is felt.

<u>Context</u>: People in love, or drunks, are not conscious of others. (One occurrence. Informant: female).

<u>Sources and Annotations</u>: Rubio, p. 95, same as A.

34 (A). Contra <u>amor</u> y fortuna no hay defensa alguna.

<u>Translation or Interpretation</u>: Against love and fortune there is no defense. A person cannot win an agreement or fight if it deals with love or money.

<u>Context</u>: My grandmother told my mother this when I began dating someone. They didn't care too much about. I was sixteen years old at the time and my mother was trying to talk me out of going to the movies with him. (One occurrence. Informant: female).

Sources and Annotations: Cobos, p. 23, same as A. Correas, p. 76, Amor y fortuna no tiene defensa alguna. Rodriguez-Marin (1926), p. 83, same as A.

36 (A). Donde hay amor hay dolor.

Translation or Interpretation: Where there is love, there is pain.

Context: This proverb is used when a person is feeling upset or depressed about losing someone. (Six occurrences. Informants: five female, one male).

Sources and Annotations: Cobos, p. 33, same as A. Conde, p. 117, same as A. De Barros, p. 180, Donde hay gran amor hay gran dolor, second same as A. Jaramillo, p. 417, Quien te quiere te hara llorar. Maldonado, p. 123, Donde hay celos hay amor; donde hay viejos hay dolor. Rodriguez-Marin (1930), p. 41, Gran amor es gran dolor. Rodriguez-Marin (1926), p. 137, same as A; p. 210, Gran amor, gran dolor; p. 450, Segun es el amor, tal es el dolor. Sbarbi, p. 72, same as A.

37 (A). El amor es ciego.

Translation or Interpretation: Love is blind.

Context: Everyone knew that R. was too good for R., but like they say "love is blind." (Two occurrences. Informants: female).

Sources and Annotations: Ballesteros, p. 3, same as A. Caballero, p. 532, same as A. Galvan, p. 125, same as A; p. 127, same as A. Jaramillo, p. 379, same as A. Rodriguez-Marin (1926), p. 14, El amor lo pintan ciego. Vasquez, p. 90, same as A.

38 (A). El amor y el interés se fueron a pasar un día. Pudo mas el interes que el amor que le tenía.

Translation or Interpretation: Love and interest went out one day, but interest gave up on love because it was stronger than affection. We choose some friends over others because we are more concerned with what they have to offer than with their friendship.

Context: Informant's cousin married her fiance because the marriage would get her U.S. citizenship. Informant thought of this proverb when she found out what happened. (One occurrence. Informant: female).

Sources and Annotation: Cerda, p. 251, El amor y el interés salieron al campo un dia y pudo mas el interes que el amor que el tenia. Santamaria, p. 97, El amor y el interes salieron al campo un día, pudo más el interes que el amor que te tenia.

39. (A). No hay _amor_ como el primero.

Translation or Interpretation: There is no love like the first.

Context: My informant had a daughter who was a divorcee. She never went out or dated. One day her mother asked her why. Her daughter answered her with this proverb. (One occurrence. Informant: female).

Sources and Annotations: Cerda, p. 251, same as A. Cobos, p. 89, same as A. Conde, p. 285, no hay amor como el primero, ni luna como en enero. Correas, p. 86, El amor primero jamás se olvida, pepita le queda por toda la vida. De Barros, p. 96, El amor primero jamas se olvida, Pepita le queda para todo la vida. Espinosa, A., p. 108, same as A; p. 113, Cuatro palomitas blancas sentadas en un romero una a la otra se decian, no hay amor como el primero. Maldonado, p. 86, El amor primero jamás se olvida; pepita le queda por toda la vida. Martinez, p. 31, Amor primero, el único verdadero. Rodriguez-Marin (1926), p. 231, no hay tal amor como el primero. Rubio, p. 26, No hay amor como el primero ni luna como en enero.

40 (A). No hay más grande _amor_ como el _amor_ de madre o padre.

Translation or Interpretation: There is no greater love than that of a mother or father.

Context: My aunt and her daughter were arguing about something. My aunt recalled once that she was arguing with her mother over something similar. My aunt's mother was advicing my cousin about something just as her mother was advicing her once, but somehow turned into an argument. She recalled how her mother loved her and was trying to help her because she loved her. She remembered this proverb. (One occurrence. Informant: female).

Sources and Annotations: Correas, p. 76, Amor de padre (madre) que todo lo otro es aire. Maldonado, p. 85, Amor de madre, que todo lo otro es aire.

41 (A). Poco es el _amor_ y lo vamos a gastar en celos.
41 (B). Poco el _amor_ y gastándolo en celo.

Translation or Interpretation: Little is the love and we are going to waste it on jealousy.

Context: People who don't trust one another. Usually referred to situations where a wife or husband are constantly suspicious about one another being unfaithful. (Two occurrences. Informants: female).

Sources and Annotations: Cerda, p. 251, Es poco el amor para gastarlo en celos. Conde, p. 367, ¡Ser poco el amor y desperdiciarlo en celos! Santamaria, p. 97, Ser poco el amor y que se vaya en celos.

42 (A). Un viejo amor ni se olvida ni se deja.

Translation or Interpretation: An old love is never forgotten or moved aside.

Context: D. said this was equivalent to saying that "there will always be a spot in my heart for you." It is used to let someone know that you still care about him even if the intensity of your relationship has decreased. It is a way of saying good-bye to an old love without totally rejecting him. (One occurrence. Informant: female).

Sources and Annotations: None.

43 (A). Amores nuevos olvidan a los viejos.

Translation or Interpretation: New loves make you forget old ones.

Context: None. (One occurrence. Informant: female).

Sources and Annotations: Correa, p. 77, Amores nuevos olvidan viejos. Maldonado, p. 41, same as A.

44 (A). Lo mismo es andar atrás que andar a ancas.
44 (B). Es igual atras que en ancas.

Translation or Interpretation: It is the same thing walking on your knees and riding in the back.

Context: Mr. G's mother told her this once when an old lady walking was given a ride and had to ride in the back of a pick-up. She said it would have been the same to her if she had walked because of the (discomfort) of the ride. (Two occurrences. Informants: one female, one male).

Sources and Annotations: Cobos, p. 73, Lo mismo de otrás que en ancas. Jaramillo, p. 391, Es lo mismo atrás qu'en las espaldas. Martinez, p. 400, Lo mismo da atrás que en las espaldas. Rodriguez-Marin (1926), p. 267, Lo mismo da atrás que en las espaldas. Santamaria, p. 155, Lo mismo es atrás que en las espaldas; p. 622, No es lo mismo atras que en las espaldas. Velasco, p. 72, Es lo mismo atras que en las espaldas.

45 (A). Nunca se levanta de sus <u>ancas</u>.

<u>Translation or Interpretation</u>: Never does he raise his bottom. It means that this person is kind of lazy. He does not like to get up if he can do things sitting down.

<u>Context</u>: One of the Spanish professors used this proverb in class. He asked one of his students to go to the board and this student took forever to get there. This is when he used the proverb. (Two occurrences. Informants: one female, one male).

<u>Sources and Annotations</u>: None.

46 (A). Cayó como <u>anillo</u> al dedo.

<u>Translation or Interpretation</u>: It was just like a ring to a finger.

<u>Context</u>: When something happens at the right time. (One occurrence. Informant: male).

<u>Sources and Annotations</u>: Adame, p. 66, same as a; p. 68, same as A. Arora, p. 60, Me cae como anillo al dedo. Caballero, p. 314, same as A. Maldonado, p. 105, Como anillo al dedo. Rubio, p. 80, Caer como anillo al dedo.

47 (A). El <u>animal</u> más raro y bruto es el hómbre.

<u>Translation or Interpretation</u>: The oddest and most stupid animal is man.

<u>Context</u>: The informant said he often exclaimed this out loud when he hears or reads about people who have killed rare animals "just for fun." (One occurrence. Informant: male).

<u>Sources and Annotations</u>: Rodriguez-Marin (1930), p. 230, No hay peor animal de conocer que el hombre.

48 (A). <u>Animas</u> que cante un gallo para saber cuando amanece, pero gallo desgraciado canta cuando le parece.

<u>Translation or Interpretation</u>: (You encourage) the rooster to crow so that you know it is morning, but that wretched rooster only crows when it feels like it.

<u>Context</u>: Mr. F. G., who was raised by his grandmother, first heard this proverb from her during a hurricane. He was only nine years old. His grandmother, on his mother's side, was of pure Mexican blood, and he explained that this proverb was usually said in a time of danger. Since the rooster would always crow in the wee hours of the morning, whenever there was

danger, and the people wanted to know when morning was nearing, they would use this proverb. (One occurrence. Informant: male).

Sources and Annotations: None.

49 (A). Tanto año en la marina y todavía no conoce el agua.
49 (B). Veinte años en la marina y no conocer el camarón.
49 (C). Cincuenta años en la marina y no conocen una ballena.

Translation or Interpretation: So many years in the navy and still doesn't know the water.

Context: A person that has been working for many years in his job makes a mistake, the thing that he did wrong should be of second nature to him. (Three occurrences. Informants: one female, two male).

Sources and Annotations: Perez, p. 119, Cincuenta años en la marina y no conoce una ballena.

50 (A). Las apariencias engañan.
50 (B). Apariencias mienten.
50 (C). No te vayas al color que también la vista engaña.

Translation or Interpretation: (Looks can be deceiving).

Context: L. was very impressed with a handsome young man who asked her out. Later she found out that his character didn't match his looks. (Three occurrences. Informants: two female, one male).

Sources and Annotations: Adame, p. 7, No te vayas por las apariencias porque engañan; same as C. Armas, p. 415, same as A. Caballero, p. 717, same as A. Conde, p. 221, same as A. Galvan, p. 130, same as A. Gamiz, p. 82, same as C. Rodriguez-Marin (1930), p. 173, same as A. Sbarbi, p. 85, same as A.

51 (A) No jusges por las apariencias si no por la calidad.

Translation or Interpretation: Judge not by appearances but by the quality.

Context: During the Mexican Revolution, my grandfather relates an interesting event which took place. It was in September when, in a village away from the city, a rich farmer received an invitation to a city reunion held by the city farmers. The mountain farmer had never been to the city, but decided to attend the meeting/reunion. He left his mountain home with his work clothes, as usual, except for the fact that he brought gold coins in case he might need them. When he reached the city he located the banquet room, but as he was about to enter the room he was (turned back) by a servant because of his appearances. He left the room confused. He reached a barber shop and the barber told him what to do. He bought a suit, shaved, bathed, and then left for the meeting. This time they let him in. Later they served him his meal, but he refused to eat. When everyone was done he poured his food into his pockets. (One occurrence. Informant: male).

Sources and Annotations: None.

52 (A). Lo que bien aprende no se olvida.

Translation or Interpretation: That which is well learned isn't forgotten.

Context: Heard this from his father, when he was a child, to encourage him to do well on his homework. (One occurrence. Informant: male).

Sources and Annotations: Cobos, p. 74, Lo que bien se aprende, tarde se le olvida. Rubio, p. 296, Lo que bien se aprende jamás se olvida.

53 (A). Para aprender nunca es tarde.
53 (B). Nunca es tarde para aprender.

Translation or Interpretation: It's never too late to learn.

Context: Heard his father say this humorously when they were discussing his uncle, who was retiring from the service to study law at the age of 45. (Three occurrences. Informants: two female, one male).

Sources and Annotations: Conde, p. 309, same as A. Rodriguez-Marin (1926), p. 357, same as A.

54 (A). Aprendiz de mucho, oficial de nada.

Translation or Interpretation: Aprentice of all trades, master of none.

Context: Jack of all trades, master of none. (One occurrence. Informant: female).

Sources and Annotations: Aranda, p. 3, Aprendiz de todo, oficial de nada. Campa, p. 63, Aprendiz de todo, oficial de nada.

55 (A). No te _apures_ para que dures.

Translation or Interpretation: Don't worry too much so you can last longer.

Context: If you are always in a hurry worrying about everything you get tired sooner. (One occurrence. Informant: male).

Sources and Annotations: Ballesteros, p. 55, same as A. Cobos, p. 93, No se apure pa que dure. Conde, p. 298, same as A. Martinez, p. 293, No se apure para que dure; p. 210, same as A.

56 (A). _Arbol_ malo no da buena fruta.

Translation or Interpretation: A bad tree will (not) produce good fruit.

Context: If you want something good you must work for it. If you don't work hard enough you won't have much or of as good quality. (One occurrence. Informant: male).

Sources and Annotations: None.

57 (A). _Arbol_ que nace torcido no se podra enderezar.
57 (B). _Arbol_ que crece torcido nunca el tronco endereza.
57 (C). _Arbol_ que nace jorobado jamaz se endereza.
57 (D). _Arbol_ que crece torcido jamás su tallo se endereza.
57 (E). _Palo_ que nace torcido nunca su rama endereza.

Translation or Interpretation: A tree that grows crooked cannot be straightened.

Context: A child (raised) without discipline cannot be disciplined when it is needed. (23 occurrences. Informants: 12 female, nine male, two not stated).

Sources and Annotations: Adame, p. 9, Arbol que nace torcido, jamas su rama endereza; p. 13, Arbol que nace torcido, jamas su rama endereza. Aranda, p. 10, El arbol que crece torcido nunca su rama endereza. Armas, p. 409, Arbol que crece torcido nunca su rama endereza. Ballesteros, p. 1, Arbol que nace torcido, nunca su rama endereza. Cobos, p. 15, same as B. Conde, p. 52, Arbol que nace torcido jamás su tronco endereza. Gamiz, p. 91, Arbol que crece torcido jamas su tronco endereza. Glazer, p. 41, same as A. Jaramillo, p. 364, Arbol que nace torcido nunca su rama endereza. Lea, p. 234, El arbol que nace torcido nunca se endereza. Lucero-White, p. 34, El arbol que nace torcido nunca su rama endereza. Rodriguez-Marin (1930), p. 33, Arbol que torcido crecio, nunca se endereza. Rodriguez-Marin (1926), p. 33, Arbol que torcido nacio, nunca se endereza. Yanez, p. 326, Arbol que crece torcido...

58 (A). Al árbol no se le arrima nomas cuando tiene sombra.

Translation or Interpretation: One never gets near a tree unless it has shade.

Context: There are things, or occurrences, which never seem
to bother people until it happens to you. Another explanation
is that people don't get near you unless they need you. (One
occurrence. Informant: male).

Sources and Annotations: De Barros, p. 88, Al que a bien
árbol se arrima, buena sombra le cobija; p. 186, Al que a
buen árbol se arrima, buena sombra le cobija. Maldonado, p.
61, Quien a buen arbol se arrima, buena sombra le cobija.
MacArthur, p. 21, El que a buen árbol se arrima, buena sombra
le cobija.

59 (A). Del árbol caido todos quieren hacer leña.
59 (B). De todos es bien sabido--no hay que hacer leña de
         árbol caido.

Translation or Interpretation: When something good falls
down, everybody wants to take advantage of it.

Context: When a child has done something wrong, everyone
gets after him, especially if he is always getting into
trouble. (Five occurrences. Informants: one female, four
male).

Sources and Annotations: Adame, p. 23, same as A; p. 25, same
as A. Aranda, p. 8, Del árbol caido todos hacen leña. Armas,
p. 411, same as A. Cobos, p. 29, Del árbol caido todos hacen
leña; p. 53, En arbol caido todos suben las ramas. Conde,
p. 105, same as A. De Barros, p. 167, El árbol caido todo el
mundo hace leña. Galvan, p. 127, Del árbol caido todos hacen
leña; p. 130, De árbol caido todos hacen leña. Gamiz, p. 79,
Del palo caido todos hacen leña. Jaramillo, p. 375, Del árbol
caido todos hacen leña. Lea, p. 233, Del árbol caido todos
hacen leña. Lucero-White, p. 33, Del árbol caido todos hacen
leña. Martinez, p. 136, Hacer leña del árbol caido. Pérez,
p. 119, Cuando ven el palo caido todos quieren hacer leña.
Rubio, p. 39, Al palo caido, hacerlo leña. Rodriguez-Marin
(1926), p. 19, Al caido todos se le atreven; p. 113, same as
A. Sbarbi, p. 89, Del árbol caido todos hacen leña. Vásquez,
p. 88, Cuando ven el palo caido todos quieren hacer leña.
Yanez, p. 208, De palo caido cortaremos leña.

60 (A). El arbol por su fruto se conoce.
60 (B). El arbol se conoce por su fruto.

Translation or Interpretation: A tree is known by its fruit.
You can judge a person by what he does and how he acts.

Context: In church the preacher was preaching and he exemplified with this proverb. (Three occurrences. Informants: female).

Sources and Annotations: Adame, p. 31, same as A; p. 35, same as A. Aranda, p. 10, El arbol se conoce por su fruto; same as b. Cobos, p. 35, same as B. Galvan, p. 125, same as B; p. 126, same as B; p. 127, same as B. Lea, p. 234, same as B. Lucero-White, p. 34, same as A. Rodriguez-Marin (1926), p. 372, Por el fruto se conoce el arbol; p. 477, Tal arbol, tal fruto.

61 (A). El árbol se enderesa desde chiquito.
61 (B). Debe de enderesar el árbol cuando esta chico porque ya grande es muy tarde.

Translation or Interpretation: A tree is straightened when it is small.

Context: If you are going to train a child correctly, you must do it when he is young. (22 occurrences. Informants: 11 female, nine male, two anonymous).

Sources and Annotations: Rodriguez-Marin (1930), p. 84, Desde chiquito se guia el arbolito. Rodriguez-Marin (1926), p. 125, Desde pequenito se endereza el arbolito; p. 146, El arbolito, desde chiquito.

62 (A). Eres como el arco iris, simpre sales después de la tempestad.

Translation or Interpretation: You are like the rainbow, always coming out after the storm.

Context: It is used to tell people that he/she were not there when you needed them the most, and now they are offering their services too late. (Two occurrences. Informants: one female, one male).

Sources and Annotations: Cerda, p. 252, Estar como el arco iris, que sale después de la tempestad.

63 (A). De ardor mueren los quemados.
63 (B). De que mueren los quemados sino es de purito ardor.

Translation or Interpretation: People who get burned more than likely burn from the pain (die from the itch).

Context: People who get by only from trials normally are affected by those trials. (Three occurrences. Informants: one female, two male).

Sources and Annotations: Adame, p. 24, ¿De que murio el quemado? De ardido; p. 27, ¿De que murio el quemado? De ardido. Cerda, p. 252, De ardor mueren los quemados y de frio
los encuerados. Cobos, p. 27, De ardor mueren los quemados
y de frio los encuerados. Martinez, p. 93, ¡De que mueren
los quemados? de ardores; Velasco, p. 55, ¿De que mueron los
quemados? de ardores. Yanez, p. 526, ¿De que mueren los quemados? no mas de ardores.

64 (A). No servir ni para el arranque.

Translation or Interpretation: No good, not even for starters.

Context: This can be many things, but it is usually said in
a horse race. When you race your horse against another better
one, then your horse is no good not even for starters. Your
horse has no chance of winning. (One occurrence. Informant:
male).

Sources and Annotations: Conde, p. 294, No me sirve ni pa'l
arranque. Yanez, p. 224, ¡Ves como ni pal arranque sirves
collón?

65 (A). Arrastrados se han de ver por el suelo.

Translation or Interpretation: You shall see yourselves
crawling on the ground.

Context: I learned this saying from my mother when I was
about nine years old. One day, the Blessed Mother was going
to visit her cousin Elizabeth. Since it was a rather long
trip, she was riding a burro. On her way the burro was
frightened by a snake and the Blessed Mother fell off the
burro. The snake was crawling with the end of its tail and
the rest of its body was standing. The Blessed Mother was
upset and cursed the saying at the snake. Ever since the
snake has crawled on its belly. (One occurrence. Informant:
female).

Sources and Annotations: None.

66 (A). De los arrepentidos se sirve Dios.

Translation or Interpretation: God feeds off those who repent.

Context: Informant says that she uses this proverb whenever
she hears someone say they've changed their minds about some
decision or act. (One occurrence. Informant: female).

Sources and Annotations: Adame, p. 23, De los arrepentidos
se vale Dios; p. 26, De los arrepentidos se vale Dios. Armas,
p. 410, De los humildes se sirve Dios. Cobos, p. 97, Para

los arrepentidos es el reino de los cielos. Conde, p. 107,
same as A. Jaramillo, p. 376, De los arrepentidos se vale
Dios. Martinez, p. 91, same as A. Robe, p. 67, same as A.
Rodriguez-Marin (1930), p. 250, Pecadores arrepentidos quiere
Dios. Rodriguez-Marin (1926), p. 84, Corazones arrepentidos
quiere Dios.

67 (A). No todo lo que chifla es <u>arriero</u>.

<u>Translation or Interpretation</u>: Not everyone that whistles is
a mule driver.

<u>Context</u>: Just because you know how to do something doesn't
mean you're an expert at it. (Nine occurrences. Informants:
five female, four male).

<u>Sources and Annotations</u>: Cerda, p. 252, Ni todos los que chi-
flan son arrieros. Cobos, p. 94, No todos los que chiflan
son arrieros. Conde, p. 279, Ni todos los que lazan son vaqueros, ni todos los que chiflan son arrieros; p. 300, Ni
todos los que lazan son vaqueros, ni todos los que chiflan
son arrieros. Espinoza, A., p. 209, No todos los que chiflan
son arrieros. Perez, p. 124, No todos los que chiflan son
arrieros. Yanez, p. 134, Ni todos los que chiflan son
arrieros.

68 (A). <u>Arrieros</u> somos y por el camino andamos.

<u>Translation or Interpretation</u>: We are mule drivers and we are
walking on the road.

<u>Context</u>: We are human beings and walk along the road of life
together. (Ten occurrences. Informants: seven female, three
male).

<u>Sources and Annotations</u>: Adame, p. 14, Arrieros somos y en el
camino andamos. Armas, p. 409, same as A. Ballesteros, p. 1,
Arrieros somos y en el camino andamos. Cobos, p. 15, same as
A. Conde, p. 52, Arrieros somos y andando vamos y en el
camino nos encontramos. Galvan, p. 125, Arrieros somos y en
el camino andamos. Jaramillo, p. 368, Arrieros somos y en el
camino andamos. Maldonado, p. 174, Somos arrieros y nos encontramos. Martinez, p. 37, same as B. Paredes, p. 29, Arrieros somos y en el camino andamos. Perez, p. 119, same as
A. Rodriguez-Marin (1926), p. 383, Pues somos arrieros en el
camino nos encontramos. Sbarbi, p. 94, Arrieros somos y en el
camino andamos. Velasco, p. 22, Arrieros somos y en el camino
andamos.

69 (A). <u>Arroz</u> con leche, me quiero casar, con un muchacho
que sepa bailar.

<u>Translation or Interpretation</u>: Rice with milk, I want to get
married, with a guy who knows how to dance.

Context: Just because you love to dance and like singing doesn't mean you'll marry some one who does too. The tables might turn and you will marry someone who hates to dance and hates music. (One occurrence. Informant: female).

Sources and Annotations: Velasco, p. 22, Arroz con leche.

70 (A). No hay atajo sin trabajo.

Translation or Interpretation: There is no herd without work.

Context: Used to describe a bunch of people gossiping. (One occurrence. Informant: female).

Sources and Annotations: Lea, p. 236, same as A. Maldonado, p. 29, same as A. Sbarbi, p. 102, same as A. Villafuerte, p. 84, same as A.

71 (A). Ya después de atole.

Translation or Interpretation: After the oatmeal.

Context: My mom gets very angry when the dishes are not done on time. When it's my little sister's turn to wash dishes she always comes too late, after my mom washes them. This is when my mom says "ya después de atole vienes." (Three occurrences. Informants: two female, one male).

Sources and Annotations: Cerda, p. 253, Después de atole. Conde, p. 246, Llegaste despues de atole. Martinez, p. 171, Llegar después de atole. Santamaria, p. 154, Después de atole. Velasco, p. 57, Después de atole.

72 (A). Sobre aviso no hay engaño.

Translation or Interpretation: If something goes wrong, it is your fault because you were advised beforehand.

Context: None given. (One occurrence. Informant: female).

Sources and Annotations: Adame, p. 86, same as A; p. 89, same as A. Conde, p. 380, same as A.

73 (A). Si no ayudas, no estorbes.

Translation or Interpretation: If you are not going to help, don't bother.

Context: A person may be trying to do something and someone else comes along and takes up that person't time by talking and not helping. (One occurrence. Informant: female).

Sources and Annotations: None.

74 (A). Eres como el azadón, todo para aquí y nada para allá.
74 (B). Eres como el azadón, todo para aca y nada para allá.
74 (C). Como el azadón - estira para acá.
74 (D). Eres como el azadón, recojes nomas para adentro.

Translation or Interpretation: You are like the hoe, everything this way and nothing that way.

Context: A person that takes and gives nothing in return.
(Six occurrences. Informants: three female, one male).

Sources and Annotations: Cerda, p. 253, Quieres como el azadón, todo para adentro y nada para afuera. Gamiz, p. 88, Tu
pareces al azadon, todo para aca. MacArthur, p. 70, same as A.

75 (A). No te andes miando afuera de la bacinica.

Translation or Interpretation: Do not piss outside the com-
mode.

Context: This proverb is used referring to people who are
always talking out of line. People who squeal about someone
else. (One occurrence. Informant: female).

Sources and Annotations: Caballero, p. 778, Mearse fuera del
tiesto. Jaramillo, p. 392, Estar miando fuera del tiesto.

76 (A). Lo barato es caro.

Translation or Interpretation: The cheap is expensive. (That
which is).

Context: My mother went to see this lawyer because he was
the cheapest one in town, but he made a mistake on the papers
and my mother had to pay him again. She told him this saying.
(Two occurrences. Informants: one female, one anonymous).

Sources and Annotations: Benavides, p. 91, Lo barato sale
caro. Cobos, p. 72, Lo barato cuesta caro. Conde, p. 231,
Lo barato es caro cuando no es necesario. Covarrubias, p.
192, same as A. De Barros, p. 251, Lo barato es caro y lo
caro es barato. Espinosa, A., p. 107, Lo barato cuesta caro.
Espinosa, F., p. 71, Lo caro es barato y lo barato es caro.
Galvan, p. 125, same as A; p. 130, Lo barato es caro. Lo
barato cuesta caro. Jaramillo, p. 399, Lo barato sale caro.
Maldonado, p. 58, same as A. MacArthur, p. 29, same as A.
Rodriguez-Marin (1926), p. 265, Lo barato es caro cuando no
es necesario; p. 457, Siempre lo barato fue caro. Rubio,
p. 292, Lo barato cuesta caro. Sbarbi, p. 116, same as A.

24

Barba / Basura

77 (A).   Le anda haciendo la <u>barba.</u>

<u>Translation or Interpretation</u>: He is buttering him up.

<u>Context</u>: Used when someone is being nice for a gain. (One occurrence. Informant: female).

<u>Sources and Annotations</u>: Sbarbi, p. 117, Hacerle la barba a alguno.

78 (A).   Cuando veas las <u>barbas</u> de tu vecino cortar, hecha
          las tuyas a remojar.

<u>Translation or Interpretation</u>: When you see a neighbor's beard cut, put yours to soak.

<u>Context</u>: Said when someone is getting ahead and should serve as an example to others. (Two occurrence. Informants: one female, one male).

<u>Sources and Annotations</u>: Adame, p. 17, Cuando veas las barbas de tu vecino pelar, pon las tuyas a remojar; p. 22, Cuando veas las barbas de tu vecino pelar, pon las tuyas a remojar. Aranda, p. 6, Cuando mires a tu vecino lavar pon la tuya a remojar. Covarrubias, p. 193, Quando vieres la barba de tu vecino pelar, echa la tuya en remojo. De Barros, p. 156, Cuando las barbas de tu vecino veas pelar, echa las tuyas a remojar. Espinosa, A., p. 103, Cuando veas la barba de tu vecino pelar, echa la tuya a remojar. Espinosa, F., p. 54, Cuando vieres la barba de tu vecino rapar (que no se puede rapar) echa la tuya a remojar. Camiz, p. 77, Cuando veas la barba de tu vecino pelar, hecha la tuya a remojar; p. 93, Si ves a otro resurar, pon tu barba a remojar. Maldonado, p. 53, Cuando vieres la barba de tu vecino pelar, echa la tuya a remojar. Robe, p. 69, Cuando veas las barbas de tu vecino afeitar, pon las tuyas a remojar. Rodriguez-Marin (1926), p. 461, Si las barbas de tu vecino rapar, echa las tuyas a re- mojar. Sbarbi, p. 117, Cuando la barba de tu vecino veas pelar, echa la tuya a remojar.

79 (A).   No cabe duda que la <u>basura</u> siempre flota.

<u>Translation or Interpretation</u>: There is no doubt, garbage always rises to the top. (There is no doubt, garbage always floats). There is no room for doubt since the truth always turns out. Meaning: No matter how doubtful a person is of a situation sooner or later the truth floats to the top.

<u>Context</u>: A man always is friendly with ladies. A particular woman frequently visits him at his office, supposedly for business. It is a few months later, and the wife finds out they had been seeing each other. (One occurrence. Informant: female).

<u>Sources and Annotations</u>: None.

80 (A). Hemos perdido la <u>batalla</u> pero no hemos perdido la
        guerra.

<u>Translation or Interpretation</u>: We've lost a battle but we
haven't lost the war.

<u>Context</u>: When I was in Viet Nam, I was at a base camp called
<u>Khe Sahn</u>, in April 1968. During that time the camp was over-
run by the North Vietnamese and the Viet Cong, and we suffered
heavy casualties. We were evacuated by helicopter during the
day and part of the night. I still remember flying over the
case camp, smothered in smoke, when an officer piloting the
ship said "Don't worry men, we've lost the battle but we sure
as hell haven't lost the war." Through the stupidity of the
officers we were sent back to recapture the basecamp, suffering heavy losses once again. We managed to gain what we had
lost, but I never managed to forget that phrase. "Khe Sahn
Overrun." (One occurrence. Informant: male).

<u>Sources and Annotations</u>: None.

81 (A). Eres como la <u>becerra</u> de Tía Cleta, con cualquier
        atajo te pegas.

<u>Translation or Interpretation</u>: You are like Tía Cleta's calf,
you attach yourself to any herd.

<u>Context</u>: Used whenever someone just comes and joins your
group without being invited, or whenever you are going somewhere and that person just assumes and gets in with you without being asked. (One occurrence. Informant: female).

<u>Sources and Annotations</u>: None.

82 (A). Al que <u>bien</u> haces bien no esperes.
82 (B). Al que <u>bien</u> le haces con un mal te paga.

<u>Translation or Interpretation</u> : (To) whom you do good do not
expect good in return. You may always do something to help
someone, but when it comes to them doing something for you no
one returns the favor.

<u>Context</u>: A friend of mine always used to help others around
work. One day she asked another girl if she could do (her a
favor). The girl just ignored her as if she hadn't heard and
left. (Two occurrences. Informant: one female, one male).

<u>Sources and Annotations</u>: None.

83 (A). El que <u>bien</u> hace, mal no espera.
83 (B). Hacer <u>bien</u> hacer, nunca se pierde.

<u>Translation or Interpretation</u>: He who does good things won't
expect bad things.

Bien / Bien

Context: My informant told this to her children, when they
moved out of her house, so that they might live a good life
and please the Lord. (Two occurrences. Informants: one female, one male).

Sources and Annotations: Cobos, p. 61, same as B. Rodriguez-
Marin (1926), p. 149, El buen trigo hace el pan bueno; p. 215,
Same as B.

84 (A). Has bien y no te fijes a quien.
84 (B). Has el bien y no te fijes a quien.
84 (C). Has un bien y no te fijes a quien.
84 (D). Hace el bien por donde pases sin pensar para quien es.
84 (E). Has el bien y no mires a quien.

Translation or Interpretation: Do right and worry not whom it
might benefit.

Context: If a person needs help don't ever say no, if you can
help him, because you don't know him, but you should help because you just feel like helping. (Sixteen occurrences.
Informants: 12 female, three male, one anonymous).

Sources and Annotations: Adame, p. 52, Haces el bien sin ver
a quien; p. 53, Haces el bien sin ver a quien. Aranda, p. 16,
Haz bien y no acartes a quien. Ballesteros, p. 28, Haz el
bien sin ver a quien. Cobos, p. 62, Same as E; Haz el bien
y no acates a quien. Conde, p. 192, Haces el bien sin ver a
quien. Covarrubias, p. 215, Hace el bien y no cates a quien.
Chavez, p. 47, same as E. Espinosa, A., p. 101, Haz el bien
y no acates a quien. Espinosa, F., p. 124, Haz bien y no
cates a quien. Galvan, p. 129, Haz bien y no mires a quien;
p. 131, Haz bien y no mires a quien. Gamiz, p. 90, same as
E. Glazer, p. 51, Haz bien y no veas a quien. Jaramillo, p.
394, Haz bien y no mires a quien. Lea, p. 325, same as E.
Lucero-White, p. 34, same as E. Maldonado, p. 28, Haz bien y
no cantes a quien. Paredes, p. 92, Haz bien y no mires a
quien. Perez, p. 122, Haz bien y no mires a quien. Robe, p.
69, Haces el bien sin ver a quien. Rodriguez-Marin (1930),
p. 219, Haz el bien aunque no sepas a quien; Haz bien sin
mirar a quien. Rodriguez-Marin (1926), p. 466, Si quieres
hacer bien no mires a quien. Rubio, p. 257, Haz el bien y no
veas a quien. Sbarbi, p. 131, same as A.

85 (A). No hay bien que dure, no mal que no se acabe.

Translation or Interpretation: There is no good that lasts,
nor bad that does not end. It is a long lake that has no
turning.

Context: There are many problems in our life but...in some
moment of life there is always laughter or happiness. (One
occurrence. Informant: female).

27

Sources and Annotations: Alcala, p. 87, No hay bien ni mal
que cien años dure. Correas, p. 241, same as A. Espinosa, F.,
p. 57, No hay bien que dure cien años ni mal que dure ciento y
veyente. Galvan, p. 130, No hay mal que cien años dure. Maldonado, p. 158, No hay mal que cien anos dure ni bien que los
ature. Pérez, p. 124. No hay mal que por bien no venga ni
enfermedad que dure cien años. Rodriguez-Marin (1930), p.
226, No hay bien que dure cien años, ni mal que a ellos llegue. Sbarbi, p. 132, No hay bien ni mal que cien años dure.

86 (A). No hay **bien** que mal no venga.

Translation or Interpretation: There is not any good from
which bad will come. Meaning: just when everything was going
right it all went wrong.

Context: R.'s daughter was married. She had a child. She
was very happy and so was her husband. Mrs. C. and her husband, after a year's time, got word that her daughter was
getting a divorce. (One occurrence. Informant: female).

Sources and Annotations: Conde, p. 286, No hay bien sin mal,
ni daño sin provecho. Maldonado, p. 30, Quien bien tiene y
mal escope, por mal que le vengo no se encoje. Rodriguez-
Marin (1926), p. 333, No hay bien fin por mal camino.

87 (A). Un **bien** con un mal se paga.

Translation or Interpretation: One favor pays with a bad
favor.

Context: Once some school boys were working in a school project. This guy, named José, helped his friend with his part
in the project because his friend, Juan, was behind with another assignment. When the teacher graded the project, Juan
did not give enough credit to his friend, Jose, who had done
all of the project. Jose got a lower grade. After class Jose
told his friend, Juan, "un bien con un mal se paga." This
means that if you do a favor to someone he or she will pay you
with a bad favor. My informant can remember this since he was
a junior in school and he also used it whenever somebody else
does something wrong to him. (One occurrence. Informant:
male).

Sources and Annotations: Maldonado, p. 64, Yo te perdono el
mal que me haces por el bien que me sabes. Robe, p. 72, same
as A. Rubio, p. 206, same as A.

88 (A). ¿Con esa **boca** comes?

Translation or Interpretation: Do you eat with that mouth?

Context: Used when someone is speaking vulgar language and is trying to tell them that their mouth might be very dirty and needs to be washed out with soap -- before being able to eat again. (One occurrence. Informant: male).

Sources and Annotations: Martinez, p. 68, same as A.

89 (A). En boca cerrada no entran moscas.

Translation or Interpretation: No fly will get in a closed mouth.

Context: This proverb is used whenever you are asked to divulge a secret and you would get in trouble if you do. (31 occurrences. Informants: 22 female, seven male, two anony- mous).

Sources and Annotations: Adame, p. 33, En boca cerrada no entra mosca. Alcala, p. 91, same as A. Aranda, p. 4, same as A. Armas, p. 414, same as A. Ballesteros, p. 58, En boca cerrada no pesca moscas. Benavides, p. 90, same as A. Caba- llero, p. 553, same as A. Campa, p. 64, same as A. Cobos, p. 53, same as A. Conde, p. 156, same as A. Covarrubias, p. 223, same as A. Chavez, p. 45, En boca cerrada no entra mosca. Espinosa, A., p. 106, En boca cerrada no entra mosca. Galvan, p. 128, same as A; p. 131, same as A. Gamiz, p. 80, same as A. Glazer, p. 43, same as A. Jaramillo, p. 386, En boca cerrada no entra mosca. Maldonado, p. 27, En boca cerra- da no entra mosca. MacArthur, p. 24, En boca cerrada no entra mosca. Perez, p. 118, same as A. Robe, p. 66, same as A. Vasquez, p. 88, En boca cerrada no entra mosca. Wesley, p. 215, same as A.

90 (A). En boca del mentiroso la verdad se hace dudosa.

Translation or Interpretation: In (the) mouth of the liar the truth becomes doubtful.

Context: I first heard this proverb a couple of weeks ago when my informant came over to my house. We were all in the living room and were discussing what a liar my brother was. He was saying that he had come in about 4:30 A.M. He didn't like being put on the spot, so he abruptly changed the subject and said he was going to work for twelve hours the next day. My mother didn't believe him and asked him several times "are you sure you're going to work 12 hours tomorrow?" He reas- sured her that he was. It was at that moment that I heard my informant say "en boca del mentiroso, la verdad se hace dudosa."(One occurrence. Informant: female).

Sources and Annotations: Aranda, p. 14, En boca de mentiroso lo cierto se hace dudoso. Rubio, p. 209, En boca de mentiroso lo cierto se hace dudoso.

91 (A). No te hagas <u>boca</u> chiquita.

<u>Translation or Interpretation</u>: Don't be shy at the table.
(Don't pretend to be a small mouth.)

<u>Context</u>: I heard this proverb last week at my boyfriend's
house. His mother had made a barbeque in honor of my boyfriend's birthday. I was invited to go, and when it came time
to eat I was a little hesitant since I was not too acquainted
with his family. I began serving myself small amounts of food,
then my boyfriend said come on "no te hagas de boca chiquita."
In other words, "eat, you're among friends anyway." He said
this to make me feel more at home. I had heard this <u>dicho</u>
before but this was the first time it had been directed at me.
This <u>dicho</u> is very common among Mexican families since it is
the custom to always serve your visitor something to eat.
(Three occurrences. Informants: male).

<u>Sources and Annotations</u>: Armas, p. 228, same as A. Benavides,
p. 89, same as A. Santamaria, p. 216, Hacerse uno de boca
chiquita. Villafuerte, p. 106, Hacerse de boca chiquita.

92 (A). A <u>boda</u> ni a bautismo no vayas sin ser llamado.
92 (B). Quien va a la <u>boda</u> y no es (invitado), vuelve de ella
         avergonzado.
92 (C). Quien va a la <u>fiesta</u> y no es (invitado), bien le esta
         si no es hechado.

<u>Translation or Interpretation</u>: Who goes to a wedding uninvited
is likely to be slighted, and who crashes a party unannounced
is lucky if he is not bounced.

<u>Context</u>: If a person is not invited means the people didn't
feel comfortable with his presence so why go and ruin their day
or night. (One occurrence. Informant: female).

<u>Sources and Annotations</u>: Correas, p. 16, A boda ni a bautiza-
do. De Barros, p. 62, A bodas y a niño bautizado, no vayas sin
ser llamado.

93 (A). No hay <u>borracho</u> que coma lumbre.
93 (B). No hay <u>borracho</u> que trage lumbre.
93 (C). No hay <u>borracho</u> que lumbre coma.

<u>Translation or Interpretation</u>: There's no drunkard that will
(eat) fire.

<u>Context</u>: The student that told me this proverb heard it ever
since she was very small. It is used very much in her family.
She tells me that her family uses this proverb when people try
to make excuses to get away with something. It is mainly said
when a drunk person does something wrong or says something he
later doesn't remember. She says there is no excuse why the
drunk should not remember because he did know what he was saying and doing since everyone knows that no drunk will eat fire

if you give it to him. That means that he knows what fire is
and what it can do, then he knows what he is saying and doing.
(Five occurrences. Informants: two male, two female, one
anonymous).

Sources and Annotations: Adame, p. 70, No hay loco que coma
lumbre; p. 74, No hay loco que coma lumbre. Ballesteros, p.
53, same as A. Cerda, p. 256, same as A. Cobos, p. 89, same
as A. Conde, p. 288, No hay loco que coma lumbre. Gamiz, p.
92, No hay loco que coma lumbre. Rodriguez-Marin (1930), p.
228, No hay loco que coma lumbre. Rubio, p. 27, same as A.
Santamaria, p. 189, Ningún loco come lumbre o candela. Vasquez, p. 89, same as A.

94 (A). Con pequena braza se suele quemar la casa.

Translation or Interpretation: It only takes one spark to
burn a house. It only takes one word to get an argument going.

Context: My mom and I have arguments every day, usually over
the same thing. If only I could learn to keep my mouth shut
and not say a word back to anything she says I could save a
lot of arguments. (One occurrence. Informant: female).

Sources and Annotations: Sbarbi, p. 153, Con chica braza se
enciende una braza.

95 (A). Para que son tantos brincos estando el suelo parejo.
95 (B). Para que son tantos saltos estando el suelo tan parejo.
95 (C). Para que tantos brincos y saltos estando el suelo tan
         parejo.

Translation or Interpretation: Why beat around the bush. (Why
so much jumping when the floor is straight).

Context: When you are trying to say something you don't want
to say and you say a lot of things that do not make sense, you
avoid saying what you really want to say. (Four occurrences.
Informants: two female, two male).

Sources and Annotations: Adame, p. 79, Para que tantos brincos
estando el suelo parejo; p. 81, Para que tantos brincos estando
el suelo tan parejo. Armas, p. 222, Andar con Brincos; p. 313,
No andarse con brincos; p. 338, Porque tanto brinco, estando el
suelo tan parejo. Cerda, p. 257, same as B. Conde, p. 312,
¿Para que son tantos brincos estando el suelo tan parejo?
Espinosa, A., p. 109, Pa que es tanto brinco estando el suelo
tan parejo. Galvan, p. 125, same as A; p. 132, same as A.
Martinez, p. 218, same as C. Robe, p. 67, Para que tantos
brincos si el suelo esta parejo. Santamaria, p. 234, same as
A. Velasco, p. 128, same as A. Yanez, p. 51, Ni tantos brin-
cos estando parejo el llano.

96 (A). Arrimate con los <u>buenos</u> y serás uno de ellos.

<u>Translation or Interpretation</u>: Be friends with good people and you will become a good person.

<u>Context</u>: My mother always wanted me to be friends with the son of a preacher, who was a very good boy, so some of his goodness would rub off on me. (One occurrence. Informant: female).

<u>Sources and Annotations</u>: Aranda, p. 2, Allégate a los buenos y serás uno de ellos; p. 17, Juantate a los buenos y serás uno de ellos. Cobos, p. 15, Arrimate a los buenos y serás uno de ellos; p. 64, Júntate a los buenos y serás uno de ellos; p. 72, Llegate a los buenos y serás uno de ellos. Correas, p. 576, Llegate a los buenos y serás uno de ellos. Covarrubias, p. 91, Allegate a los buenos y serás uno de ellos; p. 152, Arrimate a los buenos y serás uno de ellos; p. 910, Arrimate a los buenos y serás uno de ellos. De Barros, p. 92, Allegate a los buenos y serás uno de ellos. Espinosa, F., p. 62, Llegate a los buenos y serás uno de ellos; Gamiz, p. 79, Juntate con los buenos y serás uno de ellos. Lea, p. 233, Allegate a los buenos y serás uno de ellos. Lucero-White, p. 33, Allegate a los buenos y serás uno de ellos. Maldonado, p. 24, Allegate a los buenos y serás uno de ellos. Rodriguez-Marin (1930), p. 61, Convesar con los buenos y serás uno de ellos. Rodriguez-Marin (1926), p. 5, Acompanate con los buenos y serás uno de ellos; p. 46, Arrimate a los buenos y serás uno de ellos. Sbarbi, p. 160, same as A.

97 (A). De los <u>buenos</u> se sirve Dios.

<u>Translation or Interpretation</u>: It means that when someone dies and people say he was good, God wanted him to die and keep him. (God serves himself from the good).

<u>Context</u>: My informant said that her grandmother used to say this after she came from a funeral. (One occurrence. Informant: female).

<u>Sources and Annotations</u>: None.

98 (A). ¿A dónde ira el <u>buey</u> que no trabaje?
98 (B). ¿A dónde a de llegar el <u>buey</u> que no are?

<u>Translation or Interpretation</u>: Everywhere the ox goes he is put to plow. Everywhere the poor man goes he must work.

<u>Context</u>: According to my informant this proverb means that when a person is meant to do or be something there is no way to change the situation. It can be used whenever a person complains that his or her job is too hard, and that he/she wishes to seek an easier one. If one feels that the person complaining will not be able to find a better job because of

his physical or mental capability, then you may use this line.
My informant first heard this proverb from her mother while in
her childhood. My informant had many chores to do and was
usually complaining about this to her mother. Since she was
the only girl in the family her mother felt that was only my
informant's responsibility to fulfill them, and used this line
to do so. This occurred in San Pedro, Nuevo Leon. (Two occurrences. Informant: one female, one male).

Sources and Annotations: Armas, p. 407, ¿A donde ha de ir el
buey que no are? Caballero, p. 515, ¿Donde ira el buey que no
are? Cobos, p. 10, ¿A donde ira el buey que no are?; p. 34,
Donde vaya el buey que no are. Conde, p. 22, A donde ira el
buey que no are. Correas, p. 13, same as A. De Barros, p.
180, ¿Donde ira el buey que no are? Jaramillo, p. 337, Donde
ira el buey que no are. Maldonado, p. 23, A donde ira el buey
que no are. Martinez, p. 16, same as A. Rodriguez-Marin
(1926), p. 7, A donde ira el buey que no are, sino al matadero;
p. 138, Donde ira el buey que no are; Sbarbi, p. 161, ¿Donde
ira el buey que no are? Villafuerte, p. 124, Adonde ira el
buey que no are.

99 (A). Los bueyes y los caballos pintos, de lejos se conocen.

Translation or Interpretation: A man of low morals is like a
spotted horse you can recognize them from far away.

Context: This proverb says that the men of low morals are
like a spotted horse. You can see from far off what kind of
person he is, just like you can see far off a spotted horse
that is a spotted horse. (One occurrence. Informant: male).

Sources and Annotations: None.

100 (A). No hay peor burla que la verdadera.

Translation or Interpretation: A truth that's told with bad
intent beats all the lies you can invent.

Context: In some things that we do in life we may be ashamed,
and there will always be somebody to remind us. (One occurrence. Informant: female).

Sources and Annotations: Maldonado, p. 94, Burlando se dicen
las verdades.

101 (A). Cuando te digo que la burra es parda es porque trai-
           go los pelos en la mano.
101 (B). Cuando digo ques el buey/burra es gris es porque
           traigo los pelos en la mano.
101 (C). Si te digo que la mula es prieta es porque traigo
           los pelos en la mano.

33

Translation or Interpretation: When I say that the mule is brown its because I have a bunch of hairs in my hand.

Context: Before you say something make sure of what you're going to say first. (Six occurrences. Informants: three female, three male).

Sources and Annotations: Adame, p. 17, Cuando digo que la mula es pinta, es porque traigo los pelos en la mano; p. 20, Cuando digo que la mula es pinta, es porque traigo los pelos en la mano. Ballesteros, p. 60, Cuando digo que el caballo es pardo es porque tengo los pelos en la mano. Cerda, p. 257, Cuando digo que la burra es pinta, es porque traigo los pelos en la mano. Conde, p. 94, Cuando yo digo que la burra es parda, es porque traigo los pelos en la mano. Galvan, p. 125, Cuando digo que la burra es parda...; p. 126, same as A. Martinez, p. 252, same as A. Rubio, p. 108, same as A. Velasco, p. 149, Si digo que la burra es parda es porque tengo los pelos en la mano.

102 (A). Otra vez, la burra al maiz.

Translation or Interpretation: Again the donkey to the corn.

Context: This is when someone commits the same mistake twice. Someone who is very stubborn. (Two occurrences. one female, one male).

Sources and Annotations: Adame, p. 86, Sigue la burra al maiz; p. 87, Sique la burra al maiz.

103 (A). El burrito adelante, para que no se espante.

Translation or Interpretation: Put the donkey first, so he will not be frightened.

Context: Always the little boys/girls should go first so they would not get scared in the years to come. (One occurrence. Informant: female).

Sources and Annotations: Conde, p. 414, Y el burrito delante, para que no me espante. Santamaria, p. 241, same as A. Sbarbi, p. 167, El burro delante, para que no se espante. Villafuerte, p. 126, El burro adelante para que no se espante.

104 (A). Al burro dado no se le busca colmillo.

Translation or Interpretation: Accept a gift and do not complain about it. To a gift donkey you should not check to see if it has teeth.

Context: About five years ago, when I graduated from high school, I got a 1970 Maverick Ford as a graduation present.

When I saw the car, I told my mother that I wanted a newer car.
She then told me the proverb mentioned above. (One occurrence.
Informant: female).

Sources and Annotations: Cobos, p. 9, A burro dado no se le
ve el colmillo. Conde, p. 20, A caballo dado no se le busca
el colmillo. Galvan, p. 124, A caballo dado no hay que mirarle el colmillo; p. 126, A caballo dado no hay que mirarle el
colmillo; p. 127, A caballo dado no hay que mirarle el colmillo. MacArthur, p. 39, A caballo regalado, no se le mira el
colmillo. Martinez, p. 13, A caballo dado no se le ve colmillo.

105 (A). El burro de Don Vicente carga gente y no lo siente.

Translation or Interpretation: Don Vicente's burro carries
people and doesn't tire.

Context: Could be used as a way of describing the way a person's stamina should be tireless and endless like Don Vicente's
burro. (One occurrence. Informant: female).

Sources and Annotations: Caballero, p. 330, Como el borrico
de San Vicente, que lleva la carga, y no la siente. Conde, p.
126, El burro de San Vicente, lleva la carga, y no la siente.

106 (A). Entras como burro sin mecate.

Translation or Interpretation: (You) enter like a donkey without a rope. You come in like a lose donkey.

Context: My parents would tell us this proverb when we would
not greet visitors. (Two occurrences. Informants: one female, one male).

Sources and Annotations: Arora, p. 96, Se fue como burro sin
mecate. Caballero, p. 569, Entrar como los burros en la cua-
dra. California Spanish Proverbs and Adages, p. 123, Se fue
como burro sin mecate. Conde, p. 44, Anda como burro sin
mecate; p. 78, Como burro sin mecate; p. 366, Se mete como
burro sin mecate. Santamaria, p. 24, Meterse como burro sin
bozal o sin mecate.

107 (A). Hasta que hubo burro que no le gusto lo verde.

Translation or Interpretation: Since when is there a donkey
who does not like green grass?

Context: I first recall hearing this proverb when I was about
15 years old. This proverb was usually heard among the older
generation, perhaps in controversial issues. Therefore, I
don't recall specifically the person who first said it. I
asked my mother what it meant. She states that when a majority

in a group of people oppose a certain way, and one or two dis-
agree, they refer to these persons as donkeys who are stubborn
and no longer satisfied with eating only green grass. She
also added that this is often heard among two people who are
arguing about something. I believe this proverb can relate to
most. Many times we encounter stubborn people who are persis-
tent in their views. (One occurrence. Informant: female).

Sources and Annotations: Cerda, p. 258, Estás como el burro,
deseando morder lo verde.

108 (A). Tanto le picas al burro hasta que respinga.

Translation or Interpretation: One can bug a donkey so long
(until) it will come at you.

Context: My informant has two brothers. One is very passive
and the other is quick to anger. The quick to anger was pok-
ing fun at his passive brother. The passive brother took all
he could of it, and beat up his brother. (Two occurrences.
Informants: one female, one male).

Sources and Annotations: None.

109 (A). Un burro rasca a otro.

Translation or Interpretation: One burro scratches the other.
When two persons help one another.

Context: I heard a conversation between a man and some teenagers. The teenagers had done something wrong. They had
broken a window of a car and each one was covering for the
other, and the truth was never really discovered. (One occurrence. Informant: female).

Sources and Annotations: Aranda, p. 39, same as A.

110 (A). Entre menos burros más elotes.
110 (B). Entre menos burros alcansamos más elotes.
110 (C). Entre menos marranos mas elotes.

Translation or Interpretation: The fewer the better.

Context: There is more to go around if there are fewer people.
(Fifteen occurrences. Informants: six female, nine male).

Sources and Annotations: Adame, p. 34, same as A; p. 49, same
as A. Ballesteros, p. 62, same as A. Benavides, p. 89, same
as A. Cerda, p. 258, Mientras menos burros, más olotes. Chavez, p. 45, same as A. Cobos, p. 56, same as A. Conde, p.
263, Mientras menos burros, más olotes. Espinosa, A., p. 106,
Entre menos burros más olotes. Gamiz, p. 90, Mientras menos
burros, más olotes. Glazer, p. 43, same as A. MacArthur, p.

2, Menos burros, más elotes. Martinez, p. 183, same as A.
Paredes, p. 31. Entre menos burros, más olotes. Pérez, p. 122,
same as A. Rubio, p. 328, Mientras menos burros, más olotes,
Santamaria, p. 241, same as A.

111 (A). Los burros se buscan para rascarse.

Translation or Interpretation: People with a common interest
tend to stick together. Donkeys look for each other so they
can scratch each other.

Context: There was a bunch of guys that like drugs, and they
were always together. (One occurrence. Informant: male).

Sources and Annotations: Jaramillo, p. 400, same as A.
Rodriguez-Marin (1926), p. 496, Un asno rasca a otro. Santamaria, p. 210, Los machos viejos se buscan para rascarse.

112 (A). Caballo ajeno, espuelas propias.

Translation or Interpretation: With a borrowed horse you use
your spurs.

Context: This was said to a boy after borrowing his father's
car and driving around recklessly. (One occurrence. Informant: male).

Sources and Annotations: Maldonado, p. 95, Caballo ajeno, ni
come ni se cansa. Rodriguez-Marin (1926), p. 3, same as A.
Sbarbi, p. 169, same as A.

113 (A). Caballo alazan tostado primero muerto que cansado.

Translation or Interpretation: Horse that would rather die
than quit.

Context: This proverb was told by my father. It is about a
very fast horse that would prefer to die than to give up the
race. (One occurrence. Informant: male).

Sources and Annotations: Conde, p. 28, Alazan tostado, antes
muerto que cansado; p. 67, same as A. Covarrubias, p. 62,
Alazan tostado, antes muerto que cansado; p. 124, Alazan tostado, antes muerto que cansado. Martinez, p. 24, Alazan tostado, primero muerto que cansado.

114 (A). Caballo viejo mata potrillo.

Translation or Interpretation: An older person is wiser than
a younger person.

Context: When a father gives advice to his son it is because his dad has the wisdom and experience in life. (Two occurrences. Informants: two female).

Sources and Annotations: Adame, p. 16, same as A; p. 17, same as A. Conde, p. 68, same as A.

115 (A). A caballo grande, grandes espuelas.

Translation or Interpretation: For a big horse wear big spurs.

Context: Don E. says this dicho is told whenever there is a big job that needs to be done, and one needs to brace himself to accomplish it. (One occurrence. Informant: male).

Sources and Annotations: Rodriguez-Marin (1926), p. 3, same as A. Sbarbi, p. 169, same as A.

116 (A). A caballo regalado no se le mira el diente.
116 (B). A caballo regalado no se le mira el colmillo.

Translation or Interpretation: Don't look the gift horse in the mouth.

Context: When my informant got married he got a lot of presents. When opening them up he found a cheap coffee pot. His wife told him this proverb. (Four occurrences. Informants: one female, three male).

Sources and Annotations: Armas, p. 407, A caballo regalado no se le busca colmillo. Correas, p. 18, A caballo dado, no le mires el diente si a cerrado. De Barros, p. 63, A caballo regalado no hay que mirarle el diente. Espinosa, A., p. 103, A caballo regalado no hay que mirarle el diente. Gamiz, p. 78, A caballo dado no se le busca colmillo. Jaramillo, p. 360, A caballo regalado no le mira el diente. Maldonado, p. 77, A caballo dado no le mires el diente, si a cerrado. Molera, p. 65, Caballo dado no le mires el diente. Robe, p. 67, A caballo dado no le veas el diente. Rodriguez-Marin (1930), p. 4, Al caballo que te regalan, no pongas reparos a la capa. Rodriguez-Marin (1926), p. 18, Al caballo de presente, no mires el diente. Rubio, p. 6, A caballo dado no se le busca colmillo. Sbarbi, p. 169, A caballo regalado, no hay que mirarle el diente.

117 (A). Al caballo con la rienda y a la mujer con la
          espuela.

Translation or Interpretation: To a horse with the rein and to a woman with the spur. You can control a horse with the rein and a woman with the spurs.

Context: This proverb is usually said among the macho type men in Mexico and here among the Mexican Americans. Some of us say it because we mean it, and some of us say it because we want to make women angry. (One occurrence. Informant: male).

Sources and Annotations: None.

118 (A). Al caballo lo puedes llevar al agua, pero no lo puedes hacer tomar.

Translation or Interpretation: You can lead a horse to water but you can't make him drink.

Context: In many cases people can be forced to do things to a point, but no further. (One occurrence. Informant: female).

Sources and Annotations: Cobos, p. 109, Se lleva el asno al agua pero no lo hacen beber. Espinosa, A., p. 110, Se lleva al asno al agua pero no se fuerza a beber.

119 (A). Lo que es tu caballo, tu pistola y tu mujer, ni a tu buen amigo se lo prestas.

Translation or Interpretation: (Your horse, your gun or your woman, not even to your best friend should you lend). Very personal things are not to be lent, not even to a good friend. This proverb includes a horse, pistol and a woman.

Context: Informant had lent his pocket knife to his cousin and he broke the blade. Informant's uncle then told him this proverb. (One occurrence. Informant: male).

Sources and Annotations: Rodriguez-Marin (1930), p. 46, Caballo, mujer y escopeta son prendas no se prestan. Rodriguez-Marin (1926), p. 248, La mujer, el caballo y la escopeta no se prestan.

120 (A). Si no ves caballo ensillado no se te antoja viaje.
120 (B). Cuando el caballo esta ensillado todos quieren montar.
120 (C). Nomas ves caballo ensillado y se te antoja viaje.

Translation or Interpretation: If you do not see a harnessed horse (don't yearn for a trip).

Context: Used whenever you say you are going somewhere and your friend, or neighbor, or other members of the family suddenly has an errand, or trip to where you are going. (Three occurrences. Informants: two female, one male).

Sources and Annotations: Ballesteros, p. 65, Viendo caballo ensillado se les ofrece viaje. Cerda, p. 259, Cuando ve ca-

ballo ensillado, se le ofrece viaje. Conde, p. 92, Cuando hay
caballo ensillado a todos se les ofrece viaje. Espinosa, A.,
p. 108, No mas ven caballo gordo y se les ofrece viaje. Martinez, p. 199, Nomas ves burro y se te ofrece viajar. Rodriguez-Marin (1926), p. 1, En cuanto vez caballo, se te ofrece
viaje. Sbarbi, p. 170, En cuanto ves caballo, se te antoja
viaje.

121 (A). Cada <u>cabeza</u> es un mundo.

<u>Translation or Interpretation</u>: Each head is his own world.

<u>Context</u>: My mother used to remind us of this <u>dicho</u> when I was
<u>telling</u> her about some of the strangest ideas that some one
had expressed in my classes at school. (Seven occurrences.
Informants: four female, three male).

<u>Sources and Annotations</u>: Adame, p. 16, same as A; p. 17, same
as A. Benavides, p. 91, same as A. Cobos, p. 18, same as A.
Conde, p. 68, same as A. Espinosa, A., p. 103, same as A.
Vasquez, p. 90, same as A.

122 (A). Más vale ser <u>cabeza</u> de ratón que cola de leon.

<u>Translation or Interpretation</u>: It is better to be the head
of a mouse than the lion's tail.

<u>Context</u>: It is better to be the leader of a small group than
the one with the say so in a large group. (One occurrence.
Informant: male).

<u>Sources and Annotations</u>: Aranda, p. 20, same as A. Conde, p.
173, Es mejor ser cabeza de ratón que cola de león. De Barros,
p. 98, Antes cabeza de ratón que cola de león. Espinosa, F.,
p. 64, Más vale cabeza de gato que cola de león. Gamiz, p. 93,
Ser cabeza, aun de ratón; ser cola ni de león. Jaramillo, p.
403, same as A. MacArthur, p. 56, same as A. Maldonado, p.
51, Antes cabeza de ratón que cola de león. Sbarbi, p. 174,
same as A.

123 (A). Dos <u>cabezas</u> son mejor que una.

<u>Translation or Interpretation</u>: Two heads are better than one.

<u>Context</u>: I hear this when three or more people are working on
a project--they get more ideas than just their own. (Two
occurrences. Informants: one female, one male).

<u>Sources and Annotations</u>: Lea, p. 236, Más valen dos cabezas
que una. Lucero-White, p. 35, Mas valen dos cabezas que una.

124 (A). La <u>cabra</u> tira al monte.

Translation or Interpretation: The goat will return to the woods. Example: if a poor person from low economic standards moves up he will always go back to be with the same people before he becomes rich.

Context: My informant knew a couple that was lucky enough to make a small fortune. Even though they had luxuries, like a car and a better home, they kept the same acquaintances. The proverb above was applied in this case. (One occurrence. Informant: male).

Sources and Annotations: Armas, p. 415, La cabra siempre tira el monte. Ballesteros, p. 62, La cabra siempre tira el monte. Caballero, p. 710, same as A. Cobos, p. 65, La cabra siempre tira el monte. Conde, p. 205, same as A. Espinosa, A., p. 107, La cabra le tira al monte. Gamiz, p. 80, La cabra siempre aspira al monte. Jaramillo, p. 396, La cabra tira pal monte. Rodriguez-Marin (1926), p. 233, same as A. Santamaria, p. 248, same as A. Sbarbi, p. 178, same as A. Yanez, p. 143, same as A; p. 213, La cabra tira el monte y el capon al muladar.

125 (A). Por donde brinca la <u>cabra</u> brinca el cabrito.

Translation or Interpretation: Where the goat jumps, jumps the kid.

Context: This proverb was said to my brother, that if a girl's mother was a prostitute chances were that the girl would turn out to be like her mother. (Three occurrences. Informants: female).

Sources and Annotations: Ballesteros, p. 59, A donde vaya la cabra, brincan los chivos. Cerda, p. 259, same as A. Cobos, p. 100, same as A. Covarrubias, p. 255, Por donde salta la cabra, salta la que la mama. Rodriguez-Marin (1930), p. 298, Salto la cabra en la vina; tambien saltara la hija. Rodriguez-Marin (1926), p. 371, Por donde el rey pasa, todo lo arrasa. Sbarbi, p. 178, Por donde salta la cabra, el chivo.

126 (A). Hecha la <u>caca</u> de vaca aunque me escurra la mano.

Translation or Interpretation: (Throw) the excrete of the cow (even though it drips in my hand). It means that you nag your parents until they give you permission for what you want to do.

Context: My informant's daughter wanted to go to the swimming pool. This went on for an hour. My informant got tired of this and said her daughter could go. Her mother told her this proverb. (One occurrence. Informant: female).

Sources and Annotations: Cobos, p. 123, Yo no le suelto la cola aunque me cague la mano. Martinez, p. 198, No le sueltes la cola aunque te cague la mano.

127 (A). Es del otro <u>cachete</u>.

<u>Translation or Interpretation</u>: A person from Mexico.

<u>Context</u>: A <u>barrio</u> term to refer to a person from Mexico.
(One occurrence. Informant: male).

<u>Sources and Annotations</u>: Cerda, p. 259, El otro cachete.

128 (A). Eres como la <u>calabaza</u>, pedorra y entripadora.

<u>Translation or Interpretation</u>. You are like a pumpkin: (full
of it) and a stinker. A person who thinks so conceited of
himself, but isn't worth beans.

<u>Context</u>: My uncle would tell this saying to one of his work-
ers, because he would always be showing off and ordering the
other workers to do the job right. (One occurrence. Informant: male).

<u>Sources and Annotations</u>: Robe, p. 72, ¡Uy! ¡Hasta eso tiene
la calabaza...mala y entripadora.

129 (A). Salio más caro el <u>caldo</u> que los frijoles.

<u>Translation or Interpretation</u>: The soup turned out to be
more expensive than the beans.

<u>Context</u>: Informant said this because the girl wanted to go to
a movie theater, but it was too expensive. She then decided
to go to the drive-in movie, but it turned out she spent more
in the drive-in and did not enjoy the movie. (One occurrence. Informant: female).

<u>Sources and Annotations</u>: Armas, p. 357, Salir más caro el
caldo que los frijoles. Chavez, p. 47, Sale más caro el caldo
que las albondigas. Jaramillo, p. 422, Salir más caro el
caldo que los huevos.

130 (A). Más vale <u>callar</u> que mal hablar.

<u>Translation or Interpretation</u>: It's better to be quiet than
to talk bad.

<u>Context</u>: None given. (One occurrence. Informant: female).

<u>Sources and Annotations</u>: Ballesteros, p. 10, Mas vale callar
que mucho hablar. Cobos, p. 120, Vale más callar que loca-
mente hablar. Conde, p. 253, same as A; p. 311, Para mal
hablar, más vale callar. De Barros, p. 275, same as A. Lea,
p. 236, Más vale buen callar que mal hablar. Lucero-White,
p. 35, Más vale buen callar que mal hablar. Maldonado, p.
148, Mal para quien calla y peor para quien habla. Rodriguez-

Marin (1930), p. 247, Para mal hablar, más vale callar. Rodriguez-Marin (1926), p. 295, Más vale callar que errar. Sbarbi,
p. 187, Más vale buen callar que mal hablar.

131 (A). <u>Camaron</u> que se duerme se lo lleva la corriente.
131 (B). El que se duerme se lo lleva la corriente.
131 (C). Pescado que se duerme se lo lleva la corriente.

<u>Translation or Interpretation</u>: Shrimp that sleeps will be
taken by a current.

<u>Context</u>: My informant told me that when she was taking a
class in school she did not keep up with her studies. By the
time she knew it she had fallen too far behind to catch up
with her assignments, and had to drop the class. She heard
the proverb from her father. (40 occurrences. Informants:
20 female, 17 male, three not stated).

<u>Sources and Annotations</u>: Adame, p. 16, same as A; p. 18, same
as A. Armas, p. 409, same as A. Ballesteros, p. 59, same as
A. Cerda, p. 260, same as A. Cobos, p. 36, El camarón que se
duerme se lo lleva la corriente. Conde, p. 72, same as A.
Galvan, p. 125, same as A; p. 126, same as A. Gamiz, p. 87,
same as A. Glazer, p. 44, same as A. Jaramillo, p. 370, same
as A. MacArthur, p. 37, same as A. Robe, p. 69, same as A.
Rodriguez-Marin, p. 67, same as A. Wesley, p. 218, Al pescado
que se duerme se lo lleva la corriente.

132 (A). Andas por mal <u>camino</u>.

<u>Translation or Interpretation</u>: You are in the wrong business.
(You're walking the wrong road).

<u>Context</u>: A friend of ours was trying to sell drugs in school,
and the coach told him this proverb. (One occurrence. Informant: male).

<u>Sources and Annotations</u>: Armas, p. 223, Andar por mal camino.
Maldonado, p. 168, Quien malos caminos anda, malo abrojos
halla.

133 (A). De un <u>camino</u> dos mandados.

<u>Translation or Interpretation</u>: In one road, two errands. To
kill two birds with one stone.

<u>Context</u>: Informant was told this by her husband when he asked
her to go back to school, and as long as she would do that to
lose a few pounds also. He said "ya que vas de un camino has
dos mandados." (One occurrence. Informant: female).

Sources and Annotations: Armas, p. 385, Hacer un viaje y dos
mandados. Jaramillo, p. 394, Hacer en un viaje dos mandados.
Rodriguez-Marin (1926), p. 497, Un camino y dos mandados.
Sbarbi, p. 190, Hacer de un camino dos mandados.

134 (A). No dejes <u>camino</u> por vereda.
134 (B). No agarres veredas por <u>caminos</u>.
134 (C). Nunca largues <u>camino</u> por vereda.
134 (D). Nunca dejes <u>camino</u> por un sendero.
134 (E). No dejas el <u>camino</u> andado por uno desconocido.
134 (F). No dejes <u>camino</u> andado por una vereda.
134 (G). Nunca dejes <u>camino</u> real por vereda.
134 (H). No dejes <u>caminos</u> por veredas, ni preguntes que no te
          importa.

Translation or Interpretation: It is better to do what you
are accustomed to doing than to take a different route.

Context: A friend of mine has constantly bugged me to leave
school for a job in which I see no future. (18 occurrences.
Informants: 11 female, seven male).

Sources and Annotations: Ballesteros, p. 13, Para que andar
por veredas habiendo camino real. Cobos, p. 87, same as A.
Conde, p. 281, No dejes camino real por vereda. Covarrubias,
p. 1002, Quien deja el camino real por vereda prensa atajar y
rodea. Espinosa, A., 108, same as A. Glazer, p. 44, same as
A. Maldonado, p. 160, Nunca dejes el camino llano por el atajo. Rodriguez-Marin (1930), p. 200, Mas vale camino viejo que
sendero nuevo; p. 223, No dejes camino real por vereda; p.
257, Por el camino que va la vida, viene la muerte apercibida;
p. 271, Quien deja el camino viejo por el nuevo, halla el mal
que va buscando; Quien deja el camino viejo por el nuevo, tiene
mal acuerdo. Rodriguez-Marin, p. 5, Acertar piensa y yerra
quien deja el camino real por la vereda; p. 328, No dejes
camino por sendero nuevo; p. 400, Quien deja camino por vereda, atras se queda; Quien deja camino real por vereda, piensa
atajar y rodea; Quien deja camino y toma vereda, dara menos
pasos, pero atras se queda. Yanez, p. 137, No dejen camino
por vereda; p. 353, same as A.

135 (A). No te metas en <u>camisa</u> de once baras.
135 (B). Para que meterse en <u>camisa</u> de once baras.

Translation or Interpretation: Don't get yourself in problems.
In other words, don't get married. (Don't get into a shirt
with stays).

Context: I heard it from my dad when my brother told him that
he wanted to get married. So my dad told my brother that he
was too young and "que no se metiera en camisa de once baras,"
because he was going to regret it later on. (Three occurrences. Informants: female).

Sources and Annotations: Adame, p. 90, Te andas metiendo en camisa de once varas; p. 92, Te andas metiendo en camisa de once varas. Armas, p. 310, Meterse en camisa de once varas. Caballero, p. 789, Meterse en camisa de once varas. Conde, p. 298, same as A. Jaramillo, p. 405, Meterse en camisa de once varas. Sbarbi, p. 192, Meterse en camisa de once varas.

136 (A). Come camote y no te de pena, cuida tu casa y deja
la ajena.

Translation or Interpretation: Eat sweet potatoes without
embarrassment, (take care of your house not someone else's).

Context: Used when trying to tell people not to meddle in
other's lives, but to take care of their own affairs. (One
occurrence. Informant: female).

Sources and Annotations: Adame, p. 17, Cuida tu casa y deja
la ajena; p. 22, Cuida tu casa y deja la ajena. Conde, p. 96,
Cuida tu casa y deja la ajena come camote y no te de pena.
Galvan, p. 124, Cuida tu vida y deja la ajena; p. 126, Cuida
tu vida y deja la prójima. Cuida tu vida y deja la del vecino. Gamiz, p. 86, Cuida tu casa y deja la ajena. Martinez,
p. 59, same as A. Rodriguez-Marin (1930), p. 311, Si quieres
vivie sin pena, cuida de tu casa y deja la ajena. Santamaria,
p. 284, same as A. Yanez, p. 54, Cuiden sus casas y dejen la
ajena.

137 (A). Eres como la campana que todos vienen y te tocan.

Translation or Interpretation: You are like a bell; everyone
comes and rings you.

Context: It is used as a pun when someone likes to be touched
a lot. (One occurrence. Informant: male).

Sources and Annotations: Arora, p. 110, Estar campana.

138 (A). Las canas no quitan ganas.

Translation or Interpretation: Just because you are old and
have grey hair doesn't mean you don't have desire.

Context: My informant's mother would tell her husband this
proverb all the time when they grew old together. (One occurrence. Informant: female).

Sources and Annotations: Aranda, p. 18, same as A.

139 (A). Las canas salen de ganas.

Translation or Interpretation: White hairs come out because
of your will.

Context: Sometimes a person will worry too much and will be affected by what he is thinking. (One occurrence. Informant: female).

Sources and Annotations: Cerda, p. 260, same as A. Cobos, p. 70, Las canas salen de ganas, la arruga saca de duda. Conde, p. 222, same as A.

140 (A). Candil de la calle, obscuridad en tu casa.
140 (B). Eres luz de la calle y obsuridad de tu casa.

Translation or Interpretation: Light of the street, darkness in your home.

Context: Said to someone who is sweet to everyone except his own family. (11 occurrences. Informants: six female, four male, one anonymous).

Sources and Annotations: Adame, p. 34, Eres candil de la calle y obsuridad de tu casa; p. 49, Eres candil de la calle y obscuridad de tu casa. Cerda, p. 261, same as B. Cobos, p. 20, Candil de la calle y obscuridad de su casa. Conde, p. 72, Candil de la calle y obscuridad de su casa. Espinoza, A., p. 110, Eres candil de la calle y obscuridad de tu casa. Galván, p. 125, same as A; p. 128, Farol de la calle, obscuridad de la casa; p. 132, Farol de la calle, obscuridad de su casa. Gamiz, p. 81, Ser candil de la calle y obscuridad de su casa. Rodriguez-Marin (1926), p. 68, Candil de la calle, alumbra a los que pasan y oscurena su casa. Santamaria, p. 291, Candil de la calle y obscuridad de su casa. Yanez, p. 253, Ser candil de la calle y obscuridad de su casa.

141 (A). Tanto va el cántaro al agua hasta que se quiebra.
141 (B). Tanto va el cántaro al agua hasta que se rompe.
141 (C). Tanto va el cántaro a la fuente que al final se rompe.

Translation or Interpretation: A clay pot can only go for water until it is broken.

Context: Professor used this proverb to mean that student will say the same excuse everytime they miss a test or class. He said that they wear off the excuse, just as the pitcher, until it is finally broken. (18 occurrences. Informants: 11 female, six male, one not stated).

Sources and Annotations: Adame, p. 90, Tanto baja el cantaro al agua hasta que se quiebra; p. 91, Tanto baja el cántaro al agua hasta que se quiebra. Aranda, p. 28, same as A. Armas, p. 421, Tanto va el cántaro al agua que al fin se rompe. Ballesteros, p. 15, same as A. Caballero, p. 229, Cantarito que va mucho a la fuente a fin se rompe; p. 1046, Tanto va el cántaro a la fuente... Cerda, p. 261, same as A. Cobos, p.

46

115, same as A. Conde, p. 384, same as B. Covarrubias, p. 289, Cantarío que muchas veces va a la fuente alguna vez se ha de quebrar. Espinosa, A., p. 102, Tanto va el cántaro al agua hasta que se cae. Galvan, p. 125, same as A; p. 133, same as A; p. 134, same as A. Gamiz, p. 79, same as A. Glazer, p. 45, same as A. Jaramillo, p. 424, Tanto va el cántaro a la fuente que al fin se rompe. Lea, p. 238, same as B. Lucero-White, p. 35, Tanto ca el cántaro al agua hasta que por fin se rompe. MacArthur, p. 15, Tanto va el cántaro al agua, que al fin se rompe. Maldonado, p. 25, Cantarillo que muchas veces va a la fuente o deja el asa o la fuente. Rodriguez-Marin (1926), p. 68, Cántaro que mucho ca a la fuente al fin se quiebra; p. 479, Tantas veces va el cántaro a la fuente que al fin se quiebra; p. 480, Tanto va el cántaro a la fuente hasta que al fin se quiebra. Sbarbi, p. 199, Tanto va el cántaro a la fuente que al fin se quiebra. Yanez, p. 320, Tanto va el cántaro al pozo.

142 (A). Defender a <u>capa</u> y espada a defender con uñas.

<u>Translation or Interpretation</u>: To guard with one's life, to defend to the last ditch.

<u>Context</u>: This problem happens very often. It happened to my sister. My father, in the beginning, did not like her boy-friend and he would say things. She would defend him to the last ditch. (One occurrence. Informant: female).

<u>Sources and Annotations</u>: Sbarbi, p.   , Defender a capa y espada.

143 (A). Donde manda <u>capitán</u> no govierna marinero.

<u>Translation or Interpretation</u>: Where a captain orders, the (sailor) does not. In other words, the boss gives the orders.

<u>Context</u>: I once asked my mother how come she did everything that my dad told her to do. She told me that she just followed instructions, and then, she said the above proverb. (Two oc-currences. Informants: female).

<u>Sources and Annotations</u>: Adame, p. 24, same as A; p. 30, same as A. Ballesteros, p. 27, same as A. California Spanish Pro-verbs and Adages, p. 122, Donde manda capitán no manda mari-nero. Cerda, p. 261, Donde manda capitán no manda marinero. Cobos, p. 34, Donde manda capitán no manda marinero. Conde, p. 118, same as A. De Barros, p. 180, Donde hay patron no manda marinero. Galvan, p. 125, same as A; p. 127, same as A. Jaramillo, p. 377, Donde manda capitán no manda marinero. Santamaria, p. 304, Donde manda capitán no manda marinero. Velasco, p. 58, Donde manda el coparal no gobiernan los va-queros.

144 (A). <u>Caras</u> vemos corazones no sabemos.

<u>Translation or Interpretation</u>: Faces we see, hearts we don't know.

<u>Context</u>: This was mentioned while talking about people in general, and the fact that all we see is the face. Yet, many times never get to know what is in their hearts or their real intentions. (13 occurrences. Informants: nine female, four male).

<u>Sources and Annotations</u>: Adame, p. 16, same as A; p. 18, same as A; p. 78, Ojos vemos, corazones no sabemos. Aranda, p. 4, Caras vemos pero corazones no sabemos. Ballesteros, p. 13, Ojos vemos, corazones no sabemos. Cerda, p. 263, same as A. Cobos, p. 20, Cara vemos, corazón no sabemos; p. 95, Ojos vemos, corazón no sabemos. Conde, p. 73, same as A. Espinoza, A., p. 99, same as A; p. 103, Caras vemos pero corazones no. Glazer, p. 46, same as A. Jaramillo, p. 370, Caras se ven pero corazones no. Lea, p. 233, same as A. Lucero-White, p. 33, same as A. MacArthur, p. 29, same as A. Paredes, p. 30, same as A. Robe, p. 65, same as A. Rubio, p. 82, same as A.

145 (A). El <u>carbón</u> que a sido braza con facilidad se prende.

<u>Translation or Interpretation</u>: A person with experience in something will easily do the same thing with ease.

<u>Context</u>: A certain individual has quit drinking, but his friends insisted not to give it up. He started the habit all over again, because of the influence of others. (One occurrence. Informant: male).

<u>Sources and Annotations</u>: Cerda, p. 263, El carbón que ha sido braza, con poquita lumbre tiene. Conde, p. 73, Carbón que a sido braza con poco fuego vuelve a arder. Santamaria, p. 315, El carbón que ha sido braza, con facilidad enciende. Sbarbi, p. 208, El carbón que ha sido braza, con poco lumbre se enciende. Yanez, p. 59, El carbón que ha sido braza, facilmente vuelve a arder.

146 (A). En la <u>cárcel</u> y en la cama se conocen los amigos.
146 (B). Debe uno visitar a sus amigos en el hospital o en la <u>cárcel</u>.

<u>Translation or Interpretation</u>: In jail and at your bedside you will know who your friends are.

<u>Context</u>: My father had an accident nineteen years ago, and was in the hospital for a year. To my father, and mother, this proverb tells it all. My father did have visitors every night while in the hospital, but he says there were other patients who no one ever went to see. (Two occurrence. Informants: one female, one male).

Sources and Annotations: Adame, p. 34, En la cárcel y en la cama, los amigos se conocen; p. 47, En la cárcel y en la cama, los amigos se conocen. Armas, p. 409, Cama y cárcel, prueba de amigos y venganza de enemigos. Cerda, p. 263, En la cárcel y en la cama, los amigos se conocen. Cobos, p. 55, same as A. Conde, p. 161, En la cama y en la cárcel se conocen los amigos; p. 165, En prision y enfermedad se conoce la amistad. Gamiz, p. 90, En la cárcel y en la cama se experimentan los amigos. Maldonado, p. 99, Carceles y caminos, hacen amigos. Robe, p. 69, same as A. Rodriguez-Marin (1930), p. 125, En la cárcel y en la cama veras quien te ama; p. 238, Nunca se conoce al buen amigo con en la cárcel y en la cama. Rodriguez-Marin (1926), p. 192, En prision y enfermedad se conoce la amistad. Rubio, p. 215, same as A.

147 (A). Ahora que tengo medio para carne es vigilia.

Translation or Interpretation: Now that I have means for meat I have to fast.

Context: Years back Catholics were not allowed to eat meat on Friday. Mom and dad were paid on Friday, so mother bought meat but didn't eat it until Saturday. (One occurrence. Informant: female).

Sources and Annotations: Adame, p. 17, Cuando el pobre tiene pa carne es vigilia; p. 21, Cuando el pobre tiene pa carne es vigilia. Conde, p. 92, Cuando hay carne es vigilia. Martinez, p. 74, Cuando hay medio para carne nos salen con que es vigilia. Rubio, p. 110, Cuando el pobre tiene medio para carne, se vigilia.

148 (A). Dicen que carne de burro no es transparente.

Translation or Interpretation: They say that donkey meat is not transparent.

Context: My informant is in the eight grade at Ringgold Junior High School. She has heard her math teacher use this proverb several times. She informed me that he often uses it when students stay in front of the chalk board and the other students complain that they can't see the writing on the board. She explained that her teacher also uses other ways to put things across, both in English and in Spanish. (One occurrence. Informant: female).

Sources and Annotations: Martinez, p. 151, same as A.

149 (A). A ese carro nuevo le suenan las puertas.

Translation or Interpretation: That new car's doors rattle. Meaning that every month the payment is due so the knock is at the door.

Context: My father said this to my friend who came home to show her new car to us. My father said the above to her and she didn't know what he meant. He stated that the bill collector will be at her door to collect the monthly bill if she didn't pay. (Two occurrences. Informants: one female, one male).

Sources and Annotations: None.

150 (A). A casa de tío, pero no cada día.
150 (B). A casa de primo pero no todo el día.

Translation or Interpretation: To uncle's house, but not every day.

Context: A person that visits another person every day may become a burden. (Two occurrences. Informants: one male, one anonymous).

Sources and Annotations: Cobos, p. 54, En casa de tía, pero no cada día. Conde, p. 157, A casa de mi tía, pero no cada día. Correas, p. 17, A casa de tu tía, mas no cada día. Covarrubias, p. 162, A casa de tu tía, mas no cada día. De Barros, p. 63, A casa de tu tía pero no cada día. Rodriguez-Marin (1930), p. 5, A casa de mi tía, entrada por salida; p. 335, Visita a tu tía, mas no cada día. Rodriguez-Marin (1926), p. 178, En casa de tía -o- de tu tía-, mas no cada día. Sbarbi, p. 217, A casa de tu tía, mas no cada día.

151 (A). Del que de su casa se aleja no la halla como la deja.

Translation or Interpretation: He who leaves his home will not find it the same when he returns.

Context: Informant was told this proverb by her parents once when she returned home from an outing and complained because someone had moved things around. (One occurrence. Informant: female).

Sources and Annotations: Cerda, p. 264, Quien de su casa se aleja, no ha halla como la deja. Conde, p. 338, Quien de su casa se aleja no la halla como la deja. Gamiz, p. 94, Quien de su casa se aleja, no la halla como la deja. Yanez, p. 297, El que de su casa se aleja nunca la encuentra como la deja.

152 (A). En casa chica y en largo camino se conoce el buen amigo.

Translation or Interpretation: In close quarters, and on a long journey, one gets to know one's fellow traveller.

Context: If two persons take or make a long journey many problems can occur, and if the person that's near you helps you and
cares for you is when you really feel his/her companionship or
friendship. (One occurrence. Informant: female).

Sources and Annotations: Rodriguez-Marin (1926), p. 179, En
chica cama y largo camino se conoce el buen amigo.

153 (A). En la casa del herrero se come con cuchara de palo.
153 (B). En la casa del herrero asador de palo.

Translation or Interpretation: In the house of the (blacksmith) one eats with a wooden spoon.

Context: A blacksmith should use his iron to barbeque meat,
instead he uses one made of wood. Like a carpenter building
homes while he lives in a shack. (Two occurrences. One female, one male).

Sources and Annotations: Adame, p. 35, En la casa del herreno, cuchara de palo; p. 47, En la casa del herreno, cuchara
de palo. Armas, p. 414, En casa de herrero, cuchillo de palo.
Caballero, p. 556, En casa del herrero cuchillo de palo. Conde, p. 157, same as B. Covarrubias, p. 131, En casa del herrero peor apero. Espinosa, F., p. 73, En casa de herrero cuchillo mangorrero. Gamiz, p. 74, En casa del herrero, cuchillo
de palo. Jaramillo, p. 381, En casa de herrero, azadon (o
cuchillo) de palo. Maldonado, p. 27, En casa de herrero cuchillo mangorrero. Robe, p. 67, En casa de herrero, cuchara
de palo. Rodriguez-Marin (1930), p. 122, En casa de herrero,
asador de palo y cuchillo de madero. Sbarbi, p. 219, En casa
de herrero, badil de madero o chuchillo de manogorrero, o
cuchillo de palo o asador de palo.

154 (A). No te arrojes en casa ajena, toca de afuera y espera.

Translation or Interpretation: Don't barge into (a strange)
house, knock at the door and wait.

Context: Better be calm before you rush into very serious
problems. (One occurrence. Informant: male).

Sources and Annotations: Cobos, p. 26, Cuando vayas a casa
ajena, llama a la puerta.

155 (A). Quemas tu casa por ver arder la ajena.

Translation or Interpretation: You burn your own house just
to see your neighbor's house burn.

Context: You cut your nose to spite your face. (One occurrence. Informant: female).

Sources and Annotations: Cerda, p. 264, Por ver la casa arder, le prenden fuego a la mía. Rubio, p. 107, Por ver arder la casa del vecino le prenden fuego a la propia.

156 (A). La casada le pide a la viuda.

Translation or Interpretation: The married woman begs from the widow.

Context: Used when one is asking a favor from one who really needs one. (One occurrence. Informant: male).

Sources and Annotations: Cobos, p. 65, same as A. Martinez, p. 152, same as A. Rubio, p. 273, same as A. Velasco, p. 90, same as A.

157 (A). Al mejor casador se le va una liebre.

Translation or Interpretation: Even the best of hunters will occasionally miss a rabbit.

Context: I have heard this dicho used many times to try to sober an individual who was expressing an overly confident attitude in his ability to complete a task. A similar thing in English that I've heard is that nothing is as easy as it looks.

Sources and Annotations: Conde, p. 32, same as A. Jaramillo, p. 361, same as A. Rodriguez-Marin (1926), p. 24, same as A. Santamaria, p. 295, same as A; p. 365, same as A.

158 (A). Te casaste, te fregaste.

Translation or Interpretation: You got married you bombed out. Or you buried yourself.

Context: Usually said to a young man who has just gotten married. It is said because of his new responsibilities of his future married life. (One occurrence. Informant: male).

Sources and Annotations: Caballero, p. 1048, Te casate, te enterraste. Cerda, p. 264, same as A. Cobos, p. 115, same as A. Conde, p. 385, same as A. Espinosa, A., p. 102, Te casaste-te cagates. Galván, p. 128, same as A; p. 134, same as A. Gamiz, p. 91, Te casaste, te amolaste. Martínez, p. 260, Te casaste, te amolaste. Rodriguez-Marin (1930), p. 318, Te casaste, te cagaste; Te casaste, diste al traste. Rodriguez-Marin, P. 481, Te casaste, te enterraste.

159 (A). La cáscara guarda al palo.

Translation or Interpretation: The bark takes care of the tree. The skin takes care of the body. It means if you don't take a bath it will not harm you or kill you.

Context: Her younger brother hated to take a bath and she kept after him. His father said that saying so she would stop pestering him. (Six occurrences. Informants: four female, two male).

Sources and Annotations: Ballesteros, p. 28, same as A. Cobos, p. 67, same as A. Conde, p. 206, same as A. Gamiz, p. 84, same as A. Jaramillo, p. 396, same as A. Martinez, p. 152, same as A. Robe, p. 65, same as A. Santamaria, p. 331, same as A. Velasco, p. 90, same as A.

160 (A). Antes que te cases mira lo que haces.
160 (B). Mira lo que haces, antes que te cases.

Translation or Interpretation: Before you get married look at what you do.

Context: E. got married to a young man who she had just met, because of family pressure. Shortly after the ceremony she regretted not taking time enough to analyze the situation. (Ten occurrences. Informants: eight female, two anonymous).

Sources and Annotations: Aranda, p. 3, same as A. Balleste- ros, p. 43, same as A. Cobos, p. 14, same as A. Conde, p. 45, Antes que te cases mira bien lo que haces. Correas, p. 60, Antes que te cases mira lo que haces, que no es nudo que así lo desates. Covarrubias, p. 314, same as A. De Barros, p. 100, same as A. Espinoza, A., p. 98, Antes de que te cases- mira lo que haces. Espinosa, F., p. 74, Antes que te cases mira (muy bien) lo que haces. Galvan, p. 125, same as A; p. 131, same as A. Gamiz, p. 93, Mucho antes de que te cases, mira y piensa lo que haces. Jaramillo, p. 364, same as A. Lucero-White, p. 33, same as A. MacArthur, p. 3, same as A. Maldonado, p. 24, Antes que cases, cata que haces: que no es nudo que asi desates. Perez, p. 122, Hasta que te cases mira lo que haces. Santamaria, p. 330, Same as A. Sbarbi, p. 30, same as A; p. 225, same as A.

161 (A). Quitada la causa se quita el pecado.

Translation or Interpretation: Do away with the cause and you do away with the sin.

Context: Used to point out that one can solve a problem by doing away with the seed of the problem. (One occurrence. Informant: female).

Sources and Annotations: Cobos, p. 44, El que evita la tentación, evita el pecado; p. 106, Quien quita la ocasión quita el pecado. Espinosa, F., p. 75, Quita la causa, y quitarás el pecado; p. 170, Quita la ocasión y quitarás el pecado. Lucero-White, p. 36, Quien quita la ocasión quita el pecado. Rodriguez-Marin (1926), p. 426, Quien quita la causa, quita el pecado. Sbarbi, p. 230, same as A.

162 (A). A cena de vino desayuno de agua.

Translation or Interpretation: After a dinner of wine a breakfast of water.

Context: This is used when one observes that somebody is drinking water boraciously in the morning. (One occurrence. Informant: male).

Sources and Annotations: Rodriguez-Marin (1926), p. 5, same as A; p. 436, Quien vino cena, agua almuerza.

163 (A). Viejos los cerros y todavía enverdecen.

Translation or Interpretation: Old are the hills yet they still become green.

Context: A young man might say to an old person "you're too old to learn a new trade." (One occurrence. Informant: male).

Sources and Annotations: Arora, p. 131, Es tan viejo como los cerros y cada año enverdece.

164 (A). Del cielo a la tierra no hay nada oculto.

Translation or Interpretation: There is no secret between the sky and the earth.

Context: My daughter asked me for permission to go to the movies with her girl friends. Instead she went with her boy friend to the movies. She was surprised to find out that I knew everything. So I told her to keep in mind this proverb. (Two occurrences. Informants: females).

Sources and Annotations: Cobos, p. 29, same as A. Conde, p. 106, same as A. Chavez, p. 50, De la tierra al cielo no hay nada oculto. Espinosa, A., p. 104, same as A. Jaramillo, p. 387, same as A; p. 408, No hay nada oculto bajo el sol. Rodriguez-Marin (1926, p. 196, Entre el cielo y la tierra no hay nada oculto - o que no se sepa. Rubio, p. 139, Del cielo a la tierra nada hay oculto. Sbarbi, p. 239, same as A.

165 (A). Se me junta el cielo con la tierra.

Translation or Interpretation: I feel the sky gets too close to the earth. This is used when something sad happens and you feel bad.

Context: I heard my mother use it in a conversation about my grandfather, who was very sick and everyone felt badly. (One occurrence. Informant: female).

Sources and Annotations: Aranda, p. 27, Se le junta el cielo con la tierra. Armas, p. 298, Juntarse el cielo con la tierra. Cerda, p. 264, Juntarse el cielo con la tierra. Conde, p. 366, Same as A. Rubio, p. 268, Juntársele (a uno) el cielo con la tierra. Santamaria, p. 350, Juntársele a uno el cielo con la tierra. Sbarbi, p. 239, Juntársele a alguno el cielo con la tierra.

166 (A). A las mejores cocineras se les queman los frijoles.

Translation or Interpretation: Even the best cooks burn the beans.

Context: My aunt, who is an excellent cook, says this dicho to her husband whenever he complains about dinner. (One occurrence. Informant: female).

Sources and Annotations: Aranda, p. 1, A la mejor cocinera se le ahuma la olla. Cobos, p. 11, A la mejor cocinera se le ahuma la olla. Martinez, p. 22, Al mejor cocinero se le queman lo frijoles. Rubio, p. 26, A la mejor cocinera se le va un tomate entero; p. 183. Sopa de muchas cocineras sale quemada. Santamaria, p. 365, A la mejor cocinera se le va un tomate entero; p. 295, A la mejor cocinera se le va un tomate entero.

167 (A). Es bien codo.

Translation or Interpretation: He is very stingy. This is used to describe a greedy person.

Context: Informant told me that at work usually someone takes something in the morning, and she used this phrase to refer to that person who always went to get but never took anything. (One occurrence. Informant: female).

Sources and Annotations: Armas, p. 53, "ser muy codo".

168 (A). Levantar el codo.

Translation or Interpretation: Raise the elbow, as in a person always drinking booze.

Context: My informant's father used to drink a lot of booze in his younger days, and his wife would tell him this before he would leave with his friends, or buddies, to go to the cantinas. (One occurrence. Informant: female).

Sources and Annotations: Caballero, p. 73¹, same as A.

169 (A). Habla hasta por los codos.

Translation or Interpretation: He or she talks even through the elbows.

Context: My mother said this about a neighbor lady. She carried her gossip too far. She also said this about a sister of hers who would never stop talking when she was on the phone with my mother. (One occurrence. Informant: male).

Sources and Annotations: Armas, p. 278, same as A. Caballero, p. 657, Hablar por los codos. Conde, p. 187, same as A. Espinosa, A., p. 122, same as A. Vásquez, p. 89, same as A.

170 (A). Cojera de perro y llanto de mujer no hay que creer.

Translation or Interpretation: Seldom believe the tears of a woman or the limp of a dog.

Context: My mother once said this after a neighbor left our house where she spent the afternoon talking about her problems. (One occurrence. Informant: female).

Sources and Annotations: Caballero, p. 296, Cojera de perro. Gamiz, p. 76, En cojera de perro y lagrimas de mujer no hay que creer. Rodriguez-Marin (1930), p. 290, Llanto de mujer, engaño es; p. 219, Ni de lágrimas de puta ni de fieros derufian hagas caudal. Sbarbi, p. 250, En cojera de perro y en lágrimas o llanto de mujer no hay que creer.

171 (A). Está como la cola de la vaca, siempre esta creciendo para abajo.

Translation or Interpretation: Short people are like the cow's tail, always growing towards the ground.

Context: My brother and his friends would usually ridicule a store owner who was so short that they would usually poke fun at him, constantly making jokes and proverbs. (One occurrence. Informant: male).

Sources and Annotations: Jaramillo, p. 374, Crecer de p'abajo como la col'e las vacas.

172 (A). Te salio más cola que un chango.

Translation or Interpretation: You grew a longer tail than a monkey.

Context: This is something like Pinochio and his nose. (One
occurrence. Informant: male).

Sources and Annotations: Conde, p. 229, No tiene cola que le
pisen.

173 (A). Sana, sana colita de rana, que llueva ahora o mañana.

Translation or Interpretation: The proverb is supposed to
bring rain. While stroking the tail of a frog you say the
proverb. Roughly translated it says: Heal, heal, little
frog's tail, hope it rains today or tomorrow.

Context: The proverb is mainly said by children as a game.
(One occurrence. Informant: male).

Sources and Annotations: Cerda, p. 264, Sana, sana, colita de
rana, con un besito para hoy y manana. Maldonado, p. 171,
Sana, sana, culo de rana, tres pedos para hoy y tres para
manana.

174 (A). No te vayas al color, mira que la vista engaña.
          No te vayas a quedar como la masorca en caña.

Translation or Interpretation: Don't judge something by its
color, sight is sometimes deceiving. Don't be left behind
like dried corn on the stem.

Context: T Sr. wanted to buy an expensive pair of pants once.
Even though they were extremely good looking his mother replied with the proverb. (One occurrence. Informant: male).

Sources and Annotations: Cerda, p. 264, No te vayas al color,
mira que el color engaña; no te vayas a quedar como jilote en
la caña.

175 (A). Cuando las comadres riñen es cuando se dicen las
          verdades.
175 (B). Peléense las comadres y diganse las verdades.

Translation or Interpretation: The truth comes out when there
is an argument between people who always seem to be on very
good terms.

Context: My neighbor used this proverb when a couple of ladies
on the block had a very large, and loud argument. These ladies
were always seen together, and were the best of friends. When
they got into an argument, though, they told each other how
really felt. Our neighbor was commenting on the out come of
the inseparable friends and then said the proverb. (Two occurrences. Informants: female).

Sources and Annotations: Armas, p. 419, Peleense las comadres, y sepanse las verdades. Cerda, p. 267, Se enojaron las
comadres y se dijeron las verdades. Cobos, p. 26, Cuando se
enojan las comadres se dicen las verdades; p. 106, same as A.
Conde, p. 359, Riñen las comadres, y salen las verdades.
Covarrubias, p. 340, Riñen las comadres y dicense las verdades, Espinosa, A., p. 104, Cuando se enojan las comadres se
dicen las verdades. Gamiz, p. 91, Enojense las comadres y
sáquense las verdades. Martinez, p. 222, Same as B. Paredes,
p. 30, Cuando se pelean las comadres salen las verdades.
Velasco, p. 130, same as B.

176 (A). El comal le dice a la olla no me llenes de contil.

Translation or Interpretation: (None given).

Context: A person who is accustomed to lie while asking
another person why he had lied to him. The other person then
said the above proverb. Both persons were the same, liars,
but they were sort of upset because each had lied to each
other. (One occurrence. Informant: female).

Sources and Annotations: Adame, p. 31, El comal le dice a la
olla, haste un lado porque me tiznas; p. 35, El comal le dice
a la olla, haste un lado porque me tiznas. Armas, p. 55, same
as A; p. 256, El comal le dijo a la olla, que tiznada estás;
p. 411, El comal le dijo a la olla, que tiznada estás. Caballero, p. 503, Dijo la sartén al cazo: ¡Apate, gorrinazo que
me tizna! Cerda, p. 276, El comal le dijo a la olla: que
cola tan prieta tienes. Cobos, p. 36, El comal le dijo a la
olla- ¡Que cola tan prieta tienes! El comal le dijo a la
olla, ¡Que tiznada estás! Conde, p. 127, El comal le dijo a
la olla...culo prieto. Covarrubias, p. 929, Dijo la sartén a
la caldera. Galvan, p. 127, El comal le dijo a la olla; que
cola tan prieta tienes; p. 132, El comal le dijo a la olla...
Martinez, p. 104, El comal le dijo a la olla, que tiznada
estás. Robe, p. 71, El comal le dijo a la olla: Nalgas tiz-
nadas. Rubio, p. 164, El comal le dice a la olla. Velasco,
p. 130, same as A.

177 (A). Te comen vivo.

Translation or Interpretation: They eat you alive.

Context: My mother tells one of my sisters this because when
it comes to someone saying something to her, she probably
doesn't or won't answer. The answer my mother always gets
from either of us is they taught us to respect rather than to
be answering back to others. (One occurrence. Informant:
female).

Sources and Annotations: Aranda, p. 18, Lo comi vivo.

Comer / Comes

178 (A). Comer para vivir y no vivir para comer.
178 (B). ¿Comes para vivir, o vives para comer?

Translation or Interpretation: Eat to live and not live to
eat.

Context: I have often heard this proverb from my wife when I
over eat. (Four occurrences. Informants: two female, two
male).

Sources and Annotations: Caballero, p. 307, Comer para vivir.
Cobos, p. 104, Quien come para vivir se alimenta; quien vive
para comer, revienta. Conde, p. 335, Quien come para vivir
se alimenta; quien vive para comer, revienta. De Barros, p.
138, same as A. Jaramillo, p. 394, Hay que comer para vivir,
y no vivir para comer. Maldonado, p. 104, Come por vivir y
bebe por comer; Come por vivir y no vivas por comer y beber.
Martinez, p. 59, same as A. Rodriguez-Marin (1926), p. 76,
Come para vivir, y no vivas para comer.

179 (A). Hasta lo que no comes te hace daño.

Translation or Interpretation: Even what you don't eat does
you harm.

Context: One day at work, she was talking and talking to a
friend when a customer remarked that she talked a lot. Her
friend told him the proverb. (One occurrence. Informant:
female).

Sources and Annotations: Conde, p. 189, Hasta lo que no come
le hace daño. Galvan, p. 129, same as A. Martinez, p. 139,
Hasta lo que no come le hace daño. Velasco, p. 83, Hasta lo
que no come le hace daño.

180 (A). Ni comes ni dejas comer.

Translation or Interpretation: You don't eat nor let others
eat.

Context: Informant always says this when someone is talking
about someone else, so she doesn't let them eat or be on their
own, nor does she eat or be on her own, for just keeping up
with the others. (One occurrence. Informant: female).

Sources and Annotations: Arora, p. 358, Ese es como perro de
rancho: ni come ni deja comer. Caballero, p. 97, Al perro del
hortelano, que no come ni deja comer; p. 334, Como el perro
hortelano, que ni deja comer. Conde, p. 280, No come ni deja
comer. Covarrubias, p. 864, El perro del hortelano, que ni
come las bercas ni las deja comer a otra. Maldonado, p. 27,
El perro del hortelano, ni come las berzas ni las deja comer.
Rodriguez-Marin (1926), p. 167, El perro del hortelano, que
no roe el hueso ni lo deja roer al extraño.

181 (A). ¿Qué comes que adivinas?

Translation or Interpretation: What do you eat that you guess correctly?

Context: When, for example, you are going to tell someone something and just before you do they tell you exactly what you were going to say. (One occurrence. Informant: female).

Sources and Annotations: Martínez, p. 234, same as A. Velasco, p. 136, same as A.

182 (A). Comida reposada y cena paseada.

Translation or Interpretation: After a quiet meal a good long walk.

Context: My mom always believed that after eating supper we should go for a long walk. This is to exercise and not to have nightmares if you go to bed right before you eat. (One occurrence. Informant: female).

Sources and Annotations: Conde, p. 206, La comida, a reposar; y la cena a pasear. Maldonado, p. 105, La comida reposada y la cena paseada. Rodriguez-Marin (1930), p. 323, Tras la cena, pasea; tras la comida, siesta tranquila.

183 (A). Si comienzas mal acabas peor.
183 (B). El que mal anda mal acaba.
183 (C). Quien mal anda mal acaba.

Translation or Interpretation: If you start out wrong you'll finish even worse.

Context: The proverb would be in just about any situation when something needs to be done. It could be used to stress the importance of beginning a talk properly or else it will not come out right. (Seven occurrences. Informants: one female, five male, one not stated).

Sources and Annotations: Armas, p. 420, same as C. Conde, p. 146, El que mal comienza mal acaba. Galvan, p. 124, same as C; p. 125, same as C. Jaramillo, p. 418, same as C. Rodriguez-Marin (1926), p. 29, Al mal empezar, peor acabar; p. 411, Quien mal empieza mal acaba.

184 (A). No vale ni tres cominos.

Translation or Interpretation: To have no worth or value.

Context: I had broken up with my boyfriend. A friend was trying to cheer me up and said "no le llores, alcabo no vale ni tres cominos." (One occurrence. Informant: female).

Sources and Annotations: None.

185 (A). Si no compras no mayugues.

Translation or Interpretation: If you don't buy don't handle the merchandise.

Context: Don't touch if you're not buying. (Five occurrences. Informants: one female, three male, one anonymous).

Sources and Annotations: Ballesteros, p. 58, Si compran, no manoseen. Cerda, p. 268, same as C. Martinez, p. 254, Si no compra no mallugue. Velasco, p. 150, Si no compra no magulle.

186 (A). La conciencia es a la vez testigo, fiscal y juez.

Translation of Interpretation: Let your conscience be your guide. Your conscience is witness, judge and jury, at the same time.

Context: If a person does wrong he will never forget because her/his mind will always remind him of it. (One occurrence. Informant: female).

Sources and Annotations: Conde, p. 207, same as A. Lucero-White, p. 36, Una conciencia culpable no necesita fiscal. Rodriguez-Marin (1926), p. 233, La buena conciencia vale por mil testigos; p. 236, La conciencia vale por cien testigos.

187 (A). Condiciones rompen leyes.

Translation or Interpretation: Circumstances and conditions break laws.

Context: When the situation calls for sometimes a law is broken. This can be related to social, economic, or political unrest, or just simple need. (Two occurrences. Informants: one female, one male).

Sources and Annotations: Cobos, p. 22, same as A. Conde, p. 81, same as A. Rodriguez-Marin (1926), p. 79, same as A. Sbarbi, p. 260, same as A.

188 (A). Después de conejo ido tira piedras al matorral.

Translation or Interpretation: After the rabbit is gone (he/she) throws stones at the brush.

Context: Used like: don't cry over spilled milk. (One occurrence. Informant: female).

Sources and Annotations: Cerda, p. 268, Después de conejo ido,
garrotazo al chaparro; same as A.

189 (A). A falsa confesión, falsa absolución.

Translation or Interpretation: If one gives a false confes-
sion, one's forgiveness will also be false.

Context: My brother always says to be sincere when asking for
forgiveness of another, or else, his forgiveness will not be
sincere towards me. (One occurrence. Informant: female).

Sources and Annotations: Conde, p. 22, same as A. Espinosa,
F., p. 83, same as A. Rodriguez-Marin (1926), p. 8, same as A.

190 (A). La confianza mata al hombre.

Translation or Interpretation: Trust will kill a man.

Context: A person would have to be very careful and alert.
Trust, or being too confident can be dangerous. (One occurrence. Informant: female).

Sources and Annotations: Adame, p. 56, same as A; p. 58, same
as A. Conde, p. 207, same as A. Rodriguez-Marin (1926), p.
236, same as A.

191 (A). Conmigo no andan con que a Chepa le dan calambres.
191 (B). Pa que andamos con que a Pancha le dan calambres.

Translation or Interpretation: Let's not waste any time because of minor things or happenings. Don't come telling me
that Chepa gets cramps.

Context: Whenever there is a party and the person who came
with you wants to go home, this dicho is said. (Two occurrences. Informants: one female, one male).

Sources and Annotations: None.

192 (A). Al buen consejo no se le haya precio.

Translation or Interpretation: Good advice has no price.

Context: Personal friends of mine are constantly seeking my
advice. I will not advise them, but will counsel them on what
I would do in the same circumstances. Upon telling me that
they owe me on--a favor--I reply with the proverb. (Two occurrence. Informants: one female, one anonymous).

Sources and Annotations: Conde, p. 125, El buen consejo no tiene precio. De Barros, p. 78, same as A. Rodriguez-Marin (1930), p. 100, El buen consejo no merece menos precio; p. 328, Un buen consejo vale mas que un buen dinero. Rodriguez-Marin (1926), p. 497, Un buen consejo no es pagado con dinero. Sbarbi, p. 262, same as A.

193 (A). Da consejo y se queda sin el.

Translation or Interpretation: He gives advice and remains without it. It means that the person giving advice will usu-ally apply it to someone else, but will not take it herself.

Context: My informant's son likes to go out and have fun. His father gives him advice on how to behave and what things to look for. One day my informant went out and did exactly what he tells his son not to do. He used this proverb on himself. (One occurrence. Informant: male).

Sources and Annotations: Adame, p. 23, Das el consejo y te quedas sin el; p. 25, Das el consejo y te quedas sin el. Ba-llesteros, p. 23, Das consejo y te quedas sin el. Conde, p. 99, Da el consejo y se queda sin el. Galvan, p. 126, Dar con-sejo y quedarse sin el. Martinez, p. 83, Da el consejo y se queda sin el.

194 (A). El consejo no es bien recibido donde no es pedido.

Translation or Interpretation: Advice is not well received when it is not requested.

Context: If a person is not welcomed in someone's house, why visit that house? (One occurrence. Informant: female).

Sources and Annotations: Conde, p. 90, Cuando el consejo no ha sido pedido el aconsejado queda ofendido. De Barros, p. 144, same as A. Gamiz, p. 93, Los consejos no pedidos, los dan los entrometidos. Rodriguez-Marin (1930), p. 60, Consejo no pedido, consejo mal oido. Santamaria, p. 389, Los consejos no pedidos los dan los entrometidos.

195 (A). No hay (mejores) consejos que los que el tiempo da.

Translation or Interpretation: There isn't any advice better than the one that time gives.

Context: Informant claims that advices are better acclaimed from own experience. An example that he has heard given quite often is when men go out to drink and have a hangover. The next day they say the above--so learn, they say, from exper-ience. (One occurrence. Informant: male).

Sources and Annotations: Cobos, p. 53, El tiempo da consejos.
Correas, p. 45, Al tiempo, el consejo. Rodriguez-Marin (1926),
p. 172, El tiempo da buen consejo. Yanez, p. 129, El tiempo
es buen consejero y sabe desengañar.

196 (A). Adonde el corazón se inclina el pie camina.

Translation or Interpretation: Our feelings determine what we
will do, where we will go. Our heart guides us in decisions.
Where the heart is inclined the foot will go.

Context: A friend of my informant, who was very much in love
with a man who moved to California, soon moved there to be
with him. (One occurrence. Informant: female).

Sources and Annotations: Conde, p. 22, same as A. Maldonado,
p. 120, Dice el refrán: Alla ván los pies donde el corazón
esta. Rodriguez-Marin (1930), p. 188, Los pies se mueven hacia
donde el corazón quiere. Rodriguez-Marin (1926), p. 7, Adonde
el corazón se inclina, el pie camina. Sbarbi, p. 266, same as
A.

197 (A). El corazón no envejese, es la piel la que se arruga.

Translation or Interpretation: The heart doesn't get old, it's
the skin that gets wrinkled.

Context: This proverb is commonly used by older people. It
is especially used by older people who are young at heart.
Even though they are old, and their skin is wrinkled, their
heart is still very young. (One occurrence. Informant: female).

Sources and Annotations: Conde, p. 128, El corazón no envejece, el cuero es el que se arruga; p. 283, No es lo viejo lo
que acaba, el cuero es el que se arruga. Rubio, p. 165, El
corazón no envejece, el cuero es el que se arruga; p. 163, Si
la cabeza encanece, el corazón no envejece. Yanez, p. 63, El
corazón no envejece, el cuero es el que se arruga.

198 (A). El que se descuida se lo lleva la corriente.

Translation or Interpretation: The one who is caught off guard
is taken by the wave.

Context: This proverb means that if you don't attempt to do or
get something fast someone else will get it before you. An
example for this proverb could pertain to someone looking for
a job. If a person forgets to return his application form in
time, someone else is more than likely going to get the job
because he followed procedures correctly. In another instance, when I have heard this proverb, was in my house. One
day, circa, 1978, my parents brought home a limited supply of

sodas. I heard a commotion from my room, and by the time I got to the kitchen I said I hadn't gotten any soda; they were all gone. My brother looked at me and told me "ni modo, el que se descuida se lo lleva la corriente." I was very angry, but it was true. They, my brothers, had beat me to it. I heard this proverb from my brother, circa 1978. (One occurrence. Informant: female).

Sources and Annotations: Sbarbi, p. 270, Dejarse llevar la corriente.

199 (A). Lo cortés no le quita al hombre ser valiente.

Translation or Interpretation: Courtesy does not make a man less valiant.

Context: Said to a man who had either been rude or discourteous to a woman. Usually said to a man who is very much into "machismo." (One occurrence. Informant: female).

Sources and Annotations: Adame, p. 57, Lo cortes no quita lo valiente; p. 62, Lo cortes no quita lo valiente. Armas, p. 415, Lo cortes no quita lo valiente. Ballesteros, p. 10, Lo cortes no quita lo valiente. Caballero, p. 844, No quita lo cortes a lo valiente. Cobos, p. 73, Lo cortes no le quita a lo valiente; p. 85, Nada quita lo valiente a lo cortes. Conde, p. 231, Lo cortes no quita lo valiente. Espinosa, A., p. 108, Lo valiente no quita lo cortes. Galvan, p. 130, Lo cortes no quita lo valiente; p. 134, Lo cortes no quita lo valiente. Jaramillo, p. 399, Lo cortes no quita lo valiente. Rodriguez-Marin (1926), p. 266, Lo cortes no quita lo valiente. Sbarbi, p. 271, No quita lo cortes a lo valiente.

200 (A). Cortesía de boca mucho vale y poco cuesta.

Translation or Interpretation: A word of praise is worth a lot and costs little.

Context: "It doesn't take much effort to give a kind word to someone," my informant said. "And when it's sincerely given it's sincerely received." He did not remember when or where he first heard this saying, although it was sometime during his childhood. (One occurrence. Informant: male).

Sources and Annotations: Cobos, p. 24, Cortesia de boca, mucho consugue y nada cuesta. Conde, p. 88, Cortesia si es de boca, gana mucho y poco cuesta. Lucero-White, p. 33, El hablar bien no cuesta dinero. Maldonado, p. 110, same as A. Rodriguez-Marin (1930), p. 144, Hablar bien no cuesta dinero; p. 152, Honra de palabra, vale mucho y no cuesta nada. Rodriguez-Marin (1926), p. 85, Cortesia de lengua vale mucho y poco cuesta. Sbarbi, p. 271, same as A.

201 (A). Cada <u>cosa</u> se parese a su dueño.
201 (B). Dicen que el dueño y su mueble se parecen iguales.

<u>Translation or Interpretation</u>: Everything looks like its owner.

<u>Context</u>: Your appearance tells people what you are like. (Two occurrences. Informants: female).

<u>Sources and Annotations</u>: Aranda, p. 4, same as A. Cobos, p. 18, same as A; p. 70, Las cosas se paecen a sus duenos. Conde, p. 389, Todas las cosas se parecen a su dueño. Jaramillo, p. 398, Las cosas se parecen al dueño. Rubio, p. 195, Todas las cosas se parecen a su dueño.

202 (A). Las <u>cosas</u> dejadas a Dios son muy buenas.
202 (B). <u>Cosas</u> dejadas a Dios son mejor.

<u>Translation or Interpretation</u>: Things left up to God are very good.

<u>Context</u>: My mother uses this proverb very much. When it means is that God remembers everything, and He is the one who punishes or rewards. If a person does something to hurt someone else, God will give him his due. There is no need to take a personal revenge. God will take care of them sooner or later. (Three occurrences. two female, one male).

<u>Sources and Annotations</u>: None.

203 (A). No hagas <u>cosas</u> buenas que parezcan malas.

<u>Translation or Interpretation</u>: Avoid things that are innocent but appear bad.

<u>Context</u>: A young girl is not supposed to go to boys' homes if his parents are not there. If she does this, then an innocent meeting takes form of a "wild and crazy time," in the eyes of malicious gossipers. (Two occurrences. Informants: female).

<u>Sources and Annotations</u>: Adame, p. 52, Hay que hacer cosas malas que parezcan buenas y no cosas buenas que parezcan malas; p. 54, Hay que hacer cosas malas que parezcan buenas y no cosas buenas que parezcan malas. Cobos, p. 89, No hagas cosas buenas que a la vista parezcan malas. Conde, p. 285, No hagas cosas buenas que parezcan malas, ni malas aunque parezcan buenas. Espinoza, A., p. 107, Hay cosas buenas que parecen malas y hay cosas malas que parecen buenas. Gamiz, p. 90, No hagas cosas buenas que parezcan malas. Robe, p. 72, Has cosas malas que parezcan buenas pero no buenas que parezcan malas. Rubio, p. 24, same as A.

204 (A). A la mala <u>costumbre</u> quebrarle la pierna.

<u>Translation or Interpretation</u>: If you have a bad habit, you
are likely to have an accident.

<u>Context</u>: A friend had a bad habit of mowing the yard without
footwear. One time he disappeared for a couple of weeks. Then
we were told that he had severely chopped off a couple of toes.
(One occurrence. Informant: female).

<u>Sources and Annotations</u>: Covarrubias, p. 366, same as A; p.
988, Al mal uso quebrarle la pierna. Espinosa, F., p. 87,
same as A. Sbarbi, p. 276, A la mala costumbre quebrarle la
pierna o cortarle las piernas.

205 (A). La <u>costumbre</u> hace ley.

<u>Translation or Interpretation</u>: Customs make the law.

<u>Context</u>: "If you have certain habits, they become the way
things should be done," he said. If they are good habits that's
the way you should behave. He said he heard this saying from
his parents and grandparents. (One occurrence. Informant:
male).

<u>Sources and Annotations</u>: Caballero, p. 711, same as A. De
Barros, p. 147, same as A. Lea, p. 235, same as A. Lucero-
White, p. 35, same as A. Maldonado, p. 11, same as A. Rodri-
guez-Marin (1926), p. 236, La costumbre tiene fuerza de ley;
La costumbre hace ley y mata ley. Sbarbi, p. 276, La costum-
bre hace ley o tiene fuerza de ley.

206 (A). Ser mas listo que un <u>coyote</u>.

<u>Translation or Interpretation</u>: To be as fast, or alert, as a
coyote.

<u>Context</u>: Usually said to people who are always alert, or
ready to do something. People who are very smart are always
one step ahead of the others. (One occurrence. Informant:
male).

<u>Sources and Annotations</u>: Arora, p. 148, Mas ligero que un
coyote. Cerda, p. 270, same as A.

207 (A). Somos como los <u>cubos</u> de noria, unos suben y otros
          bajan.

<u>Translation or Interpretation</u>: We are like (well buckets) one
goes up and the other comes down.

<u>Context</u>: M. tells her brothers that all your life you will be
in the same situation. (One occurrence. Informant: female).

Sources and Annotations: Cobos, , p. 26, Cuando un cubo sube, otro baja; p. 109, Somos como los cubos de noria, unos hoy otros mañana. Conde, p. 190, Es como los cubos de noria, que suben y bajan mas no a la gloria; p. 381, Somos cual cubos de malacete, arriba o abajo, mas del mecate. Espinoza, A., p. 110, Somos como los cubos de noria, cuando unos suben otros bajan. Martinez, p. 64, same as A. Rodriguez-Marin (1926), p. 500, Unos suben y otros bajan, unos hinchen y otras vacian como arcaduces que andan. Velasco, p. 39, Como los cubos de noria, unos suben y otros bajan.

208 (A). Cuchillo de palo no corta pero mayuga.
208 (B). Cuchillo que no mocha pero maliga.

Translation or Interpretation: A (wooden knife) does not cut, but it does hurt.

Context: Told when a person is bothering someone. He may not hurt him by calling, or following them around, but they do frustrate them. (Five occurrences. Informants: three female, two male).

Sources and Annotations: Cerda, p. 271, Cuchillo de palo no corta, pero incomoda. Rubio, p. 117, Cuchillito de palo no corta, pero incomoda.

209 (A). Cuentas claras, amistades largas.

Translation or Interpretation: Clear understandings enhance long friendships.

Context: Whenever we borrow anything from friends, we make sure that we return it in the same condition in which we received it. (One occurrence. Informant: female).

Sources and Annotations: Aranda, p. 4, Buenas cuentas, buenos amigos. Ballesteros, p. 9, Las cuentas claras guardan las amistades. Cerda, p. 271, Las cuentas claras hacen buenos amigos. Cobos, p. 70, Las cuentas claras hacen buenos amigos. Conde, p. 95, same as A. Lea, p. 233, Buenas cuentas, buenos amigos. Lucero-White, p. 33, Buenas cuentas, buenos amigos. Rodriguez-Marin (1926), p. 99, same as A; p. 100, Cuentas claras y amistad que dure; p. 257, Las cuentas claras hacen buen amigos. Rubio, p. 285, Las cuentas claras hacen los buenos amigos.

210 (A). A ver de cual cuero salen mas correas.

Translation or Interpretation: Let's see which hide will produce more straps.

Context: Usually said among the men in our culture, like in a fight, to see which man is bravest, or a better fighter. Does not necessarily have to be a fight, as long as a man does not back-off. (Three occurrences. Informants: one female, two male).

Sources and Annotations: Adame, p. 9, same as A; p. 14, same as A. Conde, p. 57, same as A. Gamiz, p. 94, same as A. Martinez, p. 41, same as A. Santamaria, p. 429, same as A. Velasco, p. 23, same as A. Yanez, p. 207, Vamos a ver de que cuero salen mas correas.

211 (A). Del mismo cuero salen las correas.

Translation or Interpretation: It all comes from the same source. From the rawhide come the straps.

Context: My brother and I resemble our father, because we both come from the same source--our father. (Three occurrences. Informants: one female, two male).

Sources and Annotations: Adame, p. 23, same as A; p. 25, same as A. Armas, p. 248, same as A. Conde, p. 106, Covarrubias, p. 382, Del cuero salen las correas. Espinosa, F., p. 85, Del cuero salen las correas. Jaramillo, p. 375, Del cuero salen las correas. Rodriguez-Marin (1926), p. 115, Del cuero salen las correas. Santamaria, p. 403, same as A. Sbarbi, p. 294, De cuero ajeno, correas largas. Villafuerte, p. 221, same as A.

212 (A). No te arruges cuero viejo que te quiero--para tambor.

Translation or Interpretation: Don't shy away from your responsibilities.

Context: A worker backing off from an unfinished job. (Six occurrences. Informants: three female, three male).

Sources and Annotations: Ballesteros, p. 55, same as A. Cerda, p. 271, same as A. Conde, p. 298, same as A. Gamiz, p. 87, No te arruges cuero viejo, que te quiero "pa" tambor. Martinez, p. 206, same as A. Velasco, p. 55, same as A.

213 (A). Entre más cueros más correas.

Translation or Interpretation: The more skins the more straps.

Context: Used whenever there are more people than needed at a job. (One occurrence. Informant: female).

Sources and Annotations: Rubio, p. 62, A ver de cual cuero salen mas correas; p. 140, Del mismo cuero salen las correas.

214 (A). Cuerpo de tentación y cara de arrepentimiento.
214 (B). Cuerpo de uva y la cara de arrepentimiento.

Translation or Interpretation: Tempting body but face of regret.

Context: Some girls may have a beautiful body but when boys see their face it sure is of regret. Informant said this to her some day. (Nine occurrences. Informants: five female, four male).

Sources and Annotations: Aranda, p. 28, same as A. Ballesteros, p. 44, same as A. Cerda, p. 271, same as A. Conde, p. 96, same as A. Jaramillo, p. 426, Tener cuerpo de tentacion y cara de arrepentimiento. Martinez, p. 76, same as A. Robe, p. 65, same as A.

215 (A). Cria cuervos y te sacarón los ojos.

Translation or Interpretation: Raise crows and they will poke your eyes out.

Context: When children are little they should be taught to obey because if you wait until they're older they may not listen to you anymore and they will do what they want. (Nine occurrences. Informants: two female, two male).

Sources and Annotations: Adame, p. 16, Cria cuervos para que te saquen los ojos; p. 20, Cria cuervos para que te saquen los ojos. Aranda, p. 6, same as A. Arora, p. 154, Los hijos son como los cuervos: los crias y despues te sacan los ojos. Ballesteros, p. 63, No crias cuervos porque te sacan los ojos. Caballero, p. 409, same as A. Cobos, p. 24, same as A. Conde, p. 88, same as A. De Barros, p. 148, same as A. Espinoza, F. p. 91, Cria cuervos y sacarte el ojo. Gamiz, p. 78, same as A. Jaramillo, p. 371, Cria cuervos y te arrancaran los ojos. Lea, p. 233, same as A. Lucero-White, p. 33, same as A. MacArthur, p. 64, same as A. Maldonado, p. 25, Cria cuervo, sacarte ha el ojo. Sbarbi, p. 295, same as A. Yanez, p. 127, Cria cuervos y te sacaran las tripas.

216 (A). No tiene la culpa el indio sino el que lo hace compadre.

Translation or Interpretation: The Indian (isn't at fault), it is the one who trusts him. At times it's difficult to trust others.

Context: Heard someone talking about another person who messed up by not paying $20 he borrowed. (Ten occurrences. Informants: eight female, two male).

Sources and Annotations: Adame, p. 70, same as A; p. 77, same as A. Ballesteros, p. 55, same as A. Cerda, p. 272, No tiene la culpa el indio, sino el que lo hizo compadre. Cobos, p. 94, same as A. Conde, p. 299, same as A. Espinosa, A., p. 108, No culpes al indio sino al que lo hizo compadre. Gamiz, p. 82, same as A. Glazer, p. 46, same as A. Martinez, p. 208, same as A. Rubio, p. 63, same as A. Santamaria, p. 120, same as A. Velasco, p. 121, same as A.

217 (A). No tiene la culpa el ladrón sino el que le deja la
         puerta abierta.
217 (B). No tiene culpa el ladrón hallando la puerta abierta.

Translation or Interpretation: It is not the thief's fault.
It's the fault of the person who left the door open.

Context: This is giving the thief a chance to steal. This
means that people have a lot to blame when accidents happen.
(Two occurrences. Informants: one female, one male).

Sources and Annotations: None.

218 (A). No tiene la culpa el sol que ese indio no tenga
         techo.

Translation or Interpretation: It is nobody's fault if you
have not progressed or kept up with society.

Context: My aunt and uncle have been married for about fifteen years, and up until now they do not own a piece of furni-
ture. They are living in a house of rent, when on the other
hand, if my uncle would have done something to progress they
wouldn't be living in this situation. (One occurrence. Informant: female).

Sources and Annotations: None.

219 (A). Que culpa tiene San Pablo que San Pedro esta calvito.

Translation or Interpretation: St. Paul is not responsible
for St. Peter being bald.

Context: I am not responsible for your mistakes. (One occurrence. Informant: female).

Sources and Annotations: Aranda, p. 25, Que culpa tiene San
Pablo que San Pedro sea calvo.

220 (A). La cuna para que apriete tiene que ser de la misma
         madera.

Translation or Interpretation: (For the crib) to be tighten
it has to be of the same wood.

Context: This means that if someone is talking about you, especially if it is one of the family, they will never be that much of the family. My informant also told me this proverb because she said that her mother, who lives in Veracruz, began distrusting her own people because they talked about her. Things that weren't even true. My informant told it to me at her home. (One occurrence. Informant: female).

Sources and Annotations: Adame, p. 70, No hay mejor astilla que la de la misma madera; p. 74, No hay mejor astilla que la de la misma madera. Camps, p. 64, No hay peor cuna que la del mismo palo. Cobos, p. 90, No hay cuna peor que la del mismo palo. Conde, p. 312, Para que la cuna apriete, debe ser del propio palo. Espinosa, A., p. 108, No hay cunas más malas que la del propio palo. Gamiz, p. 78, No hay más mala cuna que la del propio palo. Maldonado, p. 60, No hay tal cuna como la del mismo palo. Martinez, p. 152, same as A. Rodriguez-Marin (1930), p. 71, cuna de la misma madera, poco aprieta. Rodriguez-Marin (1926), p. 338, No hay peor cuna que la de madera- o que la del mismo palo. Santamaria, p. 439, La cuna para ser buena o para que apriete debe ser del mismo palo. Velasco, p. 91, La cuna que apriete ha de ser de el mismo palo. Yanez, p. 199, Para que la cuna apriete ha de ser del mismo palo; p. 200, Para que la cuna apriete ha de ser del mismo palo; p. 219, Para que la cuna apriete...

221 (A). Lo que se aprende en la cuna siempre dura.

Translation or Interpretation: What is learned in the cradle lasts forever.

Context: Things learned in childhood are always remembered. (One occurrence. Informant: female).

Sources and Annotations: Sbarbi, p. 300, same as A.

222 (A). Chancla que yo tiro no vuelvo a levantar.

Translation or Interpretation: Shoes that I throw away I will never pick up again.

Context: This is when your boyfriend left you and you were really hurt. If he comes back you won't take him back because of your pride. (Two occurrences. Informants: one female, one male).

Sources and Annotations: Cerda, p. 272, Chancla tirada, no se levanta. Conde, p. 207, La chancla que yo tiro no la vuelvo a levantar.

223 (A). Cada chango a su mecate.

Translation or Interpretation: Every monkey to his own (rope).

Context: My informant said that this proverb was used when
ever someone wanted to ask you to leave. She said that it was
mostly used on children. (Four occurrences. Informants: four
male).

Sources and Annotations: Aranda, p. 4, Cada chango en su mecate y yo con mi mecatito. Cerda, p. 272, same as A. Cobos,
p. 18, same as A. Conde, p. 69, same as A. Galvan, p. 125,
Cada chango su mecate y a darse vuelvo; p. 131, same as A.
Martinez, p. 53, Cada perico a su estaca y cada chango a su
mecate. Robe, p. 68, same as A. Santamaria, p. 466, same as
A. Velasco, p. 29, Cada perico a su estaca y cada chango a
su mecate.

224 (A). Hay chaparros como abunden y altos como estorban.

Translation or Interpretation: Shorties are too many, and tall
ones get in the way.

Context: Only used because there are more short guys than tall
ones. (One occurrence. Informant: female).

Sources and Annotations: Martinez, p. 42, same as A.

225 (A). No vales chiches de gallina.

Translation or Interpretation: You're not worth a hen's bust.
Meaning that you're not worth much since hens don't have busts.

Context: When trying to repair a roof at home I was told "no
vales chiches de gallinas," because I didn't know how to do
it. (One occurrence. Informant: male).

Sources and Annotations: Cerda, p. 273, No valer chiches de
gallina.

226 (A). Peor es chile, el agua lejos y un muchacho mal man-
          dado.

Translation or Interpretation: The chile is worse when the
water is far away and a boy is given wrong directions to get
it.

Context: The proverb means that if you are given something as
a gift, or some situation arises, and you don't like it. The
proverb says there are worse things that can happen which
could make it worse. Mr. V. says there is a lot of truth behind this proverb. He learned from his grandmother in Linares,
Mexico. One day his grandmother gave him a small toy, but he
did not like it. It was at this time that his grandmother
said this proverb. (One occurrence. Informant: male).

Sources and Annotations: Adame, p. 79, Peor es chile y el agua
lejos; p. 81, Peor es chile y el agua lejos. Conde, p. 315,
Peor es chile y la agua lejos. Martinez, p. 222, Peor es chile
y l' agua lejos. Santamaria, p. 493, Peor es chile, y agua
lejos. Velasco, p. 130, Peor es chile y l' agua lejos.

227 (A). Chiquito pero picoso.
227 (B). Chiquito pero picoso, aparente nada pero es muy
          mañoso.

Translation or Interpretation: Little but hot. Meaning someone small can have just as much force, or power, regardless of
his or her size.

Context: My neighbor's son is about two years old. He came
over one day to play with my eight year old son. Suddenly
they were engaged in a fight. The two year old beat up my
eight year old, so I used this proverb. (Seven occurrences.
Informants: four female, three male).

Sources and Annotations: Conde, p. 170, Es como chile piquin,
chiquito pero picoso; Gamiz, p. 83, Ser como la pimienta, chiquita pero picosa. Martinez, p. 62, Como el chile piquin:
chiquito pero picoso. Velasco, p. 36, Como el chile piquin:
chiquito pero picoso.

228 (A). Ahora sí, chispas queman.

Translation or Interpretation: Now the sparks burn.

Context: It is used to refer to someone who is usually never
prepared for anything. Informant remembers it being used by
someone who used to sit around the campfire, and because he
didn't have any shoes he couldn't work. One day he was given
a pair of shoes, and then said "Ahora sí, chispas queman" --
para decir ya estoy listo para trabajar y preparado para las
chispas de la lumbre. (He meant to say that he was ready for
work and also for the sparks from the campfire). (One occurrence. Informant: male).

Sources and Annotations: Galván, p. 124, Ahora si chispas,
quemenme.

229 (A). Estan haciendo de chivo los tamales.

Translation or Interpretation: The tamales are being made
out of goat.

Context: Sometimes when we buy something that is supposed to
be authentic, it turns out to be false. (One occurrence.
Informant: female).

Sources and Annotations: Armas, p. 280, Hacer de chivo los
tamales. Ballesteros, p. 57, Que no te hagan de chivo los
tamales. Cerda, p. 274, Hacer de chivo los tamales. Conde,
p. 228, Le hace de chivo los tamales. Martinez, p. 135, Hacer
de chivo los tamales. Santamaria, p. 525, same as A. Velasco,
p. 80, Hacer de chile los tamales.

230 (A). Un chivo tiro un reparo y en el viento se detuvo.
230 (B). Hay chivos que tienen madre pero este ni madre tuvo.

Translation or Interpretation: A kid threw a kick but it
stopped in mid-air. There are kids that have mothers, but this
kid never had one.

Context: My friend, who my parents thought were usually bums
and hoodlums. My parents would always comment that my friends
never had parents. (Two occurrences. Informants: one female, one male).

Sources and Annotations: Adame, p. 52, Hay chivos que tienen
madre pero este ni madre tuvo; p. 54, Hay chivos que tienen
madre pero este ni madre tuvo. Conde, p. 400, Un chivo pego
un reparo y en el viento se deturo, hay chivos que tienen
madre, pero este ni madre tuvo. Rubio, p. 206, Un cojo brinco
un estanque y en el aire se deturo, hay cojos que tienen madre
pero este ni madre tuvo.

231 (A). Da y ten y harás bién.

Translation or Interpretation: Give and take and you will do
good.

Context: A good friend of mine gave me this one recently during a conversation, when we started discussing the issue of
generosity. (One occurrence. Informant: female).

Sources and Annotations: Correas, p. 307, same as A. Paredes,
p. 30, same as A. Sbarbi, p. 130, same as A; p. 314, same as
A.

232 (A). A lo dado no se le busca lado.
232 (B). A lo dado no se le pone pero.

Translation or Interpretation: To that which is given do not
look for a side.

Context: Mrs. R. gave her daughter her old car when she got
her new one. The inspection sticker was due the following
month, and there were a few minor adjustments which needed to
be made before the car passed the inspection. Her daughter
complained about this and her mother quoted the above. (24
occurrences. Informants: 11 female, 13 male).

Sources and Annotations: Aranda, p. 2, A lo dado no se le da fin; A lo dado, no se le ve colmillo. Ballesteros, p. 19, same as A. Benavides, p. 91, same as A. Cerda, p. 275, same as A. Cobos, p. 12, same as A. Chavez, p. 43, A lo dado no se le da fin. Galvan, p. 124, same as A; p. 130, same as A. Glazer, p. 47, same as A. Robe, p. 67, same as A. Rodriguez-Marin (1930), p. 18, A lo dado no le mires el pelo. Rubio, p. 38, same as A.

233 (A). **Dar** para recibir no es dar sino pedir.

Translation or Interpretation: Giving to receive is not giving but asking.

Context: Mother used to say this dicho when we were growing up and started buying gifts. She wanted to let us know and understanding that giving comes from the heart, not to give a gift in hopes of receiving one from the other person. (One occurrence. Informant: female).

Sources and Annotations: Conde, p. 111, Dar por recibir no es dar sino pedir.

234 (A). **Debo** no niego, pago no tengo.

Translation or Interpretation: I owe and don't deny it, pay I don't have.

Context: Once my brother borrowed some money from me. I would remind him, and since he had no money, he would say, "debo no niego, pago no tengo." (One occurrence. Informant: female).

Sources and Annotations: Adame, p. 23, Debo no niego, pago no tengo y cuando tengo no me acuerdo; p. 25, Debo no niego, pago no tengo y cuando tengo no me acuerdo. Conde, p. 101, same as A. Martinez, p. 87, same as A. Velasco, p. 52, same as A.

235 (A). No tener dos **dedos** de frente.

Translation or Interpretation: Not to have two fingers in front. Not to have common sense at all.

Context: Informant's grandmother used this when informant made a very bad investment. (One occurrence. Informant: female).

Sources and Annotations: Caballero, p. 854, same as A.

236 (A). Todos los **dedos** son de la misma mano pero ninguno se parece.

Translation or Interpretation: All fingers are from the same hand, but none of them are alike.

Context: None given. (One occurrence. Informant: male).

Sources and Annotations: Caballero, p. 356, Como los dedos de la mano tampoco son iguales; p. 747, Los dedos de la mano no son iguales. Conde, p. 300, No todos los dedos de la mano son iguales. Covarrubias, p. 446, No son todos los dedos de la mano iguales. De Barros, p. 166, Los dedos de la mano no son iguales. Espinosa, A., p. 109, No todos los dedos de la mano son iguales; p. 111, Todos los dedos no son iguales. Jaramillo, p. 400, Los dedos de la mano no son iguales. Lucero-White, p. 3, No todos los dedos de la mano son iguales.

237 (A). No me den, ponganme donde lo haga.

Translation or Interpretation: Don't give me -money- put me where I can make it.

Context: Proverb used for the ones who do not like to take from others. (One occurrence. Informant: male).

Sources and Annotations: Adame, p. 70, No le pido a Dios que me de, nomas que me ponga donde hay; p. 75, No le pido a Dios que me de, nomas que me ponga donde hay. Ballesteros, p. 53, No le pido a Dios que me de- nomas que me ponga donde hay. Martinez, p. 201, No pido que me den. Sino que me pongan donde hay. Rodriguez-Marin (1930), p. 89, Dios me ponga donde haya; y lo demás a mi cuenta caiga. Velasco, p. 116, same as A. Yanez, p. 320, No quiero que Dios me de, sino que me ponga donde.

238 (A). Despacio pero seguro.

Translation or Interpretation: Slowly but surely.

Context: When you are doing something, it is better to do it slowly and be sure of it. (One occurrence. Informant: female).

Sources and Annotations: Cobos, p. 39, same as A. Conde, p. 110, same as A; p. 385, Tardio, pero seguro.

239 (A). Lo que de día se piensa, de noche se sueña.

Translation or Interpretation: What you think of during the day is what you dream of at night.

Context: My informant says that if one is a good person, he/she will have peaceful sleep with pleasant dreams. (One occurrence. Informant: female).

Sources and Annotations: Rodriguez-Marin (1926), p. 268, Lo que de día se piensa, a la noche se suena.

240 (A). El diablo no duerme.
240 (B). El diablo nunca duerme.

Translation or Interpretation: The devil doesn't sleep.

Context: My cousin was going to stay by herself one weekend. My aunt was supposed to take a trip somewhere. After a while she said she wouldn't go because no telling what her boyfriend would be up to. (Two occurrence. Informants: female).

Sources and Annotations: Ballesteros, p. 40, same as B. Caballero, p. 534, same as B. Conde, p. 129, El diablo no duerme mas se hace el dormido pero eso convence. Correas, p. 94, same as A. Maldonado, p. 119, same as A. Rodriguez-Marin (1926), p. 153, El diablo y todo lo anascan. Sbarbi, p. 332, El diablo no duerme y todo anasca.

241 (A). El diablo sabe bién a quién se le aparece.

Translation or Interpretation: The devil knows to whom he will appear.

Context: A little boy was being punished for wrong doings, and his aunt replied to him with this proverb. (One occurrence. Informant: female).

Sources and Annotations: Cerda, p. 276, Bien sabe el diablo a quien se le aparece. Conde, p. 62, Bien sabe el diablo a quien le aparece. Espinosa, A., p. 103, same as A. Yanez, p. 200, Bien sabe el diablo a quien se le aparece.

242 (A). Hablando del diablo.

Translation or Interpretation: Speaking of the devil.

Context: When a person is talking about someone and that person suddenly appears. (One occurrence. Informant: female).

Sources and Annotations: Cerda, p. 276, Hablando del Diablo, se aparece.

243 (A). Mas sabe el diablo por viejo que por diablo.
243 (B). El diablo no es malo por diablo sino por viejo.
243 (C). El viejo sabe más por viejo que por diablo.
243 (D). Dicen que el diablo sabe por viejo y no por diablo.
243 (E). El diablo tiene más experiencia por ser viejo, no siendo diablo.
243 (F). El diablo no es diablo por diablo sino por viejo.

Translation or Interpretation: The devil knows more for being old than for being the devil.

Context: None given. (14 occurrences. Informants: seven male, seven female).

Sources and Annotations: Adame, p. 31, same as F. Armas, p. 416, same as A. Ballesteros, p. 52, same as A. Cobos, p. 37, El diablo lo que sabe es por viejo y no por diablo; p. 78, same as A. Conde, p. 252, same as A. De Barros, p. 273, same as A. Glazer, p. 47, same as A. Jaramillo, p. 402, same as A. MacArthur, p. 15, same as A. Maldonado, p. 165, Por eso el diablo sabe mucho, porque es viejo. Rodriguez-Marin (1930), p. 104, same as A. Rodriguez-Marin (1926), p. 153, El diablo save mucho porque es viejo. Sbarbi, p. 333, same as A. Yanez, p. 62, same as A; p. 82, same as A; p. 203, Por viejo el diablo sabe más que por diablo.

244 (A). No todos los días se muere un burro.

Translation or Interpretation: A donkey doesn't die everyday.

Context: Take advantage of the present situation, chances are they will not come again so easy. (One occurrence: Informant: anonymous).

Sources and Annotations: Cerda, p. 277, same as A. Cobos, p. 94, same as A. Conde, p. 300, same as A.

245 (A). Dicho y hecho.

Translation or Interpretation: Said and done.

Context: A man bought his son a bicycle and he said the boy was so reckless that the bike would be flat the first day. As the man was telling someone else, he said, "dicho y hecho." The boy came back with a flat bike. (Three occurrences. Informants: two female, one male).

Sources and Annotations: Aranda, p. 9, same as A. Caballero, p. 502, same as A. Espinosa, F., p. 99, same as A; Gamiz, p. 84, Se dice: dijo y hago. Rodriguez-Marin (1930), p. 34, Así dicho, así hecho. Yanez, p. 313, same as A.

246 (A). Del dicho al hecho hay mucho trecho.
246 (B). Del dicho al hecho hay gran trecho.
246 (C). De dichos y hechos a los trechos.

Translation or Interpretation: More easily said than done.

Context: To describe somebody who is always saying "I will do this or that," but never gets anything done. (18 occurrences. 12 female, six male).

Sources and Annotations: Adame, p. 23, same as A; p. 25, same as A. Aranda, p. 8, same as A. Caballero, p. 472, De lo dicho al hecho va mucho trecho. Camps, p. 64, De lo dicho a lo hecho hay largo trecho. Correas, p. 320, same as B; Chavez, p. 43, same as A. De Barros, p. 167, same as A. Glazer, p. 48, same as A. Lea, p. 234, same as A. Maldonado, p. 54, same as A. Robe, p. 64, Del dicho al hecho hay un gran trecho. Sbarbi, p. 334, same as B. Vasquez, p. 89, Entre el dicho y el hecho está el trecho.

247 (A). Lo dicho es dicho.

Translation or Interpretation: What is said, is said.

Context: If you say you will do something then you are expected not to go back on your word. (One occurrence. Informant: male).

Sources and Annotations: Alcalá, p. 227, Lo dicho y la jara en la puerta.

248 (A). De los dientes para afuera.

Translation or Interpretation: From the teeth out.

Context: My aunt and uncle had invited me to Mexico. My mother said the above proverb because she felt they had just done it for the courtesy, since they did not bother to call again to tell me if they were really going. (Three occurrences. Informants: female).

Sources and Annotations: Caballero, p. 458, De dientes a fuera. Conde, p. 107, De los dientes para fuera quiere la suegra a la nuera. Jaramillo, p. 378, Decir algo de dientes p'a fuera. Santamaria, p. 25, Reir de dientes para a fuera. Villafuerta, p. 251, Reir de los dientes para fuera.

249 (A). Están más cerca mis dientes que mis parientes.
249 (B). Están más cerca los dientes que los parientes.

Translation or Interpretation: My teeth are closer than my relatives.

Context: I use the above proverb when friends or parents have cooked something they know I like and don't even save some for me. Also I use it when somebody asks me how come I didn't save some of what I had for lunch. (12 occurrences. ten female, two male).

Sources and Annotations: Adame, p. 34, Están primero mis dientes, que mis parientes; p. 50, Están primero mis dientes, que mis parientes. Aranda, p. 15, same as A; Cobos, p. 14,

Antes son mis dientes que mis parientes; p. 57, same as A; p. 78, Más cerca están mis dientes que mis parientes; p. 102, primero mis dientes que mis parientes. Conde, p. 177, same as A. Covarrubias, p. 471, Más cerca están mis dientes que mis parientes; p. 854, Más cerca están mis dientes que mis parientes. De Barros, p. 100, Antes son mis dientes que mis parientes; p. 270, Más cerca están mis dientes que mis parientes. Espinosa, F., p. 99, Más cerca están mis dientes que mis parientes. Lea, p. 235, same as A. Lucero-White, p. 34, same as A. MacArthur, p. 5, Los dientes están más cerca que los parientes. Maldonado, p. 44, Más cerca están mis dientes que mis parientes. Rodriguez-Marin (1930), p. 197, Más lo quiero para mis dientes que para mis parientes. Rodriguez-Marin (1926), p. 34, Antes mis dientes que mis parientes; p. 382, Primero son mis dientes que mis parientes. Rubio, p. 84, Coman mis dientes y renieguen mis parientes. Yanez, p. 282, Coman mis dientes y renieguen mis parientes.

250 (A). No hay mayor dificultad que poca voluntad.

Translation or Interpretation: There is no major difficulty than little determination.

Context: In life there are always very hard decisions to be made, because it's difficult to make them, but they have to be made. If a person is sick and he needs to be operated, and he is not in danger of dying in the operating room, and if he doesn't get operated he will die anyway. (One occurrence. Informant: female).

Sources and Annotations: Conde, p. 288, same as A.

251 (A). Nunca digas sape hasta que no escape.

Translation or Interpretation: Never say scat until you see it escape.

Context: Used when someone jumps to a conclusion, then you can quote the proverb. (One occurrence. Informant: female).

Sources and Annotations: Adame, p. 70, No hay que decir ape, hasta que no escape; p. 75, No hay que decir ape, hasta que no escape.

252 (A). Más se fué en el diluvio.

Translation or Interpretation: More was lost in the flood.

Context: My informant uses this proverb when some days go bad more than others. (One occurrence. Informant: female).

Sources and Annotations: Conde, p. 252, Mas se perdio en diluvio. Gamiz, p. 87, Más se perdio el año del diluvio. Jaramillo, p. 405, Más se perdio en diluvio. Santamaria, p. 448, Más se perdio en diluvio. Yanez, p. 31, Más se perdio en el diluvio universal.

253 (A). Dime cuanto traes y te digo cuanto vales.
253 (B). Dime cuanto tienes y te diré cuanto vales.
253 (C). Si nada tienes, nada vales.

Translation or Interpretation: Tell me how much money you have and I'll tell you how much you are worth.

Context: My father always tells me to save money, not to go much with my friends. He tells me to save for the future—mañana. Sometimes, when I forget this proverb, he makes sure to remind me of it by saying it to me. (Six occurrences. Informants: three female, three male).

Sources and Annotations: Adame, p. 90, Tanto tienes, tanto vales; p. 92, Tanto tienes, tanto vales. Ballesteros, p. 44, Cuanto tienes, cuanto vales. Cobos, p. 32, same as A; p. 114, Tanto tienes, tanto vales. Rodriguez-Marin (1926), p. 480, Tanto tienes, tanto vales; Tanto tienes, cuanto vales; no tienes nada, no vales nada.

254 (A). Acabándoce el dinero se termina la amistad.

Translation or Interpretation: When you're out of money, you are out of friends.

Context: You have friends when you have money, when you don't have money you don't have friends. Money makes, or buys, friends. Money is a form of interest. (One occurrence. Informant: male).

Sources and Annotations: Cobos, p. 9, same as A. Conde, p. 20, same as A. Martinez, p. 13, same as A. Rubio, p. 6, same as A.

255 (A). Con dinero baila el chango.

Translation or Interpretation: With money the monkey will dance.

Context: Isabel's daughter likes to go out a lot. With plenty of money in her purse nothing can keep her settled down. Her mother says she is like one of those monkeys who dance up and down, and around, each time it has money. (Three occurrences. Informants: female).

Sources and Annotations: Adame, p. 79, por dinero baila el perro, y por pan también; p. 82, Por dinero baila el perro, y

por pan también. Aranda, p. 6, Con dinero hasta la mona baila.
Ballesteros, p. 59, Con dinero baila el perro. Caballero, p.
915, Por dinero baila el perro. Cobos, p. 100, Por dinero
baila el perro. Conde, p. 81, Con dinero baila el perro; p.
321, Por dinero baila el perro y por pan si se lo dan. Correas, p. 25, El dinero hace bailar al perro. Covarrubias, p.
473, Por dinero baila el perro; p. 864, Por dinero baila el
perro. De Barros, p. 176, Dinero hace bailar el perro. Espinosa, A., p. 101, Por dinero baila el perro. Espinosa, F., p.
100, Por dinero baila el perro. Galván, p. 125, Por dinero
baila el perro; p. 126, Por dinero baila el perro; p. 127, Por
dinero baila el perro; p. 132, Por dinero baila el perro; p.
133, Por dinero baila el perro, y por pan si se lo dan. Gamiz,
p. 87, Por dinero baila el perro y por dinero si se lo dan.
Jaramillo, p. 414, Por la plata baila el perro. Maldonado, p.
30, Por el dinero baila el perro; p. 122, El dinero hace bailar
al perro; p. 165, Por dinero baila el perro, y por pan si se
lo dan. Martinez, p. 68, Con dinero baila el perro. Robe, p.
67, same as A. Rodriguez-Marin (1930), p. 371, Por dinero
baila el perro, no por el son que lo toca el ciego.

256 (A). Con dinero no se olvida lo encargado.
256 (B). Con dinero no se olvidan los encargados.

Translation or Interpretation: With money your request, or
order, is not forgotten.

Context: When one orders something from the store make sure
you give them money or it is likely they'll forget. (One occurrence. Informant: female).

Sources and Annotations: Cobos, p. 22, same as B. Conde, p.
81, Con dinero no se olvidan los mandados. Martinez, p. 68,
same as B. Rubio, p. 97, same as B. Velasco, p. 42, same
as B.

257 (A). Cuando yo tenía dinero me decian Don Tomás. Ahora
          que no tengo me dicen Tomás nomas.

Translation or Interpretation: When I had money I was called
Don Tomás. Now that I don't have anything, they only call me
Tomás.

Context: When I used to be working, at the time I was in high
school, everybody always came to my house. Then I stopped
working, no money came in, everybody stayed away as much as
possible. (One occurrence. Informant: male).

Sources and Annotations: Conde, p. 94, same as A. Galván, p.
126, same as A; p. 134, same as A. Martinez, p. 76, same as
A. Rubio, p. 117, same as A. Yanez, p. 173, Cuando yo tenia
dinero me llamaban don Tomas y ahora que no tengo dinero me
llamo Tomas nomas.

258 (A). El _dinero_ busca al _dinero_.

Translation or Interpretation: Money looks for money.

Context: My informant used this proverb to try and persuade a young friend from falling in love with a very rich girl. She felt that the rich girl would find someone from her status group to marry, while she was in college, and forget about her poor boyfriend at home. (One occurrence. Informant: female).

Sources and Annotations: Adame, p. 31, El dinero se va al dinero. Armas, p. 411, Dinero llama dinero. Ballesteros, p. 3, Dinero attrae dinero. Cobos, p. 32, Dinero llama dinero; p. 37, El dinero llama al dinero. Conde, p. 113, Dinero llama al dinero. De Barros, p. 176, Dinero gana dinero; Dinero llama dinero. Galván, p. 127, Dinero trae dinero. Jaramillo, p. 398, La plata busca la plata. Maldonado, p. 121, Dinero busca dinero. Rodriguez-Marin (1930), p. 88, Dinero cria dinero. Rodriguez-Marin (1926), p. 154, same as A. Sbarbi, p. 339, same as A.

259 (A). El _dinero_ es la perdición del hombre.

Translation or Interpretation: Money is the perdition of man.

Context: Men will do anything in order to have money. (One occurrence. Informant: female).

Sources and Annotations: Adame, p. 31, same as A; p. 36, same as A.

260 (A). El _dinero_ habla.

Translation or Interpretation: Money talks.

Context: My informant was going on vacation to México. The Mexican officers were taking a lot of time getting her papers ready, so my informant gave them some money, and added this proverb. (One occurrence. Informant: female).

Sources and Annotations: None.

261 (A). Sacar _dinero_ hasta de las piedras.

Translation or Interpretation: To get money even from the rocks.

Context: There was a boy in high school who, even for lending a piece of paper to somebody, would charge them. (One occurrence. Informant: female).

Sources and Annotations: Pérez, p. 125, same as A.

262 (A). Los dineros del sacristan cantando se vienen y cantando se van.

Translation or Interpretation: The money of the sacristan singing comes and singing goes.

Context: If a person who works goes and buys something he doesn't really need he will regret it, and always be crying about why giving or spending money, if he doesn't need it. (One occurrence. Informant: male).

Sources and Annotations: Caballero, p. 327, Como dineros de Sacristan, cantando se vienen y cantando se van; p. 535, El dinero de Sacristan. Espinosa, A., p. 99, same as A. Jaramillo, p. 400, same as A. Lea, p. 234, Dineros de sacristan cantando vienen cantando van. Maldonado, p. 146, same as A. Sbarbi, p. 341, same as A.

263 (A). Dios aprieta, pero no ahorca.

Translation or Interpretation: God squeezes but doesn't choke.

Context: This dicho is used to bring solace to a person in times of trouble. It is to remind us that no matter how hard things get, they'll eventually let up. (One occurrence. Informant: male).

Sources and Annotations: Adame, p. 24, same as A; p. 28, same as A. Ballesteros, p. 39, Dios aprieta pero no ahoga. Caballero, p. 504, Dios aprieta pero no ahoga. California Spanish Proverbs and Adages, p. 121, same as A. Cobos, p. 32, Dios aprieta pero no ahoga. Conde, p. 114, same as A. De Barros, p. 176, Dios aprieta pero no ahoga. Martinez, p. 96, same as A. Rodriguez-Marin (1926), p. 132, Dios aprieta pero no ahoga. Rubio, p. 150, Dios aprieta pero no ahoga. Sbarbi, p. 344, Dios aprieta pero no ahoga. Yanez, p. 99, same as A.

264 (A). Dios castiga sin palo y sin cuarta.

Translation or Interpretation: God punishes without a club or whip.

Context: Usually said when a person does something wrong to another person. After a few days, an accident happens, or something, to the first person that did wrong. That's why people say this proverb. (Two occurrences. Informants: female).

Sources and Annotations: Ballesteros, p. 39, Dios castiga sin palo ni cuarta. Cobos, p. 32, Dios castiga sin palo ni cuarta. Conde, p. 114, same as A. De Barros, p. 176, Dios castiga sin piedra ni palo. Espinosa, A., p. 104, Dios no castiga con palos ni azotes. Jaramillo, p. 403, Mi Dios no castiga ni con palo ni con rejo sino con su machetico viejo. Martinez, p. 96, same as A. Rodriguez-Marin (1926), p. 132, Dios castiga sin palo ni piedra. Rubio, p. 150, Dios castiga sin palo y sin cuarta. Santamaria, p. 19, Dios castiga sin cuero ni palo; p. 577, Dios castiga sin cuero y sin palo. Sbarbi, p. 344, Dios castiga sin piedra ni palo. Velasco, p. 57, same as A.

265 (A). <u>Dios</u> considera pero no para siempre.

<u>Translation or Interpretation</u>: God considers but not forever.

<u>Context</u>: None given. (One occurrence. Informant: male).

<u>Sources and Annotations</u>: De Barros, p. 176, Dios consiente mas no para siempre. Sbarbi, p. 344, same as A.

266 (A). <u>Dios</u> dice: "ayudate, que yo te ayudaré."
266 (B). Al que se ayuda, <u>Dios</u> le ayuda.
266 (C). Ayudate que <u>Dios</u> te ayudará.
266 (D). Ayudate a ti mismo que <u>Dios</u> te ayudará.
266 (E). <u>Dios</u> dice: "has la lucha y yo te ayudaré."
266 (F). Has la lucha que <u>Dios</u> te ayudará.

<u>Translation or Interpretation</u>: God says: "help yourself and I'll help you."

<u>Context</u>: My mother told me when I was losing interest in attending school. (Seven occurrences. Informants: female).

<u>Sources and Annotations</u>: Adame, p. 24, same as A; p. 29, same as A. Cobos, p. 13, same as B. Conde, p. 114, same as A. Correas, p. 31, same as A. Espinosa, F., p. 51, Ayudate tu y ayudar te ha Dios. Galvan, p. 125, same as A; p. 127, same as C; Gamiz, p. 73, same as A. Robe, p. 70, same as A. Rodriguez-Marin (1930), p. 37, same as A; p. 256, same as A. Rodriguez-Marin (1926), p. 42, A quien no se ayuda, Dios no le ayuda; p. 52, Ayudate tu, y Dios te ayudará; p. 132, Dios ayuda a los ayudan. Yanez, p. 142, same as B.

267 (A). <u>Dios</u> es muy grande.

<u>Translation or Interpretation</u>: God is great.

<u>Context</u>: My neighbor was worried because his wife was having surgery. I tried to comfort him by telling him this proverb. (One occurrence. Informant: female).

<u>Sources and Annotations</u>: Sbarbi, p. 345, Dios es grande.

268 (A). <u>Dios</u> lo da, <u>Dios</u> lo quita.

<u>Translation or Interpretation</u>: God gives it, God takes it away.

Context: Meaning that God gives life and God takes it away.
I have often heard this at funerals. (One occurrence. Informant: male).

Sources and Annotations: Cobos, p. 32, Dios da y Dios quita.

269 (A). Dios los cría y el diablo los junta.

Translation or Interpretation: God raises them and the devil
brings them together.

Context: This means that God brings little children into the
world, and the devil tempts them, and tries to get them on his
side. (One occurrence. Informant: female).

Sources and Annotations: Caballero, p. 506, Dios los cria y
ellos se juntan. MacArthur, p. 42, same as A.

270 (A). Dios no cumple antojos ni endereza jorobados.

Translation or Interpretation: God doesn't perform capricious
desires, neither does He straighten hunchbacks.

Context: It's used when someone wishes something bad to happen
to another person. (Three informants: two female, one male).

Sources and Annotations: Adame, p. 24, same as A; p. 29, same
as A. Cerda, p. 279, same as A. Cobos, p. 33, same as A.
Conde, p. 114, same as A. Martinez, p. 96, same as A. Rubio,
p. 150, same as A. Velasco, p. 58, same as A.

271 (A). A cada quién Dios le dá lo que El cree que le con-
          viene.

Translation or Interpretation: God gives to each what He
thinks we (need).

Context: Usually when a person lives a good normal life, does
everything in an honest way, God will grant him better things
than to a person who lives a corrupt life and does not handle
responsibilities of himself and his family. (One occurrence.
Informant: female).

Sources and Annotations: Conde, p. 20, same as A.

272 (A). A Dios rogando y con el mazo dando.

Translation or Interpretation: Praying to God and hurting
people.

Context: People who are very religious, or who think they are.
They think that they can cheat and deceive others while they

go to church, and think that they can get away with it, pretending to be good. (Three occurrences. Informants: female).

Sources and Annotations: Armas, p. 420, Rezando, rezando, y con el mazo dando. Ballesteros, p. 37, same as A. Caballero, p. 52, same as A. Cobos, p. 10, same as A. Conde, p. 21, same as A. Covarrubias, p. 475, A Dios rogando y con el maco dando; p. 776, A Dios rogando y con el maco dando; p. 913, A dios rogando y con el maco dando. Espinosa, F., p. 155, A Dios rogando y con maco dando; A Dios rogando y con el maco dando se acaba el carro. Jaramillo, p. 360, same as A. Maldonado, p. 78, same as A. Rodriguez-Marin (1926) p. 6, A Dios rogando y al macho dando. Sbarbi, p. 341, same as A. Yanez, p. 86, same as A; p. 142, same as A.

273 (A). Al que <u>Dios</u> le a de dar, por la puerta le a de entrar.
273 (B). Al que <u>Dios</u> le quiera dar, por detras le ha de entrar.
273 (C). Si <u>Dios</u> me quiere dar, por la tronera me ha de entrar.

Translation or Interpretation: If God is going to give you something, it'll come easy.

Context: Informant says she overheard this proverb when this woman, willing to help someone else, but was unable because she lacked the means, was given something by some friends. (Three occurrences. Informants: two female, one male).

Sources and Annotations: Adame, p. 8, Al que Dios le ha de dar, por la tronera le ha de entrar; p. 11, Al que Dios le ha de dar, por la tronera le ha de entrar. Cerda, p. 277, Al que Dios le ha de dar, por la trasera le ha de entrar. Conde, p. 35, Al que Dios le ha de dar por la tronera le ha de entrar. Gamiz, p. 73, Al que Dios le ha de dar, por la tronera le ha de entrar. Robe, p. 63, Al que Dios le ha de dar, por la tronera le ha de entrar. Santamaria, p. 577, Al que Dios le quiere dar, por la tronera le ha de entrar. Wesley, p. 218, Al que Dios le ha de dar por la trasera ha de entrar.

274 (A). Así como manda <u>Dios</u> el pesar manda el consuelo.

Translation or Interpretation: God sends grief just as He sends consolation.

Context: Heard at funerals of many relatives recently. (One occurrence. Informant: female).

Sources and Annotations: Sbarbi, p. 342, Como Dios manda.

275 (A). Lo que <u>Dios</u> le dé San Pedro se lo bendice.

Translation or Interpretation: May St. Peter bless whatever God gives you.

Context: My informant's family would say this proverb at the dinner table every night. (One occurrence. Informant: female).

Sources and Annotations: Armas, p. 408, Al que Dios se la da, San Pedro se la bendice. Caballero, p. 99, Al que Dios se la de, San Pedro se la bendiga; p. 143, Al que Dios se la de, San Pedro se la bendiga. Cobos, p. 15, A quien Dios se la diera, San Pedro se la bendiga. Conde, p. 35, Al quien Dios se la dio, San Pedro se la bendiga. Espinosa, F., p. 103, Al que Dios se la tiene, San Pedro se la bendiga. Jaramillo, p. 363, Al que mi Dios se la dio, San Pedro se la bendiga. Maldonado, p. 88, A quien Dios se la diera, San Pedro se la bendiga.

276 (A). Lo que Dios no quiere, santos no pueden.
276 (B). Cuando Dios no quiere, santos no pueden.

Translation or Interpretation: What God doesn't want, Saints can't do.

Context: When a person will ask a saint for a particular wish and the saint doesn't comply. Someone might say to that person "lo que Dios no quiere, santos no pueden." (One occurrence. Informant: female).

Sources and Annotations: Cobos, p. 24, same as B. Conde, p. 90, same as B. Espinosa, F., p. 216, Cuando Dios no quiere, los santos no han de poder. Jaramillo, p. 371, Cuando Dios no quiere, el santo no puede. MacArthur, p. 10, Cuando Dios no quiere los santos no pueden.

277 (A). Saber lo que es amar a Dios en tierra ajena.

Translation or Interpretation: To know what it is to love God in a strange land.

Context: My mother usually says this to my married brothers because, now, they are on their own and have their own responsibilities. (One occurrence. Informant: female).

Sources and Annotations: Conde, p. 312, Para que lo sepas lo que es amar a Dios en tierra extraña. Martinez, p. 203, No sabes lo que es amar a Dios en tierra de indios. Rubio, p. 139, same as A. Santamaria, p. 51, same as A; p. 577, Amar a Dios en tierra ajena. Velasco, p. 117, No sabes lo que es amar a Dios en tierra.

278 (A). Sólo te acuerdas de Dios cuando te aprieta el zapato.

Translation or Interpretation: You only remember God whenever your shoe tightens.

Context: My mother always says this to me right before finals, when I begin to panic and to go to church to pray. (One occurrence. Informant: female).

Sources and Annotations: None.

279 (A). Más vale doblarse que quebrarse.

Translation or Interpretation: It's better to bend than to break.

Context: One should not hold out until the last minute because in doing so, you might lose completely. Instead, compromise and settle for something instead of nothing. (One occurrence. Informant: female).

Sources and Annotations: Cobos, p. 79, same as A. Conde, p. 45, Antes doblar que quebrar. Rodriguez-Marin (1930), p. 205, Mejor es descoser, que romper; p. 206, Menos es torcer que quebrar. Rodriguez-Marin (1926), p. 296, Más vale doblar que quebrar.

280 (A). También de dolor se canta cuando llorar no se puede.

Translation or Interpretation: One can also sing from pain when unable to cry.

Context: The proverb could be used to mean that just because you are singing doesn't mean you're not hurting. (One occurrence. Informant: male).

Sources and Annotations: Adame, p. 90, same as A; p. 91, same as A.

281 (A). ¿Quién manda, Don Joaquin o los burros?

Translation or Interpretation: Who is boss, Don Joaquin or the donkeys?

Context: Sometimes I try to convince my grandmother to try a new dress on and tell her why she should wear it. She ends up saying "no, I won't wear it because I don't feel like it." (One occurrence. Informant: female).

Sources and Annotations: Martinez, p.240, ¿Quién manda, Chepe o los burros?

282 (A). Más vale dudar que lamentar.

Translation or Interpretation: It's better to doubt than to regret.

Context: Informant says it's better for her to doubt something she is told, which might be true, rather than to ignore it and later regret it because it was true. (One occurrence. Informant: female).

Sources and Annotations: None.

283 (A). El ejercicio hace al maestro.
283 (B). La práctica hace el maestro.

Translation or Interpretation: Practice makes perfect.

Context: None given. (Four occurrences. Informants: one female, three male).

Sources and Annotations: Cobos, p. 37, same as A. Lucero-White, p. 34, El ejercicio hace al hombre. Rodriguez-Marin (1926), p. 155, El ejercicio hace al maestro al novicio. Sbarbi, p. 365, El ejercicio hace maestro.

284 (A). El que a buen árbol se arrima, buena sombra lo cobija.
284 (B). Al que buen árbol se arrima, buena sombra le cubre.
284 (C). El que de buen árbol se coje, buena sombra le dará.
284 (D). El que a buen árbol se arrima, buena sombra lo pro-
          teje.
284 (E). El que a buen árbol se arrima, buena sombra espera.

Translation or Interpretation: He who gets close to a good tree (gets a) good shade.

Context: My mother used to tell me this proverb when she wanted me to hang around with the good bunch. (Twenty-four occurrences. Seventeen female, seven male).

Sources and Annotations: Armas, p. 225, Arrimarse a buen palo; p. 412, same as A. Ballesteros, p. 19, same as A. Caballero, p. 543, El que a buen árbol se arrima. Cobos, p. 41, same as A; p. 103, Quien a buen árbol se arrima, buena sombra lo cobija. Conde, p. 101, De buen árbol, buena sombra; p. 142, same as A. Espinosa, F., p. 46, Quien a buen árbol se arrima, buena sombra lo cobija. Gamiz, p. 81, Al que a buen palo se aloja, buena sombra le cobija. Glazer, p. 42, same as A. Jaramillo, p. 363, same as A. Maldonado, p. 61, Quien a buen árbol se arrima, buena sombra le cobija. Martinez, p. 109, same as A. Rodriguez-Marin (1926), p. 39, same as A; p. 388, Quien a buen árbol se arrima buena sombra le cobija. Sbarbi, p. 89, Quien a buen árbol se arrima buena sombra le cobija.

285 (A). El que a dos ama, con uno queda mal.

Translation or Interpretation: One who loves two, will end up in good terms with one.

Context: She used it on whoever wasn't sure who they really cared for. If her daughter was going out with two guys she would use this proverb. (One occurrence. Informant: female).

Sources and Annotations: Rubio, p. 180, El que a dos amos sirve, con alguno queda mal.

286 (A). El que a hierro mata, a hierro muere.

Translation or Interpretation: He who kills with a weapon, will die the same way.

Context: Meaning, if you kill with a weapon or knock people down by cheating them, you also will die or fall by the same manner. (Ten occurrences. Informants: seven female, three male).

Sources and Annotations: Adame, p. 32, same as A; p. 35, same as A. Armas, p. 412, same as A. Caballero, p. 543, same as A. Cobos, p. 41, same as A. Conde, p. 142, same as A. De Barros, p. 186, same as A. Espinosa, A., p. 105, El que hierro mata a fuerza muere. Gamiz, p. 91, El que a fierro mata, a fierro muere. Jaramillo, p. 383, El que a cuchillo mata, a cuchillo muere. MacArthur, p. 24, same as A. Rodriguez-Marin (1926), p. 388, Quien a hierro mata, a hierro muere. Sbarbi, p. 469, Quien a hierro mata, a hierro muere. Yanez, p. 353, El que yerro mata...

287 (A). El que a su hijo consiente, va engordando una serpiente.

Translation or Interpretation: He that does not correct his child is feeding a snake.

Context: When I was about 10 years old I used to hate very much for my mother to punish me, or hit me. One day I received my grade report, and I found that I had failed two courses. Knowing that my mother was going to hit me, I decided to change the grades in my report card. Of course, when she found out later, she hit me worse, and then told me this proverb. The meaning of this proverb is that if you let your son get away with doing whatever he wants, you will be creating a bad person. Parents have the responsibility to correct the children because if they don't they will be making bad people out of them. (One occurrence. Informant: male).

Sources and Annotations: Yanez, p. 326, Madre que consiente, engorda una serpiente.

288 (A). El que a un palo se aloja, dos veces se moja.

Translation or Interpretation: He who to a tree lodges, gets
wet twice.

Context: Informant claims one time it had rained really hard.
Rain started letting down as we were walking home from school.
We ran under some trees and I remembered this saying, and said
it to my friend. I heard the saying in a conversation at my
home. (One occurrence. Informant: male).

Sources and Annotations: Rodriguez-Marin (1926), p. 428, Quien
se mete debajo de hojas, dos veces se moja.

289 (A). El que anda entre la miel algo se le pega.

Translation or Interpretation: He who is (in) the honey will
get sticky.

Context: A person who mingles the most will eventually get the
most of life. (Two occurrences. Informants: one female, one male).

Sources and Annotations: Adame, p. 32, same as A; p. 39, same
as A. Aranda, p. 11, same as A. Armas, p. 408, El que entre
la miel anda, algo se le pega. Conde, p. 35, same as A. Gamiz, p. 79, El que entre la miel anda, algo se le pega. Jaramillo, p. 363, Al que entre la miel anda, algo se le pega.
MacArthur, p. 40, same as A. Rodriguez-Marin (1930), p. 259,
¿Por que el muchacho a la miel se llega? Por lo que se le pega;
p. 265, Quien a la miel se allega, algo se le pega; p. 280,
Quien miel menea, pegasele della. Rodriguez-Marin (1926), p.
39, A quien castra la colmena, miel se le pega de ella; p.
391, Quien anda con miel, se chupa los dedos; p. 404, Quien
entre miel anda, untarse tiene; p. 409, Quien la miel menea,
siempre se le pega de ella.

290 (A). El que aprisa vive, pronto acaba.
290 (B). El que pronto vive, pronto acaba.
290 (C). El que recio vive, pronto acaba.
290 (D). El que recio vive, pronto acaba.

Translation or Interpretation: He who lives a hurried life
will soon die.

Context: My informant first heard this proverb from his father when he was carelessly riding his horse extremely fast.
(Four occurrences. Informants: one female, three male).

Sources and Annotations: Conde, p. 149, El que recio vive,
recio acaba; p. 338, Quien de prisa vive, de prisa muere.
Rodriguez-Marin (1926), p. 401, Quien de prisa fue, de prisa
volvio. Rubio, p. 59, No te apures pa' que dures.

291 (A). <u>El</u> que boca tiene, a Roma va.

<u>Translation or Interpretation</u>: He who has a mouth goes to Roma.

<u>Context</u>: Informant used it to tell someone that if, you can use your mouth to ask questions, you can obtain information. (Two occurrences. Informants: one female, one male).

<u>Sources and Annotations</u>: Alcala, p. 505, Quien pregunta a Roma va. Aranda, p. 11, same as A. Ballesteros, p. 3, same as A. Cobos, p. 42, same as A; p. 45, El que lengua tiene, a Roma va. Conde, p. 351, same as A. Covarrubias, p. 760, Quien lengua tiene a Roma va; p. 913, Quien lengua tiene a Roma va. Espinosa, A., p. 105, El que tiene boca a Roma va. Galván, p. 125, El que boca tiene... p. 128, same as A. Gamiz, p. 81, same as A. Maldonado, p. 30, Quien lengua ha, a Roma va. Pérez, p. 121, same as A. Rodríguez-Marín (1926), p. 394, Quien boca lleva, Roma llega; p. 410, Quien lengua ha, a Roma va; p. 432, Quien tiene boca, va a Roma; p. 433, Quien tiene lengua, a Roma llega. Santamaria, p. 42, same as A.

292 (A). <u>El</u> que come más pronto alcanza más.

<u>Translation or Interpretation</u>: One who eats fast will get more, or the one who eats fastest will get the most.

<u>Context</u>: Usually at a family get-together someone yelled this out just for fun. (One occurrence. Informant: female).

<u>Sources and Annotations</u>: None.

293 (A). <u>El</u> que come y canta, loco se levanta.

<u>Translation or Interpretation</u>: He who eats and sings, will wake up crazy.

<u>Context</u>: I remember my mother telling us this when my brother and I would misbehave at the table. This would quiet us down and make us eat our meal quicker. (Nine occurrences. Informants: seven female, two male).

<u>Sources and Annotations</u>: Cobos, p. 42, same as A; Conde, p. 143, same as A; p. 333, Quien bebe y canta, loco se levanta; p. 335, Quien comiendo canta, sino esta loc6 poco le falta. Gamiz, p. 91, same as A. Robe, p. 64, same as A. Rodriguez-Marin (1926), p. 396, Quien come y canta de locura se levanta.

294 (A). <u>El</u> que compra barato, compra cada rato.

<u>Translation or Interpretation</u>: He who buys cheap, buys very often.

Context: This proverb means that a person who buys cheap things will have to buy very often, because cheap items do not last long. (Seven occurrences. Informants: one female, six male).

Sources and Annotations: None.

295 (A). El que con lobos se junta, a aullar se enseña.
295 (B). El que con lobos anda, a aullar se enseña.
295 (C). El que con coyotes se junta, a aullar se enseña.

Translation or Interpretation: He who hangs around with wolves, learns to howl.

Context: If you hang around with people who have bad habits, you will also pick up bad habits. (Twenty occurrences. Informants: ten female, ten male).

Sources and Annotations: Adame, p. 32, same as A; p. 39, same as A. Ballesteros, p. 61, same as A. Caballero, p. 543, same as B. Cobos, p. 41, El que anda entre los lobos, a aullar se enseña; p. 42, same as B; p. 109, Si con lobos anda, a aullar te enseñas. Conde, p. 143, El que con coyotes anda, a aullar se enseña. De Barros, p. 391, Quien con lobos anda a aullar se enseña. Espinosa, A., p. 104, same as A. Glazer, p. 52, same as A. Lucero-White, p. 34, El que entre lobos anda a aullar se enseña.

296 (A). El que con niño se acuesta, mojado se levanta.
296 (B). El que con niño se acuesta amanece orinado.

Translation or Interpretation: He who sleeps with a baby will wake up wet.

Context: When an older person runs around with a younger mate, and ends up in trouble. (Three occurrences. Informants: one female, one male, one anonymous).

Sources and Annotations: Adame, p. 32, El que con niños se acuesta...sucio amanece; p. 39, El que con niños se acuest... sucio amanece. Armas, p. 420, Quien con criaturas se acuesta, mojado amanece. Ballesteros, p. 46, El que con niños se acuesta, mojado se levanta. Cobos, p. 42, El que con ninos se acuesta, amanece mojado; p. 50, El que con niños se acuesta, ya sabe como amanece. Conde, p. 143, El que con muchachos se acuesta, cagado se levanta; p. 336, El que con muchachos se acuesta, cagado se levanta. De Barros, p. 187, El que con niños se acuesta, cagado se levanta. Espinosa, A., p. 106, El que con niños duerme sucio amanece, o a lo menos todo miado. Jaramillo, p. 382, El que con chiquito se acuesta, cagao. amanece. Martinez, p. 239, El que con muchachos se acuesta, cagado despierta. Rodriguez-Marin (1926), p. 397, Quien con niños se acuesta, cagado etcetera. Rubio, p. 124, Quien con muchachos se acuesta...

297 (A). El que dá razón del camino es que andado ya lo
          tiene.
297 (B). El que habla del camino, ya lo tiene caminado.

Translation or Interpretation: He who gives information on the
road has already walked it.

Context: When someone tells you that you were at a certain
place, or doing a certain thing. (Fourteen occurrences. Seven
female, seven male).

Sources and Annotations: Adame, p. 69, Nadie puede hablar del
camino, hasta que no lo tiene andado; p. 71, Nadie puede hablar
del camino, hasta que no lo tiene andado. Cobos, p. 42, El
que da razón del camino es porque lo tiene andado; p. 45, El
que da razón del camino es porque lo tiene andado. Glazer, p.
45, same as A.

298 (A). El que da y quita, con el diablo se desquita.

Translation or Interpretation: He who gives and takes, will
get even with the devil.

Context: This proverb is used when a person gives a present
to someone and later wants it back. (Two occurrences. Informants: female).

Sources and Annotations: Cobos, p. 43, same as A. Chavez, p.
43, El que da y quita, le sale una corbita. Espinosa, A., p.
98, Al que da y quita- le sale una corcovita y viene el diablo
y se la corta con su navajita. Martinez, p. 109, same as A.
Rodriguez-Marin (1930), p. 271, Quien da y quita lo dado, se
lo lleva el diablo. Rodriguez-Marin (1926), p. 39, El que da
y quita, se lo lleva la perra maldita. Santamaria, p. 557,
same as A; Velasco, p. 64, same as A. Villafuerte, p. 49, Al
que da y quita, se le cría una jorobita.

299 (A). El que de ajeno se viste, en la calle lo desvisten.
299 (B). Lo ajeno siempre pido por su dueño.

Translation or Interpretation: He who dresses with loaned
clothes, will be undressed in the street.

Context: A person who borrows someone else's clothes is liable
to be asked for them by the owner when he/she leasts expects
it. (Ten occurrences: Informants: female).

Sources and Annotations: Adame, p. 32, same as A; p. 40, same
as A. Armas, p. 412, same as A. Ballesteros, p. 24, El que
de prestado se viste, en la calle lo desvisten. Cobos, p. 43,
El que de ajeno viste, en la calle lo desnudan. Espinosa, A.,
p. 105, El que de ajeno se viste en la calle lo desnudan.

Jaramillo, p. 385, El que con lo ajeno se viste, en la calle
lo desvisten. Lucero-White, p. 34, El que de otro se viste en
la calle lo desnudan. Martinez, p. 239, same as A. Rodriguez-Marin (1930), p. 31, Aquien se viste de lo ajeno, le
desnudan en concejo. Rodriguez-Marin (1926), p. 39, A quien
de ajeno se viste, en la calle lo desnudan; p. 436, Quien viste lo ajeno, en la plaza lo pide su dueño. Sbarbi, p. 48, Quien
de ajeno se viste, en la calle le desnudan.

300 (A). <u>El</u> que dice lo que quiere, oye lo que no quiere.

<u>Translation or Interpretation</u>: He who says what he wants,
hears what he doesn't want.

<u>Context</u>: Informant knew of a situation in which this lady
offended another lady in a personal matter. She, being hurt,
responded with something personal about her too. (One occurrence. Informant: female).

<u>Sources and Annotations</u>: Conde, p. 338, same as A. Jarami-
llo, p. 383, same as A. Rodriguez-Marin (1926), p. 401, Quien
dice lo que quiere, oye lo que le duele- o lo que no quiere.

301 (A). <u>El</u> que duerme con los perros, con las pulgas se
           levanta.

<u>Translation or Interpretation</u>: He who sleeps with the dogs,
wakes up with fleas.

<u>Context</u>: This proverb has one meaning. It means that a per-
son, or persons, may pick up habits from people with whom they
hang around with. I heard this proverb about two years ago,
while I was listening to a Spanish program on the radio. The
radio station was KGBT in Harlingen, Texas. (One occurrence.
Informant: male).

<u>Sources and Annotations</u>: Chavez, p. 47, El que se acuesta con
perros, con garrapatas se levanta. MacArthur, p. 60, El que
con perros se acuesta, con pulgas se levanta.

302 (A). <u>El</u> que duerme en casa ajena temprano se levanta.

<u>Translation or Interpretation</u>: If you sleep in someone else's
house (you) always get up early.

<u>Context</u>: We went to California, to visit, last year, and my
uncle told us if we woke up this early. We said no. Then he
said this saying. (One occurrence. Informant: male).

<u>Sources and Annotations</u>: Aranda, p. 12, El que duerme en casa
ajena de manaña se levanta con su cachucha en la mano mirando
a ver para donde se aranca. Cobos, p. 43, El que duerme en
casa ajena de manana se levanta.

303 (A). El que es buen gallo, en cualquier gallinero canta.
303 (B). El pájaro que puede, donde quiera canta.
303 (C). El gallo que es bueno, en donde quiera canta.
303 (D). El que es buen gallo, donde quiera canta.
303 (E). El que es buen gallo, en cualquier muladar canta.

Translation or Interpretation: A good rooster crows in any
chicken coop.

Context: A person who is good can perform well anywhere.
(Nineteen occurrences. Informants: eight female, ten male,
one anonymous).

Sources and Annotations: Adame, p. 7, same as A; p. 32, same
as A; p. 40, same as A. Ballesteros, p. 61, same as D. Cobos,
p. 43, same as A. Conde, p. 144, same as A. Chávez, p. 49,
Un buen gallo, en cualquier gallinero canta. Glazer, p. 49,
Un buen gallo en cualquier gallinero canta. Martinez, p. 109,
same as A. Robe, p. 68, El que es buen gallo en cualquier
parte canta. Velasco, p. 65, same as A.

304 (A). El que es buen juez, por su casa empieza.
304 (B). El que es buen juez que por su casa comience.

Translation or Interpretation: He who is a good judge, starts
at his house.

Context: This means that good parents begin at home. They
discipline their children in having good manners. Parents
shouldn't talk about their neighbor's kids before they see
theirs. (Thirteen occurrences. Informants: nine female,
three male, one anonymous).

Sources and Annotations: Adame, p. 32, same as A; p. 40, same
as A. Cobos, p. 44, same as B. Conde, p. 125, El buen juez
por su casa empieza. Gamiz, p. 77, same as A. Glazer, p. 52,
same as A.

305 (A). El que es barrigón ni aunque lo fajen se enflaca.
305 (B). El que es pansón, aunque lo fajen y el que es flaco,
         aunque lo soplen.
305 (C). El que es pansón, aunque lo fajen.
305 (D). El que es pansón, ni aunque lo fajen.
305 (E). El que nace pansón aunque lo fajen de chico.
305 (F). El que nace pansón aunque de chico lo fajen.
305 (G). El que ha de ser barrigón, ni aunque lo fajen de
         chico.

Translation or Interpretation: He who is fat, not even with
a girdle will become thin.

Context: She said that when she was young, she was always a
little chubby. She would wear a dress and try to tighten up

her stomach, but you could still see she was chubby. Her mother would tell her, jokingly, this phrase. (Eight occurrences.
Informants: five female, three male).

Sources and Annotations: Adame, p. 32, same as G; p. 38, same
as G. Ballesteros, p. 47, El que nace pansón aunque lo fajen.
Cobos, p. 12, El que nace pa pansón aunque lo fajen; p. 35, El
barrigón ni aunque lo fajen; p. 43, El que es barrigón aunque
lo fajen un arriero; p. 44, El que ha de ser barrigón aunque
lo fajen; p. 47, El que nace pa pansón aunque lo fajen de niño.
Conde, p. 145, El que ha de ser barrigón...aunque lo cinchen.
Chávez, p. 49, El que es barrigón, ni aunque lo fajen. Espinosa, A., p. 105, El que ha de ser barrigón aunque lo fajen de
chiquito. Lea, p. 234, El que es barrigón mas que lo fajen.
Lucero-White, p. 34, El que es barrigón mas que lo fajen.
Martinez, p. 110, El que nace barrigón aunque lo fajen de chico. Paredes, p. 31, El que ha de ser barrigón, aunque lo
fajen. Robe, p. 63, El que ha de ser barrigón, aunque lo fajen de chiquito. Rodriguez-Marin (1930), p. 248, Para quien
nace barrigón, pocas viente fajas son. Rubio, p. 188, El que
ha de ser barrigón, aunque lo fajen. Santamaria, p. 192, Al
que nació barrigón ni que lo fajen; p. 299, Al que nació
barrigón ni que lo fajen. Sbarbi, p. 121, El que ha nacido
barrigón, es al nudo que lo fajen. Velasco, p. 66, El que
nace para barrigón aunque lo fajen.

306 (A). El que escupe para arriba, a la cara le cae.
306 (B). El que escupe al cielo, a la cara le cae.
306 (C). Quien al cielo escupe, a la cara le torna.
306 (D). No escupas para arriba, porque a la cara te cae.
306 (E). Nadie escupe al aire que no le caiga en la cara.

Translation or Interpretation: Who ever spits upward, to
heaven, will have it fall on his face.

Context: You shouldn't criticize someone else because those
things may develop in your family.

Sources and Annotations: Adame, p. 79, Para arriba no has de
escupir, porque en la cara te ha de caer; p. 80, Para arriba
no has de escupir, porque en la cara te ha de caer. Aranda,
p. 21, No escupas al cielo porque a la cara te cae. Armas,
p. 412, same as B. Benavides, p. 91, same as A. Caballero,
p. 543, El que escupe al cielo, en la cara le cae. Campa, p.
63, Quien al cielo escupe, a su cara le cae. Cobos, p. 41, El
que al cielo escupe, en la cara le cae. Conde, p. 142, same
as B. Correas, p. 148, Escupí al cielo, y me cayo en la cara.
Covarrubias, p. 415, El que escupe al cielo, a la cara se le
vuelve; p. 545, El que escupe al cielo, a la cara se le vuelve. De Barros, p. 88, Al que al cielo escupe, en la cara le
cae. Espinosa, A., p. 104, El que al cielo escupe, en la
cara le cae. Espinosa, F., p. 108, Es escupir al cielo y que
le caiga sobre los ojos. Gamiz, p. 77, El que al cielo escupe,
en la cara le cae. Glazer, p. 49, No escupas al cielo porque

a la cara te cae. Jaramillo, p. 386, El que p' arriba escupe,
en la cara le cae. Lea, p. 236, Nadie escupe a los cielos que
a la cara no le caiga. Lucero-White, p. 35, Nadie escupe a los
cielos que a la cara no le caiga. Maldonado, p. 30, Quien al
cielo escupe a su cara le cae. Robe, p. 64, same as A. Rodriguez-Marin (1930), p. 244, Palabras blandas te pondran en las
andas. Rodriguez-Marin (1926), p. 39, Al quien al cielo escupe,
en el nostro le cae; p. 200, Escupe al cielo y te caera en los
ojos; p. 388, Quien a Dios escupe, en la cara le cae; 389,
Quien al cielo escupe, en la cara le cae; p. 404, Quien escupe
al cielo, en la cara le cae. Sbarbi, p. 239, El que al cielo
escupe, en la cara le cae, o de baba se llena.

307 (A). El que espera, desespera.

Translation or Interpretation: One who waits will lose hope.

Context: Waiting for something to show up, or for an event,
can be very tiresome. (Five occurrences. Informants: four
female, one male).

Sources and Annotations: Adame, p. 32, same as A; p. 40, same
as A. Ballesteros, p. 4, same as A. Cobos, p. 44, same as A.
Conde, p. 145, same as A; El que espera, desespera, pero el
que espera se Prep.se sabarca; El que espera, desespera, aunque
esperar ñe consuelo. Espinosa, A., p. 99, same as A. Espinosa,
F., p. 110, Quien espera, desespera. Gamiz, p. 89, same as A.
Jaramillo, p. 382, same as A. Maldonado, p. 45, Quien espera,
desespera. Rodriguez-Marin (1930), p. 274, Quien espera, desespera; y quien viene nunca llega; Quien espera, non desespera, si tiene esperanza vera. Rodriguez-Marin (1926), p. 405,
Quien espera, desespera. Yanez, p. 149, same as A.

308 (A). El que es perico, donde quiera es verde.

Translation or Interpretation: He who is a parrot, is green
anywhere.

Context: M. says that anybody who is smart will be noticed
anywhere. (Two occurrences. Informants: female).

Sources and Annotations: Armas, p. 412, same as A. Conde, p.
145, El que es perico en donde quiera es verde; y el que es
pendejo en donde quiera pierde. Martinez, p. 109, El que es
perico donde quiera es verde; y el que es pendejo donde quiera
pierde. MacArthur, p. 16, Al que es perico, donde quiera es
verde. Santamaria, p. 449, same as A. Velasco, p. 65, same as
A.

309 (A). El que está en el lodo quisiera meter a otro.

Translation or Interpretation: He who is in the gutter, would
like to drag someone else with him.

Context: If someone is in trouble, he would almost do anything to get himself out of it. To do this, he will try to get
another person to take his penalty. (One occurrence. Informant: female).

Sources and Annotations: Correas, p. 101, same as A. De Barros, p. 188, El que esta en el lodo querria meter a otro.

310 (A). El que feo ama, lindo le parece.

Translation or Interpretation: He who loves the ugly sees
it beautiful.

Context: My grandmother always said this to my uncle when he
got married. She didn't care too much for her daughter-in-
law, but since my uncle never listened she would quote this
proverb often. (Two occurrences. Informants: female).

Sources and Annotations: Aranda, p. 25, Quien a fea ama, hermosa le parece. Campa, p. 64, Quien a feo ama, hermosa le parece. Cobos, p. 41, El que fea ama, hermosa le parece; p. 103,
Quien a fea ama, hermosa le parece. Conde, p. 188, Hace el
deseo, hermoso lo feo; p. 339, Quien feo ama, bonito le parece. Covarrubias, p. 587, Quien feo ama, hermoso le parece;
p. 683, Quien feo ama, hermoso le parece. Espinosa, F., p.
112, Quien feo ama, hermoso le parece. Galván, p. 129, Quien
a feo ama, hermoso...; p. 133, Quien a feo ama, hermoso le
parece. Gamiz, p. 75, Al que feo ama, hermoso le parece.
Jaramillo, p. 362, El que feo ama, bonito le parece. Lucero-
White, p. 36, Quien fea ama, hermosa le parece. Robe, p. 63,
same as A. Rodriguez-Marin (1930), p. 278, Quien lo feo ama,
bello lo halla. Rodriguez-Marin (1926), p. 40, A quien feo
adama- o ama-, bonito- o hermoso le parece; p. 405, Quien feo
ama, bonita- o hermoso le parece. Sbarbi, p. 64, Quien feo
ama, hermoso le parece.

311 (A). El que fiaba se murió, Mala paga lo mató.

Translation or Interpretation: He who sold on credit died,
Bad debts killed him.

Context: Informant said he has heard it being used by some
business men in response to their customers who may want credit. (One occurrence. Informant: male).

Sources and Annotations: Jaramillo, p. 384, El que fiaba se
murio, mil saludes le dejo.

312 (A). El que hace mal, no espere bién.

Translation or Interpretation: He who does wrong, should not
expect good.

Context: A father giving advice to his son. (One occurrence. Informant: female).

Sources and Annotations: Ballesteros, p. 4, El que la hace la paga.

313 (A). El que ha de ser tostón aunque ande entre los pesos.

Translation or Interpretation: He who is mediocre will stay the same, even though he hangs around with rich people.

Context: Some people think that if they rub shoulders with upper class people, somehow they will be considered in the same category. (One occurrence. Informant: male).

Sources and Annotations: Espinosa, A., p. 105, El que ha de ser barrigón aunque lo fajen chiquito. Rubio, p. 188, El que ha de ser centavo aunque ande entre los pesos; p. 192, El que nació siendo flaco aunque ande entre tostones.

314 (A). El que hace más, lo agradecen menos.

Translation or Interpretation: The person who does more is appreciated less. This means that the more favors you do for others, the more you will be taken for granted.

Context: None given. (One occurrence. Informant: female).

Sources and Annotations: Rubio, p. 40, Al que hace más se le agradece menos.

315 (A). El que hambre tiene, en tortillas piensa.

Translation or Interpretation: When one is hungry, one thinks about food.

Context: My informant first heard about this dicho five years ago, when she was having dinner at her mother-in-law's. While they were setting the table she said something, like she wished she could be eating tacos. Then her mother-in-law told her the following dicho: "El que hambre tiene en tortillas piensa." This means when one is hungry one only thinks of tortillas. My informant said that this dicho was true, because when she is hungry she thinks of food. (Three occurrences. Informants: female).

Sources and Annotations: Ballesteros, p. 47, El que hambre tiene en gordas piensa. Cobos, p. 45, Same as A. Espinosa, A., p. 105, El que hambre tiene en comer piensa. Gamiz, p. 73, same as A. Robe, p. 64, El que hambre tiene en pan piensa. Rodriguez-Marin (1930), p. 276, Quien hambre tiene, del pan se

acuerda. Rodriguez-Marin (1926), p. 407, Quien hambre tiene,
con pan sueña. Santamaria, p. 90. same as A; p. 206, same as
A.

316 (A). El que juega con lumbre, las manos se quema.

Translation or Interpretation: He who plays with fire, burns
his hands.

Context: When her children would play with bad kids she would
tell them this proverb, and also that they would eventually
get hurt. (One occurrence. Informant: female).

Sources and Annotations: Conde, p. 332, Quien anda entre
fuego, quémase luego. Rodriguez-Marin (1930), p. 266, Quien
a pie y descalzo camina, no se litra de espinas. Rodriguez-
Marin (1926), p. 408, Quien juega, no asa castañas.

317 (A). El que juega limpio, limpio se queda.

Translation or Interpretation: He who plays clean, will remain clean.

Context: When a person is always honest he will never be well
off financially. Or, if a person is always truthful, he will
never get into trouble. (One occurrence. Informant: female).

Sources and Annotations: Adame, p. 32, El que limpio juega,
limpio se queda; p. 41, El que limpio juega, limpio se queda.
Conde, p. 341, Quien limpio juega, limpio se queda.

318 (A). El que lo hace, lo paga.

Translation or Interpretation: He who does it, pays for it.

Context: Whenever there is a case in which someone kills a
person, my mother will say "el que lo hace, lo paga." (Three
occurrences. Informants: females).

Sources and Annotations: Armas, p. 413, El que la debe, la
paga. Ballesteros, p. 4, same as A. Caballero, p. 544, El
que la haga que la pague; p. 947, Quien la haga que la pague;
Quien me la hace que me la pague. California Spanish Proverbs and Adages, p. 123, El que la debe la paga. Cobos, p.
45, same as A. Conde, p. 146, same as A; p. 395, Tu me la
hiciste, tu me la pagas. Espinosa, F., p. 124, Quien mal hace,
que lo pague. Galvan, p. 127, same as A; p. 132, same as A.
Perez, p. 121, El que la hace la paga. Rodriguez-Marin (1930),
p. 277, Quien la hace, que la pague. Rodriguez-Marin (1926),
p. 409, Quien la hace, la paga.

319 (A). <u>El</u> que le da pan a perro ajeno, pierde el pan y pier-
<u>de</u> el perro.

319 (B). No le des pan a perro ajeno porque pierdes pan y
perro.

<u>Translation or Interpretation</u>: He who gives bread to another's
dog, loses the bread and loses the dog.

<u>Context</u>: Once a stray dog was around Mrs. R.'s father's house.
He fed it for a couple of days, and after that, he never did see
that dog again. (Four occurrences. Informants: three female,
one male).

<u>Sources and Annotations</u>: Aranda, p. 12, El que da de comer al
perro ajeno, pierde el perro y pierde el pan. Armas, p. 420,
Quien da pan a perro ajeno pierde el pan y pierde el perro.
Cobos, p. 42, same as A; p. 104, Quien da pan a perro ajeno
pierde el pan y pierde el perro. Conde, p. 143, same as A.
Espinosa, A., p. 100, same as A. Gamiz, p. 76, Quien da pan
a perro ajeno, pierde el pan y pierde el perro. Lucero-White,
p. 36, Quien da pan a perro ajeno pierde el pan y pierde el
perro. Paredes, p. 33, Quien da pan a perro ajeno pierde el
pan y pierde el perro. Rodriguez-Marin (1930), p. 270, Quien
da pan a ajeno can, pierde el can y pierde el pan. Rodriguez-
Marin (1926), p. 399, Quien da pan a perro ajeno, pierde el
pan y pierde el perro.

320 (A). El que madruga, Dios lo ayuda.
320 (B). Al que madruga, Dios le ayuda.
320 (C). A quién madruga, Dios le ayuda.
320 (D). Se dice que <u>el</u> que se levanta temprano, Dios le
ayuda.

<u>Translation or Interpretation</u>: He who early rises will be
helped by God.

<u>Context</u>: Earlier in the summer I was looking for a job. My
mother recited her wise words, which, in essence, meant that
the jobs are given "first come, first served." (Thirty-eight
occurrences. Informants: twenty-four female, fourteen male).

<u>Sources and Annotations</u>: Adame, p. 9, same as C; p. 12, same
as C. Aranda, p. 2, same as A. Armas, p. 408, same as B.
Ballesteros, p. 37, same as B. Benavides, p. 89, same as B.
Caballero, p. 143, same as C. Cobos, p. 12, same as B. Conde,
p. 36, same as B. De Barros, p. 89, same as B. Espinosa, F.,
p. 98, Más vale a quien Dios ayuda que quien mucho madruga.
Galván, p. 124, same as B; p. 127, same as B. Gamiz, p. 89,
same as B. Glazer, p. 52, same as A. Jaramillo, p. 363, same
as B. Lea, p. 233, same as C. Lucero-White, p. 33, same as
B. Maldonado, p. 167, Quien madruga, Dios lo ayuda. Rodriguez-Marin (1930), p. 30, A quien madruga, le ayuda Dios, si
madruga con buena intención. Rodriguez-Marin (1926), p. 41,
same as C. Yanez, p. 20, same as B.

321 (A). El que mal busca, mal halla.

Translation or Interpretation: He who looks for evil, finds
evil.

Context: A friend of mine, joking, said he felt like fighting.
He wound up getting bruised by another dude. (One occurrence.
Informant: female).

Sources and Annotations: Aranda, p. 11, El que busca, halla.
California Spanish Proverbs and Adages, p. 123, El que la busca la halla.

322 (A). El que más sirve, menos vale.

Translation or Interpretation: He who strives to do his best,
what he does has no value.

Context : Today I frequently find myself using this proverb.
When I found myself using it the most was when I was employed,
last summer through December. I was employed part-time as a
secretary, but it turned out, soon afterwards that I became
their faithful slave. At first they asked a personal favor, and
I could never say no. This was how I eventually became their
slave/servant. I had to be there earlier in the morning and
expected to only be out to go to class. They wanted me to
work late and not count my time. When I asked for a transfer,
I was told that my boss had to evaluate me before I could begin
working elsewhere. For five days I hunted my boss but was unable to find him. I finally gave the evaluation sheet to the
secretary. Everyday I would go and ask if the evaluation sheet
was returned and each time I got the same answer--"no". I
waited two weeks and still no response. I was becoming impa-
tient. When I went and told him that I had been waiting for
two weeks, I was considered for another job without being eval-
uated. He did not seem to care whether or not I got another
job. Even recently, when I have met with him, he does not even
say "hello." So for this reason I use the proverb. (One occurrence. Informant: female).

Sources and Annotations : Conde, p. 146, same as A. Gamiz, p.
90, El que hace más es el que vale menos.

323 (A). El que mete paz, saca más.

Translation or Interpretation: He who imposes peace, gets the
most.

Context: The two parties in an argument should settle their
own differences. (One occurrence. Informant: female).

Sources and Annotations: Robe, p. 67, same as A. Rubio, p.
189, same as A.

324 (A). El que mucho abarca, poco aprieta.
324 (B). El que mucho abarca, poco coje.
324 (C). El que abraza mucho, no aprieta.
324 (D). El que abarca mucho, poco pellisca.
324 (E). El que más abarca, menos aprieta.
324 (F). El que mucho abarca, nunca aprieta.
324 (G). Quien mucho abarca, poco aprieta.
324 (H). El que abarca mucho, poco aprieta.

Translation or Interpretation: He who embraces a lot, squeezes less.

Context: Told to a person who has much enthusiasm and ambition, and tries to do too many things at one time. (Forty-seven occurrences. Informants: twenty-three female, twenty-four male).

Sources and Annotations: Adame, p. 32, same as A; p. 42, same as A. Aranda, p. 12, same as A. Armas, p. 413, same as A. Ballesteros, p. 24, same as A. Benavides, p. 89, same as H. Cobos, p. 46, same as A. Covarrubias, p. 25, same as G; p. 135, same as G. Espinosa, A., p. 105, El que mucho abraza, poco aprieta. Espinosa, F., p. 33, same as G. Galván, p. 125, Quien mucho abarca, aprieta...; p. 127, Quien mucho aprieta poco abarca; p. 133, Quien mucho abarca, poco aprieta. Gamiz, p. 74, same as A. Glazer, p. 41, same as A. Jaramillo, p. 383, same as A. Maldonado, p. 47, Quien mucho abraza, poco aprieta. Robe, p. 69, same as G. Rodriguez-Marin (1930), p. 211, Mucho abarcar y poco apretar andan a la par. Rodriguez-Marin (1926), p. 913, Quien mucho abarca, poco ata. Sbarbi, p. 24, same as G. Wesley, p. 216, El que mucho abarca, poco aprieta.

325 (A). El que mucho habla, poco sabe.

Translation or Interpretation: He who talks too much, knows too little.

Context: This is usually said when a person brags too much. Some people will talk and talk for hours and pretend to know a lot, when they actually don't know much. The saying makes sense because people who spend all their time talking don't spend enough time listening or reading. Therefore, they don't learn as much as people who listen or read. (One occurrence. Informant: male).

Sources and Annotations: MacArthur, p. 61, Quien mucho habla, mucho yerra. Robe, p. 66, El que mucho habla, mucho yerra.

326 (A). El que mucho se despide, no tiene ganas de irse.
326 (B). El que mucho se despide, pocas ganas tiene de irse.

Translation or Interpretation: He who bids farewell too often, doesn't really want to leave.

Context: My grandmother said this when people kept saying good-bye, or that they were leaving, but yet, kept lingering around. At times an hour or so would go by and you would still find them there. (Three occurrences. Informants: one female, two male).

Sources and Annotations: Cobos, p. 47, same as B; Conde, p. 147, same as B. Jaramillo, p. 384, same as B. Rubio, p. 190, same as B.

327 (A). El que nace para maseta, no sale del corredor.
327 (B). El que nace para maseta, no pasa del corredor.
327 (C). El que para maseta nace, del corredor no pasa.
327 (D). El que nace pa maseta, no pasa del corredor.

Translation or Interpretation: He who is born to be a potted plant, will not go beyond the porch.

Context: My informant had a granddaughter who wanted to be just a plain housewife. (Five occurrences. Informants: four female, one male).

Sources and Annotations: Ballesteros, p. 25, El que nace para maceta del corredor no sale. Cobos, p. 47, same as A. Conde, p. 147, same as A. Martinez, p. 110, same as D. Santamaria, p. 45, El que para guaje nace, hasta jicara no para; p. 204, El que nacio para maceta no pasa del corredor; p. 299, El que nacio para maceta no pasa del corredor. Velasco, p. 66, same as A.

328 (A). El que nació para ser real, aunque ande entre los pesos.
328 (B). El tostón es tostón aunque entre los pesos ande.

Translation or Interpretation: He who was born to be poor, even if he hangs around with the rich.

Context: Not just because one goes around with rich people will make you rich. (Two occurrences. Informants: one female, one male).

Sources and Annotations: Rubio, p. 188, El que ha de ser centavo aunque ande entre los pesos; p. 192, El que nacio siendo tlaco aunque ande entre tostones.

329 (A). El que nace para sufrir desde la cuna comienza.

Translation or Interpretation: He who is born to suffer, will start from the cradle.

Context: David tried to get a job with a company that meant success for him. He tried hard to get the job, but he did not get it. One of David's friends said, "el que nace para sufrir

desde la cuna comienza." (Two occurrences. Informants: one
female, one male).

Sources and Annotations: None.

330 (A). El que nace pa tamal, del cielo le cain las hojas.
330 (B). El que nace para tamal, del cielo le caen las hojas.
330 (C). Si para tamal naciste, del cielo te caerán las hojas.
330 (D). El que nació pa tamal, del cielo le caen las hojas.
330 (E). El que ha de ser tamal, del cielo le caen las hojas.

Translation or Interpretation: He who is born to be a tamal,
from the skies gets the leaves.

Context: This proverb is usually aimed at someone whose fate
follows him. (Twenty-five occurrences. Informants: thirteen
female, twelve male).

Sources and Annotations: Adame, p. 32, same as A; p. 42, same
as A. Ballesteros, p. 47, same as B. Cobos, p. 13, Al que
nace pa tamal, del cielo le caen las hojas; p. 47, same as A.
Glazer, p. 55, same as B. Martinez, p. 29, same as A; p. 110,
same as A. Paredes, p. 31, same as A. Robe, p. 64, El que
nade pa tamal, hasta del cielo le caen las hojas. Rubio, p.
41, Al que nace pa tamal del cielo le caen las hojas; p. 196,
El que para tamal nace vive ajeno de comojas: le dan manteca
fiada, del cielo le caen las ojas. Santamaria, p. 123, Al que
nace para tamal, del cielo le caen las hojas; p. 321, same as
A. Velasco, p. 66, same as A. Wesley, p. 217, same as B.

331 (A). El que nada debe, nada teme.

Translation or Interpretation: He who doesn't owe anything,
has nothing to fear.

Context: When accused of a wrong doing, a person will not
fear and run if he is innocent. (Five occurrences. Informants: four female, one male).

Sources and Annotations: Armas, p. 413, same as A. Conde, p.
345, Quien no teme no estemido. Galván, p. 127, same as A; p.
128, same as A. Gamiz, p. 89, same as A. Rodriguez-Marin
(1930), p. 74, Debe el que tiene; que el que nada tiene nada
debe; p. 282, Quien no debe, no le teme. Rodriguez-Marin
(1926), p. 391, Quien nadie debe, a nadie teme; p. 413, Quien
mucho teme, algo debe. Yanez, p. 298, same as A.

332 (A). El que no acude--parcha--una gotera, no cude una
          casa entera.

Translation or Interpretation: He who doesn't patch a leakage
doesn't patch up a whole house.

Context: There is a hole in our roof, it has been there for
about two years now. My dad never had it fixed when my mother
asked him, therefore, everytime it rains, the water comes
through the hole. (One occurrence. Informant: female).

Sources and Annotation: Covarrubias, p. 651, Quien no quita
gotera haze casa entera.

333 (A). El que no agarra consejo de viejo, no llega a pendejo.

Translation or Interpretation: He who doesn't take advice,
will not get to be dumb.

Context: A person who has been open and has learned through
his youth will be respected in his adulthood. Furthermore, he
has learned, and knows what is good and bad. (One occurrence.
Informant: male).

Sources and Annotations: Aranda, p. 12, El que no agarra consejo no llega a viejo. Lea, p. 234, El que no agarra consejo
no llega a viejo. MacArthur, p. 35, El que no oye consejo, no
llega a viejo.

334 (A). El que no conoce a Dios, donde quiera se anda
incando.

Translation or Interpretation: He who doesn't know God is
kneeling everywhere.

Context: When a person praises someone who is no good. (One
occurrence. Informant: female).

Sources and Annotations: Adame, p. 33, El que no conoce a
Dios, en cualquier basurero se hinca; p. 42, El que no conoce
a Dios, en cualquier basurero se hinca. Rubio, p. 193, same
as A; Yanez, p. 54, same as A.

335 (A). El que no fía, no vende.

Translation or Interpretation: He who doesn't give credit,
doesn't sell.

Context: If you have a store and don't give credit to your
customers, you aren't going to sell much. (One occurrence.
Informant: female).

Sources and Annotations: Aranda, p. 13, same as A. Rodriguez-Marin (1926), p. 416, Quien no fía no vende.

336 (A). El que no ha tenido y tiene, que hacer le viene.
336 (B). El que nunca tiene y llega a tener, loco se quiere
          volver.
336 (C). Cuando el ciego llega a ver, hasta loco se quiere
          volver.

Translation or Interpretation: He who has not had and now has,
will have more to do.

Context: Used to point out that the more one has, the more
the responsibility he has. (Four occurrences. Informants:
female).

Sources and Annotations: Ballesteros, p. 4, El que nunca ha
tenido y llega ha tener, loco se quiere volver. Cobos, p. 48,
El que nunca ha tenido y llega a tener, loco se quiere volver.
Conde, p. 148, El que nunca ha tenido y llega a tener, loco
se quiere volver. Martinez, p. 111, El que nunca ha tenido y
llega a tener, quehacer le viene. Velasco, p. 66, same as A.

337 (A). El que no habla, Dios no lo oye.
337 (B). A quien no habla, Dios no lo oye.
337 (C). El que no habla, Dios no lo ayuda.

Translation or Interpretation: He who doesn't talk, God
doesn't hear.

Context: I have been working at the same place for over a
year, and I haven't gotten a raise. I realized that if I
didn't speak up I wouldn't get a raise, but I did ask and I
was heard. (39 occurrences. Informants: 26 female, 12 male,
one anonymous).

Sources and Annotations: Adame, p. 8, Al que no habla Dios no
lo oye; p. 33, same as A; p. 43, same as A. Armas, p. 408,
same as A. Ballesteros, p. 37, Al que habla, Dios lo oye.
Benavides, p. 90, same as A. Cobos, p. 15, same as B; p. 48,
same as A. Conde, p. 50, A quien no habla, Dios no lo oye.
Espinosa, A., p. 110, Quien no habla Dios no lo oye. Galvan,
p. 124, same as A; p. 127, Al que no hable...; p. 128, same as
A; p. 129, same as A; p. 132, El que no habla... Gamiz, p.
75, Al que no habla, Dios no lo oye. Glazer, p. 50, A el que
no habla, Dios no lo oye. Martinez, p. 35, same as B. Paredes, p. 31, same as A; Pérez, p. 121, El que no habla nadie
le oye. Rodriguez-Marin (1930), p. 233, No oye Dios a quien
no le llama.

338 (A). El que no habla, los santos no lo lloran.

Translation or Interpretation: He who does not speak, the
saints will not cry for him.

Context: Those who do not ask, or lack enthusiasm, will be

left behind. Meaning, behind in economic status, or society, sometimes upward mobility. (One occurrence. Informant: female).

Sources and Annotations: Galván, p. 129, El que no habla...

339 (A). El que no le guste el jiste, que lo tire y monte a palo.

Translation or Interpretation: He who doesn't like the saddle, should throw it away and mount bare back.

Context: Meaning, if you don't like something don't just complain and do nothing, but do something about it. (Two occurrences. Informants: female).

Sources and Annotations: Conde, p. 36, Al que le guste el fuste, que lo tire y monte en pelo. Espinosa, A., p. 105, El que no le guste el fuste que se suba y monte a raiz. Gamiz, p. 82, Al que no le guste el fuste, que lo tire y monte en pelo. Martinez, p. 29, Al que no le guste el fuste, que lo tire y monte en pelo. Pérez, p. 119, same as A. Santamaria, p. 657, same as A. Velasco, p. 18, Al que no le guste el fuste que lo tire y monte en pelo. Yanez, p. 52, same as A.

340 (A). El que no mantiene, no detiene.

Translation or Interpretation: He who doesn't support, doesn't stop.

Context: My informant wanted to go to the dance. Her ex-husband told her she couldn't go. She said she could, and used the proverb. (One occurrence. Informant: female).

Sources and Annotations: Martinez, p. 110, El que tiene, mantiene. Santamaria, p. 236, El que mantiene, detiene, y si no ni cara tiene.

341 (A). El que no mira adelante, atrás se queda.
341 (B). El que no vé adelante, atrás se queda.
341 (C). El que adelante no vé, atrás se queda.
341 (D). El que adelante no pienza, atrás se queda.
341 (E). El que adelante no va, atrás se queda.

Translation or Interpretation: He who doesn't look ahead stays behind.

Context: If you do not plan for the future, your advancement will not be rapid. (Seven occurrences. Informants: four female, three male).

Sources and Annotations: Adame, p. 32, El que adelante no mira, atrás se queda; p. 38, El que adelante no mira, atrás se queda. Aranda, p. 11, El que adelante no mira, atrás se queda. Armas, p. 417, same as A. Benavides, p. 91, same as A. Caballero, p. 544, same as A. Cobos, p. 41, same as E; p. 48, same as A; p. 104, Quien adelante no mira, atrás se queda. Conde, p. 142, same as C. De Barros, p. 190, El que no mira hacia adelante, atrás se queda. Espinosa, A., p. 104, El que adelante no mira, atrás se queda. Espinosa, F., p. 160, quien adelante no mira, atrás cae. Gamiz, p. 73, same as C. Lucero-White, p. 34, same as A. Rodriguez-Marin (1926), p. 388, Quien adelante no mira, atrás se queda; p. 416, Quien no mira adelante, atrás se halla- o se queda. Sbarbi, p. 33, Quien adelanta no cata, o no mira, atrás se halla, o se queda, no se ve.

342 (A).   El que no oye consejo, no llega a viejo.
342 (B).   El que no agarra consejo, no llega a viejo.
342 (C).   El que no coje consejo, no llega a viejo.
342 (D).   El que nunca escucha consejo, lo llegará a viejo.
342 (E).   Oir buen consejo si quieres llegar a viejo.
342 (F).   Aquél que no oye consejo, nunca a viejo llegará.
342 (G).   Quien no toma consejos, no llega a viejo.

Translation or Interpretation: He who doesn't listen to advice, will not live to grow old.

Context: It's used when a young person doesn't want to listen, or obey, his parents or older people. (22 occurrences. Informants: ten female, 12 male).

Sources and Annotations: Adame, p. 33, same as A; p. 42, same as A. Aranda, p. 12, same as B; Armas, p. 413, same as A. Ballesteros, p. 26, El que no toma consejo, no llega a viejo. Benavides, p. 89, same as A. Cobos, p. 15, same as F; p. 48, same as A. Conde, p. 148, same as A. Galván, p. 133, same as A; p. 135, Quien no oye consejos... Gamiz, p. 82, same as B. Glazer, p. 46, El que no oye consejos no llegará a viejo. Jaramillo, p. 384, same as A. Lucero-White, p. 33, same as B. Rodriguez-Marin (1926), p. 417, Quien no oye consejos, no llega a viejo; p. 420, Quien no toma consejo, no llega a viejo. Sbarbi, p. 262, same as A.

343 (A).   El que no quiere ruido que no críe cochinos.

Translation or Interpretation: He who does not want noise should not raise pigs.

Context: This proverb does not have anything to do with noise or hogs. It means: Do not make, or look for, trouble if you don't want trouble yourself. (One occurrence. Informant: female).

Sources and Annotations: None.

344 (A). El que no se arriesga, no pasa la mar.
344 (B). Quien no se aventura, no pasa la mar.
344 (C). El que no se arriesga, no cruza el río.

Translation or Interpretation: He who doesn't risk it will not (cross) the sea.

Context: When my brother started to ride a bike, he would always fall down and get hurt. He stopped riding it. My grandmother told him this proverb. (Four occurrences. Informants: two female, one male, one anonymous).

Sources and Annotations: Adame, p. 33, same as C; p. 43, same as C. Aranda, p. 13, same as C. Caballero, p. 544, same as A. Cobos, p. 105, same as B. Espinosa, A., p. 105, same as A. Espinosa, F., p. 51, Quien no se aventura, no medra. Jaramillo, p. 383, same as A; p. 386, same as A. Rodriguez-Marin (1930), p. 283, Quien no se arriesga, no pesca. Rodriguez-Marin (1926), p. 418, Quien no se arriesga, no gana nada. Sbarbi, p. 107, same as B.

345 (A). El que no siembra, no cosecha.
345 (B). El que no siembra no levanta.

Translation or Interpretation: He who doesn't sow, doesn't get a crop.

Context: One must toil his fields in order for them to produce, as one must save now for tomorrow will come. (Two occurrences. Informants: one female, one male).

Sources and Annotations: Conde, p. 345, Quien no siembra, no cosecha. Espinosa, F., p. 218, Quien poco siembra, poco coje. Rodriguez-Marin (1926), p. 418, same as A.

346 (A). El que no tiene más, se acuesta con su mujer y se levanta con su suegra.

Translation or Interpretation: He who doesn't have anyone else, goes to sleep with his wife and wakes up with his mother-in-law.

Context: None given. (One occurrence. Informant: female).

Sources and Annotations: Jaramillo, p. 383, El que no tiene mas, con su mujer se acuesta. Rodriguez-Marin (1926), p. 419, Quien no tiene con quien duerma, con su madre se acuesta.

347 (A). El que no trabaja no come.

Translation or Interpretation: He who does not work does not eat.

Context: I first heard this proverb at the place my mother works. They had just hired a new worker who seemed not to be doing satisfactory work. He was standing around, not approaching any of the customers in the store. One of the other workers then went up to him and told him the proverb. (One occurrence. Informant: female).

Sources and Annotations: Conde, p. 148, El que no trabaja que no coma. Espinosa, A., p. 105, same as A. Rodriguez-Marin (1926), p. 420, Quien no trabaja, no coma- o no come.

348 (A). El que paga lo que debe, sabe lo que tiene.

Translation or Interpretation: He who pays what he owes, knows what he has.

Context: If a person has no debts he has nothing to worry about. (One occurrence. Informant: female).

Sources and Annotations: Cobos, p. 48, same as A; p. 96, Paga lo que debes sabrás lo que tienes. Conde, p. 307, Paga lo que debes y sabrás lo que tienes. Jaramillo, p. 382, same as A. Lucero-White, p. 36, Paga lo que debes y sabes lo que tienes. Rodriguez-Marin (1930), p. 310, Si quieres saber lo que tienes, paga lo que debes. Rodriguez-Marin (1926), p. 317, Nadie sabe lo que tiene, hasta que pague lo que debe.

349 (A). El que paga lo que debe, sana del mal que padese.

Translation or Interpretation: He who pays his debts is cured from his illness.

Context: When a person pays what he owes, he will have good credit. (One occurrence. Informant: female).

Sources and Annotations: Armas, p. 413, same as A. Conde, p. 148, same as A. Gamiz, p. 89, same as A. Rubio, p. 195, same as A.

350 (A). El que para pobre nace, aunque ande entre los pesos, nada mas se alisa.

Translation or Interpretation: He who was born to be poor, even if he is among money, he'll shake it off.

Context: My informant had a friend who married a doctor. Her family had always been poor, while he had always been rich. She couldn't get accustomed to her new life. So the proverb was used on her. (One occurrence. Informant: female).

Sources and Annotations: Cobos, p. 44, El que ha de ser pobre mas que ande entre el dinero. Espinosa, A., p. 104, El que

114

nace pa pobre nunca será rico. Lucero-White, p. 34, El que
ha de ser pobre, mas que ande entre el dinero. Rodriguez-
Marin (1930), p. 285, Quien por pobre se tiene, no es rico
aunque el oro apalee.

351 (A). El que para tonto nace hasta guaje no pasa.

Translation or Interpretation: He who is born to be stupid
(even as a) gourd he will not pass.

Context: A poor young ranch hand had been engaged to be married three or four times prior to his present engagement. As
the wedding day drew nearer, his fianceé seemed restless and
uneasy about the marriage. Finally she got the courage to
tell him that she didn't want to marry him anymore. The other
ranch hands cruelly mocked him and told him, "once a fool,
always a fool." (One occurrence. Informant: male).

Sources and Annotations: Pérez, p. 119, same as A.

352 (A). El que persevera, alcanza.

Translation or Interpretation: He who preseveres will acquire.

Context: My father always told me this dicho when I found a
penny and picked it up. (One occurrence. Informant: male).

Sources and Annotations: Adame, p. 33, same as A; p. 43, same
as A. Cobos, p. 49, same as A. Conde, p. 148, same as A.
Espinosa, A., p. 105, same as A. Gamiz, p. 74, same as A.
Rodriguez-Marin (1930), p. 284, Quien persevero, alcanzo.

353 (A). El que por otro se muere ni el campo santo se
merece.

Translation or Interpretation: He who dies for another doesn't
even deserve the holy ground.

Context: None given. (One occurrence. Informant: female).

Sources and Annotations: Conde, p. 149, El que por otro pad-
dece, es necio y se lo merece. Rodriguez-Marin (1930), p.
288, Quien se pierde por otro, o es tanto, o es laco.

354 (A). El que por su gusto es buey, hasta la coyunda lame.

Translation or Interpretation: He who likes to be an ox is
even grateful of the yoke.

Context: Heard many times when a man's wife is fooling around
with other men, and he keeps on living with her. (Six occur-

rences.   Informants: female).

Sources and Annotations: Adame, p. 32, El que es buey hasta
la coyunda lambe; p. 40, El que es buey hasta la coyunda lambe.
Ballesteros, p. 61, same as A. Cobos, p. 49, same as A.   Conde, p. 149, same as A. Espinosa, F., p. 105, El que por su
gusto es guey hasta la coyunda lambe. Martinez, p. 112, same
as A. MacArthur, p. 16, same as A. Perez, p. 121, El que por
su cuenta es buey hasta la coyunda lambe. Robe, p. 64, same
as A. Rubio, p. 198, same as A. Santamaria, p. 237, same as
A. Velasco, p. 67, same as A. Wesley, p. 213, same as A; El
que es buey hasta la correa lame. Yáñez, p. 52, same as A.

355 (A). El que por su gusto muere, hasta la muerte le sabe.

Translation or Interpretation: He who does of his own free
will, finds death sweet.

Context: None given. (One occurrence. Informant: female).

Sources and Annotations: Adame, p. 33, same as A; p. 44, same
as A. Rubio, p. 198, El que por su gusto muere aunque lo en-
tierren parado.

356 (A). El que porfía, mata venado.

Translation or Interpretation: He who persists, kills deer.

Context: If you want something and you don't get it, keep
trying, you will soon succeed. (Six occurrences. Informants:
two female, four male).

Sources and Annotations: Adame, p. 33, same as A; p. 43, same
as A. Ballesteros, p. 61, same as A. Cobos, p. 49, same as
A; p. 52, El que terquea mata venado. Conde, p. 149, El que
porfía, mata venado o lo matan por porfíado. Covarrubias, p.
257, Porfía mata la caca. Gamiz, p. 74, same as A. Martinez,
p. 111, El que porfía mata venado o lo matan por porfíado.
MacArthur, p. 25, El que porfía mata venado, o lo matan por
porfíado. Rodriguez-Marin (1926), p. 374, Porfíar, para al-
canzar; p. 423, Quien porfía, alcanza hoy u otro día; Quien
porfía, caza mata. Rubio, p. 197, El que porfia mata venado
o lo matan por porfíado. Santamaria, p. 517, same as A. Velasco, p. 67, El que pofía mata venado, o lo matan por porfíado.

357 (A). El que quiera celeste, que le cueste.
357 (B). El que quiera azul celeste, que le cueste.

Translation or Interpretation: He who wants blue should pay
for it.

Context: Things in life are not easy to come by, but if you want them you can have them, provided you pay the price.

Sources and Annotations: Adame, p. 33, same as B; p. 44, same as B. Aranda, p. 14, same as A. Cobos, p. 49, same as B. Conde, p. 149, same as B. Galvan, p. 125, El que quiera azul. ..; p. 127, El que quiera azul... Gamiz, p. 73, same as G. Jaramillo, p. 363, same as B. Molera, p. 65, same as B. Rodriguez-Marin (1926), p. 410, Quien quiera azul celeste, que le cueste. Santamaria, p. 172, same as B.

358 (A). El que reparte y comparte siempre deja para sí lo mejor.

Translation or Interpretation: He who distributes and shares, always leaves the best for himself.

Context: If you want the best piece of something, volunteer your services to distribute it, and then you are assured of it. (One occurrence. Informant: female).

Sources and Annotations: Ballesteros, p. 5, El que parte y reparte al partir tiene tino, siempre deja para sí la mejor parte. Cobos, p. 49, El que parte y comparte guarda para sí la mejor parte; p. 50. El que reparte y comparte y al repartir tiene tino siempre deja para sí la mejor parte. Conde, p. 149, El que reparte y comparte para sí deja la mejor parte. Espinosa, A., p. 111, El que comparte y reparte y en repartir tiene tino, siempre deja, de contino, para sí la mejor parte. Gamiz, p. 89, El que parte y recomparte siempre deja para sí la mayor parte. Rodriguez-Marin (1926), p. 422, Quien parte, toma para sí mejor parte; Quien parte y reparte, cabea mayor parte; Quien parte y reparte guarda para sí-o se lleva- la mejor parte. Santamaria, p. 548, Quien parte y comparte, y en el partir tiene tino, siempre deja de contino para sí la mejor parte. Yanez, p. 56, El que parte y recomparte, se queda con la mayor parte.

359 (A). El que ríe al último, ríe mejor.

Translation or Interpretation: He who laughs the last, laughs the best.

Context: A friend was being teased once, because his girl was dating someone else. The teaser's girlfriend broke up with him to marry another guy. (16 occurrences. Informants: 13 female, three male).

Sources and Annotations: Adame, p. 33, same as A; p. 45, same as A. Armas, p. 420, Quien ríe el último, ríe mejor. Ballesteros, p. 26, same as A. Cobos, p. 50, same as A; p. 51, El que ríe al ultimo, se ríe más bonito. Conde, p. 149, same as

A. Espinosa, A., p. 104, El que se ríe al último se ríe mas
bonito. Galván, p. 133, same as A. Glazer, p. 58, El que ríe
al último, se ríe mejor. Jaramillo, p. 382, same as A. Yañez,
p. 203, El que río, al último lo hace más a sus anchas.

360 (A). El que pregunta, no hierra.

Translation or Interpretation: He who asks, makes no mistakes.

Context: In a job, when you go in and you don't know something, the best thing to do is to ask so you won't make mistakes.

Sources and Annotations: Adame, p. 83, Quien pregunta, no
yerra   p. 84, Quien pregunta, no yerra. Conde, p. 149, El
que pregunta, no yerra. Covarrubias, p. 683, El que pregunta
no yerra, si la pregunta no es necia. Rodriguez-Marin (1926)
p. 169, El preguntar no es errar, si no es necio el preguntar.
Rubio, p. 196, El que poco habla, poco yerra.

361 (A). El que ríe en viernes, llora en domingo.
361 (B). Ríe el viernes, llora el domingo.
361 (C). Quién ríe en viernes, llora en domingo.

Translation or Interpretation: He who laughs on Friday, cries
on Sunday.

Context: Sometimes we tend to laugh at things thinking they
would never happen to us, then, before we know it, it happens
to us. (Three occurrences. Informants: two female, one male.

Sources and Annotations: Rodriguez-Marin (1926), p. 38, Aquél
que ríe ahora, mañana llora; p. 395, Quien canta en viernes,
llora en Domingo; p. 408, Quien hoy llora, mañana ríe; p. 426,
Quien ríe ahora, manana llora; p. 428, same as C; p. 478, Tal
que ríe ahora, acabo de rato llora. Sbarbi, p. 87, Aquél que
rie ahora, manana llora.

362 (A). El que sabe dos lenguas, vale por dos.
362 (B). Saber dos lenguas es ser dos personas.

Translation or Interpretation: He who knows two languages is
worth two.

Context: My father is all for bilingual education, and he
says the above proverb at times. (Two occurrences. Informants: female).

Sources and Annotations: Cobos, p. 106, Quien sabe dos lenguas
vale por dos.

363 (A). <u>El</u> que se aleja lo olvidan y el que se muere lo en-
tierran.

<u>Translation or Interpretation</u>: He who goes away is forgotten,
and he who dies is buried.

<u>Context</u>: None given. (One occurrences. Informant: female).

<u>Sources and Annotations</u>: None.

364 (A). <u>El</u> que se fué para la villa. perdió su silla.
364 (B). <u>El</u> que se fué para la villa. le ganaron su silla.
364 (C). <u>El</u> que se levanta a comer sandía, le ganaron su silla.
364 (D). <u>El</u> que se va al convento, pierde el asiento.
364 (E). <u>El</u> que se levanta a bailar, pierde su lugar.

<u>Translation or Interpretation</u>: He who left for <u>la villa</u>, lost
his chair.

<u>Context</u>: When a person goes somewhere and leaves his seat,
the person who occupies the seat will use this proverb as the
former returns. (Nine occurrences. Informants: seven female, one male, one anonymous).

<u>Sources and Annotations</u>: Adame, p. 33, same as A; p. 45, El
que se fue a la villa, perdio su silla. Aranda, p. 13, El que
sale a bailar pierde su lugar. Armas, p. 413, El que va a
Santa Lucia, pierde su silla. Caballero, p. 545, El que se a
Sevilla perdio su silla. Cobos, p. 50, same as A; p. 51, El
que se va para la villa, pierde su silla. Conde, p. 150, El que
se va pa' Sevilla pierde su silla. Covarrubias, p. 938, Quien
se fue a Sevilla perdio su silla. De Barros, p. 393, Quien se
fue a Sevilla perdio su silla. Espinosa, A., p. 99, El que
sale a bailar pierde su lugar. Gamiz, p. 88, El que se va para
la villa, pierde su silla. Jaramillo, p. 385, El que se va
para la villa pierde su silla. Martinez, p. 112, El que se va
a la villa pierde su silla. Robe, p. 70, same as A. Rodriguez-Marin (1930), p. 289, Quien se va de Sevilla, pierde la
silla; que se va y vuelve, nunca la pierde. Rodriguez-Marin
(1926), p. 406, Quien fue a Sevilla, perdio su silla; Quien va
a mear, pierde su lugar. Rubio, p. 201, El que se fue a la
villa, perdio su silla. Santamaria, p. 262, same as A. Velasco, p. 68, same as A.

365 (A). <u>El</u> que se mete de vendedor, sale crucificado.
365 (B). <u>El</u> que se mete de redentor sale crucificado.

<u>Translation or Interpretation</u>: He who works as a sales person,
ends up crucified.

<u>Context</u>: This proverb is usually applied to some persons who
get involved in some cause they really believe in. (Two occurrences. Informants: one female, one male).

Sources and Annotations: Caballero, p. 918, Por meterse de Redentor le crucificaron. Conde, p. 150, El que se mete a Redentor, sale cricificado. Gamiz, p. 78, Métete a redentor y saldrás crucificado. Rodriguez-Marin (1930), p. 288, Quien se mete de redentor, lo cricifican. Rodriguez-Marin (1926), p. 43, A quien se mete de redentor lo cricifican; p. 499, Uno que se metio a redentor lo cricificaron.

366 (A). El que se quema con leche, hasta al jocoque le sopla.
366 (B). El que con leche se quema, hasta al jocoque le sopla.
366 (C). El que está quemado con jocoque, hasta a la leche le sopla.

Translation or Interpretation: He who gets burned with milk, blows even on the buttermilk.

Context: If you have had bad experiences, later you are very cautious and never take chances. (Five occurrences. Informants: three female, two male).

Sources and Annotations: Ballesteros, p. 24, same as B; Cobos, p. 42, same as B. Conde, p. 143, same as B. Martinez, p. 112, same as D. Rubio, p. 201, El que se quemo con la leche, hasta al jocoque le sopla. Santamaria, p. 176, same as B. Yanez, p. 208, El que se quemo con la leche hasta al jocoque le sopla.

367 (A). El que se va, se va cantando. El que se queda, se queda llorando.

Translation or Interpretation: He who leaves, goes singing. He who stays, stays crying.

Context: Informant was told this proverb by his girlfriend when he came to the United States from Mexico. She stayed behind and was very sad. (One occurrence. Informant: male).

Sources and Annotations: Rubio, p. 202, El que se va, se divierte con lo verde del camino, y el que se queda, se queda a luchar con el destino.

368 (A). El que siembra vientos, cosecha torbellinos.

Translation or Interpretation: He who plants wind, will harvest whirlwinds.

Context: You harvest whatever you plant. Sara formed very good relations with people and consequently she got some very nice friends. (One occurrence. Informant: female).

Sources and Annotations: Adame, p. 33, El que siembra vientos, levanta tempestades; p. 45, El que siembra vientos, levanta tempestades. Gamiz, p. 77, Siembra vientos, y recogerás tempestades. Rodriguez-Marin (1930), p. 289, Quien siembra odio recoge venganza. Rodriguez-Marin (1926), p. 429, Quien siembra vientos, recoge tempestades.

369 (A). El que sirve a dos amos, con alguno queda mal.
369 (B). El que sirve a dos amos con todos queda mal.

Translation or Interpretation: He who serves two masters, ends up disappointing one of them.

Context: You can never please two persons at the same time. (Five occurrences. Informants: female).

Sources and Annotations: Adame, p. 32, El que a dos amos sirve, con alguno queda mal; p. 38, El que a dos amos sirve, con alguno queda mal. Armas, p. 419, Quien a dos amos sirve a uno sirve y a otro engana. Cobos, p. 41, same as A. Conde, p. 142, El que a dos amos sirve, con alguno queda mal. Correas, p. 299, same as A. Gamiz, p. 89, El que a dos amos sirve, con alguno queda mal. Rodriguez-Marin (1930), p. 265, Quien a dos señores sirve, a alguno de ellos sirve a alguno guez-Marin (1926), p. 388, Quien a dos amos o señores a alguno de ellos o a uno ha de mentir. Rubio, p. 180, same as A. Yañez, p. 354, same as A.

370 (A). El que solo se ríe, de sus maldades se acuerda.

Translation or Interpretation: He who laughs on his own, remembers his doings.

Context: When a person has done something wrong, or when a funny incident has happened to this individual in the past. (Two occurrences. Informants: female).

Sources and Annotations: Aranda, p. 13, same as A. Cobos, p. 41, El que asolas se ríe, de sus maldades se acuerda; p. 51, same as A. Conde, p. 150, same as A. Jaramillo, p. 385, El que asolas se ríe, de sus picardías se acuerda. Lucéro-hite, p. 34, same as A. MacArthur, p. 2, El que a solas se ríe, de sus maldades se acuerda. Martinez, p. 238, Quien a solas se ríe, de sus maldades se acuerda. Santamaria, p. 25, El que solo se ríe, de sus picardía se acuerda.

371 (A). El que solo vive, solo muere.

Translation or Interpretation: He who lives by himself, dies by himself.

Context: Told to a bachelor, when someone wants him to think about marriage. (One occurrence. Informant: female).

Sources and Annotations: Conde, p. 350, same as A. Jaramillo, p. 386, El que come solo, muere solo. Perez, p. 121, same as A.

372 (A). El que temprano se moja, tiene tiempo de secarse.
372 (B). El que temprano se moja, tiempo tiene para secarse.

Translation or Interpretation: He who gets wet early has time to dry up.

Context: This proverb means that if a person starts a job early, he/she will have enough time to finish it. (Two occurrences. Informants: one female, one male).

Sources and Annotations: Cobos, p. 51, same as A. Conde, p. 151, El que temprano se moja, tiempo tiene de secarse. Espinosa, A., p. 105, El que de mañana se moja lugar tiene de secarse. Gamiz, p. 74, El que temprano se moja, lugar tiene de secarse. Martinez, p. 112, same as A. Rubio, p. 203, El que temprano se moja, lugar tiene de secarse.

373 (A). El que tenga hambre, que le atize a la olla.

Translation or Interpretation: He who is hungry should stir the pot.

Context: I remember my mother saying this to us when we were kids, and would take out time about coming to dinner when playing outdoors. We would come in late and she would say this. (One occurrence. Informant: male).

Sources and Annotations: Adame, p. 32, El que hambre tiene, atiza la olla; p. 41, same as A. Conde, p. 145, El que tiene hambre, atiza la olla. Gamiz, p. 73, Quien tiene hambre, atiza la olla. Robe, p. 64, El que tiene hambre atiza la olla. Rubio, p. 104, El que tiene hambre atiza la olla.

374 (A). El que tiempo agarra, tiempo le sobra.

Translation or Interpretation: He who grasps time will have time left over. He who takes his time will have time left over.

Context: This proverb means that a person who gets a head start, will finish early and have extra time. Also means better to do it now than later. (Three occurrences. Informants: two female, one male).

Sources and Annotations: Gamiz, p. 73, Al que tiempo "agarra"
tiempo le sobra.

375 (A). El que tiene más saliva, traga más pinole.

Translation or Interpretation: He who has more saliva, swal-
lows more cereal meal.

Context: Her friend told her that when a person is very con-
vincing he/she usually gets the better jobs; the best piece
of the pie. (15 occurrences. Informants: 11 female, four
male).

Sources and Annotations: Armas, p. 346, Quien tiene más saliva traga más pinole; p. 413, same as A. Cobos, p. 52, same
as A. Conde, p. 151, same as A. Gamiz, p. 83, same as A.
Glazer, p. 58, same as A. Jaramillo, p. 383, El que tiene más
saliva, traga más hojaldra. MacArthur, p. 16, same as A.
Martinez, p. 112, same as A. Paredes, p. 31, same as A. Rubio, p. 204, same as A. Santamaria, p. 59, same as A; p. 479,
same as A. Velasco, p. 68, same as A.

376 (A). El que tiene peones y no los vé, se queda en cueros
         y no lo cree.

Translation or Interpretation: He who has laborers and does
not look at them, is left naked and does not believe it.

Context: What this proverb tries to tell you is that when
someone has people working for him, this person has to be
keeping an eye on his employees. Otherwise, they can be
stealing from you, and whenever you find yourself with no
money, or properties at all, it is going to be because you
trusted them, and you don't believe it. The other meaning
that this proverb could possibly have is, never trust your
employees. (One occurrence. Informant: male).

Sources and Annotations: Conde, p. 352, Quien tiene peones y
no los ve, se queda en cueros y no lo cree. Martinez, p. 112,
same as A. Rodriguez-Marin (1926), p. 438, Quiereste perder
y no lo sientas? Lleva peones y no los veas. Rubio, p. 205,
same as A.

377 (A). El que tiene tienda que la atienda y si no que la
         venda.

Translation or Interpretation: He who owns a store should
care for it, if not, sell it.

Context: My informant told this dicho to her children when
they had a pet. (One occurrence. Informant: female).

Sources and Annotations: Adame, p. 33, El que tiene tienda
que la atienda sino mejor que la venda; p. 45, El que tiene
tienda que la atienda sino mejor que la venda. Alcala, p.
605, Quien tiene tienda que la atienda. Aranda, p. 14, El
que tiene tienda que la atienda sino que la venda. Ballesteros, p. 26, El que tenga tienda que la atienda. Cobos, p.
52, same as A. Conde, p. 151, same as A; p. 387, Tienda y
atienda quien tenga tienda. Covarrubias, p. 961, Quien tiene
tienda, que atienda. Espinosa, A., p. 100, El que tiene
tienda- que atienda- o si no que la venda. Galvan, p. 125,
Quien tiene tienda...; p. 133, Quien tiene tienda y no la
atienda que la venda. Jaramillo, p. 384, same as A; Martinez, p. 113, same as A. Molera, p. 67, same as A. Santamaria, p. 168, same as A.

378 (A).   El que vive en casa de vidrio no debe de tirar
           piedras.

Translation or Interpretation: He who lives in a glass house
should not throw stones.

Context: This happened in a wild political campaign. One of
the candidates made some wild accusations about my informant.
The informant pulled the opponent's skeleton from the closet,
and made the above remark. (One occurrence. Informant: male).

Sources and Annotations: Armas, p. 324, No tirar piedras en
tejado ajeno; p. 418, No hay que lanzar piedras en tejado
ajeno. Cobos, p. 52, El que tiene tejado de vidrio que no
tire piedras al de su vecino. Covarrubias, p. 959, El que
tiene tejado de vidrio, no tire piedras al de su vecino; p.
1006, El que tiene tejado de vidrio, no tire piedras al de tu
vecino. De Barros, p. 193, El que tiene el tejado de vidrio,
no tire piedras al del vecino. Jaramillo, p. 384, El que
tenga tajeo de vidrio, no tire piedras al del vecino. Rodriguez-Marin (1926), p. 423, Quien tuviere el tejado de vidrio
no tire piedras a su vecino.

379 (A).   El que vive en tinieblas, ciego es.
379 (B).   El que vive en tinieblas, cojo es.

Translation or Interpretation: He who lives in darkness is
blind.

Context: When a child, I used to ask my mother why people
fought, killed, drank, etc. My mother being religious replied
with this. (Two occurrences. Informants: one female, one
male).

Sources and Annotations: None.

380 (A). Más hace el que quiere que el que puede y no quiere.
380 (B). Hace más el que quiere que el que puede.

Translation or Interpretation: He who wants to, does more,
than he who can and does not want to. Does more, he who
wants, than he who can.

Context: My mother says that when she was young, her parents
always used to say this proverb to their children. They used
to say that if their children had an ambition they could
reach their goal despite the fact that the parents could not
afford to give them much of an education. (Six occurrences.
Informants: two female, four male).

Sources and Annotations: Benavides, p. 89, same as A. Cobos,
p. 78, Más hace el que quiere que el que puede. Conde, p.
188, same as B. Lucero-White, p. 35, Más hace el que quiere
que el que puede.

381 (A). ¿Quién te hace rico? El que te mantiene el pico.

Translation or Interpretation: Who makes you rich? He who
gives you to eat.

Context: Talk which criticizes the abusing of people. (One
occurrence. Informant: male).

Sources and Annotations: Conde, p. 351, same as A. Gamiz,
p. 92, No sabes quien te hace rico? El que te mantiene el
pico. Santamaria, p. 38, same as A; p. 548, Quién te hace
rico? Quién te mantiene el pico? Yañez, p. 128, same as A.

382 (A). Peca más el que juzga que el que roba.

Translation or Interpretation: Whoever judges someone sins
more than the one who steals.

Context: Meaning that a person who is always judging someone
sins more than the persons who steals. (One occurrence. Informant: female).

Sources and Annotations: None.

383 (A). Se quedó como el que chifló en la loma.
383 (B). Te vas a quedar como el de las dos bodas, chiflando
          en la loma.
383 (C). No te vayas a quedar como el que chifló en la loma.
383 (D). Quedaste como el que chifló en la loma.

Translation or Interpretation: He stayed like the one who
whistled on the hill.

125

Context: When a person is going somewhere and is kept waiting. The ride never shows up. Or when someone goes shopping and ends up without buying anything. (Five occurrences. Informants: four female, one male).

Sources and Annotations: Adame, p. 91, Te quedaste chiflando en la loma; p. 93, Te quedaste chiflando en la loma. Conde, p. 232, Lo dejaron chiflando en la loma. Martinez, p. 62, Como el que chiflo en la loma. Paredes, p. 34, Como el que chiflo en la loma. Santamaria, p. 490, Quedarse como el que chiflo en la loma; p. 541, Quedarse uno como el que chiflo en la loma. Velasco, p. 36, Como el que chifló en la loma. Wesley, p. 213, Lo dejaron como el que silbó en la loma.

384 (A). Se quedó como el de las dos bodas, sin uno y sin la otra.

Translation or Interpretation: He stayed like the one with the two weddings, without one or the other.

Context: Informant's son had two girlfriends. He was going out with both of them. He planned to get married with one of them, but when they discovered him, he ended up with neither of them. (Two occurrences. Informants: female).

Sources and Annotations: None.

385 (A). Siembra el que habla y recoje quien calla.

Translation or Interpretation: He who speaks sows, and he who keeps silent gathers.

Context: A person who speaks with the truth and the person who is listening may get a little wiser with that speech. (One occurrence. Informant: female).

Sources and Annotations: Rodriguez-Marin (1926), p. 406, Quien habla, siembra; quien escucha, siega. Quien hablo, sembró; y quien oyo, sego.

386 (A). Solo el que carga el costal sabe lo que lleva dentro.
386 (B). Nomás el que lleva el costal sabe lo que lleva dentro.   .
386 (C). Cada quién sabe lo que carga en su costal.
386 (D). Nadie sabe lo que trae en el saco más el que lo carga.
386 (E). Solamente el que carga el morral sabe que peca.
386 (F). Nadie sabe lo que el otro sabe aunque tenga talento, sólo el que trae su petaca sabe lo que trae adentro.

Translation or Interpretation: Only he who carries the sack knows what he has in it.

126

Context: Nobody knows what you think, or feel, but yourself.
(Ten occurrences. Informants: six female, three male, one
anonymous).

Sources and Annotations: Benavides, p. 91, Nadie sabe lo que
trae el morral nomas el que lo carga. Cobos, p. 19, Cada
quien sabe lo que lleva su costal; p. 92, Nomás el que carga
el saco sabe lo que lleva dentro; p. 113, Sólo el que carga
el cajón sabe lo que pesa el muerto. Espinosa, A., p. 108,
Nomas el que carga el costal sabe lo que lleva dentro. Lucero-
White, p. 35, same as B. Martinez, p. 255, same as A. Paredes, p. 31, El que carga el costal sabe lo que lleva dentro.
Santamaria, p. 406, El que carga su costal, sabe lo que lleva
dentro. Velasco, p. 150, same as A.

387 (A). Tanto peca el que mata a la vaca como el que le
          detiene la pata.
387 (B). Tanto peca el que se roba la vaca como el que le
          detiene la pata.
387 (C). Tanto peca el que mata a la vaca como el que le es-
          tira la pata.
387 (D). Tanto peca el que mata como el que le tiene la pata.

Translation or Interpretation: The one who kills the cow sins
as much as the one that holds its leg.

Context: When two people do something wrong, but one of them
does almost everything the other has as much fault as the other one, because he witnessed whatever happened. (20 occurrences. Informants: ten female, ten male).

Sources and Annotations: Adame, p. 90, Tanto peca el que mata
la vaca, como el que le jala la pata; p. 92, Tanto peca el que
mata la vaca, como el que le jala la pata. Ballesteros, p.
64, Tanto peca el que mata a la vaca como el que le detiene la
pata. Benavides, p. 91, Tanto peca el que se roba la vaca
como el que le detiene la pata. Cobos, p. 73, Lo mismo peca
el que mata la vaca como el que come la pata. Conde, p. 384,
Tanto peca el que mata como el que le tiene la pata. Espinosa, A., p. 102, Tanto peca el que mata la vaca-como el que
agarra la pata. Gamiz, p. 89, Tanto peca el que mata la vaca
como el que tiene la pata. Glazer, p. 57, Tanto peca el que
mata a la vaca como el que le detiene la pata. Lucero-White,
p. 36, Tanto peca el que come la vaca como el que le detiene
la pata. Rodriguez-Marin (1930), p. 317, Tanto peca el que
roba en la huerta como el que queda a la puerta. Rodriguez-
Marin (1926), p. 267, Lo mismo peca el que mata la vaca que
el que la tiene por las patas; p. 480, Tanto peca el que
tiene la pata como el que ordena la vaca. Sbarbi, p. 179,
Tanto peca el que tiene la cabra como el que la mama. Yanez,
p. 33, Tanto peca el que mata la vaca como el que le tiene la
pata.

388 (A). Si, pero el que de mañana se levanta pierde de dormir un sueño y cualquier bulto lo espanta.

Translation or Interpretation: Yes, but he who gets up early
loses some sleep and any shadow scares him.

Context: Reply to the proverb: "El que madruga, Dios lo
ayuda." (One occurrence. Informant: female).

Sources and Annotations: Cobos, p. 51, El que temprano se
levanta con cualquier bulto se espanta.

389 (A). A enemigo que huye, puente de plata.

Translation or Interpretation: To the enemy that flees, silver bridge.

Context: This dicho is to teach us that it is not wise to
dagger or corner someone if they have given indications that
they wish to back out of a confrontation or compromise in an
argument. (One occurrence. Informant: male).

Sources or Annotations: Caballero, p. 56, A enemigo que huye,
puente de plata; Conde, p. 22, A enemigo que se ausenta, con
musica y con fiesta; p. 30, A enemigo que huye, puente de
plata. Correas, p. 38, A enemigo que huye hazle puente de
plata. Covarrubias, p. 886, Al enemigo que se retira, la
puente de plata. Espinosa, A., p. 106, Al enemigo puente de
plata. Rodriguez-Marin (1930), p. 7, A enemigo que vuelve la
espalda, las puentes de plata; p. 19, A los enemigos, barre-
lles el camino; p. 64, Cuando el énemigo vuelve la espalda,
hacalle la puente de plata. Rodriguez-Marin (1926), p. 7, A
enemigo que huye, puente de plata. Sbarbi, p. 370, Al enemigo
que huye, la puente de plata.

390 (A). Enero y febrero esta loco y marzo otro poco, y si
abril da una rabiada ni perro queda en la mojada.

Translation or Interpretation: January and February are crazy
and March a little bit more, and if April turns around for the
worse not even a dog would be left around.

Context: An old dicho, said when the weather was nasty. (One
occurrence. Informant: female).

Sources and Annotations: Ballesteros, p. 60, Cuando marzo de
una rabiada ni perros quedan en la mojada. Martinez, p. 125,
Febrero loco, marzo otro poco. Sbarbi, p. 372, En enero y
febrero saca la vieja sus madejas alhumero; en marzo, al pra-
do; en abril, a urdir.

391 (A). _Enfermo_ que come y mea, el diablo que se lo crea.

Translation or Interpretation: Sick person that eats and uri-
nates, let the devil believe him.

Context: When informant was a little kid, he used to stay
home from school by playing sick. After a while his mother
would catch on and send him off quoting this _dicho_. (One
occurrence. Informant: male).

Sources and Annotations: Adame, p. 34, Enfermo que come y
orina, el diablo que se lo crea. Rubio, p. 215, same as A.

392 (A). No lo _engendran_, lo heredan.

Translation or Interpretation: They don't engender it, they
inherit it.

Context: Said about patience, understanding, looks, etc. You
aren't born with patience, you work at it and also inherit
some of its characteristics from parents. (One occurrence.
Informant: male).

Sources and Annotations: Adame, p. 57, Lo que se hereda, no
se hurta; p. 64, Lo que se hereda, no se hurta.

393 (A). Si quieres _enriquecer_ compra lo que has de menester,
           si quieres _empobrecer_ compra lo que has de amenester.

Translation or Interpretation: If you want to be rich, buy
what you need. If you want to be poor, buy what you don't
need.

Context: Advice on how to preserve money. (One occurrence.
Informant: male).

Sources and Annotations: Jaramillo, p. 421, Si quieres empobrecer, compra lo que no has de menester. Rodriguez-Marin
(1926), p. 424, Quien quiera empobrecer compra lo que no ha
de menester; p. 466, Si quieres empobrecer compra lo que no
has de menester.

394 (A). Al buen _entendedor_, pocas palabras.
394 (B). Al buen _entendedor_, con cuatro palabras.
394 (C). A un buen _entendedor_, pocas palabras bastan.

Translation or Interpretation: He who understands needs only
a few words.

Context: If a person is a good listener, he will get the most
out of a conversation or assignment. (Seven occurrences. Informants: four female, three male).

129

Sources and Annotations: Adame, p. 79, Para el buen entendedor, con pocas palabras; p. 81, Para el buen entendedor, con
pocas palabras. Aranda, p. 1, A buen entendedor, pocas palabras bastan. Ballesteros, p. 20, A pocas palabras buen en-
tender. Caballero, p. 96, Al buen entendedor, pocas palabras
le bastan. Cobos, p. 11, Al buen entendedor, pocas palabras.
Conde, p. 29, Al buen entendedor, pocas palabras. Covarrubias, p. 523, A buen entendedor pocas palabras; p. 845, A
buen entendedor pocas palabras. De Barros, p. 63, A buen entendedor pocas palabras bastan. Espinosa, F., p. 107, same
as A. Galván, p. 124, A buen entendedor pocas palabras; p.
125, A buen entendedor...; p. 128, A buen entendedor...; p.
132, A buen entendedor... Jaramillo, p. 360, same as C. Lea,
p. 233, same as A. MacArthur, p. 32, same as C. Maldonado,
p. 23, same as A. Rodriguez-Marin (1926), p. 18, Al buen entendedor con media palabra basta. Al buen entendedor, pocas
palabras, y esas sabias. Sbarbi, p. 111, A buen entededor,
breve hablador.

395 (A). Le entra por una y le sale por la otra.

Translation or Interpretation: It goes in one ear and out the
other.

Context: Often used when people don't listen to someone else.
(One occurrence. Informant: female).

Sources and Annotations: Aranda, p. 15, Entra por aquí y sale
por allá. Caballero, p. 916, Por este oido me entra y por el
otro me sale. Conde, p. 325, Por un oido le entra y por el
otro le sale. Espinosa, A., p. 110, Por un oido le entra y
por otro le sale. Maldonado, p. 117, Dale, dale; por un oido
le entra y por otro le sale.

396 (A). Si la envidia fuera tiña, ¡Que de tiñosos habría!

Translation or Interpretation: If envy were tinted there
would be lots of tinted people.

Context: In our lifes every person has envy of somebody,
something, or for the wealth of life. (One occurrence. Informant: male).

Sources and Annotations: Adame, p. 86, Si la envidia tiznara,
cuantos tiznados no habría; p. 87, Si la envidia tiznara,
cuantos tiznados no habría. Aranda, p. 27, Si la envidia
fuera tinta todo el mundo se tiñiera. Ballesteros, p. 58, Si
la envidia fuera tiña estuvieramos todos tinosos. Caballero,
p. 1025, Si la envidia fuera tiña. Conde, p. 373, Si la envidia tiña fuera...que de tinosos hubiera. Espinosa, A., p.
110, Si la envidia fuera tinta todos tiñeran con ella. Maldonado, p. 62, Si envidia fuese tiña. ¿Que pez lo bastaria?
Si la envidia fuera tiña, cuantos tinosos habiera. Martinez,

p. 253, same as A. Rodriguez-Marin (1930), p. 306, Si la envidia tiña fuera, que de tiñosos hubirea. Rodriguez-Marin
(1926), p. 460, Si la envidia fuera tiña como se pegaria.
Sbarbi, p. 378, same as A. Velasco, p. 149, same as A.

397 (A). La escoba nueva bien barre.

Translation or Interpretation: The new broom sweeps well.

Context: None given. (One occurrence. Informants: female).

Sources and Annotations: Armas, p. 414, Escoba nueva barre
bien. Conde, p. 170, Escoba nueva barre bien. Jaramillo, p.
387, Escoba nueva barre bien. Rodriguez-Marin (1926), p. 56,
Bien barre la escoba nueva, mas pronto se hace vieja. Santamaria, p. 617, Escoba nueva barre bien.

398 (A). Desde que se inventaron las excusas se acabaron las
          derrotas.

Translation or Interpretation: Since excuses were invented
defeats no longer exist.

Context: People always have excuses for whatever they fail
in, therefore, they are never at fault. (One occurrence. Informant: male).

Sources and Annotations: Conde, p. 110, Desde que se inventaron las disculpas se acabaron los pendejos.

399 (A). Estoy entre la espada y la pared.
399 (B). Entre la espada y la pared.

Translation or Interpretation: I am between the sword and the
wall.

Context: When a person has to make a decision that involves
the concerns, or feelings of another person(s). (Two occurrences. Informants: one female, one male).

Sources and Annotations: Armas, p. 291, Hallarse entre espada y el pared. Caballero, p. 294, Cogerle entre espada y la
pared; p. 466, Cogerle entre la espada y la pared; p. 571,
same as B; p. 907 Poner a uno entre la espada y la pared.
Conde, p. 178, same as A. Jaramillo, p. 391, Estar entre
l'espada y la pare'. Pérez, p. 122, same as B. Sbarbi, p.
385, Poner o estar o hallarse. Vasquez, p. 88, same as B.

400 (A). Está como la espada de Santa Catalina, relumbre pero
          no corta.

Translation or Interpretation: It's like Santa Catalina's sword, it sparkles but doesn't cut.

Context: One who boasts but really had nothing to brag about. (One occurrence. Informant: female).

Sources and Annotations: Rubio, p. 90, Como la espada de Santa Catarina: relumbra pero no corta. Sbarbi, p. 385, Ser como la espada de Bernardo, que ni pincha ni corta.

401 (A). El que vuelve las espaldas al enemigo, en sus manos se muere.

Translation or Interpretation: He who turns his back at the enemy dies in his hands.

Context: Informant knew a person who was mad at his friends, and when he was dying, he would call for her. (One occurrence. Informant: female).

Sources and Annotations: Maldonado, p. 50, Al enemigo, si vuelve la espalda, la puente la plata.

402 (A). En este espejo no te has de ver.

Translation or Interpretation: In this mirror you shall not see yourself.

Context: Used mostly when a guy is trying to get a coveted girl, and the girl does not want to go out with him because she is too proud. (One occurrence. Informant: female).

Sources and Annotations: Sbarbi, p. 388, No te verás en ese espejo.

403 (A). La esperanza es la última que muere.

Translation or Interpretation: Hope is the last to die.

Context: Never lose hope. Never give up. (Two occurrences. Informants: one female, one male).

Sources and Annotations: Cobos, p. 66, same as A. Espinosa, A., p. 107, La esperanza es lo ultimo que se pierde. Gamiz, p. 89, La esperanza es lo último que se pierde. Jaramillo, p. 397, La esperanza es lo último que se pierde. Maldonado, p. 134, Esperanza me consuela, que no muera. Rodriguez-Marin (1926), p. 238, La esperanza es lo último que se pierde. Rubio, p. 227, La esperanza muere al último. Sbarbi, p. 327, La esperanza muere al último.

404 (A). La _esperanza_ no engorda pero mantiene.

Translation or Interpretation: Hope doesn't make one fat, but it keeps you going.

Context: Having hope gives a person the will to live. (One occurrence. Informant: female).

Sources and Annotations: Aranda, p. 7, same as A. Cobos, p. 70, Las esperanzas engordan pero no mantienen. Espinosa, A., p. 107, same as A. Espinosa, F., p. 109, De esperanza me mantengo. Lea, p. 235, same as A. Lucero-White, p. 35, same as A. Rodriguez-Marin (1930), p. 161, La esperanza es el pan del alma. Rodriguez-Marin (1926), p. 238, La esperanza me consuela...de comer de la cazuela.

405 (A). Por eso _estamos_ como _estamos_, por eso nunca progresamos.

Translation or Interpretation: That's why we are like we are, that's why we never progress.

Context: My dad would say that when he saw me doing something wrong or in a hurry, he would tell me that's why sometimes my efforts in a task were futile. (One occurrence. Informant: anonymous).

Sources and Annotations: None.

406 (A). _Estás_ de mírame y no me toques.

Translation or Interpretation: To be like, see me but don't touch me.

Context: Usually said to a woman who thinks she has a sexy body and a pretty face. (One occurrence. Informant: female).

Sources and Annotations: Conde, p. 178, Estoy de mirame y no me tientes. Santamaria, p. 283, same as A.

407 (A). La _experiencia_ es el mejor maestro.

Translation or Interpretation: Experience is the best teacher.

Context: Your experience is worth a lot when it comes to look for a job. (One occurrence. Informant: female).

Sources and Annotations: Cerda, p. 280, La experiencia es gran maestro. De Barros, p. 282, El mejor maestro es el tiempo y la mejor maestra es la experiencia. Maldonado, p.

152, El mejor maestro es el tiempo, y la mejor maestra es la experiencia. Rodriguez-Marin (1930), p. 161, La experiencia es gran maestra.

408 (A). Agarra <u>fama</u> y acuéstate a dormir.
408 (B). Agarra <u>fama</u> y échate a dormir.
408 (C). Cria buena <u>fama</u> y echate a dormir.
408 (D). Criala mala y tírate a morir.
408 (F). Cria <u>fama</u> y olvídate de todo.

<u>Translation or Interpretation</u>: Gain fame and go to sleep.

<u>Context</u>: Someone said that a particular person had worked hard for a couple of years and was now a lazy person. (Four occurrences. Informants: female).

<u>Sources and Annotations</u>: Adame, p. 16, Cría fama y échate a dormir; p. 20, Cría fama y échate a dormir. Ballesteros, p. 22, Cría fama y acustate a dormir. Cobos, p. 10, Agara fama y échate en la cama; p. 24, Cría fama y échate en la cama. Conde, p. 77, Cobra buena fama y échate a dormir, mas no tanto duermas, que se te pueda ir; p. 88, Cría fama y acuestate a dormir. De Baros, p. 120, Buena fama, hurto encubre; p. 136, Cobra buena fama y échate a dormir, cobrala mala y échate a morir; p. 136, Cobra buena fama y échate a dormir, y mira no te duermas por que no la pierdas. Espinosa, A., p. 99, Cobra buena fama y echate a dormir, cobra mala fama y échate a huir. Jaramillo, p. 371, Cría fama y échate a dormir. Lea, p. 233, Cobra buena fama y echate a dormir. Lucero-White, p. 33, Cobra buena fama y echate a dormir. Maldonado, p. 102, Cobra buena fama y echaté a dormir. MacArthur, p. 47, Cría fama y héchate a dormir. Rodriguez-Marin (1930), p. 42, Cobra buena fama y échate a dormir; p. 53, Cobra buena fama y túmbate en la cama; p. 146, Hasta cobrar fama, vela ya afamado, duerme a pierna suelta. Rodriguez-Marin (1926), p. 86, Cría buena fama y échate a dormir, criala mala y echate a morir. Sbarbi, p. 398, Cobra buena fama y échate a dormir.

409 (A). Más vale <u>fama</u> que riqueza.

Translation or Interpretation: Fame is worth more than riches.

<u>Context</u>: It is better to be poor and have a lot of friends, than to be rich and not to have true friends. (One occurrence. Informant: female).

<u>Sources and Annotations</u>: None.

410 (A). Sin fé se cierra el mundo.

Translation or Interpretation: Without faith the world closes
on you.

Context: When things go wrong faith can pull you through.
(One occurrence. Informant: female).

Sources and Annotations: None.

411 (A). Febrero loco y marzo otro poco.

Translation or Interpretation: February is crazy and March a
little bit more.

Context: A. was born in February and T. was born in March.
A. always acted crazy, but T. was really witty. Their mother
told them the above proverb. (Three occurrences. Informants:
female).

Sources and Annotations: Adame, p. 51, Febrero loco, marzo
otro poco, y de marzo y abril, no hay a cual ir. Aranda, p.
15, Febrero loco, marzo airoso, abril lluvioso, sacan a mayo
floreado y hermoso. Cobos, p. 57, Febrero loco y marzo otro
poco. Conde, p. 181, Febrero loco y marzo otro poco. Gamiz,
p. 91, Febrero locò y marzo otro poco. Rodriguez-Marin, p.
205, Febrero es loco y marzo no poco.

412 (A). Lo fiado es pariente de lo dado.

Translation or Interpretation: Credit is related to what's
given.

Context: My mother used to have a small business and people
would always ask things on credit. My mother would say no,
and tell them the above proverb. (One occurrence. Informant:
female).

Sources and Annotations: Adame, p. 57, Lo fiado es hermano
de lo dado; p. 63, Lo fiado es hermano de lo dado. Cobos, p.
73, Lo prestado es hermano de lo dado. Gamiz, p. 82, Lo fiado
es pariente de lo dado. Robe, p. 67, Lo fiado es pariente de
lo dado. Santamaria, p. 523, Lo prestado es pariente de lo
dado. Yañez, p. 280, Lo fiado es pariente de lo dado.

413 (A). No te fijes como vengo, fíjate que ya llegué.
413 (B). No te fijes como vengo, lo bueno es que ya estoy
          aquí.

Translation or Interpretation: Do not look at how I came,
notice that I'm here.

Context: When a man who has been drinking all night tells his wife not to place so much emphasis on his present condition, she should be content that he has arrived. (Two occurrences. Informants: one female, one male).

Sources and Annotations: None.

414 (A). Al flojo le ayuda Dios.
414 (B). Al flojo Dios lo ayuda.
414 (C). Dios ayuda al flojo.
414 (D). A los flojos todo el tiempo los ayuda Dios.
414 (E). Al más flojo le ayuda Dios.

Translation or Interpretation: God helps the lazy one.

Context: When an event happens, preventing a task one was not too eager to start. (Ten occurrences. Informants: nine female, one male).

Sources and Annotations: Galvan, p. 124, Al flojo lo ayuda Dios; p. 124, Al perezoso lo ayuda Dios; p. 125, Al perezoso Dios lo ayuda; p. 127, Al flojo Dios lo ayuda; p. 128, Al flojo Dios lo ayuda. Villafuerte, p. 45, Al tonto, Dios lo ayuda.

415 (A). El flojo y el mesquino anda dos veces el mismo camino.

Translation or Interpretation: The lazy and the stingy walk twice the same road.

Context: A person who is in a hurry to finish something much too quickly will eventually have to redo it. (Eight occurrences. Informants: six female, two male).

Sources and Annotations: Armas, p. 411, El haragán y el mezquino andan dos veces el camino. Cerda, p. 281, El flojo y el mesquino andan dos veces el camino. Cobos, p. 37, El flojo y el mesquino andan dos veces el camino. Conde, p. 131, El flojo y el mesquino andan dos veces el mismo camino, Gamiz, p. 93, Todo el que es flojo y mesquino, dos veces anda el camino. Lucero-White, p. 34, El dinero de mezquino anda dos veces el camino. Martínez, p. 106, El flojo y el mesquino anda dos veces el mismo camino. Paredes, p. 30, El flojo y el mesquino andan dos veces el camino. Pérez, p. 120, El flojo y el mezquino dos veces andan el camino. Santamaria, p. 642, El flojo y el mezquino andan dos veces el camino. Yañez, p. 100, El flojo y el mesquino andan dos veces el camino.

416 (A). Gracias por la <u>flor</u>, mañana vengo por la maceta.

<u>Translation or Interpretation</u>: Thanks for the flower, I'll come back tomorrow for the pot.

<u>Context</u>: This means that when somebody is constantly insulting without knowing it, you should graciously ignore their lack of manners. (One occurrence. Informant: female).

<u>Sources and Annotations</u>: Conde, p. 265, Muchas gracias por una flor ya vendré por la maceta. Martinez, p. 185, Muchas gracias por la flor mañana vengo por la maceta. Robe, p. 85, Muchas gracias por la flor, ya volveré por la maceta.

417 (A). <u>Fondo</u> salido, busca marido.
417 (B). <u>Fondo</u> salido, buscando marido.

<u>Translation or Interpretation</u>: Slip showing, looking for a husband.

<u>Context</u>: Said whenever a woman's or girl's slip is showing. (Three occurrences. Informants: female).

<u>Sources and Annotations</u>: Cerda, p. 281, Fondo salido, busca marido. Cobos, p. 58, Fondo salido, busca marido.

418 (A). El <u>fruto</u> prohibido es el más apetecido.

<u>Translation or Interpretation</u>: The forbidden fruit is the most appealing.

<u>Context</u>: None given. (One occurrence. Informant: female).

<u>Sources and Annotations</u>: Conde, p. 182, Fruta prohibida, mas apetecida. Jaramillo, p. 400, Lo prohibido sabe mejor. Rodriguez-Marin (1930), p. 138, Fruta prohibida, mas apetecida. Rodriguez-Marin (1926), p. 156, El fruto prohibido es el más apetecido; p. 268, Lo prohibido es más apetecido; p. 316, Nada es más apetecido como lo prohibido.

419 (A). Ni <u>fu</u> ni fa.

<u>Translation or Interpretation</u>, (Neither here nor there; it's irrelevant.)

<u>Context</u>: None given. (One occurrence. Informant: female).

<u>Sources and Annotations</u>: Caballero, p. 813, Ni fu, ni fa. Conde, p. 276, Ni fu, ni fa, "haste pa'lla. Sbarbi, p. 416, Ni fu, ni fa.

420 (A). Lo que _fue_ amargo de pasar es dulce de recordar.

Translation or Interpretation: What was bitter in passing is sweet in recalling.

Context: My informant uses this proverb when talking about a young girl who was once ill and had to take very ugly tasting medicine. She became well and was glad she had taken the medicine. (One occurrence. Informant: female).

Sources and Annotations: Conde, p. 236, Lo que fue amargo de pasar, es dulce de recordar. Rodriguez-Marin (1930), p. 270, Lo que fue amargo de pasar, es dulce de recordar.

421 (A). Gallina vieja hace buen caldo.
421 (B). Gallina vieja hace mejor caldo.

Translation or Interpretation: An old hen makes good broth.

Context: None given. (Two occurrences. Informants: one female, one unstated).

Sources and Annotations: Ballesteros, p. 62, Gallina vieja hace buen caldo. Caballero, p. 712, La gallina vieja hace mejor caldo. Cobos, p. 59, La gallina vieja hace buen caldo. Conde, p. 185, La gallina vieja hace buen caldo. De Barros, p. 214, La gallina vieja hace bueno caldo. Espinosa, A., p. 107, Gallo viejo mejor caldo. Jaramillo, p. 393, Gallina vieja da buen caldo. Martinez, p. 129, Gallina vieja hace buen caldo. Rodriguez-Marin (1930), p. 333, Vieja gallina hace buena la cocina. Rodriguez-Marin (1926), p. 208, Gallina vieja hace buen caldo; p. 239, Gallina vieja hace buen caldo. Rubio, p. 243, Gallina vieja hace buen caldo. Sbarbi, p. 245, Gallina vieja, buen caldo. Velasco, p. 78, Gallina vieja hace buen caldo. Yanez, p. 315, Gallina vieja hace buen caldo.

422 (A). Mas vale que digan; corrio gallina y no murio gallo.
422 (B). Corrio gallina y no murio gallo.
422 (C). Mejor correr gallina que morir gallo.
422 (D). Mas vale correr gallina que morir gallo.

Translation or Interpretation: It's better if they say a chicken ran, and not a rooster died.

Context: It means that it's better to run away from a fight and be called a chicken, than to get involved in a fight and be hurt. (Four occurrences. Informants: two female, two male).

Sources and Annotations: Adame, p. 98, Vale mas que digan aqui corrio, y no que digan aqui quedo; p. 99, Vale mas que digan aqui corrio, y no que digan aqui quedo. Ballesteros, p.

138

65, Vale mas correr gallina que morir gallo; p. 50, Es mejor
que digan "corrio por cobarde" y no "murio por valiente".
Covarrubias, p. 160, Mas vale digan de aqui muyo, que aqui;
p. 704, Mas vale que digan que aqui huyo, que aqui murio.
Jaramillo, p. 387, Es mejor que digan: aqui corrio uno, que
no: aqui murio uno. Rodriguez-Marin, p. 200, Mas vale decir
"Aqui corri" que "Aqui mori". Wesley, p. 220, Vale mas que
digan que aqui corrio una gallina, que no aqui murio un gallo.
Yanez, p. 52, Mas vale que digan aqui corrio y no aqui
petateo.

423 (A). Poquito por poquito llena la _gallina_ el buche.

Translation or Interpretation: Little by little the hen fills
her gizzard.

Context: One day a friend of mine wanted to quit her job and
go up north to make more money. Her father told her this proverb, soon she knew he was right. (One occurrence. Informant: female).

Sources and Annotations: Cobos, p. 28, De grano en grano
llena la gallina el buche. MacArthur, p. 33, De grano en
grano se llena la gallina el buche. Rodriguez-Marin (1926), p.
500, Un poquito por otro poquito hacen un muchito. Wesley, p.
218, Grano a grano llena la gallina el buche.

424 (A). Mas vale _gallina_ viva que gallo muerto.
424 (B). Mejor una _gallina_ viva que un gallo muerto.
424 (C). Mas vale ser _gallina_ viva y no gallo muerto.

Translation or Interpretation: It's better to be a live
chicken than a dead rooster.

Context: It's better to run away from a fight than to act
"brave" and really accomplish nothing. (Four occurrences.
Informants: two female, two male).

Sources and Annotations: None.

425 (A). Cuidado con sus _gallinas_ que mis gallos andan suel-
          tos.
425 (B). Encierre sus _gallinas_ porque mis gallos andan suel-
          tos.
425 (C). Cuide a sus hijas que mi gallo anda suelto.

Translation or Interpretation: Take care of your chickens
because my roosters are loose.

Context: Lady said that mothers should take care of their
daughters because her sons were not responsible if anything
happened to them. (Three occurrences. Informants: female).

Sources and Annotations: Adame, p. 17, Cuiden sus gallinas
que mis gallos andan sueltosñ p. 22, Cuiden sus gallinas que
mis gallos andan sueltos. Aranda, p. 27, Sujeten sus pollos
que mis gallos andan libres. Martinez, p. 30, Amarren a sus
gallinas porque mis gallos andan sueltos. Rubio, p. 119,
Cuiden sus gallinas que mi coyote anda suelto. Velasco, p. 19,
Amarren a sus gallinas porque mi gallo anda suelto.

426 (A). Donde hay gallinas hay gallos.

Translation or Interpretation: Where there are chickens there
are roosters.

Context: Females attract males. (One occurrence. Informant:
not stated).

Sources and Annotations: Perez, p. 118, Al haber gallinas
hay gallos.

427 (A). No cuentes tus gallinas antes de que las tengas.
427 (B). No cuentes las gallinas antes de nacer.
427 (C). No cuentes los pollos antes de nacer.

Translation or Interpretation: Don't count your chickens
before you have them.

Context: Don't include what you have not accomplished yet.
It might not happen the way you have planned it. (Three
occurrences. Informants: two female, one male).

Sources and Annotations: Lea, p. 236, No cuentes las ganan-
cias antes de empezar la obra.

428 (A). A cada gallo se le llega el día.

Translation or Interpretation: The day comes for every
rooster.

Context: None given. (One occurrence. Informant: not
stated).

Sources and Annotations: Vasquez, p. 89, A cada gallo se
le llega su día.

429 (A). Ese gallo no canta, algo tiene en la parganta.

Translation or Interpretation: That rooster doesn't sing,
it has something in its throat.

Context: The one who is always quiet arouses suspicion.
(One occurrence. Informant: female).

Sources and Annotations: Caballero, p. 612, Este gallo que
no canta, algo tiene en la garganta. De Barros, p. 82, Al
gallo que canta le aprietan la garganta; p. 214, Gallo que no
canta, algo tiene en la garganta. Sbarbi, p. 426, Cuando este
gallo no canta, algo tiene en la garganta.

430 (A). Más claro no canta un gallo.

Translation or Interpretation: A rooster doesn't sing any
clearer.

Context: The informant said she often caught herself using
the proverb with her students when, after a long process of
trying to get them to understand a particular math problem,
they would explain, "Oh! You mean..." She would respond with
the proverb. (Three occurrences. Informants: female).

Sources and Annotations: Armas, p. 230, Cantar claro; p. 306,
Más claro no canta un gallo. Arora, p. 210, Más claro no canta un gallo. Caballero, p. 763, Más claro no canta un gallo.
Chavez, p. 50, Más claro no canta un gallo. Conde, p. 412,
Ya más claro no canta un gallo. Galvan, p. 128, Más claro no
canta un gallo; p. 130, Más claro no canta un gallo. Jaramillo, p. 405, Más claro no canta un gallo. Martinez, p. 211,
¡Oh; ... Más claro no canta un gallo. Yanez, p. 192, Más
claro no canta el gallo, sí, el gallo.

431 (A). Oye los gallos cantar pero no sabe donde cantan.

Translation or Interpretation: Hears the roosters crow, but
doesn't know where they are.

Context: His sister-in-law thought he had heard his brother
say something he hadn't. She brought it up. He clarified
his meaning and quoted this proverb. (One occurrence.
Informant: male).

Sources and Annotations: Conde, p. 305, Oye cantar el gallo
y no sabe por donde. Covarrubia, p. 625, Oyó el gallo cantar,
y no supe en que muladar. De Barros, p. 351, Oye al gallo
cantar y no supo en que muladar. Espinosa, A., p. 109, Oyen
cantar el gallo y no saben por onde. Espinosa, F., p. 116,
Oyotes gallo cantar y no sabeys en que muradal. Jaramillo,
p. 413, Oyo el gallo cantar, y no supo en que mulado.
Maldonado, o. 98, Cantó el gallo: no supo cómo ni cuando.
Villafuerte, p. 138, Oye cantar el gallo y no sabe donde.

432 (A). Eres como una garrapata en la oreja de un perro.

Translation or Interpretation: You are like a tick in a dog's ear.

Context: When a person keeps on bothering someone. (One occurrence. Informant: male).

Sources and Annotations: Arora, p. 214, Prendido como garapata.

433 (A). Es la misma gata rebolcada.

Translation or Interpretation: It's the same cat, but dusty.

Context: Meaning that it is the same thing only disguised. (One occurrence. Informant: female).

Sources and Annotations: Adame, p. 34, Es la misma gata, nomas que revolcada y sin cola; p. 49, Es la misma gata, nomas que revolcada y sin cola. Conde, p. 172, Es la misma gata nomas revolcada. Espinosa, A., p. 106, Es la misma gata nomas que se revolco. Santamaria, p. 293, Ser una cosa la misma mona, nomas que revolcada. Yanez, p. 186, La misma gata.

434 (A). Gato con guantes no caza ratones.

Translation or Interpretation: A cat with mittens doesn't catch mice.

Context: I would say this proverb deals with people who are ill prepared. (One occurrence. Informant: male).

Sources and Annotations: Armas, p. 414, Gato con guantes no caza ratones. Ballesteros, p. 62, Gato que duerme no casa ratón. Caballero, p. 646, Gato con guantes no caza. Cerda, p. 283, Gato que duerme no caza ratones. Cobos, p. 59, Gato que duerme no casa ratón. Lea, p. 235, Gato enguantado no caza ratones. Lucero-White, p. 34, Gato enguantado no caza ratones. Rodriguez-Marin (1930), p. 140, Gato que duerme no caza ratones. Rodriguez-Marin (1926), p. 209, Gato con guantes no caza ratones.

435 (A). Aquí hay gato encerrado.

Translation or Interpretation: There's a cat locked up in here.

Context: Meaning something suspicious is going on. (Two occurrences. Informants: female).

Sources and Annotations: Adame, p. 9, Aquí hay gato encerrado; p. 13, Aquí hay gato encerrado. Caballero, p. 143, Aquí hay gato encerrado. Jaramillo, p. 394, Haber gato encerrado.

Sbarbi, p. 433, Aquí hay gato encerrado. Yáñez, p. 243, Que había gato encerrado.

436 (A). Cuando el gato se va los ratones juegan.

Context: The situation can be an office where the manager leaves on a business or pleasure trip and the other employees don't do their work while he is away. (One occurrence. Informant: female).

Sources and Annotations: Adame, p. 17, Cuando el gato no está en casa, los ratones hacen fiesta; p. 21, Cuando el gato no está en casa, los ratones hacen fiesta. Aranda, p. 6, Cuando el gato esta, el ratón se pasea. Cobos, p. 25, Cuando el gato no está en casa, los ratones se pasean. Robe, p. 70, Cuando el gato no esta en casa, los ratones se pasean. Rodriguez-Marin (1926), p. 89, Cuando el gato está ausente los ratones se divierten; p. 94, Cuando los gatos salen de casa los ratones estan de danza. Rubio, p. 109, Cuando el gato no está en casa, los ratones se pasean; p. 160, Si el gato sale de casa de fiesta estan los ratones. Sbarbi, p. 433, Cuando el gato está fuera los ratones se divierten.

437 (A). Para gato viejo, ratón tierno.

Translation or Interpretation: For an old cat, a young rat.

Context: Used when referring to an old man married to a young woman. (Two occurrences. Informants: male).

Sources and Annotations: Aranda, p. 1, Para gato viejo, ratón tierno. Armas, p. 407, A gato viejo, raton tierno. Ballesteros, p. 56, Para gato viejo, ratón tierno. Cobos, p. 10, A gato viejo, ratón tierno. Conde, p. 310, Para gato viejo, ratón tierno. Camiz, p. 82, A gato viejo, ratón tierno. Jaramillo, p. 360, A gato viejo, ratón tierno. Martinez, p. 17, A gato viejo, ratón tierno. Robe, p. 72, A gato viejo, ratón tierno. Rodriguez-Marin (1930), p. 8, A gato viejo, rata tierna; A gato viejo, raton nuevo. Rodriguez-Marin, (1926), p. 8, A gato viejo, ratón nuevo. Rubio, p. 17, A gato viejo, ratón tierno. Sbarbi, p. 440, A gato viejo, rata tierna; A gato viejo, ratón nuevo.

438 (A). Te dieron gato por liebre.
438 (B). Dar gato por liebre.
438 (C). Vender gatos por liebres.

Translation or Interpretation: They gave you cat instead of jack-rabbit.

Context: My grandfather used this proverb when he was buying some milking cows. He told my grandmother that he himself was going to do the milking and checking of the cows. (Four occurrences. Informants: Two female, one male, one anonymous).

Sources and Annotations: Adame, p. 90, Te dieron gato por liebre; p. 92, Te dieron gato por liebre. Armas, p. 239, Dar gato por liebre; p. 308, Meter gato por liebre. Ballesteros, p. 64, Que no te den gato por liebre. Caballero, p. 433, Dar gato por liebre; p. 439, Darle gato por liebre; p. 646, Gato por liebre. Conde, p. 261, Me quiere dar gato por liebre. Covarrubias, p. 632, Vender el gato por liebre. Espinosa, p. 118, Vender gato por liebre. Galvan, p. 126, Dar gato por liebre; p. 130, Dar gato por liebre. Maldonado, p. 132, En todas artes hay engaño, sino en el que vende estopa por cerro, y el vinagre por vino, y el gato por liebre. Perez, p. 120, Dar gato por liebre. Rodriguez-Marin (1926), p. 505, Véndese el gato por liebre, con sus pebre. Sbarbi, p. 433, Dar o vender gato por liebre. Wesley, p. 212, Ten cuidado que no te den gato por liebre.

439 (A). No todos los gatos son pardos.

Translation or Interpretation: Not all cats are spotted.

Context: Not everyone is alike. (One occurrence. Informant: male).

Sources and Annotations: Aranda, p. 8, De noche todos los gatos son pardos. Correas, p. 314, De noche los gatos todos son pardos. Lea, p. 234, De noche los gatos son pardos. Maldonado, p. 54, De noche los gatos son pardos. Sbarbi, p. 434, De noche todos los gatos son pardos.

440 (A). Genio y figura hasta la sepultura.
440 (B). Forma y figura hasta la sepultura.

Translation or Interpretation: Genius and shape until the grave.

Context: If a person has a certain personality she'll always be that way. (Four occurrences. Informants: female).

Sources and Annotations: Adame, p. 69, Natural y figura hasta la sepultura; p. 92, Natural y figura hasta la sepultura. Armas, p. 414, Genio y figura hasta la sepultura. Ballesteros, p. 7, Genio y facha hasta la sepultura. Campa, p. 64, Genio y figura hasta la sepultura. Cobos, p. 59, Genio y figura hasta la sepultura; p. 86, Natural y figura hasta la sepultura. Conde, p. 185, Genio y figura hasta la sepultura; p. 243, Genio y figura hasta la sepultura. Espinosa, A., p. 101, Natural y figura hasta la sepultura. Gamiz, p. 91, Natural y figura, hasta la sepultura; p. 93,

Muere el genio y la figura solo all en la sepultura. Jaramillo, p. 393, Genio y figura hasta la sepultura. Rodriguez-
Marin (1930), p. 56, Condición y figura hasta la muerte dura.
Rodriguez-Marin (1926), p. 55, Bella por natura, hasta la
sepultura; p. 209, Genio y figura, hasta la sepultura; p. 318,
Natural y figura hasta la sepultura; Muere el genio y la
figura solo all en la sepultura. Sbarbi, p. 436, Genio y
figura hasta la sepultura.

441 (A). <u>Gente</u> parada no gana nada.

<u>Translation or Interpretation</u>: People standing idle don't
gain anything.

<u>Context</u>: None given. (One occurrence. Informant: female).

<u>Sources and Annotations</u>: Sbarbi, p. 437, same as A.

442 (A). Andando caliente aunque se ría la <u>gente</u>.

<u>Translation or Interpretation</u>: As long as I am warm, it
doesn't matter if people laugh.

<u>Context</u>: When someone is wearing old clothing, or mismatched
attire. (One occurrence. Informant: female).

<u>Sources and Annotations</u>: Ballesteros, p. 43, Andando calien-
te aunque se ría la gente. Conde, p. 44, Andando yo caliente
aunque se ría la gente. Correas, p. 59, Andeme yo caliente, y
ríase la gente. Covarrubias, p. 269, Andeme yo caliente y
ríase la gente. Espinosa, F., p. 67, Ande me yo caliente,
ríase la gente. Gamiz, p. 80, Ande yo caliente, ríase la
gente. Jaramillo, p. 364, Ande yo caliente y ríase la gente.
Lucero-White, p. 33, Andando yo caliente más que se ría la
gente. Maldonado, p. 87, Ande yo caliente, y ríase la gente.
Martinez, p. 33, Ande yo caliente y ríase la gente. Sbarbi,
p. 77, Ande yo caliente y ríase la gente; p. 185, Andeme yo
caliente y riase la gente. Villafuerte, p. 58, Andoy como
quiera y como cual quiera.

443 (A). Para donde va la <u>gente</u> va Vicente.

<u>Translation or Interpretation</u>: Wherever the people go,
Vicente goes.

<u>Context</u>: None given. (One occurrence. Informant: female).

<u>Sources and Annotations</u>: Armas, p. 407, ¿Adónde va Vicente?
Adónde va la gente. Caballero, p. 54, ¿A dónde vas Vicente?
A dónde va la gente; p. 515, ¿Dónde va Vicente? Dónde va la
gente. Cobos, p. 10, A dónde va Vicente va la gente; p. 97,
Para dónde va Clemente, va la gente. Conde, p. 22, ¿A dónde

va Vicente? A donde va la gente. Gamiz, p. 92, Siempre camina Vicente donde va toda la gente. Jaramillo, p. 413, Para
dónde va Vicente? Para dónde va la gente. Rodriguez-Marin,
p. 7, A donde vas, Vicente? --¿A dónde va la gente; A dónde
vas, Vicente? -- Al hilo -- o con el golpe -- de la gente, p.
139, Dónde va Vicente? Con el golpe de la gente.

444 (A). Una golondrina no hace el verano.

Translation or Interpretation: A flying gurnard doesn't make
the summer. One swallow does not make it summer.

Context: Said of a person who thinks she is always needed.
(One occurrence. Informant: female).

Sources and Annotations: Caballero, p. 1100, Una golondrina
no hace verano. Lea, p. 238, Una golondrina no hace verano.
Maldonado, p. 31, Una golondrina no hace verano. Sbarbi, p.
439, same as A.

445 (A). El golpe avisa.

Translation or Interpretation: The blow lets you know.

Context: My sister was learning to drive and she asked if
any cars were coming. This lady, my mother's friend, told
her this, and got my sister more nervous. (One occurrence.
Informant: female).

Sources and Annotations: Aranda, p. 10, same as A. Cerda,
p. 238, A golpe de vista. Jaramillo, p. 380, same as A.
Martínez, p. 106, same as A.

446 (A). Los golpes hacen al jinete.

Translation or Interpretation: The blows make the rider.

Context: In order to achieve something you must face the
obstacles. (One occurrence. Informant: female).

Sources and Annotations: Martinez, p. 169, los porrazos
hacen al jinete. Perez, p. 123, same as A. Velasco, p. 97,
Los porrazos hacen la jinete.

447 (A). Por sí, por no, ponte gorro.

Translation of Interpretation: Just in case, wear a cap.

Context: It looked cloudy outside, but I didn't want to take
my umbrella to go out. My grandfather told me the proverb.
(One occurrence. Informant: female).

Sources and Annotations: Conde, p. 232, Lo dice por sí o por no. Rodríguez-Marín (1930), p. 260, Por sí o por no, Mariquita, póntelo.

448 (A). Vale más gota que dure y no chorro que apachurre.

Translation or Interpretation: It's better a drop that lasts and not a spout that crushes.

Context: It's better to take your time to do something than rush into it and not do it right. (One occurrence. Informant: male).

Sources and Annotations: Adame, p. 66, Más vale gota permanente que chorro de repente; p. 67, Más vale gota permanente que chorro de repente. Wesley, p. 218, Vale más una gota que dura que un chorro que se para.

449 (A). Más vale una gota que un aguacero.
449 (B). Vale más una gota que un aguacero.

Translation or Interpretation: It's better a drop than a heavy shower.

Context: It's better to have a job with a small salary than to have one that pays a lot of money, but only temporarily. (Four occurrences. Informants: female).

Sources and Annotations: Conde, p. 254, Más vale gota permanente que aguacero de repente.

450 (A). La gracia no es vivir, la gracia es saber vivir.

Translation or Interpretation: It is not enough to live, we must live life to the fullest and correctly. There is no grace in living, grace is knowing how to live.

Context: The proverb's main meaning is that many people are content with just living without thinking of the manner in which they live. Some people never think of making their lives worth living; they are happy with just having a life to live. (One occurrence. Informant: female).

Sources and Annotations: None.

451 (A). No te creas de un gringo que habla español o un mexicano que fuma puro.

Translation or Interpretation: Don't believe an anglo who speaks Spanish or a Mexican who smokes cigars.

Context: One is just as crooked as the other. I was brought
up on a ranch and I heard a lot of dichos, and one my grandfather told me was this one. Y lo que quiere decir es que el
mexicano que fuma puro es tan sinverguenza como el gringo que
habla español. (What it means is that the Mexican who smokes
a cigar is as much a scoundrel as the anglo who speaks Spanish). I was about fifteen years old when I first heard it.
(Two occurrences. Informants: one female, one male).

Sources and Annotations: None.

452 (A). Vale más un grito a tiempo que tres después.

Translation or Interpretation: It's better a loud cry on
time than three afterwards. One loud cry before is better
than three after.

Context: If you know of a friend of yours who is going to do
something that is going to hurt him and his family, it is
better to counsel him before and not get all upset at him
after it's too late. (One occurrence. Informant: female).

Sources and Annotations: Conde, p. 400, Un grito a tiempo
vale mucho; p. 404, Vale más un grito a tiempo que hablar a
cada momento.

453 (A). No necesito guajes para nadar.

Translation or Interpretation: I don't need gourds to swim.

Context: I invited a friend to go out with me, and she told
me that her parents might not let her go. I offered to ask
her parents for permission. Then, she said, "I can ask myself. No necesito guajes para nadar." She asked herself and
her parents let her go. (Three occurrences. Informants:
two female, one male).

Sources and Annotations: Armas, p. 96, No necesitar de tecomates para nadar; p. 318, No necesitar de tecomates para nadar. Cerda, p. 285, No necesitar guajes para nadar. Covarrubias, p. 263, Nadar sin calabazas. Martínez, p. 201, No
necesito bules para nadar. Santamaria, p. 45, No necesitar
uno de guajes para nadar; p. 257, No necesitar mates para
nadar. Velasco, p. 117, No necessito vejigas para nadar.
Sbarbi, p. 182, No necesitar de calabazas para nadar.

454 (A). De guatemala se fue a guatepeor.
454 (B). Salió de guatemala y cayó en guatepeor.
454 (C). Salí a guatemala y entré a guatepeor.

Translation or Interpretation: He went from bad to worse.

Context: My mother used this proverb when my uncle had gone from a bad situation to a worse one. (Three occurrences. Informants: two female, one male).

Sources and Annotations: Adame, p. 86, Sales de Guatemala para entrar en Guatepeor; p. 87, Sales de Guatemala para entrar en Guatepeor. Alcalá, p. 471, De mal en peor. Armas, p. 293, Ir de mal a peor. Cobos, p. 107, Salir de Guatemala para entrar en Guatepeor. Conde, p. 361, Salió de Guatemala para entrar a guatepeor. Espinosa, F., p. 109, Por salir de Guatemales entrates a Guate-peor. Galván, p. 128, Ir de guatemala a guatepeor. Gamiz, p. 90, Salir de Guatemala y entrar a Guatepeor. Jaramillo, p. 422, Salir de Guatemala pa caer en guatepeor. Martínez, p. 246, Salir de Guatemala a guatepeor. Santamaria, p. 59, Salir uno de Guatemala, para caer en guatepeor. Sbarbi, p. 477, De guatemala se fue a guatepeor. Velasco, p. 144, Salir de guatamala para entrar en guatapeor.

455 (A). A la guerra con la guerra.

Translation or Interpretation: To war with war.

Context: A friend said this when she was telling me about her meddling mother-in-law. My friend said she had been nice and considerate, but had not gotten the same in return. She was not going to be rude as her mother-in-law was. (One occurrence. Informant: female).

Sources and Annotations: Sbarbi, p. 447, same as A.

456 (A). En gustos se rompen géneros.
456 (B). Por gusto se rompen géneros.

Translation or Interpretation: Fabrics tear up in likings.

Context: My informant told me that she was looking for a material to make a dress for the dance. She wanted to buy some material, but she didn't really like any. Her mother told her the above proverb. (Two occurrences. Informants: one female, one not stated).

Sources and Annotations: Conde, p. 161, En gustos se rompen los géneros, ven los colchones frazadas. Espinosa, A., Entre gustos se rompen genias y en géneros cualidades. Gamiz, p. 87, En gustos se rompen géneros y en empedrados los zapatos. Santamaria, p. 86, Por gustos se rompen géneros.

457 (A). El hábito no hace monje.

Translation or Interpretation: The habit does not make the priest.

Context: Clothes do not make the man. Usually said about someone who is putting on a big show, or front, to cover up something they are ashamed of. (Four occurrences. Informants: two female, two male).

Sources and Annotations: Adame, p. 31, same as A; p. 36, same as A. Aranda, p. 11, El hábito no hace la monja. Ballesteros, p. 23, same as A. Caballero, p. 536, same as A. Cobos, p. 38, same as A; p. 53, El traje no hace al monje. Conde, p. 181, El hábito no hace al monje pero le da la figura. Covarrubias, p. 29, same as A. De Barros, p. 219, same as A; p. 327, No hace el hábito al monje. Espinosa, A., p. 108, No es el hábito el que hace al monje. Espinosa, F., p. 122, same as A. Galvan, p. 127, same as A; p. 131, same as A. Jaramillo, p. 380, same as A. Lea, p. 234, same as A. Lucero-White, p. 34, same as A. Maldonado, p. 59, No hace el hábito al monje. Pérez, p. 120, same as A. Robe, p. 65, El hábito no hace al monje pero le da apariencia. Rodriguez-Marin (1926), p. 157, El hábito no hace al monje, ni le venera al noble. Rubio, p. 169, El hábito no hace al monje pero le da la figura. Sbarbi, p. 453, same as A.

458 (A). Cae más pronto un hablador que un cojo.

Translation or Interpretation: A gossiper falls quicker than a cripple. Even though a cripple is crippled, a gossip will fall down quicker because he talks too much. (14 occurrences. Informants: eight female, six male).

Context: My sister was talking to her neighbor. Her neighbor was always criticizing divorcees. My sister told her this proverb. About two or three months later her husband left my sister's neighbor. She immediately started to date guys, so this proverb was true. (14 occurrences. Informants: eight female, 6 male).

Sources and Annotations: Adame, p. 16, Cae mas pronto un hablador que un cojo; p. 18, Cae más pronto un hablador que un cojo. Ballesteros, p. 57, Primero cae un hablador que un cojo. Cerda, p. 285, Cae más pronto un hablador que un cojo. Cobos, p. 20, Cae más pronto un hablador que un cojo. Conde, p. 71, Cae más pronto un hablador que un cojo. Galvan, p. 125, Cae más pronto un hablador que un cojo; p. 129, Cae más pronto un hablador que un cojo. Glazer, p. 50, Cae más pronto un hablador que un cojo. Jaramillo, p. 414, Primero cae un metiroso que un cojo. Martinez, p. 54, Cae más pronto un hablador que un cojo; p. 175, Más pronto cae un hablador que un cojo. MacArthur, p. 67, Cae más pronto un hablador que un

cojo. Robe, p. 66, Más pronto cae un hablador que un cojo.
Rubio, p. 69, Cae más pronto un hablador que un cojo. Velasco, p. 30, Cae más pronto un hablador que un cojo.

459 (A). A mucho hablar (mucho errar).

Translation or Interpretation: The more you talk, the more
liable you are to make mistakes.

Context: I, myself, have caught myself trying to defend a
point while not very well informed and have come out with the
short end of the stick. (One occurrence. Informant: female).

Sources and Annotations: Ballesteros, p. 26, El que poco
habla, poco yerre. Caballero, p. 544, El que mucho habla
mucho yerra; p. 947, Quien mucho habla mucho yerre. Cobos, p.
46, El que mucho habla mucho yerra; p. 83, A mucho hablar
mucho errar. Conde, p. 148, El que poco habla poco yerra; p.
266, A mucho hablar mucho errar; p. 343, El que mucho habla,
mucho yerra. Correas, p. 27, A mucho hablar, mucho errar. De
Barros, p. 97, A mucho hablar mucho errar. Espinosa, F., p.
123, A mucho hablar mucho errar. Jaramillo, p. 385, El que
mucho habla, mucho yerra. Maldonado, p. 28, Mucho hablar,
mucho errar; p. 41, A mucho hablar, mucho errar. Rodriguez-
Marin (1930), p. 54, Comenzar a hablar, comenzar a errar; p.
280, Quien mucho habla, mucho yerra pero en algo acierta.
Rodriguez-Marin, p. 416, Quien no habla, yo yerra.

460 (A). Al hablar, como al guisar, su granito de sal.

Translation or Interpretation: Take your food with a grain
of salt, but also take something you hear with a grain of
salt. Gossip, like cooking, with a grain of salt.

Context: A man was always telling stories and one was never
sure whether or not to believe him and my grandmother told me
this proverb. (One occurrence. Informant: female).

Sources and Annotations: Conde, p. 31, Al hablar, como al
guisar, pon un granito de sal. Martínez, p. 27, Al hablar,
como al guisar; su granito de sal. Rodriguez-Marin, p. 21, Al
hablar, como al guisar; su granito de sal.

461 (A). Hablar sin pensar es disparar sin apuntar.

Translation or Interpretation; Speaking without thinking is
shooting without aiming.

Context: When a person speaks about every one, he may get in
trouble because he may be speaking without thinking. (One
occurrence. Informant: female).

462 (A). No <u>hables</u> que te puedes escupir.

<u>Translation or Interpretation</u>: Don't talk or you may spit on yourself. This is said when you are gossiping or saying something ugly about someone else that could happen to you. (One occurrence. Informant: female).

<u>Context</u>: A lady was talking to another lady about how good her son was, and not smoking "pot" like the rest of the kids. A few days later the boy was caught with a truck load of marijuana. The other lady was telling of the incident and she said it was better "no hablar porque nos podemos escupir." (One occurrence. Informant: female).

<u>Sources and Annotations</u>: None.

463 (A). Si <u>haces</u> mal no esperes bien.

<u>Translation or Interpretation</u>: If you do evil do not expect good.

<u>Context</u>: The girl was saying that another girl had not helped her when she needed her. Proverb said to her because she was always doing things she wasn't supposed to, resulting in fights, gossip, etc. Now that she really needed the help she could not find someone to help her. (One occurrence. Informant: female).

<u>Sources and Annotations</u>: Armas, p. 420, Quien mal hace, mal espere. Cobos, p. 46, El que mal hace, bien no espere; p. 46, El que mal anda, bien no espere; p. 61, Haces mal, espera otro tal. Conde, p. 192, Haz mal y espera otro mal; p. 340, Quien haga mal, tal mal; p. 372, Si haces daño, espera daño. De Barros, p. 220, Haces mal, espera otro tal. Espinosa, A., p. 108, No hagas mal que bien esperas. Galvan, p. 125, El que haga mal no espere bien. Rodriguez-Marin (1930), p. 276, Quien hace mal, ¿qué bien debe esperar? Rodriguez-Marin (1926), p. 407, Quien hace mal, espere otro tal; p. 411, Quien mal hiciera, bien no espere; p. 421, Quien obra mal, espere otro tal; p. 462, Si mal hicieres, tal esperes.

464 (A). Al que te <u>haga</u> más mal debes hacerle más bien.

<u>Translation or Interpretation</u>: The one that does you more harm you should do the most good for.

<u>Context</u>: I recall when my mother told me that this proverb was one of the ones she like best, and which she liked to practice frequently. I found this hard to practice and even harder to believe that my mother practiced it. On one occa-

sion I found out how mistaken I was. I discovered that my
mother carried out her personal philosophy when I verified
that for some afternoons she would visit a lady that was hos-
pitalized. She would take her magazines, cigaretts, and other
personal items. She also initiated a collection in the neighborhood to defray the daily expenses of her hospitalization,
and to help her husband and children. When I found this out
it surprised me very much because this same lady, when in
perfect health, three months prior, had come to our home to
accuse my mother of stealing some clothes off her clothesline.
She was very vulgar and insulting, because she was drunk at
the time. My mother, of course, was so hurt that she cried and
cried, and even said that she would never forgive the lady for
insulting her in such a manner. Yet, here she was three
months later, still faithful to her belief of doing good to
those who do you wrong by helping this lady in every way possible. My informant says that experience happened to him in
Monterrey, Mexico, in a barrio where he lived with his mother
and sister. He must have been fifteen years old at the time,
approximately around 1949. (One occurrence. Informant:
male).

Sources and Annotations: Lucero-White, p. 36, Un mal con
bien se paga.

465 (A). No te hagas del rogar.

Translation or Interpretation: Do not let yourself be begged.

Context: If I needed a favor, like to be taken to town, I
would ask my sister and she would say no, then I would say,
"no te hagas del rogar"--Don't make me beg you to take me.
(One occurrence. Informant: female).

Sources and Annotations: None.

466 (A). Cuando hay hambre no hay mal pan.

Translation or Interpretation: With hunger everything tastes
good.

Context: I am not too crazy about vegetables, but that
doesn't mean that I'll skip lunch...When you're hungry you'll
eat anything. (16 occurrences. Informants: nine female,
seven male).

Sources and Annotations: Adame, p. 16, Con buena hambre no
hay mal pan; p. 19, Con buena hambre no hay mal pan. Aranda,
p. 16, Habiendo hambre no hay pan duro. Armas, p. 410, Con
buen hambre, no hay mal pan. Ballesteros, p. 43, Con hambre
no hay mal pan. Benavides, p. 90, Con hambre no hay mal pan.
Chavez, p. 50, Cuando hay hambre no hay mal pan. Cobos, p.
9, A buena hambre no hay pan duro; p. 98, Para un buen ham-

bre no hay pan duro; Conde, p. 20, Cuando hay hambre no hay mal
pan. Correas, p. 28, A hambre, no hay mal pan. Correas, p. 28,
A hambre, no hay mal pan. Covarrubias, p. 675, A mucha hambre
no hay pan malo; p. 848, A grande hambre no hay pan malo. De
Barros, p. 63, A buen hambre, no hay pan duro; p. 68, A grande
hambre no ay pan malo, ni duro, ni bazo; p. 222, A buen hambre,
no hay pan duro. Espinosa, F., p. 124, A hambre no hay pan duro.
Galvan, p. 124, A buen hambre no hay mal pan; p. 129, A buen
hambre no hay mal pan. Gamiz, p. 74, A buena hambre no hay pan
duro; p. 90, A buena hambre no hay pan duro. Glazer, p. 51,
Cuando hay hambre no hay mal pan. Jaramillo, p. 360, A buen
hambre no hay mal pan. MacArthur, p. 29, Con hambre no hay mal
pan. Maldonado, p. 77, A buena hambre no hay pan duro. Martínez,
p. 12, A buen hambre no hay pan duro. Paredes, p. 29, Cuando
hay hambre no hay mal pan. Pérez, p. 118, A buen hambre no hay
mal pan. Robe, p. 64, A buen hambre no hay pan duro. Rodríguez-
Marín (1926), p. 3, A buena hambre no hay pan duro; p. 3, A
buena hambre no hay pan duro ni falta salsa a ninguno; p. 3, A
buen hambre no hay pan malo, ni duro, ni bazo; p. 32, A mucha
hambre no hay pan duro; p. 124, De ruin montecillo buena es un
gazapillo; p. 124, De sancho a conde, la olla y el mote. Rubio,
p. 5, A buena hambre, gordas duras. Sbarbi, p. 459, A buen hambre no hay pan duro. Villafuerte, p. 157, Para el hambre no hay
pan duro.

467 (A). El hambre los tumba y la vanidad los levanta.

Translation or Interpretation: Hunger will make them fall, but
their pride will pick them up.

Context: Hunger will make you fall but pride will pick you up.
M.V. first heard this proverb from her mother in a story she
would tell her when she was a little girl. The story goes
something like this: There was a lady who lived by herself
with her children, but she was always trying to impress the
rest of the people, even though everybody knew they were just
as poor as everyone else. The lady was always buying the very
best for her kids, but staying without something they really
needed, like food. Just the idea that her kids were wearing
the very best would pick up the lady. (One occurrence. Informant: female).

Sources and Annotations: Ballesteros, p. 46, El hambre los
tumba y la vanidad los levanta. Cerda, p. 286, El hambre las
tumba y la vanidad las levanta. Cobos, p. 38, El hambre las
tumba y la vanidad las levanta. Conde, p. 131, El hambre lo
tumba y la vanidad lo levanta. Rubio, p. 170, El hambre los
tumba y la vanidad los levanta.

468 (A). El hambre es canija, pero más canijo es el que se
         aguanta.

Translation or Interpretation: Hunger is (weird), but more (weird) is whoever endures it.

Context: When someone arrives, especially from out of town and is very hungry. (One occurrence. Informant: female).

Sources and Annotations: Arora, p. 226, Listo como el hambre.

469 (A). Harina de otro costal.

Translation or Interpretation: Flour from another sack.

Context: This proverb was used because a lady said that her son was "harina de otro costal". This means that he now belonged to another household, and she could not really interfere with his new life. (Ten occurrences. Informants: seven female, three male).

Sources and Annotations: Alcalá, p. 315, Ser harina de otro costal. Armas, p. 369, Ser harina de otro costal. Caballero, p. 588, Eso es harina de otro costal; p. 675, Same as A; p. 1014, Ser una cosa harina de otro costal. Gamiz, p. 94, Eso es harina de otro costal. Glazer, p. 51, same as A.

470 (A). Has lo que digo no lo que hago.

Translation or Interpretation: Do as I say not as I do.

Context: P. learned this from his father when he was growing up in Willacy County. He said that his father enjoyed drinking beer but did not want P. to do the same as he did. At times, when his father did not want to show by example in teaching good behavior, he would pull out this saying. (Two occurrences. Informants: male).

Sources and Annotations: Caballero, p. 869, Oye lo que digo y no mires lo que hago. Conde, p. 192, has lo que bien digo, y no lo que mal hago. Galvan, p. 127, has lo que yo digo no lo que yo hago; p. 129, Haz lo que yo te digo y no lo que yo hago. Maldonado, p. 134, Haz lo que bien digo no lo que mal hago. Sbarbi, p. 131, Has lo que bien te digo y no lo que mal hago.

471 (A). Haste sordo y vivirás gordo.

Translation or Interpretation: Act deaf and you'll remain fat.

Context: A woman complaining of all her problems is told "haste sordo y vivirás gordo" -- Don't worry so much so you can get along fine. (One occurrence. Informant: male).

Sources and Annotations: Conde, p. 192, same as A.

472 (A). Te dan una <u>hebrita</u> y quieres todo el carretillo.

Translation or Interpretation: They give you a piece of string and you want the whole spool.

Context: Used when you try to be nice to someone, and instead of being grateful the person tries to take advantage of you. (One occurrence. Informant: female).

Sources and Annotations: None.

473 (A). Escribo en <u>hielo</u>.

Translation or Interpretation: Write on ice.

Context: My informant told me that this little saying is used in reference to a person who makes loud boasts or empty promises. He has heard it used ever since he was a little boy down in Southern Mexico. The significance of the proverb is that when you write something on ice it won't last very long. To me this proverb seems to be the ideal credo for politicians. Instead of using planks for their platforms they should use blocks of ice. (One occurrence. Informant: male).

Sources and Annotations: None.

474 (A). Oyelo tu, <u>hija</u> y entiéndelo tú, nuera.
474 (B). A ti te lo digo mi <u>hija</u>, entiende tú mi nuera.

Translation or Interpretation: Hear me daughter, but (understand) me daughter-in-law.

Context: The mother is telling her daughter something that she wants to get across to her daughter-in-law. (Four occurrences. Informants: female).

Sources and Annotations: Caballero, p. 165, A ti te lo digo suegra... Cobos, p. 15, same as B; p. 32, same as A. Conde, p. 54, same as B. Covarrubias, p. 523, A ti lo digo, mi hijuela; entiéndelo tú mi nuera; p. 690, A ti te lo digo, hijuela; entiéndelo tú mi nuera; p. 831, A ti lo digo, mi hijuela; entiendelo, tu mi nuera. Espinosa, A., p. 104, Digotelo a ti, mi hija y entiéndelo tú, mi nuera. Espinosa, F., p. 169, A ti lo digo, hijuela, entiendelo tu, mi nuera. Rubio, p. 56, A ti te lo digo, mi hija, entiendelo tu mi nuera. Yanez, p. 53, same as B.

475 (A). <u>Hijo</u> de tigre, tigirío.
475 (B). <u>Hijo</u> de gato, gatillo.

Translation or Interpretation: Son of a tiger, tiger he shall be.

Context: In my hometown there was this man who everyone said was very mean. His son was mean to everyone, too. Everyone always said this proverb when referring to them. (Three occurrences. Informants: two female, one male).

Sources and Annotations: Conde, p. 193, Hijo de tigre, tigrito.

476 (A). **Hijo** de tu nana, pariente de tu tata.

Translation or Interpretation: Son of your mother, relative of your father.

Context: My father used to play with me a lot when I was a child. I remember he used to tell me this proverb. (One occurrence. Informant: male).

Sources and Annotations: None.

477 (A). Cada hijo trae un pan bajo el brazo.
477 (B). Cada hijo viene con su torta.

Translation or Interpretation: Each son/daughter brings a loaf of bread under their arm. Those parents who have large families are rewarded.

Context: Husband used this to relieve wife's worry about being pregnant and not having enough money. (Two occurrences. Informants: female).

Sources and Annotations: Caballero, p. 213, Cada hijo que nace en la casa del pobre, trae un pan debajo del brazo. Jaramillo, p. 367, same as A.

478 (A). Mira hijo, el muchacho de el vecino, de mañana se
           levantó y una lateja de pesos se hayó. Sí apa,
           pero más madrugo el que la perdió.

Translation or Interpretation: Look son, how early the neighbor's son woke up and a tin can of dollars he has found. Yes father, but the one who lost it got up much earlier.

Context: My father was a young lad when he heard this proverb from his dad. Basically, what it says is that, sure one can get up early and find, or make, a lot of money, but someone else got up earlier and lost it. So, if one has the money what is the point of getting up real early only to lose it to someone who gets up later in the morning. This is like "the early bird gets the worm" proverb, but only it's more like "the early bird doesn't always get the worm." Later when my dad became of working age, his dad would push him and brothers to get up early to go to work and make a fortune, but my dad remembered the saying and told it back to his dad. (One occurrence. Informant: male).

Sources and Annotations: Jaramillo, p. 427, Un hombre que madrugó, una bolsa de oro s'encontro...Pero más madrugo el que la perdio. Rodriguez-Marin (1926), p. 499, Uno, por madrugar, se hallo un costal pero más madrugo el que lo perdió.

479 (A). Hijas son, madres seran.

Translation or Interpretation: Daughters they are, mothers they will be.

Context: These are the kinds of sayings that mothers tell their daughters of what might happen to them if they fool around. (One occurrence. Informant: female).

Sources and Annotations: None.

480 (A). Donde hay hijos ni pariente ni amigos.

Translation or Interpretation: Where there are children neither relatives nor friends.

Context: If in a family there are eight or ten, you don't need more persons. With them you have enough for a will. (One occurrence. Informant: male).

Sources and Annotations: De Barros, p. 180, same as A.

481 (A). Los hijos como los árboles, se deben de enderezar cuando están tiernos porque ya de grandes es demaciado tarde.

Translation or Interpretation: Children (like a tree) must be directed in a right direction when they are young. If you wait to straighten them out when they are older it is very difficult.

Context: My grandfather used this proverb very often. He was once very upset because the children of a particular daughter of his, let her children do as they pleased, and the parents never reprimanded them. When the oldest child got in trouble, my aunt asked my grandfather for some advice, and my grandfather told her the above proverb. (One occurrence. Informant: female).

Hijos / Hijos

482 (A). Los hijos y los maridos por sus hechos son queridos.

Translation or Interpretation: Sons and husbands are loved for their acts.

Context: None given. (One occurrence. Informant: female).

Sources and Annotations: Rubio, p. 304, Los hijos y los maridos por sus obras son queridos.

483 (A). Todos hijos de Dios o todos hijos del diablo.

Translation or Interpretation: All sons of god or all sons of the devil. All people are the same.

Context: R. comes from a big family and he tells this proverb to his father. Everybody should be treated the same. (Four occurrences. Informants: two female, two male).

Sources and Annotations: Cobos, p. 116, Todos hijos de Dios o todos entenados. Martinez, p. 213, O todos hijos de Dios, o todos hijos de diablo. Rodriguez-Marin (1926), p. 487, Todos somos hijos de Dios. Velasco, p. 125, O todos hijos de Dios o todos hijos del Diablo.

484 (A). Hijos de mi hijos serán. Hijos de mi hijo dudas estarán.

Translation or Interpretation: Children of my daughter will always be. Children of my son, in doubt they will be.

Context: My sister has a friend, and her mother is always using this proverb. She does not trust her daughter-in-law. She says that maybe the children are her grandchildren and maybe they are not. (Three occurrences. Informants: female).

Sources and Annotations: Conde, p. 193, Hijo de mi hija mi nieto es, hijo de mi hijo...será tal vez. Jaramillo, p. 394, Hijo de hija nieto será, hijo de hijo nadie sabrá; p. 399, Los hijos de mis hijas son mis nietos en verda, los hijos de mis hijos no lo puedo asegurar. Martinez, p. 142, Hijo de mi hija nieto será hijo de mi hijo soló Dios sabrá. Rodriguez-Marin (1930), p. 149, Hijo de mi hija estar mi nieto, hijo de mi hijo no saberto. Rubio, p. 258, Hijo de tu hija, es tu nieto; hijo de tu hijo quien sabe. Yañez, p. 76, Hijo de tu hija es tu nieto: hijo de tu hijo quien sabe.

485 (A). Todos <u>hijos</u> o todos entenados.

Translation or Interpretation: All sons or all step sons.

Context: R. says that he treats all his students alike, and that's the way it should be. (One occurrence. Informant: male).

Sources and Annotations: Cerda, p. 287, O todos hijos, o todos entenados. Cobos, p. 96, O todos hijos o todos entenados; p. 116, Todos hijos o todos entenados. Conde, p. 319, Pocos entenados hay buenos; y padrastros poco menos. Gamiz, p. 87, Todos hijos o todos entenados. Martinez, p. 213, Todos hijos o todos entenados. Velasco, p. 125, Todos hijos o todos entenados.

486 (A). No me subas tan arriba que las <u>hojas</u> en el árbol no duran toda la vida.

Translation or Interpretation: Don't raise me to high, the leaves on a tree don't last a lifetime. A friend of yours that once always said good things about you and talked very highly of you, all of a sudden she starts talking bad about you.

Context: She said that a friend of hers was real nice to her and always told her and others how sweet she was and how pretty she was. She went and told her grandmother, and she told her that phrase. She said to be careful because she may get mad one day and turn on you. That is what happened. The friend started talking bad about her. (One occurrence. Informant: female).

Sources and Annotations: Cerda, p. 287, Las hojas en el árbol no duran toda la vida.

487 (A). Acostarse temprano, levantarse temprano, hace el <u>hombre</u> activo, rico y sano.

Translation or Interpretation: To get to bed early and to get up early makes a man active, rich and healthy. Early to bed, early to rise, makes a man healthy, wealthy and wise.

Context: Informant's father always told this to his children in order to get them to go to bed early and to get them up early. Informant said his kids never believed him, but knew better than not to mind him. (One occurrence. Informant: female).

Sources and Annotations: Sbarbi, p. 31, Acostarse temprano y levantarse temprano, hace al hombre activo, opulento y sano.

488 (A). El hombre aprovechado nunca quedará vencido.

Translation or Interpretation: The man who is prepared will never be defeated.

Context: My informant recalls his father telling him this whenever he would start losing interest in something that he started. My informant is a person who is always prepared, and I have known him for quite a long time. I guess he paid attention to what his father told him. (One occurrence. Informant: male).

Sources and Annotations: MacArthur, p. 9, Hombre prevenido nunca es vencido.

489 (A). El hombre en su casa es rey.

Translation or Interpretation: Man is king in his home. A man's home is his castle .

Context: The man is the head of the home and he has the final say so on everything. (One occurrence. Informant: male).

Sources and Annotations: Aranda, p. 20, Mientras en mi casa, rey soy. Cobos, p. 38, same as A. MacArthur, p. 34, Cuando en casa estoy, rey soy.

490 (A). El hombre propone y la mujer dispone.

Translation or Interpretation: The man proposes and the woman disposes.

Context: J. wants to build a house in the country. He starts to make plans for it, and his wife disagrees with the plans. She wants a house in the city. "El hombre propone y la mujer dispone". (One occurrence. Informant: male).

Sources and Annotations: Conde, p. 133, same as A. Rodriguez-Marin (1930), p. 108, same as A. Rodriguez-Marin (1926), p. 158, El hombre pone, Dios dispone y la mujer la descompone.

491 (A). Es un hombre hecho y derecho.

Translation or Interpretation: He is a man, finished and straight. Means he is a grown and mature person.

Context: A man was telling his son of an upright and honest person, and used the above to dramatize the fact. (Three occurrences. Informants: two female, one male).

Sources and Annotations: Caballero, p. 1018, Ser un hombre

echo y derecho. Espinosa, F., p. 123, Hasta hecho y derecho.

492 (A). El <u>hombre</u> propone y Dios dispone.
492 (B). Lo que uno propone Dios dispone.
492 (C). El <u>hombre</u> propone, Dios dispone y la mujer se inter-
          pone.
492 (D). Uno pone y Dios dispone y viene la mujer y todo des-
          compone.
492 (E). Uno hace y Dios deshace.

Translation or Interpretation: Man proposes, God disposes.

Context: God has control, that is why we say "God willing."
(18 occurrences. Informants: 11 female, seven male).

Sources and Annotations: Adame, p. 31, El hombre pone y Dios
dispone; p. 36, El hombre pone y Dios dispone. Aranda, p. 11,
El hombre propone y Dios dispone. Benavides, p. 90, El hombre
propone y Dios dispone. Cobos, p. 38, El hombre hace y Dios
des hace. Conde, p. 133, El hombre propone y Dios dispone.
Correas, p. 88, El hombre propone y Dios dispone; p. 186, El
hombre propone y Dios dispone. De Barros, p. 235, El hombre
propone y Dios dispone. Espinosa, A., p. 11, El hombre propone
y Dios dispone. Espinosa, F., p. 101, El hombre pone y Dios
dispone. Galvan, p. 127, El hombre propone y Dios dispone.
Gamiz, p. 74, El hombre pone y Dios dispone. Glazer, p. 48,
Uno pone y Dios dispone. Uno hace Dios deshace. Jaramillo, p.
380, El hombre propone y Dios dispone...y el diablo lo descompone. Lea, p. 234, El hombre propone y Dios dispone. Lucero-
White, p. 34, El hombre propone y Dios dispone. Maldonado, p.
139, El hombre propone y Dios dispone. Peréz, p. 120, El hombre pone y Dios dispone. Rodriguez-Marin (1930), p. 108, El
hombre propone y la mujer dispone. Rodriguez-Marin (1926), p.
158, El hombre pone, Dios dispone, y la mujer la descompone;
p. 240, La genta compone, y Dios dispone. Sbarbi, p. 482, El
hombre propone y Dios dispone.

493 (A). Un <u>hombre</u> preparado vale por dos.
493 (B). La <u>mujer</u> precavida vale por dos.
493 (C). Una persona preparada vale por dos.

Translation or Interpretation: One prepared man is worth two.

Context: M. tells this proverb to his students, meaning that
if you learn a trade you are more likely to get a job. (11
occurrences. Informants: seven female, four male).

Sources and Annotations: Adame, p. 52, Hombre precavido,
vale por dos; p. 54, Hombre precavido, vale por dos. Armas, p.
414, Hombre precavido, vale por dos. Ballesteros, p. 8, Hombre
precavido vale por dos. Conde, p. 195, Hombre prevenido vale
por dos. Correas, p. 88, El hombre prevenido vale por dos.

De Barros, p. 235, Hombre prevenido, vale por dos. Jaramillo, p. 394, Hombre prevenido vale por dos. Rodriguez-Marin (1926), p. 222, Hombre apercibido, vale por dos.

494 (A). Los hombres no lloran, pero se aguantan.

Translation or Interpretation: Men don't cry (they just re-strain themselves.)

Context: I remember hearing this proverb as I was walking in-to a store in McAllen. A small boy, about three or four years old was crying. A woman turned to him and said the proverb. This made the little boy stop crying. (One occurrence. In-formant: female).

Sources and Annotations: None.

495 (A). Nunca te creas de los hombres aunque los mires llo-
          rar porque los hombres son como los cocodrilos, llo-
          ran para engañar.

Translation or Interpretation: Never believe what men say even if you see them cry. Men are like crocodiles that cry only to deceive.

Context: Usually said to a female when she has had some dis-appointment with a man. (One occurrence. Informant: female).

Sources and Annotations: Armas, p. 303, Llorar lágrimas de crocodrilo. Caballero, p. 344, Como lágrimas de cocodrilo. p. 355, Como llanto de cocodrilo; p. 713, Lagrimas de cocodrilo.

496 (A). Te encontraste con la horma de tu zapato.

Translation or Interpretation: You finally met your match. You found the mold for your shoe.

Context: Informant used this to tell his friends that he finally had met someone who was not afraid of him. (One oc-currence. Informant: male).

Sources and Annotations: Adame, p. 90, Te enconstraste con la horma de tu zapato; p. 93, Te encontraste con la horma de tu zapato. Aranda, p. 26, Se encontró con la horma de su zapato. Armas, p. 257, Encontrase con la horma de su zapato; p. 291, Hallar la horma de tu zapato. Caballero, p. 990, Se encontró con la horma de su zapato. Conde, p. 190, Hasta que encontró la horma de su zapato. Correas, p. 138, Econtró con horma de su zapato; p. 583, Halló horma de su zapato. Espinosa, F., p. 130, Hallado el horma de su pie. Gamiz, p. 89, Encontrarse con la horma de su zapato. Maldonado, p. 127, Encontró con horma de su zapato. Sbarbi, p. 494, Hallar un la horma de su zapato.

163

497 (A). Al pasito y con el tiempo, una hormiga se comió un elefante.

Translation or Interpretation: Slowly and with time, an ant ate an elephant.

Context: The meaning of this proverb is that any person willing to do something can, if he or she has faith and believes what he or she is doing is right. Though he or she really knows it's impossible, one should never lose hope even if it takes forever to get what they want done. Mr. Rubalcaba said that there is a lot of truth behind this meaning. He said he heard it about two months ago at a friend's house. His friend told him the meaning and said it is very true. Mr. Rubalcaba said it is a generally believed proverb, and is referred to anyone of any age. (One occurrence. Informant: male).

Sources and Annotations: None.

498 (A). No hay quien la brinque sin huarache.

Translation or Interpretation: You can't jump her without sandals. They don't do you a favor without interest.

Context: This lady came to my mother's house and she told my mom how much she missed her, and that she loved my mother so much. She beat around the bush for a favor she wanted, but she wouldn't come out and say it. So, when she was leaving she asked for a favor, and my mother told her this saying. (One occurrence. Informant: female).

Sources and Annotations: Adame, p. 69, Nadie la corre sin huarache; p. 71, Nadie la corree sin huarache.

499 (A). Donde hay humo hay fuego.

Translation or Interpretation: Where there is smoke there is fire.

Context: I was sitting in a cantina when I heard these guys arguing. I quickly drank my beer and left because I knew a fight was about to start. (One occurrence. Informant: female).

Sources and Annotations: Adame, p. 24, Donde hay humo, hay lumbre; p. 30, Donde hay humo, hay lumbre. Cobos, p. 34, Donde hay humo hay fuego. Conde, p. 117, Donde hay humo hay fuego. Lea, p. 234, Donde humo sale fuego sale. Lucero-White, p. 33, Donde humo sale fuego hay. MacArthur, p. 65, Donde

hay humo hay fuego. Rodríguez-Marín (1930), p. 109, El humo
cerca de la llama anda. Rodríguez-Marín (1926), p. 206, Fuego
hay do humo dale; p. 335, No hay humo, sin fuego. Rubio, p.
152, Donde no hay humo no hay lumbre.

500 (A). Si quieres entrar a la <u>iglesia</u> tienes que agachar
la cabeza.

<u>Translation or Interpretation</u>: If you want to enter into
church you have to lower your head.

<u>Context</u>: O. says this <u>dicho</u> is always told to girls who are
engaged to marry and are acting uppity or having too many
quarrels with their boyfriends. It advises them to compromise
if they expect to get married. (One occurrence. Informant:
female).

<u>Sources and Annotations</u>: Conde, p. 59, Baja, novia, la cabe-
za; si quieres ir a la iglesia.

501 (A). Nunca te vayas de primer <u>impulso</u>.

<u>Translation or Interpretation</u>: Do not go back on your first
impulse. This means that usually one's first answer or in-
stinct is the correct one.

<u>Context</u>: My father said that he would use this proverb when
he found somebody in a situation where they had second
thoughts about a personal matter. (Three occurrences. Informants: one female, two male).

<u>Sources and Annotations</u>: Benavides, p. 91, Nunca te vayas al
primer impulso.

502 (A). De buenas <u>intenciones</u> está lleno el infierno.

<u>Translation or Interpretation</u>: Hell is full of good inten-
tions.

<u>Context</u>: My mother used to reproach me with this <u>dicho</u> when-
ever I had failed to run some errands but kept promising that
I intended to do them in the immediate future. (One occurrence. Informant: male).

<u>Sources and Annotations</u>: None.

503 (A). El <u>interés</u> tiene pies.

<u>Translation or Interpretation</u>: Interest has feet.

Context: Girls at a night club try and get acquainted with very well dressed guys and try and find out if they are well off or not. One of my friends got very angry because a girl was following her boyfriend, and she said the above to me. (Eight occurrences. Informants: six female, two male).

Sources and Annotations: Cobos, p. 38, El interés tiene pies. Martinez, p. 106, El interés tiene pies. Rodriguez-Marin (1926), p. 159, El interés mueve los pies. Rubio, p. 171, El interés tiene pies. Yañez, p. 242, El interés tiene pies.

504 (A). Jarrito nuevo donde te pondre.

Translation or Interpretation: New jug where can I place you.

Context: When you have a new friend and you go especially out of your way to please him, or do everything for him. (One occurrence. Informant: unstated).

Sources and Annotations: Rodríguez-Marín (1930), p. 156, Jarrito nuevo, guárdase en el chinero; pasan dos semanas, y por todas partes anda.

505 (A). Todo cabe en un jarrito sabiendo acomodar.

Translation or Interpretation: Everything fits in a little jug if you know how to stack it. Everything has got its rightful place if you know how to stack it up.

Context: My family and I were trying to rearrange the old shack. There seemed to be more junk than space, but when we got through everything was in the shack. (Three occurrences. Informants: female).

Sources and Annotations: Ballesteros, p. 16, Todo cabe en el jarrito sabiendolo acomodar. Cerda, p. 280, Todo cabe en un jarrito sabiendo acomodar. Cobos, p. 115, Todo cabe en un costal, sabiendolo acomodar. Conde, p. 389, Todo cabe en un jarrito sabiendo acomodar. Martinez, p. 265, Todo cave en un jarrito sabiendo acomodar. Paredes, p. 33, Todo cabe en un jarrito sabiendo acomodar. Velasco, p. 156, Todo cabe en un jarrito sabiendolo acomodar.

506 (A). Aunque la jaula sea de oro no deja de ser prisión.

Translation or Interpretation: Although the cage is golden it is still a prison.

Context: Cannot think of an example. Only one comparison, a home is not a palace. (One occurrence. Informant: female).

Sources and Annotations: Adame, p. 56, La jaula ni aunque sea de oro; p. 59, La jaula ni aunque sea de oro. Ballesteros, p. 33, No porque la jaula sea de oro deja de ser prisión. Conde, p. 55, Aunque la jaula sea de oro no deja ser prision. Rubio, p. 59, Aunque la jaula sea de oro no deja ser prision.

507 (A). Jesús los valga.

Translation or Interpretation: God bless you.

Context: This is said after someone sneezes. (One occurrence. Informant: female).

Sources and Annotations: Aranda, p. 17, Jesús los valga.

508 (A). Jesús y cruz.

Translation or Interpretation: Jesús and cross.

Context: My informant's family would use this proverb before traveling down to Mexico to visit relatives. (One occurrence. Informant: female).

Sources and Annotations: Aranda, p. 17, Jesus y cruz.

509 (A). Juan Gómez, Tú lo traes y tú lo comes.

Translation or Interpretation: One who takes something to a party and eats most of it. Juan Gómez, you bring it and you eat it.

Context: My little sister baked a chocolate cake for my sister's anniversary party, and since chocolate is her favorite, she ate most of it when it was supposed to be for the guests at the party. (Four occurrences. Informants: three female, one male).

Sources and Annotations: None.

510 (A). Juan Guangoche, lo que no hace de día hace de noche.

Translation or Interpretation: Juan Guangoche, what he does not do during the day he does at night.

Context: Mrs. Gallardo's daughter needed a dress for the following day. Instead of working on it during the day she left with her friends and had a nice time. When she returned it was already late and was worried that she might not get the dress on time. (Four occurrences. Informants: one female, two male, one anonymous).

Sources and Annotations: None.

511 (A). Que culpa tiene Juan que Pedro este pelón.

Translation or Interpretation: What fault is it of Juan that Pedro is bald.

Context: I was working very hard one day. My boss had an argument with one of our patients. I was busy doing my work when suddenly, she started fussing at me. I used this pro-verb to describe this situation. (One occurrence. Infor-mant: female).

Sources and Annotations: Cobos, p. 102, Que culpa tiene San Pedro que San Pablo esté pelón.

512 (A). A buen juez, mejor testigo.

Translation or Interpretation: For a good judge a better witness.

Context: It happened to a judge that did not do his job well. The people of the town used to say this to his employees. (One occurrence. Informant: female).

Sources and Annotations: Conde, p. 29, A buen juez, el mejor testigo. Rodriguez-Marin (1926), p. 3, A buen juez, mejor testigo.

513 (A). Juventud perezosa, vejez menesterosa.

Translation or Interpretation: Lazy youth, needy old age.

Context: If, when young, you are lazy and do not apply your-self, then in old age you will be a miser and unable to do anything. Irma comes from a family that used many intelli-gent and meaningful proverbs. This particular one, she says, her father would repeat quite often to all of them. He want-ed them to really apply themselves in their studies so that they would be able to have a good future and a good job. (One occurrence. Informant: female).

Sources and Annotations: None.

514 (A). Si juventud supiera y vejéz pudiera.

Translation or Interpretation: If youth knew and old age could.

Context: I was doing my homework when I was in grade school,
and couldn't solve some problems. The only person to help me
was grandmother. I asked her and she told me this saying.
(Four occurrences. Informants: two female, two male).

Sources and Annotations: Conde, p. 370, Si el mozo supiera
y el viejo pudiera no habría cosa que no se haciera. Martínez, p. 253, Si juventud supiera y vejez pudiera.

515 (A). Juntos pero no revueltos.

Translation or Interpretation: Together, but not mixed.

Context: You and someone else are together in a certain
place, but you are different from your friend. You have different beliefs from him. Someone might say "juntos pero no
revueltos." (Five occurrences. Informants: four female,
one male).

Sources and Annotations: Adame, p. 55, Juntos pero no revueltos. Benavides, p. 90, Juntos pero no revueltos. Conde,
p. 200, Juntos pero no revueltos. Pérez, p. 122, Juntos pero
no revueltos. Rubio, p. 268, Juntos pero no revueltos. Vasquez, p. 88, Juntos pero no revueltos.

516 (A). Pagan justos por pecadores.

Translation or Interpretation: Just ones pay for (sinful)
ones.

Context: My informant's son is in jail. She tells me he
did not break the law. According to her, using this proverb,
others were to blame and were called innocent, while her son
is innocent and serving a sentence. (Two occurrences. Informant: one female, one male).

Sources and Annotations: Adame, p. 79, Pagan justos por pecadores; p. 80, Pagan justos por pecadores. Caballero, p.
871, Pagar justos por pecadores. Conde, p. 302, ( ). Espinosa, A., p. 109, Pagan justos por pecadores. Espinosa, p.
137, Pagan justos por pecadores.

517 (A). Cree el ladrón que todos son de su condición.
517 (B). El ladrón cree que todos son ladrones.
517 (C). Piensa el ladrón que todos son de su condición.
517 (D). Cree el león que todos son de su misma condición.
517 (E). Tú eres como el ladrón, quieres que todos sean de
          tu condición.

Translation or Interpretation: The thief believes that
everyone is the way he is.

Context: When someone thinks that just because he's a bad person so is everyone else. (Eight occurrences. Informants: six female, two male).

Sources and Annotations: Armas, p. 411, El leon cree que to-dos son de su condición; El león piensa que todos son de su condición. Ballesteros, p. 46, El león cree que todos son de su condición. Caballero, p. 901, same as C. Cobos, p. 99, same as C; p. 24, same as A. Conde, p. 88, same as C; p. 317, Piensa el ladrón que todos tienen su condición. Espinosa, A., p. 101, same as C. Espinosa, F., p. 137, Piensa el ladrón que todos son de su condición. Gamiz, p. 92, Piensa el león que todos son de su condición. Jaramillo, p. 380, El ladrón goza por su condición. Rubio, p. 32, same as C. Santamaria, p. 181, same as D.

518 (A). Ladrón que roba a ladrón tiene cien años de perdón.
518 (B). Ladrón que roba a ladrón alcanza cien años de perdón.

Translation or Interpretation: Thief who steals from thief has one hundred years of pardon.

Context: My informant's neighbor was a thief. One night he left the house early, by midnight he came in. He had left the key in the car and went to get them. When he came back the bag was gone. My informant used this proverb on him. (Six occurrences. Informants: five female, one male).

Sources and Annotations: Adame, p. 56, same as B; p. 58, same as B. Ballesteros, p. 51, same as A. Conde, p. 207, same as A. Espinosa, A., p. 100, El que le roba a otro ladrón--tiene cien años de perdon--y otros tantos de condenación. Gamiz, p. 90, same as A. Jaramillo, p. 382, El que roba a un ladrón, tiene cien años de perdón. MacArthur, p. 41, same as A. Robe, p. 65, same as A. Rodriguez-Marin (1926), p. 408, Quien hurta al lad-rón, harto digno es de perdón; p. 426, Quien roba al ladrón gana -- o tiene -- cien años de perdón. Sbarbi, p. 531, El que roba al ladrón tiene cien años de perdón.

519 (A). Lo que en la leche se mama, en la mortaja se derra-ma.

Translation or Interpretation: What's learned from mother's milk, is carried to the grave.

Context: If a person learns what he is supposed to, and prac-tices it, he will never forget it. (One occurrence. Infor-mant: male).

Sources and Annotations: Cobos, p. 75, Lo que aprende en la cuna siempre dura. De Barros, p. 254, same as A. Rodriguez-

Marin (1930), p. 181, Lo que en la leche se mama, hasta la
sepultura acompaña; p. 181, Lo que en la leche se mama, sale
en la mortaja; p. 184, Lo que se aprende en la cuna, se olvida
en la sepultura. Rodriguez-Marin (1926), p. 273, Lo que se
aprende -- o se mama -- en la cuna, hasta la muerte dura.
Sbarbi, p. 539, same as A.

520 (A). Para que compras leche teniendo tan buena vaca.

Translation or Interpretation: Why buy milk when you have
such a good cow.

Context: I was telling my aunt, the informant, that I had
gone to see the dentist that day. Then she told me why did
I go see this doctor when I had an uncle in Weslaco who could
do the job. Then she told me that I was crazy and cited the
above proverb. (Two occurrences. Informants: female).

Sources and Annotations: None.

521 (A). Me quité de lechero por no cargar los botes.

Translation or Interpretation: I quit being a milkman so
that I wouldn't have to carry the milk containers.

Context: It means, "don't ask me to do what I have already
decided not to." (One occurrence. Informant: female).

Sources and Annotations: None.

522 (A). La lengua no tiene hueso.

Translation or Interpretation: The tongue has no bone.

Context: A lady in my aunt's neighborhood is called "The
Monitor," like the newspaper. She knows all the news in the
neighborhood. People say that her tongue has no bones. She
never gets tired of talking. (Three occurrences. Informants:
female).

Sources and Annotations: Rodriguez-Marin (1926), p. 243,
La lengua no tiene huesos; pero sabe romperlos.

523 (A). Escucha, o tu lengua te hará sordo.

Translation or Interpretation: Listen or your tongue will
make you deaf.

Context: When my informant started teaching he had a couple
of students talking all the time while he was lecturing, then

171

he told the students the proverb. (Two occurrences. Informants: one male, one anonymous).

Sources and Annotations: None.

524 (A). No te asustes ni te espantes que es la lengua de
Cervantes.

Translation or Interpretation: Do not get scared or frightened, it's Cervantes' tongue.

Context: This was told to someone when others witnessed an
Anglo person speak perfect Spanish, and everyone was shocked.
(One occurrence. Informant: male).

Sources and Annotations: None.

525 (A). No te vayas a morder la lengua.
525 (B). No hables tanto porque te puedes morder la lengua.
525 (C). No digas nada porque te muerdes la lengua.

Translation or Interpretation: You might bite your tongue.

Context: When cutting down, insulting, talking about someone, it is suggested that the person talking has faults too.
(Four occurrences. Informants: two female, two male).

Sources and Annotations: Caballero, p. 797, Morderse uno la
lengua. Sbarbi, p. 541, Morderse uno la lengua.

526 (A). No es tan fiero el león como lo pintan.

Translation or Interpretation: The lion is not as fierce as
he is described.

Context: When my informant's wife was expecting the birth of
their child he was pretty depressed and anxious, so, his
mother-in-law quoted the proverb. (Three occurrences. Informants: one female, two male).

Sources and Annotations: Adame, p. 31, El león no es como lo
pintan; p. 36, El león no es como lo pintan. Aranda, p. 21,
No es el león como lo pintan. Caballero, p. 829, No es tan
fiero el león como la gente lo pinta. Chavez, p. 46, same as
A. Conde, p. 282, No es el león como lo pintan. Correas, p.
246, No es el diablo tan feo como le pintan el miedo; p. 247,
No es tan bravo el león como le pintan. De Barros, p. 324,
No es el diablo tan feo como le pintan el miedo; p. 325, No
es tan bravo el león como lo pintan. Espinosa, A., p. 108,
No es el león como lo pintan. Espinosa, F., p. 140, No es tan
brabo el león como lo pintan. Galván, p. 131, No es el león

como lo pintan; p. 131, No es la leona como la pintan; p. 132, No es el león como lo pintan. Jaramillo, p. 407, same as A. Maldonado, p. 29, No es tan bravo el león como lo pintan. Rodriguez-Marin (1930), p. 224, No es el diablo tan feo como lo pintan. Rodriguez-Marin (1926), p. 329, No es el león tan bravo como pintado. Sbarbi, p. 541, No es tan bravo a fieso el león como lo pintan o como la gente lo pinta. Yañez, p. 44, No es el león como lo pintan.

527 (A). No les tengo miedo a los leones contimas a los ratones.

Translation or Interpretation: I am not afraid of lions much less of rats.

Context: You're not afraid of anyone, even if they are bigger than you. (One occurrence. Informant: female).

Sources and Annotations: None.

528 (A). Levantarse de mal tegue.

Translation or Interpretation: To get up on the wrong side of the bed.

Context: My informant told me that she usually tells her family this when they wake up in a very bad mood. (One occurrence. Informant: female).

Sources and Annotations: None.

529 (A). Libro cerrado no saca letrado.

Translation or Interpretation: Closed book doesn't produce an intelligent person. One must read in order to learn.

Context: I was supposed to be studying, but I couldn't. I closed my book, and was just staring out the window. My Spanish teacher walked by my desk and told me the above proverb. (One occurrence. Informant: female).

Sources and Annotations: Aranda, p. 18, same as A. Conde, p. 230, Libro cerrado no hace letrado. Correas, p. 215, same as A. De Barros, p. 250, same as A. MacArthur, p. 67, same as A. Maldonado, p. 59, same as A. Sbarbi, p. 542, Libro cerrado no hace o no saca letrado.

530 (A). Cuando menos piensas salta la liebre.

Translation or Interpretation: When you least expect it, the jackrabbit jumps.

173

Context: An old lady told this to a friend while waiting to see a doctor. (One occurrence. Informant: female).

Sources and Annotations: Adame, p. 24, Donde menos se espera, salta la liebre; p. 30, Donde menos se espera, salta la liebre. Aranda, p. 25, Por donde menos piensa, salta la liebra. Ballesteros, p. 22, same as A. Cobos, p. 34, Donde menos se piensa, salta la liebre. Conde, p. 158, En donde menos se piensa salta la liebre. De Barros, p. 164, De donde no se piensa salta la liebre y andabala a buscar por lo tejados; p. 181, Donde menos se piensa salta la liebre. Espinosa, A., p. 103, Cuando menos piensa, salta la liebre. Jaramillo, p. 377, Donde menos se piensa salta la liebre. Lucero-White, p. 36, Por donde menos se piensa salta la liebre. Maldonado, p. 42, De no pensais, salta la liebre. Rodriguez-Marin (1930), p. 92, Donde menos lo piensa el galgo, da la liebre el salto. Rodriguez-Marin, p. 108, De donde no piensa, salta la liebre; p. 138, Donde menos se piensa, salta la liebre; p. 139, Donde no se piensa, salta -- o se caza -- la liebre.

531 (A). No me gusta la liebre para que sea lijera.

Translation or Interpretation: I don't believe the jackrabbit is fast.

Context: Whenever you think someone is talking or bluffing, but will not actually measure up. (One occurrence. Informant: male).

Sources and Annotations: None.

532 (A). Limosnero y con garrote.

Translation or Interpretation: A beggar and with a stick.

Context: When a person wants a handout, he or she doesn't want just any old thing. They demand the best. (Six occurrences. Informants: three female, three male).

Sources and Annotations: Rubio, p. 292, Limosnero y con garrote.

533 (A). Limosneros no pueden escojer.

Translation or Interpretation: Beggars can't be choosey.

Context: People are to take what is given to them and not be choosey when they ask and receive. (One occurrence. Informant: female).

Sources and Annotations: None.

534 (A).   De límpios y de tragones están llenos los panteones.

Translation or Interpretation: The cemeteries are full of clean-good people - and glutons.

Context: This proverb means that extremely good people, and people who eat too much are mostly the ones who die.   (One occurrence. Informant: male).

Sources and Annotations: Cobos, p. 28, De golosos y tragones están llenos los pantiones. Conde, p. 106, same as A. Jaramillo, p. 375, De baños y de cenas estan la sepulturas llenas. Martinez, p. 91, same as A. Velasco, p. 54, same as A. Yañez. p. 282, De golosos y tragones están llenos los pantiones.

535 (A).   Eres como la linterna, nomás de noche brillas.

Translation or Interpretation: You are like the lantern that sparkles at night only.

Context: Used to describe a person who is very quiet and in-active during the day, at school or at work, but has a lot of energy and is ready to go for excitement at night. (One oc-currence. Informant: male).

Sources and Annotations: None.

536 (A).   Cada loco con su tema.
536 (B).   Cada loco con su tema y cada chango a su mecate.

Translation or Interpretation: Every crazy person with his theme.

Context: Whenever two persons are talking, but each one talks of what interest themselves instead of the other per-son's interest. (Eight occurrences. Informants: seven fe-male, one male).

Sources and Annotations: Adame, p. 16, same as A; p. 17, same as A. Alcala, p. 364, same as A. Armas, p. 409, same as A. Caballero, p. 213, Cada loco con su tema. Campa, p. 63, same as A. Cobos, p. 18, same as A. Conde, p. 69, same as A. Covarrubias, p. 956, same as A. De Barros, p. 125, same as A; p. 125, Cada loco con su tema y cada llaga con su poste-ma. Espinosa, A., p. 103, Cada loco con su tema y yo con mi terqueda. Jaramillo, p. 372, same as A. MacArthur, p. 2, same as A. Peréz, p. 119, same as A. Robe, p. 68, same as A. Sbarbi, p. 555, same as A. Vasquez, p. 88, same as A.

537 (A). Más vale que haya un <u>loco</u> y no dos.
537 (B). Mejor un <u>loco</u> y no dos.
537 (C). Vale más un <u>loco</u>, no dos.
537 (D). Mejor que haya un <u>sonso</u> y no dos.
537 (E). Mejor que haya una <u>loca</u> y no dos.
537 (F). Más vale que haya un <u>loco</u> y no dos.
537 (G). Más vale un <u>loco</u> que dos.

<u>Translation or Interpretation</u>: It's better to have a crazy
person and not two.

<u>Context</u>: When we were kids my brothers picked on me. I
wanted to fight with them but my mother always told me this
so that I would cool down. (10 occurrences. Informants:
seven female, three male).

<u>Sources and Annotations</u>: Adame, p. 7, Más vale que haya un
loco que dos. Galván, p. 128, Es mejor que haya un tonto y
no dos; p. 130, Más vale que haiga un tonto y no dos; p. 134,
Más vale que haiga un tonto y no dos.

538 (A). Me tienen por <u>loco</u> pero no por tonto.

<u>Translation or Interpretation</u>: They have me here because
I'm crazy not dumb.

<u>Context</u>: A wino who gets himself thrown in jail for break-
ing a store window in the presence of a police officer, during a cold winter night. (One occurrence. Informant: female).

<u>Sources and Annotations</u>: None.

539 (A). A los <u>locos</u> se les dá la razón.

<u>Translation or Interpretation</u>: Reason is given to the crazy
ones. Don't waste time with irrational people.

<u>Context</u>: During an interview I encountered a woman who kept
arguing about very insignificant data. I caught on to her
game, and agreed with her, and consequently, acquired the
needed information. (Two occurrences. Informants: female).

<u>Sources and Annotations</u>: Conde, p. 34, A los locos hay que
darles la razon. Rodriguez-Marin, p. 25, A los locos se les
dá la razón.

540 (A). Si los <u>locos</u> usaran coronas todos fuéramos reyes.

<u>Translation or Interpretation</u>: If the crazy people would
wear crown, we all would be kings.

Context: None. (One occurrence. Informant: female).

Sources and Annotations: None.

541 (A). Cuando no hay lomo de todo como.
541 (B). Cuando no hay lomo de todo se come.
541 (C). No habiendo lomo de todo como.
541 (D). Si no hay de lomo de todo como.
541 (E). Cuando no hay carne de lomo de todo como.

Translation or Interpretation: When there's no sirlion I eat anything.

Context: Used when a person is hungry and eats a food that is not what he/she really likes. (Eight occurrences. Informants: six female, one male, one anonymous).

Sources and Annotations: Ballesteros, p. 43, same as A. Caballero, p. 413, same as A. Cerda, p. 292, same as A. Cobos, p. 25, Cuando no hay carne de lomo todo como. Conde, p. 93, same as A. Jaramillo, p. 371, Cuando no hay solomo, de todo como. Rodriguez-Marin (1926), p. 95, Cuando no hay lomo, tocino como; p. 191, En no habiendo lomo, de todo como. Sbarbi, p. 557, Cuando no tengo lomo, de todo como.

542 (A). El lugar de una mujer es en la casa.

Translation or Interpretation: A woman's place is at home.

Context: My husband at first used that proverb because he felt that a woman's place should be her home, but, with the high prices, he changed his mind. (One occurrence. Informant: female).

Sources and Annotations: Conde, p. 215, La mujer en el hogar, su marido a trabajar.

543 (A). Un lugar para cada cosa y cada cosa en su lugar.

Translation or Interpretation: A place for everything and everything in its place.

Context: Like in a meeting, this girl said: "He is from the lowest class and should never try to get out of it because he never will, and that's his place." (One occurrence. Informant: female).

Sources and Annotations: Ballesteros, p. 17, Un lugar para cada cosa, y cada cosa en su lugar. Conde, p. 400, Un lugar para cada cosa, y cada cosa en su lugar. Jaramillo, p. 424, Cada cosa a su debido tiempo; p. 372, Cada cosa a su debido tiempo. Rodriguez-Marin (1926), p. 64, Cada cosa en su lugar, ahorrar tiempo en la buscar.

544 (A). Puede andar entre la lumbre y no se quema.

Translation or Interpretation: One can walk (on) fire and doesn't get burned.

Context: One lady was giving me advice on how to act in row- dy places. She emphasized to always act with respect, and like a lady. Then she quoted the above proverb. (One occur- rence. Informant: female).

Sources and Annotations: Galván, p. 129, La gracia es andar entre las llamas y no quemarse; p. 130, La gracia es andar entre las llamas y no quemarse.

545 (A). No porque la luna es redonda crean que es queso.
545 (B). No porque ves la luna redonda vayas a creer que es queso.
545 (C). No creas que la luna es de queso porque la ves re- donda.

Translation or Interpretation: Not because the moon is round you all will think it's cheese. Don't believe the moon is cheese because it's round.

Context: My informant told me that her father was constantly saying this to her brother because everything came very easy for them. (Three occurrences. Informants: two female, one male).

Sources and Annotations: Arora, p. 261, Era tan tonto que cuando vio la luna reflegada en el agua creyo que era queso. Armas, p. 235, Creer que la luna es queso. Conde, p. 290, No hay que creer que la luna es queso. Espinosa, A., p. 109, Pensó que la luna era queso y se le volvio requeson. Gamiz, p. 86, Creer que la luna es queso. Jaramillo, p. 374, Creer que la luna es pan de queso. Paredes, p. 32, No creas que la luna es queso nomas porque la ves redonda. Pérez, p. 122, La luna no es queso porque se ve redonda. Wesley, p. 214, No creas que la luna es queso porque la ves redonda.

546 (A). El lunes ni las gallinas ponen.

Translation or Interpretation: On Mondays not even the chickens lay.

Context: There was going to be a party on Monday, and she said this proverb because it was rare for a party to be on a Monday. (One occurrence. Informant: female).

Sources and Annotations: Ballesteros, p. 49, En lunes ni las gallinas ponen. Cobos, p. 39, El lunes ni las gallinas ponen. Conde, p. 241, El lunes ni las gallinas ponen. Rubio, p. 172, El lunes ni las gallinas ponen. Velasco, p. 70, El lunes, ni las gallinas ponen.

547 (A). Más vale llegar a tiempo que ser invitado.

Translation or Interpretation: It's better to arrive on time then to be a guest/invited.

Context: When she arrived early at a friend's house she wasn't invited to dinner, and her friend told her this. (One occurrence. Informant: female).

Sources and Annotations: Cobos, p. 80, Más vale llegar a tiempo que ser convidado. Martinez, p. 176, Más vale llegar a tiempo que ser invitado. Velasco, p. 100, Más vale llegar a tiempo que ser convidado.

548 (A). No hay que llegar primero, pero hay que saber llegar.

548 (B). No hay que llegar primero, sino es como saber llegar.

Translation or Interpretation: There's no need to arrive first, but there's a need to know how to arrive.

Context: A friend and I made a bet to get at a destination He took off first and arrived at the destination, but in his attempt, got a traffic ticket. I came in second, but kept my record clean. (Three occurrences. Informants: male).

Sources and Annotations: Adame, p. 56, La gracia no es llegar, si no como llegar.

549 (A). Ya ni llorar es bueno.

Translation or Interpretation: Not even crying is worth it.

Context: A young housewife washed all her husband's clothes. They all came out different colors. She called her mother to ask what she could do. Her mother told her there was nothing to do, and then used the above proverb. (One occurrence. Informant: female).

Sources and Annotations: Ballesteros, p. 37, Ya ni llorar es bueno.

550 (A). Aquí cuando no nos llueve nos llovisna.

Translation or Interpretation: Here, when it doesn't rain it pours.

Context: When something goes wrong, usually something else goes wrong, and even worse. (One occurrence. Informant: female).

Sources and Annotations: Adame, p. 17, Cuando no llueve, llovizna; p. 21, Cuando no llueve, llovizna. Rubio, p. 113, Cuando no llueve, llovizna.

551 (A). Cuando llueve truena.

Translation or Interpretation: When it rains it thunders.

Context: When one bad thing happens a lot of things seem to follow. (One occurrence. Informant: female).

Sources and Annotations: Maldonado, p. 115, Cuando truena, o llueve o quiere llover.

552 (A). No por mucho madrugar amanece más temprano.
552 (B). No por madrugar amanece más temprano.
552 (C). No porque madrugas amanece más temprano.

Translation or Interpretation: Just because you get up earlier doesn't mean the sun will rise earlier.

Context: The proverb could be used to tell someone not to worry about something they have no control over. Just because you are always worrying about something won't make it any better. (24 occurrences. Informants: 15 female, nine male).

Sources and Annotations: Adame, p. 70, same as A; p. 76, same as A. Armas, p. 418, same as A. Ballesteros, p. 13, No por tanto madrugar amanece más temprano. Cobos, p. 93, same as A; p. 101, Por mucho madrugar no amanece más temprano. Conde, p. 294, same as A. Covarrubias, p. 109, Por mucho madrugar no amanece más aina; p. 779, Por mucho madrugar no amanece más aina. De Barros, p. 337, same as A. Espinosa, F., p. 145, Por mucho madrugar no amanece más aina. Glazer, p. 52, same as B. Gamiz, p. 74, same as A. Jaramillo, p. 408, same as A. Maldonado, p. 159, No por mucho madrugar amanece más aina; p. 378, Por mucho madrugar no amanece más temprano. Martinez, p. 202, same as A. Sbarbi, p. 572, No por mucho madrugar amanece más temprano o más aina.

553 (A). No le hace que duerman altas enseñandoles maíz se apean.

Translation or Interpretation: It doesn't matter how high they live/drop a couple ears of corn and they shall all come down.

Context: Some women will give you problems in trying to attract them to you. It just takes a different manner to win
them over. (One occurrence. Informant: male).

Sources and Annotations: Cerda, p. 293, No le haces que duer-
mas altas echandoles maiz se apean. Gamiz, p. 94, No le hacen
que duerman alto, echandoles maiz se apean. Yañez, p. 51, O
como gallinas que duermen alto: con echarles maiz se apean.

554 (A). Mal de muchos, Consuelo de tontos.

Translation or Interpretation: Evil of many, advice from
fools.

Context: Many people who steer you in a certain direction may
not be going anywhere themselves. (Two occurrences. Informants: one female, one male).

Sources and Annotations: Armas, p. 416, Mal de muchos consue-
los de tontos. De Barros, p. 264, Mal de muchos, consuelo de
bobos. Galvan, p. 126, Mal de muchos consuelo de tontos, p.
130, Mal de muchos consuelo de tontos. Gamiz, p. 81, Mal de
muchos consuelo de tontos. Jaramillo, p. 402, Mal de muchos
consuelo de tontos. Martinez, p. 173, Mal de muchos consejo
de pendejos. Sbarbi, p. 576, Mal de muchos, consuelo, o gozo
es. Velasco, p. 99, Mal de muchos consuelo de pendejos.

555 (A). De mal a peor.

Translation or Interpretation: From bad to worse.

Context: Bought a new car, but it always needed to be fixed.
(One occurrence. Informant: female).

Sources and Annotations: Alcalá, p. 471, De mal en peor.
Caballero, p. 474, De mal en peor; p. 697, Ir de mal en peor.
Conde, p. 197, Ir de mal en peor. Espinosa, p. 147, Anda de
mal en peor. Maldonado, p. 42, De mal en peor. Sbarbi, p.
574, De mal en peor.

556 (A). No hay mal que dure cien años ni enfermo que lo
          aguante.
556 (B). No hay mal que dure cien años ni cuerpo que lo
          resista.
556 (C). No hay mal que dure cien años ni cuerpo que lo
          aguante.

Translation or Interpretation: There is no illness that would
last one hundred years nor a patient who could endure it.

Context: This would more than likely be told to someone that is always talking about their illness. (11 occurrences. Informants: eight female, two male, one not stated).

Sources and Annotations: Adame, p. 70, No hay mal que dure cien años ni cuerpo que lo resista; p. 74, No hay mal que dure cien años ni cuerpo que lo resista. Alcala, p. 87, No hay bien ni mal que cien años dure. Aranda, p. 22, No hay mal que dure cien años ni enfermo que lo aguante; p. 22, No hay mal que siempre dure ni bien que nunca acaba. Armas, p. 417, No hay mal que dure cien años, ni enfermo que lo aguante. Ballesteros, p. 12, No hay mal que dure cien años ni enfermo que lo aguante. Cobos, p. 90, No hay mal que cien años dure. Conde, p. 288, No hay mal que dure cien años ni enfermo que lo aguante. Correas, p. 244, No hay mal que cien años dure, ni bien que a ellos llege. De Barros, p. 328, No hay bien ni mal que dure cien años. Espinosa, A., p. 101, No hay dolor que dure cien años ni enfermo que lo aguante; p. 108, No hay mal que dure cien años. Galvan, p. 124, No hay mal que dure cien años; p. 129, No hay mal que dure cien años; p. 130, No hay mal que dure cien años; p. 131, No hay mal que dure cien años ni enfermo que lo aguante. Glazer, p. 53, No hay mal que dure cien años. Jaramillo, p. 408, No hay mal que dure cien años, ni enfermo que los resista. Lucero-White, p. 35, No hay mal que dure cien años ni enfermo que los aguante. MacArthur, p. 42, No hay mal que dure cien años ni cuerpo que lo aguante. Peréz, p. 124, No hay mal que por bien no venga ni enfermedad que dure cien años. Rodriguez-Marin (1926), p. 333, No hay bien ni mal que cien años dure; p. 333, No hay bien que dure años cien; p. 335, No hay mal ni bien que dure años cien; p. 335, No hay mal que cien años dure, ni bien que los conserva; p. 335, No hay mal que dure años ciento, ni bien que se llegue a ellos. Sbarbi, p. 557, No hay mal que dure cien años ni cuerpo que lo resista. Yanez, p. 346, No hay mal que dure cien años, ni buey que lo resista.

557 (A). No hay mal que por bien no venga.
557 (B). No hay mal que por bien no venga ni enfermedad que dure cien años.

Translation or Interpretation: If something bad happens something good will always follow. There is no evil that will not bring good.

Context: Something good comes from every bad thing. (20 occurrences. Informants: 16 female, four male).

Sources and Annotations: Adame, p. 70, No hay mal que por bien no venga. Aranda, p. 22, No hay mal que por bien no venga. Armas, p. 417, No hay mal que por bien no venga. Ballesteros, p. 12, No hay mal que por bien no venga. Caballero, p. 833, No hay mal que por bien no venga. California Spanish Proverbs and Adages, p. 122, same as A. Cobos, p. 90, same as A.

Conde, p. 288, No hay mal que por bien no venga, ni mal que
su bien no tenga. Correas, p. 244, No hay mal que no venga por
bien. Espinosa, A., p. 108, same as A. Espinosa, F., p. 147,
No hay mal que no venga por bien. Galvan, p. 129, No hay mal
que por bien no venga; p. 130, No hay mal que por bien no venga; p. 134, No hay mal que por bien no venga. Gamiz, p. 78,
same as A. Glazer, p. 53, same as A. Jaramillo, p. 407, same
as A. MacArthur, p. 27, No hay mal que bien no traiga; p. 42,
same as A. Perez, p. 124, No hay mal que por bien no venga,
ni enfermedad que dure cien años. Rodriguez-Marin (1926), p.
334, No hay cosa tan mala que para algo no sea buena; p. 336,
same as A. Rubio, p. 33, No hay mal que por mujer no venga.
Sbarbi, p. 557, same as A.

558 (A). Si tu <u>mal</u> tiene remedio para que te apuras y si no
tiene remedio para que te apuras.

<u>Translation or Interpretation</u>: Don't worry if the thing wrong
with you has a cure, if you cannot get a cure, why are you
still worrying.

<u>Context</u>: A particular individual went to a hospital and
quickly came out cured because there was something that
could really save him. (One occurrence. Informant: male).

<u>Sources and Annotations</u>: Adame, p. 86, same as A; p. 89, same
as A. California Spanish Proverbs and Adages, p. 123, same as
A. Cobos, p. 112, Si tu mal tiene remedio, ¿para que te apuras? Conde, p. 379, same as A. Gamiz, p. 88, Si tu mal tiene
remedio, ¿para que te quejas?, y si no tiene, ¿para que te
quejas? Martinez, p. 255, Si tu mal tiene remedio, ¿para que
te apuras? y si no tiene remedio para que lloras?

559 (A). Un <u>mal</u> nunca viene solo.

<u>Translation or Interpretation</u>: One bad thing never comes by
itself.

<u>Context</u>: This means that when something goes wrong it is
probable that other things will go wrong. (One occurrence.
Informant: female).

<u>Sources and Annotations</u>: Armas, p. 410, Cuando un mal viene,
no viene solo. Conde, p. 222, Las desgracias nunca vienen
solas. Correas, p. 178, Un mal no viene solo. De Barros, p.
462, Un mal no viene solo. Espinosa, F., p. 147, Un mal otro
atrae. Rodriguez-Marin (1930), p. 320, Todo mal trae otros
detrás. Rodriguez-Marin (1926), p. 349, Nunca viene una desgracia sola; p. 490, Tras un mal, otro tal; p. 490, Tras un
mal, viene otro mal; p. 494, Una desgracia nunca viene sola;
p. 498, Un mal llama a otro mal; p. 498, Un mal otro trae

detrás. Yáñez, p. 176, Bien dicen que ninguna desgracia viene sola.

560 (A). Cuando andas de _malas_ hasta los perros te mean.

Translation or Interpretation: When you are in a bad mood even the dogs urinate on you.

Context: No actual occasion. She just heard it in conversation. (One occurrence. Informant: female).

Sources and Annotations: Conde, p. 94, Cuando uno anda de malas hasta los perros los mean. Jaramillo, p. 371, Cuando uno está de malas, hasta los perros mean. Martinez, p. 76, Cuando uno esta de malas hasta los perros lo mean. Rubio, p. 116, Cuando uno está de desgracia hasta los perros mean. Santamaria, p. 218, Cuando al pobre le va mal, o cuando a uno le va mal, o está de malas, hasta los perros lo mean.

561 (A). Más vale _malo_ por conocido que bueno por conocer.
561 (B). Más vale el camino conocido que camino para conocer.
561 (C). Más vale viejo conocido que nuevo por conocer.

Translation or Interpretation: If you are familiar with something even if it is bad it's better to stick with it rather than risk something new, even if it's good. Better the evil you know than the good you don't know.

Context: Told to someone who is considering a risk, like a job change or marital status. (22 occurrences. Informants: 14 female, eight male).

Sources and Annotations: Adame, p. 98, Vale más malo por conocido que bueno por conocer; p. 99, Vale más malo por conocido que bueno por conocer. Ballesteros, p. 30, same as A. Benavides, p. 90, same as A. California Spanish Proverbs and Adages, p. 121, Vale más malo por conocido que lo bueno por conocer. Cerda, p. 295, same as A. Cobos, p. 80, Más vale malo conocido que bueno por conocer. Conde, p. 403, same as A. De Barros, p. 277, Más vale lo malo conocido que lo bueno por conocer. Galvan, p. 126, same as A; p. 130, same as A. Glazer, p. 54, same as A. Jaramillo, p. 403, Más vale malo conocido que bueno por conocer. Martinez, p. 177, Más vale malo por conocido que bueno, con quien hablo. Paredes, p. 33, Más vale mal conocido que mejor por conocer. Perez, p. 123, Más vale malo por conocido que bueno por conocer. Rodriguez-Marin (1926), p. 297, same as A; p. 298, Más vale pan malo conocido que bueno por conocer. Rubio, p. 320, same as A. Sbarbi, p. 581, Más vale malo conocido que bueno por conocer. Yañez, p. 115, Es mejor malo conocido que bueno por conocer.

562 (A). Más vale maña que fuerza.

Translation or Interpretation: Craft is better than force.

Context: It is better to do something smoothly and in a good mood, than do it roughly and in a bad mood. (One occurrence. Informant: female).

Sources and Annotations: Armas, p. 416, same as A. Campa, p. 64, Más valen mañas que fuerzas. Cobos, p. 78, Más puede maña que fuerza; p. 80, same as A; p. 120, Vale mas maña que fuerza. Conde, p. 254, same as A. Espinosa, A., p. 111, Vale mas maña que fuerza. Galvan, p. 128, same as A; p. 130, same as A. Gamiz, p. 90, same as A. Maldonado, p. 150, same as A. Perez, p. 124, same as A. Rodriguez-Marin (1926), p. 297, Mas vale maña que fuerza, y más a quien Dios es fuerza. Sbarbi, p. 593, same as A. Yañez, p. 68, same as A.

563 (A). Mañana hay misa para los sordos.

Translation or Interpretation: Tomorrow there will be mass for the deaf.

Context: Used when someone is asked to repeat something because the other person was not listening. (Two occurrences. Informants: one female, one male).

Sources and Annotations: None.

564 (A). Mañana sera otro día.

Translation or Interpretation: Tomorrow will be another day. You don't know what is going to happen next.

Context: Informant told me she used to have a friend who always kept thinking ahead, and she told her this (saying) because she had heard her parents using it. (Three occurrences. Informants: two female, one male).

Sources and Annotations: Ballesteros, p. 30, same as A. Conde, p. 250, same as A. Rodriguez-Marin (1926), p. 288, same as A. Sbarbi, p. 594, same as A. Villafuerte, p. 68, Mañana es otro dia. Yanez, p. 118, same as A.

565 (A). No dejas para mañana lo que puedes hacer hoy.

Translation or Interpretation: Don't leave for tomorrow what you can do today. It means that if you have a choice of something to do, don't leave it for tomorrow what you can do today.

Context: I had a friend who was always saying, "I'll do it tomorrow." One day, she had to go into the hospital and had
left a lot of things pending. I told her this proverb. (37
occurrences. Informants: 22 female, 14 male, one unstated).

Sources and Annotations: Adame, p. 69, same as A; p. 73, same
as A. Aranda, p. 21, same as A. Armas, p. 417, same as A. Ballesteros, p. 32, same as A. Benavides, p. 89, Lo que puedas
hacer hoy, nunca dejes para mañana. Cerda, p. 296, same as A.
Cobos, p. 74, Lo que has de hacer hoy, no dejes para mañana;
p. 75, Lo que puedas hacer hoy, no lo dejes para mañana; p. 87,
same as A; p. 94, Nunca dejes para manana lo que puedes hacer
hoy. Conde, p. 281, same as A. De Barros, p. 255, Lo que has
de hacer hoy, no lo dejes para mañana; p. 322, same as A. Galvan, p. 127, same as A; p. 129, same as A; p. 130, same as A;
p. 131, same as A. Gamiz, p. 90, same as A. Glazer, p. 47,
same as A. Jaramillo, p. 409, same as A. Lucero-White, p. 35,
Lo que se ha de hacer tarde que se haga temprano. MacArthur,
p. 11, same as A. Maldonado, p. 146, Lo que puedes hacer hoy,
no lo dejes para mañana, no. Rodriguez-Marin (1926), p. 328,
No dejes para otra hora lo que puedes hacer ahora.

566 (A).   Es más corta que las mangas de un chaleco.

Translation or Interpretation: She is more shy than the
sleeves on a vest.

Context: A person who is shy will always stay away from social gatherings. (One occurrence. Informant: female).

Sources and Annotations: Arora, p. 270, Más corto que las
mangas de un chaleco.

567 (A).   Al que mete la mano le pica el gusano.
567 (A).   Mariquita no metas la mano porque si la metes te
           pica el gusano.

Translation or Interpretation: He who puts his hand in will
get stung by a worm.

Context: Meaning that if a person sticks his nose into other
people's business he will get what he deserves, or will suffer
the consequences. (Two occurrences. Informants: one female,
one male).

Sources and Annotations: Robe, p. 70, Al que mete la mano
le pica el gusano.

568 (A).   Le das la mano, y te quiere agarrar la pata.

Translation or Interpretation: You give them your hand and
they want your foot too.

Context: An example is when you offer some candy, or a drink,
and they want something else to fit what they have gotten.
(Three occurrences. Informants: two female, one male).

Sources and Annotations: Armas, p. 239, Dar la mano y cogerse
el pié. Cerda, p. 296, same as B. Cobos, p. 72, Le dan la mano y cogen el pie. Conde, p. 227, Le dan la mano y se toma el
pie. Covarrubias, p. 869, Al villano dalde el pie, tomaros a
la mano; p. 966, Al villano dalde el pie, tomaros a la mano.
Galvan, p. 132, Te dan la mano y quieres el pie. Gamiz, p. 82, Se les da la mano
y se cogen el pie. Martinez, p. 249, Se les da la mano y
cogen la pata.

569 (A). Te dan la mano y quieres todo el brazo.
569 (B). Te ofresen la mano y agarras el brazo.

Translation or Interpretation: They give you a helping hand
and you want the whole arm.

Context: On Monday, a student calls you up and asks for a
ride from Weslaco to Edinburg. You agree to give the guy a
helping hand. You take him there. Tuesday, however, the same
guy calls you up and asks you to take him to Edinburg the rest
of the week. (Three occurrences. Informants: two female,
one male).

Sources and Annotations: Arora, p. 273, Esa persona es tan
ventejosa que le dan la mano y se agarra del codo; p. 275,
Le dan la mano y coge el brazo.

570 (A). Manos frías, corazón caliente.
570 (B). Manos calientes, corazón frío.

Translation or Interpretation: Cold hands, warm heart. Just
because you have cold hands doesn't mean you're a bad person.

Context: Some girlfriend he knew shook his hand and told him
the proverb. (Three occurrences. Informants: two female,
one male).

Sources and Annotations: De Barros, p. 268, Manos calientes
y corazón frío, amor perdido.

571 (A). Se tapan con la misma manta.

Translation or Interpretation: They help each one, or they
are the same. (They cover themselves with the same cloth.)

187

Context: Barrio term. (One occurrence. Informant: male).

Sources and Annotations: Armas, p. 389, Taparse con la misma chamarra. Conde, p. 389, Se tapan con la misma cobija.

572 (A). Es un mar de engaños.

Translation or Interpretation: An ocean of illusions.

Context: We were trying to pick up girls and had bad luck -- no girls. My friends said "como dice el dicho--es un mar de engaños." My friends say, "like the saying goes -- it is an ocean of illusions." (One occurrence. Informant: female).

Sources and Annotations: None.

573 (A). Solo que el mar se seque no me bañaré en sus olas.
573 (B). Mientras no se seque el mar, yo me bañaré en sus olas.

Translation or Interpretation: Unless the sea (runs dry) I will not bathe in it.

Context: A friend swore that he would never go out with a particular girl. Today he is seen at her side constantly. (Three occurrences. Informants: male).

Sources and Annotations: Cerda, p. 296, Sólo que el mar se seque no me bañaré en sus olas.

574 (A). La manzana podrida pudre a su compañera.

Translation or Interpretation: The rotten apple will soon spoil the other apples around it. The rotten apple will spoil its companion.

Context: My mother always told us to choose our friends carefully, for if only one friend was bad he might make the rest to be bad also. (One occurrence. Informant: female).

Sources and Annotations: Adame, p. 95, Una manzana podrida, pudre un cajon; p. 96, Una manzana podrida, pudre un cajón. Armas, p. 415, La manzana podrida pudre a las demas. Conde, p. 212, La manzana podrida pudre a la de enseguida; p. 319, Podrida una manzana, corrompe a la cercana; p. 398, Una manzana podrida pudre la enseguida. De Barros, p. 269, La manzana podrida pierde a su companio. Rodriguez-Marin (1930), p. 165,

575 (A). No arrojes margaritas a los cerdos.

Translation or Interpretation: Don't give daisies to the pigs.

Context: Informant first heard this from an elementary teacher who taught her to lower herself to the level of certain people, and try to explain things so that they would understand.
(One occurrence. Informant: female).

Sources and Annotations: De Barros, p. 186, Echar margaritas
a puercos. Jaramillo, p. 386, No arrojes margaritas a los
cerdos. Sbarbi, p. 597, Eso es lo mismo, ovale tanto, como
echar margaritas a puercos.

576 (A). Entre marido y mujer nadie se debe meter.

Translation or Interpretation: No one should interfere between husband and wife.

Context: My informant said that he always says this proverb
to his mother-in-law, who is always trying to make their decisions. (Two occurrences. Informants: male).

Sources and Annotations: Cobos, p. 56, same as A. Conde, p.
167, same as A; p. 293, No medies en la cuestión si marido y
mujer son. Rodriguez-Marin (1926), p. 197, same as A; p. 197,
Entre marido y mujer sólo paz debes poner. Sbarbi, p. 598,
Entre marido y mujer, solo paz debes poner.

577 (A). Eres como mariposa que anda de flor en flor.

Translation or Interpretation: You are like the butterfly
that flies from flower to flower.

Context: Used to describe a person who does not make up his
mind. (One occurrence. Informant: male).

Sources and Annotations: None.

578 (A). Anda ver si puso la marrana.

Translation or Interpretation: Go check the pig. Get lost!
Go see if the pig layed an egg.

Context: A child was trying to listen in to his sister's conversation over the phone when she replied with this proverb.
(One occurrence. Informant: female).

Sources and Annotations: Armas, p. 292, Ir aver si puso huevos la cocha. Martínez, p. 275, Vete a ver si puso la puerca.

579 (A). Está como la <u>marrana</u> de tía Cleta, metiendo oreja.
579 (B). Está como la <u>marrana</u> de tía Cleta, comiendo y poniendo oreja y esperando el cascajo.

Translation or Interpretation: He is like Aunt Cleta's pig, eavesdropping.

Context: When someone is eavesdropping, yet dreading to be found out. (Two occurrences. Informants: female).

Sources and Annotations: Robe, p. 71, Está como la marrana de tía cleta, no más poniendo oreja.

580 (A). Si la <u>marrana</u> te muerde, no le aflojes al mecate.

Translation or Interpretation: If the pig bites you, don't loosen the rope.

Context: It has many meanings, but it means "don't give up when things are at its worse, keep on trying." (One occurrence. Informant: male).

Sources and Annotations: Yáñez, p. 279, Aunque te chille el cochino, nole aflojes el mecate.

581 (A). El <u>marrano</u> más trompudo se lleva la mejor mazorca.

Translation or Interpretation: The ugliest pig will get the best husk. The pig with the biggest snout will get the best husk.

Context: There is an ugly family in Weslaco called "the monsters." Their last name is Garza. All of the boys managed to marry a pretty girl. My father used this proverb to describe their situation.

Sources and Annotations: Ballesteros, p. 60, El marrano más trompudo se llena la mejor mazorka. Cerda, p. 297, Al marrano más trompudo, le toca la mejor mazorca. Cobos, p. 12, El marrano más trompudo le toca a la mejor mazorca. Glazer, p. 54, La marrana más trompuda se lleva la mejor masorca.

582 (A). El <u>martes</u> no te cases ni te embarques.
582 (B). El <u>martes</u> no te cases ni te embarques, ni de tu casa te apartes.

Translation or Interpretation: Don't get married or begin a trip on a Tuesday.

Context: My mother told me this when I told her I was going on a trip to San Antonio the following Tuesday. (10 occurrences.   Informants: five female, five male).

Sources and Annotations: Adame, p. 34, En martes ni cases ni
te embarques; p. 48, En martes ni cases ni te embarques. Ballesteros, p. 49, El martes trece no te cases, ni te embarques. Cobos, p. 31, Dia martes, ni te cases ni te embarques;
p. 39, El martes, ni te cases ni te embarques; p. 55, En martes, ni te cases ni te embarques. Conde, p. 164, same as A.
Correas, p. 135, En martes, ni tu casa mudes, ni tu hija cases,
ni tu ropa cortes; En martes, ni tu tela hurdes ni tu hija
cases. De Barros, p. 200, En martes, ni te cases, ni te embarques. Espinosa, A., p. 100, El martes- ni te cases ni te embarques. Espinosa, F., p. 153, En martes, ni tela urdas ni
hija cases. Galvan, p. 125, same as A; p. 127, same as A.
Gamiz, p. 88, En martes, ni te cases ni te embarques. Jaramillo, p. 403, Martes, ni te cases ni te embarques ni te es-
treves alpargates. Perez, p. 121, En martes ni te cases ni te
embarques. Rodriguez-Marin (1930), p. 128, En martes, ni gallinas eches, ni hija cases. Rodriguez-Marin (1926), p. 190,
En martes, ni te cases ni te embarques. Rubio, p. 219, En
martes ni te cases ni te embarques ni de tu casa te apartes.

583 (A).   Marzo ventoso y abril lluvioso, nacen en mayo, florido y hermoso.

Translation or Interpretation: Windy March, April showers
make May bloom pretty with flowers.

Context: It happens every spring. (One occurrence. Informant: female).

Sources and Annotations: De Barros, p. 270, Marzo ventoso y
abril lluvioso sacan a mayo florido y hermoso. Sbarbi, p. 605,
Marzo ventoso y abril lluvioso nacen en mayo, florido y hermoso. Maldonado, p. 58, Marzo ventoso y abril lluvioso hacen
el mayo hermoso.

584 (A).   Si me han de matar mañana que me maten de una vez.

Translation or Interpretation: If I am to be killed tomorrow,
kill me at once, right now.

Context: This is an old proverb. It is also a Mexican revo-
lutionary song, La Valentina. Usually said among the tough
men in Mexico, men who are not afraid of death. This is said
because we, the Mexican people, know that life has to come to
an end, so why wait to be killed tomorrow. (One occurrence.
Informant: male).

Sources and Annotations: Conde, p. 374, Si me han de matar
mañana que me maten de una vez. Rubio, p. 167, Si me han de
matar mañana que me maten de una vez.

585 (A). Matrimonio y mortaja del cielo baja.

Translation or Interpretation: Marriage and death come from above.

Context: When a person is past the average age for marriage and is not yet married, it's God's will. Or when a person is involved in a situation where normally he/she would die, but lived, it is God's will. (One occurrence. Informant: male).

Sources and Annotations: Adame, p. 66, same as A; p. 67, same as A. Armas, p. 409, Casamiento y mortaja, del cielo baja. Cobos, p. 82, same as A. Conde, p. 75, Casamiento y mortaja del cielo baja. Jaramillo, p. 403, same as A. Martinez, p. 274, Velo y mortaja del cielo baja. Rodriguez-Marin (1926), p. 71, Casamiento y mortaja del cielo baja. Sbarbi, p. 608, same as A. Yañez, p. 58, Alli quedé convencido de que velo y mortaja del cielo baja.

586 (A). La mentira dura mientras la verdad llega.

Translation or Interpretation: The lie lasts while the truth arrives.

Context: This was told to me several times by my mother, while growing up. Like every other little kid, when I did something wrong or went somewhere I wasn't supposed to, I would lie to my mother. That way I wouldn't get in trouble. But, like every other mother, she would find out sooner or later. I would, most of the time, get a spanking, and it wasn't so much for what I did, it was for lying, and my mother would tell me "la mentira dura mientras la verdad llega." (Eight occurrences. Informants: two female, six male).

Sources and Annotations: Adame, p. 56, same as A; p. 59, same as A. Armas, p. 415, La mentira luce mientras la verdad no llega. Ballesteros, p. 8, La mentira dura mientras la verdad llege. Benavides, p. 91, La mentira dura mientras llega la verdad. Cobos, p. 35, Dura la mentira mientras la verdad llega; p. 68, La mentira dura mientras la verdad llega. Conde, p. 213, La mentira dura hasta que la verdad llega. Galvan, p. 129, same as A; p. 134, same as A. Rubio, p. 279, La mentira dura mientras la verdad aparece. Sbarbi, p. 618, Tanto la mentira es mejor cuanto mas parece la verdadera. Vasquez, p. 90, La mentira dura mientras que la verdad llega.

587 (A). Al mentiroso cuando dice la verdad no le dan autoridad.

Translation or Interpretation: A person who lies, when he tells the truth, no one will believe him.

192

Context: Five years ago, when my little brother was eleven years old, he was one of the worst liars there could ever be. He always lied about everything. Only one time he really told the truth and he was so hurt because no one would believe him. (One occurrence. Informant: female).

Sources and Annotations: Correas, p. 103, El que por mentiroso es tenido, aunque diga verdad no es creido. De Barros, p. 65, same as A; p. 187, El que en mentira es cogida, cuando dice verdad no es creido. Maldonado, p. 126, El que en mentira es cogido, cuando dice verdad no es creido. Sbarbi, p. 619, El mentiroso no es creido cuando dice verdad.

588 (A). El miedo no anda en burro.
588 (B). Miedo no anda en burro.

Translation or Interpretation: Fear does not exist in a donkey.

Context: People are scared, they are capable of being frightened. (Two occurrences. Informants: male).

Sources and Annotations: Cobos, p. 39, same as A. Conde, p. 137, same as A. Martinez, p. 108, same as A. Rubio, p. 175, same as A. Santamaria, p. 279, same as A. Velasco, p. 63, same as A.

589 (A). Por miedo de las urracas no levantamos pero tenemos que sembrar.

Translation or Interpretation: Because of the fear of crows (we do not reap), but we still have to plant.

Context: We are expanding our house, and we wanted a larger living room and kitchen. When we asked the carpenter how much it would cost, he told us the price -- a lot of money. Then he used this saying. (One occurrence. Informant: male).

Sources and Annotations: Sbarbi, p. 625, Por miedo de goriones no se deja de sembrar cañamones.

590 (A). Nomás mira y calla.

Translation or Interpretation: Just look and don't talk.

Context: When you are listening to someone talk in a bad way and your mother does not want you to get involved in the conversation. She will tell you "nomas mira y calla." (One occurrence. Informant: female).

Sources and Annotations: Benavides, p. 91, Mira y calla.

591 (A). En todo está menos en <u>misa</u>.

<u>Translation or Interpretation</u>: He is in everything except in mass.

<u>Context</u>: When a person gets into your own personal business which is not his business. (Four occurrences. Informants: two female, one male, one not stated).

<u>Sources and Annotations</u>: Conde, p. 166, En todo esta menos en misa. Robe, p. 69, Estar en todo menos en misa. Vasquez, p. 90, En todo esta menos en misa.

592 (A). Aunque la <u>mona</u> se vista de seda, <u>mona</u> se queda.

<u>Translation or Interpretation</u>: Even if a monkey dresses in silk a monkey it remains.

<u>Context</u>: A change of clothing does not change one's personality or character. (14 occurrences. Informants: ten female, three male, one not stated).

<u>Sources and Annotations</u>: Adame, p. 9, same as A; p. 14, same as A. Aranda, p. 3, same as A. Armas, p. 409, same as A. Ballesteros, p. 51, La mona aunque se vista de seda, mona se queda. Caballero, p. 170, same as A. Cobos, p. 68, same as A. Conde, p. 55, same as A. Correas, p. 33, same as A; p. 202, La mona, aunque la vistan de seda, mona se queda. De Barros, p. 288, La mona, aunque la vistan de seda, mona se queda. Espinosa, A., p. 102, La mona aunque se vista de seda, mona se queda. Galvan, p. 125, same as A; p. 131, same as A. Gamiz, p. 76, same as A. Glazer, p. 54, same as A. Jaramillo, p. 365, same as A. Lucero-White, p. 33, same as A. MacArthur, p. 34, Aunque la mona de seda se viste, mona se queda. Maldonado, p. 90, same as A. Sbarbi, p. 635, same as A.

593 (A). No es <u>monedita</u> de oro para caerle bien a todos.
593 (B). No somos <u>monedas</u> de oro para gustarle a todos.
593 (C). No soy <u>monedita</u> de oro para caerle bien a todos.

<u>Translation or Interpretation</u>: He isn't a gold coin to be liked by everyone. He isn't perfect to be liked by everyone.

<u>Context</u>: Used when father was criticizing her boyfriend. (Three occurrences. Informants: two female, one male).

<u>Sources and Annotations</u>: Arora, p. 290, No soy monedita de oro para caerle bien a todos. Conde, p. 297, No soy monedita de oro para caerle bien a todos.

594 (A). Calmantes montes, pajarillos cantantes.

Translation or Interpretation: Calm forests, happy birds.

Context: Mr. A. recalls hearing this proverb when he was
about seven or eight years old. He states that his mother
would tell him this proverb whenever he became anxious, or upset, about something. It seems that if one tries to remain
calm during bad situations he will lead a happier and health-
ier life. He remembers this proverb used among the older
generation of that time. I believe that the proverb is most
meaningful. Many times we get too excited over certain situations, and thus, making yourself miserable. I, too, feel
people should try keeping their cool in handling problems.
(One occurrence. Informant: male).

Sources and Annotations: Cerda, p. 300, ¡Calmantes montes,
pájaros cantantes, pichicuates pintos! Conde, p. 72, Calmantes
montes, pintos pajaros cantantes. Martinez, p. 55, Calmantes
montes, alicantes pintos pajaros cantantes y elefantes vola-
dores. Velasco, p. 31, Calmantes montes, Pajaros Cantantes,
Alicantes Pintos.

595 (A). Si has de morir orcado no has de morir de un balazo

Translation or Interpretation: If you are to die by hanging
you will not die of a bullet wound.

Context: A person's destiny determines what will happen and
how it will happen. (One occurrence. Informant: female).

Sources and Annotations: Yáñez, p. 229, El que nacio para
ahorcado, no morirá de a hogado.

596 (A). Como moscas a la miel.
596 (B). Como moscas a la cagada.

Translation or Interpretation: Like flies to honey.

Context: I heard this proverb while passing by the crowded
parking lot of a food stamp office. My father angrily commented "como moscas a la miel." (Three occurrences. Informants: one female, one male, one unstated).

Sources and Annotations: Armas, p. 228, Caer como moscas.
Arora, p. 295, Acudían como moscas a la miel. Caballero, p.
350, Como las moscas a la miel; p. 359, Como moscas a la miel;
p. 924, Presas como moscas a la miel. Covarrubias, p. 804,
Acudir como moscas a la miel. Perez, p. 119, same as A.

597 (A). Hacerse la <u>mosca</u> muerta.

<u>Translation or Interpretation</u>: To become a dead fly. To act very naive or dumb. Pretend to be a dead fly.

<u>Context</u>: Informant's grandmother told this to informant's sister. The sister had come in very late the night before, and when the grandmother asked her if she had heard the cats prowling the sister said she had fallen asleep very early and hadn't heard a thing. The grandmother told her "no te hagas la mosca muerta," and gave her a good scolding. (One occurrence. Informant: female).

<u>Sources and Annotations</u>: Armas, p. 142, Ser una mosca muerta; p. 383, Ser una mosca muerta. Arora, p. 295, Se hace la mosca muerta. Caballero, p. 798, Mosca muerta; p. 1015, Ser una mosquita muerta. Conde, p. 314, Pararse por mosquita muerta, tan solo por ser discreta. Espinosa, F., p. 163, Parece mosca muerta. Santamaria, p. 303, Hacer uno la mosquita muerta. Sbarbi, p. 643, Parece una mosca muerta.

598 (A). No me saques sin <u>motivo</u> ni me guardes sin honor.

<u>Translation or Interpretation</u>: A soldier must never take out his resolve unless he has to defend himself. Don't take me out without reason nor put me away without honor.

<u>Context</u>: My husband used to say that Pancho Villa said this famous quotation to his soldiers. (One occurrence. Informant: female).

<u>Sources and Annotations</u>: Rodriguez-Marin (1926), p. 341, No me saques sin razón, ni me envaines sin honor.

599 (A). Al que le duela la <u>muela</u> que se la saque.

<u>Translation or Interpretation</u>: He whose molar hurts, take it out. Help yourself because it is unlikely that anyone else will.

<u>Context</u>: It's up to you to solve your own problems. (Three occurrences. Informants: one female, one male, one not stated).

<u>Sources and Annotations</u>: Aranda, p. 2, same as A. Cobos, p. 12, same as A. Conde, p. 49, Al que le duela la muela que la saque o se amuele. Covarrubias, p. 810, A quien le duele la muela que se la saque. Espinosa, F., p. 164, same as A. Galvan, p. 127, same as A; p. 131, same as A; p. 133, same as A. Lea, p. 233, same as A. Lucero-White, p. 33, same as A. Maldonado, p. 88, A quien duele la muela, que le eche fuera o que se la saque. Perez, p. 119, same as A. Rodriguez-Marin (1930), p. 30, A quien le duele la muela, echela fuera. Rod-

riguez-Marín (1926), p. 41, same as A.   Sbarbi, p. 650, same
as A.

600 (A).   Muerte deseada, vida sabrada.

Translation or Interpretation: Death desired, life meaning-
less.

Context: None given.   (One occurrence.   Informant: female).

Sources and Annotations: Cobos, p. 84, Muerte deseada, vida
durada. Rodríguez-Marín (1930), p. 272, Quien desea bien morir, procure bien vivir; p. 274, Quien espera la muerte de
oro, le alarga la vida; p. 310, Si quieres que viva larga
mente, deseame la muerte.

601 (A).   De la muerte no se escapa.

Translation or Interpretation: You cannot escape death.   No
matter how many problems you try to run from death will always find you.   Don't run away from your problems.

Context: Usually said to a person who is trying to run away
from his'her problems. Meant as a realization that you should
face your problems, instead of running from them because sooner or later, as with death, it catches up with you.   (One occurrence.   Informant: female).

Sources and Annotations: Cobos, p. 28, De la muerte y de la
suerte no hay quien se escape. Espinosa, A., p. 104, De la
suerte y de la muerte nadien se escapa. Lucero-White, p. 33,
De la suerte y de la muerte no hay quien se escape. Robe, p.
64, same as A. Rubio, p. 138, De la suerte y de la muerte no
hay quien escape. Yanez, p. 273, De la suerte y de la muerte
no escapa el debil ni el fuerte; p. 286, De la suerte y de la
muerte no escapa el debil ni el fuerte; p. 287, No escapa el
debil ni el fuerte...de la suerte y de la muerte no escapa.

602 (A).   Donde lloran alli esta la muerte.

Translation or Interpretation: A penny pincher, or money nag-
ger, is usually very wealthy.   Death is where there is crying.

Context: My mom says an old woman complained about a cent at
a grocery store, then jumped into a brand new Cadillac and
drove off. My mom felt the proverb was appropriate to describe this situation.   (One occurrence.   Informant: female).

Sources and Annotations: Adame, p. 24, Donde se llora esta el
muerto. Armas, p. 411, same as A. Ballesteros, p. 45, Donde

lloran está el muerto. Cobos, p. 34, Donde lloran está el muerto. Espinosa, A., p. 105, El llanto sobre el difunto. Gamiz, p. 75, Donde lloran esta el muerto. Martinez, p. 97, Donde lloran esta el muerto. Rubio, p. 152, Donde se llora está el muerto. Velasco, p. 58, Donde lloran está el muerto.

603 (A). Estás bueno para traer la <u>muerte</u>.

Translation or Interpretation: You're good for bringing death. The translation sounds funny, but when the proverb is used people usually mean that one takes too long to produce something at someone's request.

Context: My dad used to say that when we took too long to bring something to him. (One occurrence. Informant: female).

Sources and Annotations: None.

604 (A). Para la <u>muerte</u> no hay achaque.
604 (B). <u>Muerte</u> no vengas que achaques no faltan.
604 (C). Achaque quiere la <u>muerte</u> para llevarse el enfermo.

Translation or Interpretation: For death there are no excuses. Death don't come because excuses aren't scarce. Death wants an excuse to take the sick.

Context: I was told these proverbs by several people. All three say about the same thing, only in different words. I had never heard these proverb until I started asking for help for this class. I'm sure it was originally one proverb and like things usually go one person said it to someone and that person said it to someone else and probably changed the words to it, either purposefully or just simply because he forgot the words and said it the best he could. (One occurrence. Informant: female).

Sources and Annotations: Aranda, p. 20, Muerte que venga que achaque no tenga. Cobos, p. 9, Achaques quiere la muerte; p. 84, Muerte no venga que achaque no tenga. Espinosa, A., p. 101, Muerte no vengas- que achaque no tengas. Lea, p. 233, Achaque quiere la muerte para llevarse a los morales. Lucero-White, p. 33, Achaque quiere la muerte para llevarse a los morales. Rodriguez-Marin (1926), p. 6, Achaques quiere la muerte; p. 15, A la muerte nunca le falta un achaque.

605 (A). El <u>muerto</u> al hoyo y el vivo al bolo.

Translation or Interpretation: The dead to the hole and the live keep on rowing. The dead to the grave or the show must go on.

Context: My grandmother told me that when people die they must go down to their hole, and those living should keep on having fun. She always tells us that the day she dies she wants for us keep on being happy, because we are still alive and she already had her fun. (One occurrence. Informant: female).

Sources and Annotations: Armas, p. 412, same as A. Caballero, p. 539, same as A. Cobos, p. 39, same as A. Covarrubias, p. 667, El muerto a la quesa y el vivo a la mesa. De Barros, p. 279, El muerto a la huesa y el vivo a la mesa; same as A. Gamiz, p. 77, El muerto a la sepultura y los vivos a la diablura. Jaramillo, p. 380, El muerto al hoyo el vivo a la olla. Robe, p. 68, El muerto al hoyo y el vivo al pollo. Rodriguez-Marin (1926), p. 164, same as A. Santamaria, p. 313, El muerto al hoyo y el vivo a la olla. Sbarbi, p. 653, same as A.

606 (A). El muerto al poso y el vivo al negocio.

Translation or Interpretation: The dead to the grave and the live to his business.

Context: Forget what is past and begin anew. (29 occurrences. Informants: 19 female, seven male, three not stated).

Sources and Annotations: Ballesteros, p. 46, same as A. Cerda, p. 300, same as A. Cobos, p. 39, same as A. Conde, p. 138, El muerto al poso y el vivo al gozo. Espinosa, A., p. 100, same as A. Galván, p. 127, same as A; p. 133, same as A. Glazer, p. 55, same as A. Pérez, p. 123, Los muertos al pozo y los vivos al negocio.

607 (A). El muerto y el arrimado a los tres días apesta.

Translation or Interpretation: The dead and a visitor stink after the third day.

Context: My informant's aunt had had company for about ten days and the aunt told her this proverb. (15 occurrences. Informants: 12 female, two male, one not stated).

Sources and Annotations: Adame, p. 31, same as A; p. 37, same as A. Arora, p. 362, Los huespedes son como los pescados, que a los tres días hieden. Ballesteros, p. 46, same as A. Cobos, p. 40, El pescado y el arrimado a los tres días apestan. Conde, p. 138, same as A. Espinosa, A., p. 106, same as A. Martínez, p. 108, same as A. Rubio, p. 176, same as A. Santamaria, p. 142, El arrimado y el muerto a los tres dias apestan. Velasco, p. 64, same as A. Yáñez, p. 106, same as A.

608 (A). Váyase el muerto a la sepultura y el vivo a la hogaza.

Translation or Interpretation: Let the dead proceed to the burial ground and the living return to their homes.

Context: I usually hear this when people go to the cemetery and the relatives of the dead still cry a lot. (One occurrence. Informant: female).

Sources and Annotations: Cobos, p. 39, El muerto a la sepultura y vivo a la travesura. Conde, p. 138, El muerto a la sepultura y el vivo a la compostura. Covarrubias, p. 693, El muerto a la cava y el vivo a la hogaza. De Barrios, p. 297, El muerto al hoyo y el vivo al bollo. Gamiz, p. 77, El muerto al hoyo y el vivo al bollo. Maldonado, p. 55, El muerto a la fosada y el vivo a la hogaza. Martinez, p. 108, El muerto a la sepultura y el vivo a la travesura. Rodriguez-Marin (1926), p. 24, Al muerto, al mortaja; a vivo, la hogaza; p. 164, El muerto a la cava; y el vivo a la hogaza. Rubio, p. 175, El muerto a la sepultura y el vivo a la travesura. Sbarbi, p. 653, same as A. Yanez, p. 54, El muerto a la sepultura y el vivo a la travesura; p. 323, El muerto a la sepultura y el vivo a la travesura.

609 (A). Lo bueno es andar entre la mugre y no mancharse.

Translation or Interpretation: The good in being within the bad is not letting ourselves become bad. The good of being among the garbage is not getting dirty.

Context: This proverb was heard by my informant when he was about ten years old. He does not remember who he heard it from, but he is sure that it could have been one of its relatives. My informant said it meant that a person can hang around with bad people and yet be different from them. (One occurrence. Informant: male).

Sources and Annotations: None.

610 (A). Mujer fea, tropa armada.

Translation or Interpretation: Ugly woman, armored troop.

Context: Informant says that in this case an ugly woman has nothing to fear. She is not in danger of having men grab her or make passes at her. Her ugliness is her own armor. (Two occurrences. Informants: one female, one male).

Sources and Annotations: None.

611 (A). A la mujer ni todo el amor ni todo el dinero.

Translation or Interpretation: To women, not all the love (nor) all the money.

Context: R. says that a woman will get spoiled if you give her all your love and all your money. (Two occurrences. Informants: male).

Sources and Annotations: Aranda, p. 1, A la mujer ni todo el amor ni todo el dinero. Ballesteros, p. 42, A la mujer ni todo el amor ni todo el dinero. Cobos, p. 11, A la mujer ni todo el amor ni todo el dinero. Martinez, p. 24, A las mujeres ni todo el amor ni todo el dinero. Velasco, p. 15, A las mujeres ni todo el amor ni todo el dinero.

612 (A). Una mujer hermosa es muy peligrosa.

Translation or Interpretation: A beautiful woman is very dangerous. You can't keep a beautiful woman for a long time.

Context: I had a friend who liked this very pretty girl. She went out with him twice and that was it. We had told him that she wasn't his type, because it seemed as if she was only going out with him to make her ex-boyfriend jealous. (One occurrence. Informant: female).

Sources and Annotations: Aranda, p. 20, Mujer hermosa es muy peligrosa. Conde, p. 215, La mujer hermosa, si es noble, no es peligrosa. Rodriguez-Marin (1930), p. 213, Mujer hermosa, mujer peligrosa. Rodriguez-Marin, p. 306, Mientras es la mujer mas hermosa, es mas peligrosa.

613 (A). Una buena mujer, una buena mula y una buena cabra
          son tres malas bestias.

Translation or Interpretation: A good woman, a good mule, and a good goat make three bad beasts.

Context: My grandfather told me never to trust or give full freedom to a girl because you never know what they can do. (Two occurrences. Informants: male).

Sources and Annotations: Rodriguez-Marin (1930), p. 327, Unas mujeres son bobas, otras alocas, y ambas cosas las demás. Rodriguez-Marin (1926), p. 60, Buena mula, buena cabra y buena hembra, tres malas bestias.

614 (A). Bueno, le dijo la mula al freno, si hay agua y sa-
          cate todo esta bueno.

Translation or Interpretation: "All right," said the mule to the bit, "as long as there is water and feed everything is all right."

Context: This proverb is a symbol of a mule as a complaisant animal. Ironically, there are people who react much like the

mule. Their only concern is similar to that of the mule.
Their only concern is that they have food and water. All other things, such as condition, etc., are all secondary. (Two
occurrences. Informants: one female, one male).

Sources and Annotations: Conde, p. 64, Bueno le dijo la mula
al freno. Villafuerte, p. 124, Bueno el digo la mula al freno.

615 (A). La mula no era arisca, la hicieron.
615 (B). La burra no era bronca pero la hicieron.
615 (C). La mula no era bronca, la hicieron.

Translation or Interpretation: The mule wasn't wild, it was
made.

Context: This may refer to a person whose life seems too difficult, but it is all the experiences that the person may collect. Informant heard it from another person. The person
said it because it sort of fitted her. She had had a few bad
experiences and this made her feel that her life kept hitting
on her. (Five occurrences. Informants: three female, one
male, one not stated).

Sources and Annotations: Adame, p. 56, same as C; p. 59, same
as C. Ballesteros, p. 62, La mula no era arisca, los palos la
hicieron. Cerda, p. 301, La mula no era arisca, pero los palos la hicieron. Cobos, p. 65, La burra no era arisca, los
palos la hicieron. Conde, p. 205, La burra no era arisca, la
hicieron. Gamiz, p. 88, La burra no era mañosa, la hicieron.
Martinez, p. 151, La burra no era arisca, a palos la hicieron.
Velasco, p. 90, La burra no era arisca, los palos la hicieron.
Yanez, p. 35, La burra no era arisca, la hicieron.

616 (A). Huye de la multitud y tendras quietud.

Translation or Interpretation: Get away from the crowd and
you will have peace of mind.

Context: J. was constantly partying with his friends and
didn't have peace of mind. One day he stayed home and medi-
tated and obtained the tranquility he needed. (One occurrence. Informant: female).

Sources and Annotations: Rodriguez-Marin (1930), p. 153,
Huye de la multitud, si quieres tener quietud. Rodriguez-
Marin, p. 251, La multitud causa inquietud.

617 (A). Deja que el mundo ruede.

Translation or Interpretation: Let the world go in a circle.
This means you should mind your own business and let everyone
else mind theirs.

Context: Whenever I say something, especially criticizing someone else, my daddy uses this proverb. (One occurrence. Informant: male).

Sources and Annotations: Correas, p. 33, Aunque se hunda el mundo. Maldonado, p. 90, Aunque se hunda el mundo.

618 (A). Todo el mundo sonríe en el mismo idioma.

Translation or Interpretation: Everyone in the world (smiles) in the same language

Context: Our aunt tells us the above proverb when we visit her in Mexico City. When one of us was angry for something, she told us that we should give her an American smile and a Mexican smile, also. We didn't know what she meant and told us the above proverb. (Three occurrences. Informants: two female, one male).

Sources and Annotations: None.

619 (A). Vine al mundo por loco, mas no por pendejo.

Translation or Interpretation: When someone wants to trick you or make a fool out of you. I came into this world because I was crazy not stupid.

Context: A man was trying to sell me a car and he was saying what the car had, that it was really nice and neat. The interior was pathetic, so I told him this saying. The car was a disaster. (One occurrence. Informant: male).

Sources and Annotations: None.

620 (A). Música pagada hace mal sonido.

Translation or Interpretation: Music paid in advance sounds wrong.

Context: A worker that is paid in advance does not work as hard. (Seven occurrences. Informants: five female, two male).

Sources and Annotations: Adame, p. 66, Músico pagado hace mal son; p. 68, Musico pagado hace mal son. Aranda, p. 20, Músico pagado, mal trabajo. Ballesteros, p. 31, Música pagada no hace buen son. Caballero, p. 540, El musico pagado hace mal son; p. 802, Músico pagado hace mal son. Cerda, p. 301, Música pagada tiene mal son. Cobos, p. 84, same as A. Conde, p. 269, Música pagada, toca mal son. Jaramillo, p. 404, Música pagada por adelantado no suena. Martinez, p. 186, Músico

pagado toca mal son. Robe, p. 67, Música pagada toca mal son.
Rubio, p. 337, Música pagada hace mal son.

621 (A). Trae la música por dentro.
621 (B). Las muchachas calladitas tienen la música por dentro.

Translation or Interpretation: Carries the music inside.

Context: Someone who you thought you already knew is totally
a different person. You find out that someone you thought
was quiet and trustworthy is the opposite when it is to that
person's benefit. (Two occurrences. Informants: one female,
one male).

Sources and Annotations: Cerda, p. 302, Tener la musica en-
cerrada (por dentro). Gamiz, p. 87, Tener la musica por dentro. Santamaria, p. 318, Tener no la musica por dentro.

622 (A). Cuando el músico es malo, le hecha la culpa a las
cuerdas.

Translation or Interpretation: If the musician is bad, he
will usually blame it on the instrument.

Context: Mr. G. said that there is a lot of truth behind this
meaning. He learned it in Monterrey, Nuevo Leon, from his
friends at about the age of twelve. People in general will
always tend to blame others for their mistakes. This dicho
was told to Mr. G. after a band rehearsal, while joking a-
round with his friends. (One occurrence. Informant: male).

Sources and Annotations: Rubio, p. 36, Al mal músico hasta
las uñas le estoban.

623 (A). Haciendo y haciendo y nada se hizo.

Translation or Interpretation: Doing and doing and nothing
is done.

Context: When a person always says we are going to do this
and that and they end up doing nothing. (One occurrence.
Informant: female).

Sources and Annotations: None.

624 (A). Peor es nada.

Translation or Interpretation: Nothing is worse.

Context: When a person is able to salvage only a few belong-ings during a catastrophe. (Two occurrences. Informants: one female, one not stated).

Sources and Annotations: Ballesteros, p. 34, same as A. Ca-ballero, p. 895, same as A. Jaramillo, p. 361, Algo es algo y peor es nada. Santamaria, p. 81, Algo es algo, peor es nada.

625 (A). Que no hay nada oculto que no se descubra.

Translation or Interpretation: That there is nothing hidden that will not be discovered.

Context: The truth has to come out sooner or later. A daugh-ter lied to her parents about visiting a forbidden place, but her mother's friend saw her. (One occurrence. Informant: female).

Sources and Annotations: Conde, p. 287, No hay cosa oculta que no se descubra.

626 (A). Nadie muere sin pagar lo que debe.
626 (B). Nadie nos vamos de este mundo sin pagar lo que de-bemos.
626 (C). De este mundo nadie se va sin pagar las que debe.

Translation or Interpretation: Nobody dies without paying what they owe. Before anyone dies, if there is an outstanding debt, it will be paid somehow.

Context: From the way I have heard it, it can be flexed to even mean that the death of a person is seen as payment for his debt. (Three occurrences. Informants: female).

Sources and Annotations: Ballesteros, p. 11, Nadie se va de este mundo sin pagar las que debe.

627 (A). Nadie sabe el bien que tiene hasta que lo ha perdido.

Translation or Interpretation: No one values his goods until he loses them.

Context: When someone complains about something a lot and later misses it when they no longer have it. (Three occur-rences. Informants: female).

Sources and Annotations: Adame, p. 69, Nadie sabe el bien que pierde, hasta que no lo ve perdido; p. 71, Nadie sabe el bien que pierde, hasta que no lo ve perdido. Ballesteros, p. 32, Nadie sabe lo que tiene hasta que lo pierde. Benavides, p. 90, same as A. Cobos, p. 36, El bien no es conocido hasta que

205

es perdido; p. 85, same as A. Correas, p. 97, El bien es no
conocido hasta que es perdido. Covarrubias, p. 349, El bien no
es conocido, hasta que es ido. Espinosa, F., p. 57, El bien
nunca es conocido hasta que es perdido. Gamiz, p. 76, Nadie
sabe el bien que pierde hasta que lo ve perdido. Lucero-White,
p. 35, No se conoce el bien hasta que no se pierde. Martinez,
p. 188, same as A. Perez, p. 124, same as A. Rodriguez-Marin
(1930), p. 234, No sabe lo que se pierde quien no bebe con lo
verde. Rodriguez-Marin (1926), p. 147, El bien perdido, en-
tonces conocido. Rubio, p. 4, Nadie sabe el bien que tiene
hasta que lo ve perdido.

628 (A). Nadie sabe lo que está en la olla nadamás el que
          la manea.
628 (B). Nadie sabe lo que hay en la olla nadamás la cuchara
          que la manea.
628 (C). Nadie sabe lo que caldea nadamás el que la manea.

Translation or Interpretation: No one knows what's in the pot
only the one who stirs it.

Context: When a person is in a crisis or trouble only the one
in trouble can really appreciate the predicament at the time.
(Nine occurrences. Informant: six female, three male).

Sources and Annotations: Aranda, p. 21, Nadie sabe lo que
trae en el saco mas que el que lo carga. Ballesteros, p. 53,
Nadie sabe lo que contiene la olla, nomas la cuchara. Cobos,
p. 85, Nadie sabe lo que hay en l'olla como el meneador que
la menea. Conde, p. 272, Nadie sabe lo que hay en la holla.
Chavez, p. 48, Nadie sabe lo que lleva en el costal mas de el
que lo acarella. Gamiz, p. 81, Nadie sabe lo que hay en la
olla, sino la cuchara que la manea. Rodriguez-Marin (1926),
p. 317, Nadie sabe lo que tiene, si tiene quien lo mantiene.
Vasquez, p. 90, Nadie sabe lo que esta en la hiolla, nomas la
que lo esta meniando.

629 (A). Nadie sabe para quien trabaja.

Translation or Interpretation: No one knows for whom he
works.

Context: Some one was talking about all the effort and time
put into developing a plan needed as a requirement to complete a course. In actuality this plan was used to further
the benefits of a teacher and be used elsewhere. The comment
was made, "nadie sabe para quien trabaja."

Sources and Annotations: Adame, p. 69, same as A; p. 70,
same as A. Armas, p. 417, Nadie nace sabiendo. Ballesteros,
p. 32, same as A. Cerda, p. 302, same as A. Cobos, p. 85, same
as A; p. 113, Solo dios sabe para quien trabajas. Conde, p.

273, same as A. Espinosa, A., p. 108, Nadie sabe para quien trabaja. Galván, p. 134, Uno nunca sabe por quien trabaja. Jaramillo, p. 406, Nadien sabe para quien trabaja. Perez, p. 124,
same as A. Robe, p. 64, same as A. Rubio, p. 5, same as A.
Wesley, p. 216, same as A. Yáñez, p. 14, same as A.

630 (A). <u>Nadie</u> vende su mula por buena.
630 (B). <u>Nadie</u> vende su caballo por bueno.

<u>Translation or Interpretation</u>: Nobody sells his mule because
it is good.

<u>Context</u>: Informant says that he first heard this proverb from
his father when he was about nine years old and was living in
Roma at the time. My informant says that no one ever sells his
things because they are good. It was told to him when he
wanted to buy a used toy from a friend of his. (Two occurrences. Informants: male).

<u>Sources and Annotations</u>: Ballesteros, p. 69, Nadie vende su
caballo por bueno. Conde, p. 273, Nadie vende su caballo por
bueno.

631 (A). No hay <u>nadie</u> tan perfecto que no tenga un defecto.

<u>Translation or Interpretation</u>: There is (no one) so perfect
that does not have at least one flaw.

<u>Context</u>: My informant heard this proverb within the context
of: If you meet a person he is thought to be perfect, beware,
for there has got to be something wrong. (One occurrence.
Informant: female).

<u>Sources and Annotations</u>: None.

632 (A). A la <u>necesidad</u> no hay ley.

<u>Translation or Interpretation</u>: There are instances when laws
were meant to be disobeyed.

<u>Context</u>: A young man was driving his espectant wife to the
hospital. He ran a couple of red lights. The informant used
the above proverb to describe the situation. (One occurrence.
Informant: female).

<u>Sources and Annotations</u>: Conde, p. 217, La necesidad carece
de ley. Lea, p. 236, La necesidad carece de ley. Maldonado,
p. 109, Con necesidad no hay ley. Rodriguez-Marin (1926), p.
251, La necesidad hace ley. Sbarbi, p. 687, same as A.

633 (A). La <u>necesidad</u> desconoce fronteras.

<u>Translation or Interpretation</u>: Necessity knows no borders.

<u>Context</u>: Undocumented workers will do anything, even if they are not in their own country. (One occurrence. Informant: male).

<u>Sources and Annotations</u>: Adame, p. 56, same as A.

634 (A). La <u>necesidad</u> es madre de la invención.

<u>Translation or Interpretation</u>: Necessity is the mother of invention.

<u>Context</u>: A person invents something to ease his work. Necessity of not working too hard leads to invention. (Two occurrences. Informants: female).

<u>Sources and Annotations</u>: Jaramillo, p. 397, La necesidad es madre del ingenio. Perez, p. 123, same as A.

635 (A). La <u>necesidad</u> tiene cara de hereje.

<u>Translation or Interpretation</u>: Necessity -- poverty -- has the face of a heretic.

<u>Context</u>: Beggars aren't welcome. (One occurrence. Informant: female).

<u>Sources and Annotations</u>: Maldonado, p. 156, same as A.

636 (A). Más puede preguntar un <u>necio</u> que responder un cuerdo.

<u>Translation or Interpretation</u>: Any fool can ask questions, but it takes a smart man to answer them.

<u>Context</u>: A smart man always get tired of answering the same questions every minute, and he may not answer the fool that is asking him. (One occurrence. Informant: female).

<u>Sources and Annotations</u>: De Barros, p. 272, same as A. Sbarbi, p. 689, Más sabe un necio preguntar que un sabio contestar.

637 (A). Mejor ser <u>necio</u> con los demás que sabio a solas.

<u>Translation or Interpretation</u>: Better to be a fool with the crowd than wise by oneself.

Context: It's better to speak and clear your point of view
with others than to sit. Even if you know and understand a
solution for something that's going on, by shooting it down
would never help. (One occurrence. Informant: female).

Sources and Annotations: Sbarbi, p. 689, Mejor es ser necio,
que porfiado.

638 (A). Negocio es negocio.

Translation or Interpretation: Business is business.

Context: My cousin wanted an insurance form filled. I usually charge five dollars ($5) for this, but considering them my
relatives, I told them I wouldn't charge. My mother said I
should have charged them and used this proverb. (One occurrence. Informant: female).

Sources and Annotations: Jaramillo, p. 407, same as A.

639 (A). Negocio que no deja, déjalo.

Translation or Interpretation: A business that doesn't give
a profit, don't bother with it.

Context: When engaging in something that is not worth your
time or trouble. (One occurrence. Informant: female).

Sources and Annotations: Rubio, p. 6, same as A.

640 (A). Después del niño ahogado tapen el pozo.

Translation or Interpretation: After the child has drowned
cover up the hole.

Context: If a child is playing with a pencil, pokes his eye
with it, and you didn't take it away from him until he had
hurt himself. (One occurrence. Informant: female).

Sources and Annotations: Adame, p. 52, Hasta que se ahoga el
chamaco, tapamos el hoyo; p. 54, Hasta que se ahoga el chamaco, tapamos el hoyo. Cerda, p. 302, Después de niño ahogado,
a tapar el pozo. Conde, p. 110, same as A. Rodriguez-Marin
(1930), p. 85, Después de la casa robada, la puerta atranca-
da. Yáñez, p. 202, Niño ahogado, pozo tapado; p. 339, Niño
ahogado quieren tapar el poso.

641 (A). Los niños y los borrachos siempre dicen la verdad.
641 (B). Si quieres conocer un hombre, emborráchalo. Los
          niños y los borrachos no dicen mentiras.

641 (C). Los muchachos y los borrachos dicen la verdad.
641 (D). Los locos y los niños dicen la verdad.

Translation or Interpretation: Children and winos always tell the truth.

Context: A little kid was telling his mom or his father. (Five occurrences. Informants: four female, one male).

Sources and Annotations: Adame, p. 56, Las criaturas y los locos dicen la verdad; p. 60, Las criaturas y los locos dicen la verdad. Ballesteros, p. 52, same as A. Cobos, p. 76, same as D. Conde, p. 241, Los muchachos y los borachos dicen las verdades y los demás necedades. Chávez, p. 45, Los niños y los tontos dicen la verdad. Espinosa, A., p. 107, Los niños y los tontos dicen las verdades. Galvan, p. 134, Los niños y los locos dicen la verdad. Gamiz, p. 92, same as C. Jaramillo, p. 400, Los borrachos, los niños y los locos, dicen la verdad. Lucero-White, p. 35, Los niños y los locos dicen la verdad. Maldonado, p. 157, Los niños y los locos dicen las verdades; p. 316, Los niños y los locos dicen las verdades. Molera, p. 66, Los niños y los locos dicen las verdades. Rodriguez-Marin (1926), p. 278, Los niños y los orates dicen las verdades. Sbarbi, p. 695, Los niños y los locos dicen las verdades.

642 (A). De noche todos los gatos son pardos.

Translation or Interpretation: At night all cats are dark gray. It means that all cats look alike at night.

Context: My informant went to the bar one night. He got tired of drinking so he went out. In the dark he saw a woman that he thought was pretty. When she came closer, she was old and ugly. My informant said this proverb to himself. (Four occurrences. Informants: two female, two male).

Sources and Annotations: Caballero, p. 470, same as A.

643 (A). De la noche a la mañana.

Translation or Interpretation: From night to day. A person can, or is able to change from one day to the next. Money. A person is able to become rich.

Context: Some friend became rich over night. He won the lottery in Mexico. (One occurrence. Informant: female).

Sources and Annotations: Adame, p. 23, same as A; p. 27, same as A. Aranda, p. 8, same as A. Ballesteros, p. 60, same as A. Caballero, p. 476, same as A. Cobos, p. 30, same as A. Covarrubias, p. 829, same as A; p. 853, same as A. De Barros,

p. 168, same as A. Espinosa, A., p. 104, same as A. Jaramillo, p. 376, same as A. Lea, p. 234, same as A. Lucero-White, p. 33, De noche todos los gatos son pardos. Maldonado, p. 54, same as A. Martinez, p. 92, same as A. Robe, p. 65, same as A. Rodriguez-Marin (1926), p. 121, De noche todos los gatos son pardos. Sbarbi, p. 434, same as A; p. 696, same as A. Velasco, p. 55, same as A.

644 (A).   La noche es hecha para descansar y el día para tra-
           bajar.

Translation or Interpretation: The night was made to rest and the day to work. There is time for everything.

Context: My informant told me this proverb when we were in a restaurant one evening and a couple was there hugging and kissing instead of looking at the menu. (One occurrence. Informant: female).

Sources and Annotations: Sbarbi, p. 697, same as A.

645 (A).   Negro como la noche.

Translation or Interpretation: Black as the night. This means it is as black as it can be.

Context: Informant and friends were playing a game of cards when she used this proverb to describe the ace of spades. (Two occurrences. Informants: one female, one male).

Sources and Annotations: Arora, p. 311, same as A. Jarami-llo, p. 409, Negro, como la noche en que Romeo.

646 (A).   Al nopal se visita nomás cuando tiene tunas.
646 (B).   El nopal no lo van a ver solo cuando tiene tunas.
646 (C).   Tristes ingratas fortunas,
           He llegado a comprender
           Que al nopal lo van a ver
           Nomás cuando tiene tunas,
           Si no, ni se acuerdan de él.

Translation or Interpretation: The cactus is visited only when it has cactus pear, the fruit.

Context: When you visit someone only when you need something. (Six occurrences. Informants: four female, two male).

Sources and Annotations: Adame, p. 8, Al nopal lo van a ver nomás cuando tiene tunas; p. 11, Al nopal lo van a ver nomás cuando tiene tunas. Ballesteros, p. 1, Al nopal nomás lo van a ver cuando tiene tunas. Cerda, p. 302, El nopal no se visita hasta que no da tunas. Cobos, p. 12, same as A. Conde, p. 33, same as A. Gamiz, p. 81, No se visita el nopal sino cuando tiene tunas. Martinez, p. 28, El nopal se le va a ver solo cuando tiene tunas. Rubio, p. 38, El nopal no se visita hasta que no da tunas. Santamaria, p. 331, Ir al nopal sólo cuando tiene tunas.

647 (A). Eres como el <u>nopal</u>, entre más verde más baboso.

<u>Translation or Interpretation</u>: The older you get the more ignorant you become.

<u>Context</u>: Told to people when they are making a fool of themselves. (One occurrence. Informant: not stated).

<u>Sources and Annotations</u>: None.

648 (A). Estás como la <u>novia</u> de rancho, vestida y alborotada.
648 (B). Quedarse vestida y alborotada.
648 (C). Se quedó como el que chiflo en la loma, vestido y alborotado.

<u>Translation or Interpretation</u>: You were dressed and they didn't take you. You were left like the ranch bride, dressed and ready to go.

<u>Context</u>: I was going to DJ's (Disco) with a friend of mine but he never came for me. So my mother told me this saying. (Three occurrences. Informants: two female, one male).

<u>Sources and Annotations</u>: Adame, p. 90, Te dejaron como novia del rancho vestida y alborotada; p. 92, Te dejaron como novia del rancho vestida y alborotada. Alcalá, p. 428, Sacar la novia. Arora, p. 312, Estar como novia de campo. Conde, p. 257, Me dejó como novia del rancho vestida y alborotada. Rubio, p. 114, Quedarse como el que chiflo en la loma; p. 115, Quedarse como novia del rancho vestida y en la ventana. Yanez, p. 22, No me vas a dejar como las novias de rancho vestidas y alborotadas.

649 (A). <u>No vio</u>, no via.

<u>Translation or Interpretation</u>: Love is blind. He didn't see. He's blinded by her love and he didn't see.

<u>Context</u>: She said that while she was attending school, her sister started dating this real ugly boy, and she really fell for him. Her and her mother were talking about it when they said the phrase. This phrase was very popular then. (One occurrence. Informant: female).

Sources and Annotations: Covarrubias, p. 1000, No avéis visto lo que avéis hecho.

650 (A). Nunca es tarde.

Translation or Interpretation: Better late than never.

Context: I was late for school, and as I walked in the teacher said, "better late than never. (One occurrence. Informant: male).

Sources and Annotations: Aranda, p. 30, Vale más tarde que nunca. De Barros, p. 343, Nunca es tarde si la dicha es buena. Maldonado, p. 58, Más vale tarde que tarde.

651 (A). Primero la obligación que la devoción.

Translation or Interpretation: First the obligation than the devotion.

Context: C. learned this saying from both her mother and father when she was growing up in Brownsville, Texas. She preferred watching television to doing her homework and she would be reminded that school work was her obligation. Her parents recited this saying to her. (One occurrence. Informant: female).

Sources and Annotations: Sbarbi, p. 706, same as A.

652 (A). Obras son amores, no buenas razones.

Translation or Interpretation: Doing is loving, and not good advice. Practice what you preach.

Context: This proverb is referred to as you show that doing is loving and not something you just give advice about. Don't go around telling someone how wonderful it is to do good for others, and then go around hurting people and doing everything to the contrary. This came about in a conversation about her neighbor who has made her and her children's lives miserable. She was always preaching to them on how much she cares for them, but goes talking bad about her mother behind her back. (One occurrence. Informant: female).

Sources and Annotations: Cerda, p. 303, Obras son amores que no buenas razones. De Barros, p. 345, same as A. Maldonado, p. 60, Obras son amores que no buenas razones. Molera, p. 66, Obras son amores que no buenas razones. Sbarbi, p. 708, same as A.

653 (A). Si bien me quieres tus <u>obras</u> me lo dirán.

<u>Translation or Interpretation</u>: If you love me, your actions will speak louder than words.

<u>Context</u>: A's boyfriend told her that he loves her, and proved it by being nice, attentive, and faithful. (One occurrence. Informant: female).

<u>Sources and Annotations</u>: Conde, p. 368, Si bien me quieres Juan, tus obras me lo dirán. Rodriguez-Marin (1930), p. 307, Si me quieres bien, en tus hechos lo veré; si me quieres mal, tus hechos me lo dirán.

654 (A). La <u>ocasión</u> perdida no se recobra fácilmente.

<u>Translation or Interpretation</u>: If one does not take advantage of an opportunity when it knocks, it may be a while before he gets another chance. The lost opportunity is not easily recovered.

<u>Context</u>: My informant told me of a man who got a good job offer which involved a move to another state. He took the chance, and today he's a very successful man. (One occurrence. Informant: female).

<u>Sources and Annotations</u>: Conde, p. 217, La ocasión una vez ida, para siempre esta perdida; p. 303, Ocasión que se va, ¡quien sabe si volvera! Lea, p. 235, Hay que aprovechar la ocasión; p. 236, La ocasión perdida no se recoba facil. Lucero-White, p. 35, La ocasión perdida no se recoba facil. Rodriguez-Marin (1926), p. 252, same as A.

655 (A). Entre más <u>ojales</u> más botones.

<u>Translation or Interpretation</u>: The more buttonholes the more buttons. What it means is that you are going to have a lot of work to do. Usually said by a seamstress.

<u>Context</u>: The informant once exclaimed this when she had a great deal of work to do. (One occurrence. Informant: female).

<u>Sources and Annotations</u>: Cerda, p. 303, Salir con más ojales que botones. Cobos, p. 56, Entre más ojales, más botones. Rodriguez-Marin (1926), p. 84, Contra ojales, hay botones. Rubio, p. 327, Mientras más botones mas ojales. Sbarbi, p. 713, Contra botones hay ojales. Yáñez, p. 299, A que voy, si mientras más botones, mas ojales, y si lo que tiene la olla saca la cuchara.

656 (A). Ojo de chícharo y píco de séda.

Translation or Interpretation: Keep your eyes open and don't say anything.

Context: When a person sees something he should mind his own business. (One occurrence. Informant: female).

Sources and Annotations: Conde, p. 320, Ponte ojo de cícharo. Martínez, p. 224, Pico de cera. Velasco, p. 131, Pico de cera.

657 (A). Ojo por ojo y diente por diente.

Translation or Interpretation: Eye for eye and tooth for tooth.

Context: If you hurt me in any way, I shall hurt you back. (Seven occurrences. Informants: five female, one male, one not stated).

Sources and Annotations: Armas, p. 418, same as A. Balles- teros, p. 41, same as A. Caballero, p. 865, same as A. Cobos, p. 95, same as A. Conde, p. 172, Es la ley de Talion, ojo por ojo, diente por diente; p. 304, same as A. Jaramillo, p. 412, same as A. Rodriguez-Marin (1926), p. 240, same as A.

658 (A). El ojo del amo engorda el caballo.
658 (B). Al pie del amo engorda el caballo.
658 (C). Al lado del amo engorda el caballo.
658 (D). A la vista del amo engorda el caballo.

Translation or Interpretation: Under the eye of the master the horse will grow fat.

Context: The owner takes better care of his personal pro- perty.

Sources and Annotations: Adame, p. 8, same as A; p. 11, same as A. Aranda, p. 2, same as A. Ballesteros, p. 59, same as A. Caballero, p. 541, El ojo del amo engorda el caballo. Cobos, p. 39, El ojo del amo engorda el caballo. Conde, p. 33, same as A. Correas, p. 88, same as A. De Barros, p. 347, El ojo del amo engorda el caballo. Espinosa, A., p. 106, El ojo del amo engorda el caballo. Galvan, p. 124, Al ojo del amo engorda el macho; p. 130, Al ojo del amo engorda el macho. Gamiz, p. 81, Al ojo del amo engorda el caballo. Jaramillo, p. 366, same as A. Maldonado, p. 160, El ojo del amo engorda el caballo. Molera, p. 66, El ojo del amo engorda el caballo. Sbarbi, p. 713, same as A.

659 (A). Como te quedo el ojo, ¿tirante y flojo?

<u>Translation or Interpretation</u>: How did your eye stay, strained and loose?

<u>Context</u>: A young girl was wearing an outfit which I very much admired and wanted to buy it. While we were standing by a store with that outfit, my sister told me ¿como te quedo el ojo ¿tirante y flojo? (One occurrence. Informant: female).

<u>Sources and Annotations</u>: Velasco, p. 41, ¿Como te quedo el ojo?

660 (A). Donde pongo el <u>ojo</u> pongo la bala.

<u>Translation or Interpretation</u>: Where I (place) my sight, I put the bullet. Where I set my sight I place the bullet.

<u>Context</u>: Once a brother-in-law wanted to buy a car. He had looked over and over at a certain one. Finally he bought it. We, my sisters and brothers, made fun of him about how he came to end up with the car. He, very confidently, said "Donde pongo el ojo pongo la bala". (One occurrence. Informant: female).

<u>Sources and Annotations</u>: Armas, p. 333, Poner la bala donde se pone el ojo. Caballero, p. 515, Donde pone el ojo pone la bala. Conde, p. 118, Donde pone el ojo pone la bala. Martínez, p. 97, Donde pone el ojo, pone la bala.

661 (A). Te sumen un <u>ojo</u> y te pican el otro.
661 (B). Te sumen un <u>ojo</u> y te sacan el otro.

<u>Translation or Interpretation</u>: They dent one eye and poke the other one.

<u>Context</u>: I first heard this proverb on July 4, 1978, at my mother's home. My mother sent my brother to the store to get some meat. When my brother returned with the meat "¿esto es todo?", my mother asked -- is this all. My brother told her that that was all he could buy with the money she had given him. My mother told him "te sumen un ojo y te pican el otro." What my mother meant by this was that she was really being ripped off. I asked my mother where she learned this saying and she said her mother used to use it. (Five occurrences. Informants: one female, four male).

<u>Sources and Annotations</u>: Benavides, p. 90, same as B.

662 (A). <u>Ojos</u> que no ven, corazón que no siente.
662 (B). <u>Ojos</u> que no ven, corazón que no quiebra.

<u>Translation or Interpretation</u>: Eyes that don't see, heart that won't feel. Your heart will suffer no pain if your eyes

don't witness the situation.

Context: There can be a lot of bad or good things going a-
round but if you don't see them, they can't hurt you. My informant's neighbor was having an affair with a married man.
My informant asked her if she thought it was wise. Her neighbor answered her with this proverb. (52 occurrences. Informants: 42 female, nine male, three not stated).

Sources and Annotations: Adame, p. 78, same as A. Aranda, p.
23, same as A. Armas, p. 418, same as A. Ballesteros, p. 34,
same as A. Benavides, p. 90, same as A. Caballero, p. 866,
same as A. Cobos, p. 95, same as A. Correas, p. 171, same as
B; p. 217, Los ojos no ven, corazón no desea. Covarrubias, p.
1000, Ojos que no ven, corazón que no llora; p. 835, Ojos que
no veen, corazón no quebrantante. De Barros, p. 347, same as
A. Espinosa, A., p. 109, same as A. Espinosa, F., p. 240, Lo
que ojos no ven, corazón no lo desea. Galvan, p. 126, same as
A; p. 132, same as A. Glazer, p. 55, same as A. Jaramillo, p.
399, Lo que ojos no ven, corazón no siente. Maldonado, p. 30,
Ojos que no ven, corazón que no quiebra. Molera, p. 66, Ojos
que no ven corazón que quiebra. Pérez, p. 124, same as A.
Robe, p. 63, same as A. Rodriguez-Marin (1926), p. 352, same
as A. Rubio, p. 72, Ojos que no ven tienen menos que sentir.
Sbarbi, p. 717, same as A. Vasquez, p. 89, same as A. Wesley,
p. 218, same as A.

663 (A). Ojos que se quieren bien desde lejos se saludan.

Translation or Interpretation: Admiring eyes greet from afar.

Context: Mother used to say this refran to us when we were
growing up to show us how the honor of the girls were pro-
tected. They would only admire each other from a distance
with their eyes. People were very strict with their children
at that time and were not allowed to date. Usually loved ones
would look at each other in church or in the presence of other
people. (One occurrence. Informant: female).

Sources and Annotations: Conde, p. 304, same as A. Rodriguez-
Marin (1930), p. 241, Ojos que bien se quieren, desde lejos se
entienden. Sbarbi, p. 717, same as A.

664 (A). Ojos que te vieron ir cuando volveran a verte.

Translation or Interpretation: Eyes that saw you leave when
will they see you again.

Context: Informant used this when he referred to someone
close to him who was going away. (One occurrence. Informant:
female).

Sources and Annotations: Adame, p. 78, Ojos que te vieron ir, cuando te verán volver. Ballesteros, p. 34, Ojos que te vieron ir, no te volverán a ver. Caballero, p. 866, ¡Ojos que te vieron ir, cuándo te verán volver! Conde, p. 304, Ojos que te vieron ir ¿Cuando te verán volver? Maldonado, p. 160, Ojos que le vieron ir, no le verán más venir. Martínez, p. 212, Ojos que te vieron ir, ¿cuando te verán volver? Rubio, p. 72, Ojos que te vieron ir, ¿cuando te veran volver. Sbarbi, p. 717, Ojos que te vieron ir.

665 (A). Dichosos los ojos que la vieron.

Translation or Interpretation: Happy are the eyes that saw you. If someone has not seen another person for some time they are usually happy to see them.

Context: Informant used this on a young lady he hadn't seen for a long time. It was used like a casual acquaintance. (Two occurrences. Informants: male).

Sources and Annotations: Caballero, p. 501, Dichos los ojos que le ven a usted; Dichosos los ojos que te ven.

666 (A). Más ven cuatro ojos que dos.

Translation or Interpretation: Four eyes see more than two. Two heads are better than one.

Context: My mother started our restaurant business by herself. When the business grew and began to be more than she could handle, she tried to convince my father to quit his job and devote himself to the restaurant instead. She used this proverb many times during that year. (One occurrence. Informant: female).

Sources and Annotations: Ballesteros, p. 23, Cuatro ojos ven más que dos. Caballero, p. 776, same as A. Cobos, p. 82, same as A. Conde, p. 256, same as A. Correas, p. 543, same as A. De Barros, p. 281, same as A. Jaramillo, p. 371, Cuatro ojos ven más que dos. Lea, p. 236, Más ven cuatro ojos que dos. Lucero-White, p. 35, same as A. Maldonado, p. 59, same as A. Sbarbi, p. 717, Más ven cuatro ojos que no dos.

667 (A). No me mires con ojos de hambre porque no tengo cara de lonche.

Translation or Interpretation: Do not look at me with hungry eyes, my face is not lunch.

Context: Boys were looking and my mother told me to reply. (One occurrence. Informant: female).

Sources and Annotations: Cerda, p. 304, ¡No me mires con ojos de hambre, que no tengo restaurante.

668 (A). No me piques los ojos.
668 (B). No me pintes los ojos verdes.

Translation or Interpretation: Don't poke my eyes.

Context: M. tells this proverb to his students when they try to lie to him. (Two occurrences. Informants: male).

Sources and Annotations: Benavides, p. 90, Le pico los ojos.

669 (A). Eres como las olas del mar que van y vienen.

Translation or Interpretation: You are like the ocean's waves that come and go.

Context: Used to describe a person who never makes up his mind. (One occurrence. Informant: male).

Sources and Annotations: None.

670 (A). Por salir de la olla me caí en la lumbre.

Translation or Interpretation: By jumping out of the puddle you might fall in the mud. By trying to get out of the pot, I fell in the fire.

Context: If you try to get away with a bad thing you will probably end up in a worse situation. (One occurrence. Informant: female).

Sources and Annotations: Jaramillo, p. 422, Salir de las brazas para caer en las llamas. Rodriguez-Marin (1926), p. 446, Salir de llamas y caer en brazas.

671 (A). Habiendo oportunidad hasta el más santo peca.

Translation or Interpretation: With an opportunity even a saint sins.

Context: None given. (One occurrence. Informant: female).

Sources and Annotations: Adame, p. 52, same as A; p. 53, same as A.

672 (A). La oportunidad la pintan calva y con un solo pelo.

Translation or Interpretation: Opportunity knocks only once.
They paint opportunity as bald and with only one hair.

Context: When my informant got out of the service, no one in
his family had ever gone beyond a high school education. His
father told him about the proverb and going to college on the
G.I. Bill. (One occurrence. Informant: female).

Sources and Annotations: Adame, p. 56, La oportunidad la pintan calva; p. 60, La oportunidad la pintan calva. Robe, p. 70,
La oportunidad la pintan calva y cuando se presenta hay que
cogerla de los pelitos que tenga.

673 (A). Dime cuanto oras y te dire que tan buen cristiano
            eres.

Translation or Interpretation: Tell me how much you pray and
I'll let you know how good a christian you are. It means that
by your praying you will be judged, whether or not you are a
good christian.

Context: My brother likes to tease his friends because he is
always going to church. One day his friend told him this proverb. (One occurrence. Informant: male).

Sources and Annotations: None.

674 (A). Se fue a planchar oreja.

Translation or Interpretation: She went to iron the ear.

Context: This proverb is used when someone leaves to go to
sleep. (One occurrence. Informant: female).

Sources and Annotations: None.

675 (A). Una oreja te la estiras y la otra no te la vas al-
            canzar.

Translation or Interpretation: The more you have the more you
want. One ear you can stretch, the other you won't be able
to get.

Context: The informant used this proverb on her daughter --
you have a house but you still want more. (One occurrence.
Informant: female).

Sources and Annotations: Espinosa, A., p. 110, Se estira una
oreja y no se alcanza la otra.

676 (A). Puede más una **hormiga** que un buey hechado.

Translation or Interpretation: An ant can do more than an ox that is lying down.

Context: L. heard this proverb from her mother about ten years ago. According to L., her mother would ask, or tell her to do some house chore, ie., wash the dishes. L. would continue to watch television or reading a book, and tell her mother "ahorita"--just a minute. After reminding L. about the dishes several times, her mother finally said that an ant could do more than an ox lying down, or an ant could do more than L., who hadn't gotten up to do the dishes. To L. this was a subtle way of punishment for disregarding her mother's commands. (One occurrence. Informant: female).

Sources and Annotations: None.

677 (A). Llorar poco y buscar **otro**.

Translation or Interpretation: Cry a little and look for another.

Context: A friend of mine broke up with her boyfriend. Her aunt told her the above proverb, and she took her aunt's advice and found herself another boyfriend. (Three occurrences. Informants: female).

Sources and Annotations: None.

678 (A). Hoy por **otros**, mañana por los nuestros.

Translation or Interpretation: Today for others, tomorrow for our own.

Context: Informant heard this in a doctor's office. The lady sitting next to her had once helped this young girl, and never saw her again. As time passed, her own daughter found herself in a difficult situation when she wasn't around. Another lady helped her, and then she said the proverb. (Three occurrences. Informants: female).

Sources and Annotations: Ballesteros, p. 28, Hoy por ti, mañana por mí. Cobos, p. 63, Hoy por ti, mañana por mi. Conde, p. 196, Hoy por ti, mañana por mí. Gamiz, p. 83, Hoy por ti, mañana por mi. Jaramillo, p. 394, Hoy por tí, mañana por mi. Lucero-White, p. 34, Hoy unos mañana otros. Rodriguez-Marin (1930), p. 37, Ayer para mí, hoy por tí.

679 (A). No juzges a **otros** por lo que tu eres o haces.

Translation or Interpretation: Don't judge others by who you are or what you do.

Context: Usually said to someone who is gossiping or judging someone else. Said to someone. Just because you do it that way doesn't mean that anyone else has to do it the same. (One occurrence. Informant: not stated).

Sources and Annotations: None.

680 (A). Si abusas de otros no puedes protestar si algún día te dan una muestra de tu misma medicina.

Translation or Interpretation: If you abuse others you can't squak if you are given a taste of your own medicine.

Context: I remember the neighborhood bully, who would always, for no reason, beat up the little kids, me especially because I was very short. As the years went by a friend of ours really grew into a giant. P. was his name. He was around ten years of age and he could beat up the fifteen year olds. Eventually he came upon the neighborhood bully, who was now shorter than him. "Remember when you used to beat me up, Panzo" Let's see if you can still do it," P. told the fat dude. The fight ensued, and in the end P. beat the hell out of the barrio bully. Both of these guys are now some of my best friends I guess, in the end, all of us do change. (One occurrence. Informant: male).

Sources and Annotations: None.

681 (A). Cada oveja con su pareja.
681 (B). Cada oveja tiene su pareja.

Translation or Interpretation: Each sheep with his partner.

Context: People that are the same stick together. (14 occurrences. Informants: five female, six male, three not stated).

Sources and Annotations: Adame, p. 16, same as A; p. 18, same as A. Aranda, p. 4, same as A. Armas, p. 409, Cada oveja busca su pareja. Ballesteros, p. 59, same as A. Benavides, p. 90, same as A. Caballero, p. 213, same as A. Cobos, p. 19, same as A. Conde, p. 69, same as A. Covarrubias, p. 842, same as A. De Barros, p. 126, same as A. Espinosa, A., p. 99, same as A. Galván, p. 125, same as A; p. 132, same as A. Gamiz, p. 75, same as A. Glazer, p. 56, same as A. Jaramillo, p. 372, same as A. MacArthur, p. 32, same as A. Maldonado, p. 52, same as A. Paredes, p. 29, same as A. Pérez, p. 119, same as A. Vasquez, p. 88, same as A. Yáñez, p. 64, same as A.

682 (A). Con paciencia se gana el cielo.
682 (B). Con paciencia se gana la Gloria.

Translation or Interpretation: With patience one earns heaven.

Context: My grandmother said this to me when I would help her sew her quilts. I would get in a hurry and anxious to finish and would start to mess up the stitches. She would say to take my time and it wouldn't cost me as much time as if I had to rip out the messy stitches and start over again. (Two occurrences. Informants: female).

Sources and Annotations: Aranda, p. 6, Con paciencia se gana lo imposible. Cobos, p. 23, same as A; p. 23, same as B. Conde, p. 84, same as B. Espinosa, A., p. 103, same as A. Gamiz, p. 90, same as A. Robe, p. 65, same as A. Rodriguez-Marin (1926), p. 81, Con la paciencia se gana el cielo; p. 82, Con paciencia y desvelo se gana el cielo. Sbarbi, p. 732, Con paciencia se ganó el cielo.

683 (A). La paciencia todo lo alcanza.

Translation or Interpretation: Patience gains all.

Context: His mother used this proverb many times. He can remember her saying this when he was trying to learn how to ride a bicycle. (One occurrence. Informant: male).

Sources and Annotations: Conde, p. 84, Con paciencia y esperanza todo se alcanza. Lea, p. 233, Con paciencia todo se logra. Lucero-White, p. 33, Con paciencia todo se logra. Rodriguez-Marin (1930), p. 59, Con paciencia todo se logra. Rodriguez-Marin (1926), p. 81, Con la paciencia todo se logra; p. 82, Con paciencia, todo se obtiene, y sin ella todo se pierde.

684 (A). Tal padre, tal hijo.

Translation or Interpretation: Such father, such son.

Context: An uncle was laughing at the informant when he was mimicking the way his father walked. (One occurrence. Informant: male).

Sources and Annotations: Caballero, p. 495, De tal padre tal hijo. Cerda, p. 305, same as A. Cobos, p. 114, Tal el padre tal el hijo. Conde, p. 383, Tales padres tales hijos. Espinosa, A., p. 111, same as A. Rodriguez-Marin (1926), p. 478, Tales padres, tales hijos.

685 (A). Entre padres y hermanos no metas las manos.

Translation or Interpretation: Among parents and brothers do not put in the hands.

Context: If there is a fight between brothers or father and son, never interfere because you may get into trouble. (One occurrence. Informant: female).

Sources and Annotations: Cobos, p. 55, En pleitos hermanos, no metas las manos. Covarrubias, p. 531, Entre hermanos no metas tus manos. Rodriguez-Marin, p. 197, Entre padres, hijos y hermanos, nadie meta las manos- o no metas tu mano. Rubio, p. 224, Entre casados o hermanos ninguno meta las manos. Sbarbi, p. 735, Entre padres y hermanos nunca metas tus manos.

686 (A). Más vale un pájaro en la mano que cien volando.
686 (B). Es mejor un pájaro en la mano que cien volando.
686 (C). Más vale pájaro en mano que diez volando.
686 (D). Más vale un pájaro en la mano que dos en el aire.
686 (E). Más vale un pájaro en la mano y no mil volando.
686 (F). Vale mas un pájaro en la mano que no veintemil vo-
          lando.
686 (G). Un pájaro en la mano es mejor que mil volando.

Translation or Interpretation: Better to have one bird in the hand than one hundred flying.

Context: A gambler once lost his jewelry in a card game be-cause he wanted to win all of his opponents' chips. He ended up without his or his opponents' chips. (50 occurrences. Informants: 26 female, 22 male, two anonymous).

Sources and Annotations: Adame, p. 98, Vale más pajaro en mano que cien volando; p. 99, Vale más pajaro en mano que cien volando. Armas, p. 306, same as A. Ballesteros, p. 66, Un pa-jaro en la mano vale más que cien que estan volando. Benavi-des, p. 89, Más vale pajaro un mano que cien volando. Cobos, p. 80, same as A; p. 118, Un pajaro es mejor que dos en el árbol; p. 120, Vale más pajaro en mano que cien volando. Con-de, p. 255, same as A. Covarrubias, p. 242, Más vale pajaro en mano que buitre volando y más vale un toma que dos te dare. De Barros, p. 278, Más vale pajaro en mano que buitre volando; Más vale pajaro en mano que ciento volando. Espinosa, A., p. 108, same as A. Espinosa, F., p. 176, Más vale paxaro en mano que buitre volando. Galvan, p. 130, same as A; p. 135, same as A. Gamiz, p. 89, Más vale pajaro en mano que ciento volan-do. Glazer, p. 56, same as A. Jaramillo, p. 403, same as A. Lea, p. 238, Vale más pajaro en la mano que cien volando. Lucero-White, p. 36, Vale más pajaro en la mano que volando. MacArthur, p. 39, Más vale pajaro en mano, que cientos volan-do. Maldonado, p. 29, Más vale pajaro en mano que buitre vo-lando; p. 151, Más vale un pajaro en la mano que dos volando. Perez, p. 123, Más vale un pajaro en la mano que dos volando. Rodriguez-Marin (1930), p. 202, Más vale pajaro en mano que ver tres volando. Rodriguez-Marin (1926), p. 298, Más vale pajaro en la barriga que ciento en la liga. Santamaria, p. 374, Más vale pajaro en mano que ciento volando. Sbarbi, p. 740, Más vale pajaro en mano que ciento volando o que buitre volando. Wesley, p. 217, Un pajaro en la mano vale ciento volando

687 (A). ¿Si porque el <u>pájaro</u> se come el maíz no vas a sembrar?

<u>Translation or Interpretation</u>: Because the bird eats the corn you will not plant?

<u>Context</u>: My informant first heard this proverb from a neighbor who was giving him advice and telling him never to quit in life, no matter how hard it could become. (One occurrence. Informant: male).

<u>Sources and Annotations</u>: Caballero, p. 1030, Si por miedo a los gorriones no se sembraran cañamones. Rodriguez-Marin (1930), p. 223, No dejes de sembrar cebada por miedo de la cogujada.

688 (A). <u>Pájaros</u> de la misma pluma vuelan juntos.

<u>Translation or Interpretation</u>: Birds of the same feather fly together.

<u>Context</u>: These two boys always hung around together, and whenever they would get into trouble they each would cover for the other, saying that they would never do anything like that. She would always repeat that phrase to them, and they would get mad at her. (Two occurrences. Informants: female).

<u>Sources and Annotations</u>: Aranda, p. 23, same as A. Espinosa, A., p. 109, Pájaros de una pluma se reconocen. Galván, p. 131, Ser pájaros de la misma pluma; p. 132, Ser pajáros de la misma pluma; p. 133, Ser pájaros de la misma pluma. Villafuerte, p. 146, Los pájaros de igual pluma siempre vuelan juntos.

689 (A). Matar a dos <u>pájaros</u> con un solo tiro.
689 (B). Matar dos <u>pájaros</u> con la misma piedra.

<u>Translation or Interpretation</u>: To kill two birds with one shot.

<u>Context</u>: Pedro was a young man who wanted a big spread of cattle. His only problem was that he didn't have land or cattle. Thus, he did what most people hate to do, that was, to get a loan from the bank. After he got his loan, Pedro was able to solve his problems concerning his land and his cattle, thus, getting two tasks done in one. Pedro related this story to me during a social gathering in September, 1975. I was interested at the time in borrowing money from the bank, but I was reluctant to do so. (Two occurrences. Informants: one female, one male).

<u>Sources and Annotations</u>: Armas, p. 306, Matar dos pájaros de un tiro. Ballesteros, p. 63, Matar dos pájaros con una piedra. Caballero, p. 777, Matar de una pedrada dos pájaros; Matar dos

pájaros de un tiro. Correas, p. 313, De un tiro, dos pájaros.
Covarrubias, p. 870, Matar dos pájaros con una piedra; p. 858,
De un tiro, matar dos pájaros. Chavez, p. 49, Mate dos pájaros
con una piedra. De Barros, p. 145, Con un tiro matar dos pájaros. Espinosa, F., p. 229, Matar de un tiro dos pájaros.
Jaramillo, p. 405, Matar dos pájaros con una pedrada. Maldonado, p. 110, Con una piedra matar dos pájaros, (o con un tiro
matar dos pájaros). Rubio, p. 103, Con una piedra se matan
muchos pájaros. Sbarbi, p. 740, Matar dos pájaros de una piedra, o de un tiro.

690 (A). La palabra honesta mucho vale y poco cuesta.

Translation or Interpretation: An honest word is worth much
and costs little.

Context: My mother always tells us to be friendly and nice to
people because it does not cost one thing to do so and it is
good. (One occurrence. Informant: female).

Sources and Annotations: Conde, p. 54, A todo buena respuesta,
mucho vale poco cuesta. Espinosa, F., p. 177, Poco cuesta.
Espinosa, F., p. 177, Poco cuesta la buena palabra y mucho la
mala. Rodriguez-Marin (1930), p. 43, Buenas palabras, no cues-
tan nada; p. 243, Palabra cortes, vale mucho y no cuesta res.
Rodriguez-Marin (1926), p. 253, same as A. Sbarbi, p. 131, El
hablar bien poco cuesta.

691 (A). No hay palabra mal dicha no siendo mal tomada.

Translation or Interpretation: There is no word said wrong
if it is not taken wrong.

Context: My informant had a way with words. He always managed to make people laugh. It wasn't what he said, it was how
he said it. One day he surprised us by using this proverb.
(One occurrence. Informant: male).

Sources and Annotations: Caballero, p. 833, No hay palabra
mal dicha sino mal interpretada. Covarrubias, p. 845, No hay
palabra mal dicha, si no fuese mal entendida. Espinosa, F.,
p. 94, No abria cosa mal dicha si no fuese bien oyida; p. 177,
No abria palabra mala sino fuese retrayada. Rodriguez-Marin
(1930), p. 235, No son más las cosas buenas o malas de como
so tomadas. Rubio, p. 34, No hay palabras mal dichas como no
sea mal tomado. Sbarbi, p. 741, No hay mala palabra, si no es
mal tenida.

692 (A). A palabras necias, oídos sordos.

Translation or Interpretation: To foolish words, deaf ears.

Context: When my mom nags and nags about different things my dad has not done for her, my father just pretends she is not even talking. (Four occurrences. Informants: three female, one male).

Sources and Annotations: Armas, p. 407, same as A. Balles-teros, p. 20, same as A. Caballero, p. 130, same as A. Cobos, p. 14, same as A. Conde, p. 47, same as A. Correas, p. 22, A palabras locas, orejas sordas. Espinosa, A., p. 102, same as A. Jaramillo, p. 364, same as A. Lea, p. 233, same as A. Lucero-White, p. 33, same as A. MacArthur, p. 25, same as A. Rodriguez-Marin (1926), p. 7, A discursos necios, oídos sordos; p. 37, same as A. Santamaria, p. 375, same as A.

693 (A). Quieres todo a paleta de otro.

Translation or Interpretation: You want everything on another's shoulder.

Context: About seven months ago a cousin of my wife's moved in with us. He brought his family along. They stayed with us for two full weeks. During that time they used our phone to call long distance, they ate our food without buying any themselves, etc. We didn't get back a single penny. (One occurrence. Informant: female).

Sources and Annotations: None.

694 (A). Palo dado, ni Dios lo quita.

Translation or Interpretation: Stick given, not even God can take away.

Context: If something is given from one person to another, and either the giver or a third party wants it, this proverb is said in order to make it clear that they will not get the possession. (Two occurrences. Informants: one female, one male).

Sources and Annotations: Adame, p. 79, same as A; p. 80, same as A. Ballesteros, p, 41, same as A. Cobos, p. 96, same as A. Conde, p. 308, same as A. Espinosa, A., p. 109, Palo dado no hay quien lo quite; p. 111, Palo dado ni San Juan lo quita. Gamiz, p. 78, same as A. Martinez, p. 216, same as A. Rodriguez-Marin (1930), p. 244, Palo dado ni Dios lo ha quitado. Velasco, p. 127, same as A.

695 (A). De tal palo tal astilla.
695 (B). De tal palo salta la astilla.
695 (C). De tal palo tal astilla, entre más adentro más
          amarilla.
695 (D). De tal palo sale la astilla.

227

695 (E). En tal palo está la astilla.
695 (F). De tal árbol tal astilla.

Translation or Interpretation: From such a stick such a
splinter.

Context: One night my grandfather and my uncle came home drunk
together, and they were laughing and hugging each other. My
grandmother was mad and she said this saying. (56 occurrences.
Informants: 34 female, 18 male, four anonymous).

Sources and Annotations: Adame, p. 24, same as A; p. 28, same
as A. Aranda, p. 8, same as B. Armas, p. 410, same as A. Ballesteros, p. 45, same as A. Benavides, p. 90, same as A.
Caballero, p. 495, same as A. Campa, p. 63, same as A. Cerda,
p. 306, same as A. Cobos, p. 31, same as A. Conde, p. 111,
same as A. De Barros, p. 166, De casta le viene al galgo el
ser rebilargo; p. 170, same as A. Espinosa, A., p. 104, same
as A. Galvan, p. 125, same as A; p. 127, same as A. Glazer, p.
56, same as A. Jaramillo, p. 376, same as A. Pérez, p. 120,
same as A. Rodriguez-Marin (1926), p. 127, same as A. Sbarbi,
p. 745, same as A. Yáñez, p. 199, same as A.

696 (A). Tú eres como el palo blanco en el campo.

Translation or Interpretation: You are like the hackberry
tree in the field.

Context: When you tell another person this proverb (it means)
that person is useless, just taking up space. (One occurrence. Informant: female).

Sources and Annotations: Cerda, p. 306, ¡Eres como el palo
blanco, ni das nada,   ocupando campo!

697 (A). Come pan y bebe agua y viviras vida larga.

Translation or Interpretation: Eat bread and drink water and
you will live a long life.

Context: Informant's neighbor uses this proverb whenever her
husband goes out drinking. The neighbor claims he is over in-
dulging and that he will not live long if he does not take
care. (One occurrence. Informant: female).

Sources and Annotations: Cobos, p. 21, Come pan y bebe agua
y vivirás large vida. Rodriguez-Marin (1926), p. 76, same as
A. Sbarbi, p. 747, Come pan y bebe agua y vivirás vida larga.

698 (A). El pan ajeno hace al hijo bueno.

Translation or Interpretation: Another's bread makes the son
good.

Context: When you have to work for something you tend to appreciate it more. (One occurrence. Informant: female).

Sources and Annotations: Vásquez, p. 88, same as A.

699 (A). El pan, pan y el vino, vino.

Translation or Interpretation: The bread, bread and wine, wine.

Context: Things should be called as they are. They should not be covered up. Informant heard this when a mutual friend was making excuses for her husband's drinking. The friend's mother then said the proverb. This happened about two years ago. (One occurrence. Informant: female).

Sources and Annotations: Alcalá, p. 448, same as A. Armas, p. 301, Llamar al pan, pan y al vino, vino. Ballesteros, p. 3, same as A. Caballero, p. 97, Al pan, pan y el vino, vino. Conde, p. 34, Al pan, pan y el vino, vino. Covarrubias, p. 848, Pan por pan y vino por vino, hablar llanamente. De Barros, p. 356, Pan por pan y vino por vino. Gamiz, p. 78, Llamar al pan, pan y al vino, vino. Paredes, p. 29, same as A. Rodriguez-Marin (1930), p. 245, Pan por pan, vino por vino; que yo no soy griego ni latino. Rodriguez-Marin (1926), p. 26, Al pan, pan y al vino, vino. Sbarbi, p. 749, same as A. Yáñez, p. 204, De gente ocupada, que le gusta ir al grano y llamar al pan, pan.

700 (A). Le dan pan y pide jalea.
700 (B). Le dan pan y quiere jalea.

Translation or Interpretation: They give him bread and he asks for jelly.

Context: She said that it was used when people were given something as a favor, or gift, and they the receiver would ask for more. She further said that it was good in a derrogatory way, as to criticize a person for being greedy. This saying is used by close family members where the members know the meaning. The mother uses it to point out the moral "it is best to be modest." The interviewer liked the proverb for it depicts the necessity of being modes and good mannered. The interviewer was intrigued, as she had not ever heard it. The proverb is a good one, as bread and jelly go hand in hand. Furthermore, it is amusing and easy to make the point. The interviewer felt that she wanted to share it with everyone. (Two occurrences. Informants: one female, one male).

701 (A). Panza de pobre, mejor que reviente y no que le sobre.

Translation or Interpretation: Belly of poor, better to burst and not to have leftover.

Context: None given. (One occurrence. Informant: female).

Sources and Annotations: Conde, p. 60, Barriga de pobre, primero reventar que sobre; p. 309, Panza de pobre, primero reventar que sobre. Espinosa, A., p. 98, Barriga de pobre - primero reviente que sobre. Rodriguez-Marin (1930), p. 125, En
la casa del pobre, reventan antes que sobre; p. 274, Quien es
pobre, antes revienta que sobre.

702 (A). Panza llena, corazón contento.
702 (B). Barriga llena, corazón contento.
702 (C). Estómago contento, corazón contento.

Translation or Interpretation: Belly full, heart content.
Full belly, happy heart.

Context: My grandmother was advising my cousin about keeping
a husband happy. She said food was very important in marriage,
and she said the above saying. (36 occurrences. Informants:
21 female, 14 male, one anonymous).

Sources and Annotations: Aranda, p. 24, same as A. Armas, p.
409, same as B. Ballesteros, p. 56, same as A. Benavides, p.
90, same as A. Cobos, p. 97, same as A. Conde, p. 60, same as
B. Chavez, p. 48, same as A. Espinosa, A., p. 103, same as B.
Galvan, p. 126, same as A; p. 132, same as A. Gamiz, p. 74,
same as B. Glazer, p. 57, same as A. Jaramillo, p. 368, same
as B. MacArthur, p. 43, same as B. Martinez, p. 46, same as
B. Perez, p. 124, same as A. Rodriguez-Marin (1926), p. 54,
same as B. Santamaria, p. 191, same as B; p. 207, same as B.
Vasquez, p. 89, same as A. Villafuerte, p. 100, same as A.
Wesley, p. 216, same as A.

703 (A). Si me he de morir, mejor con panza llena que con
barriga vacía.

Translation or Interpretation: If I am to die, better with
belly full than with belly empty.

Context: María Guillen, who was born in San Pedro Piedra Gor-
da, in Guadalajara, México, recalls she first heard this saying
when she was fifteen, and heard it from her father when the
family lived in México City. This saying was said very often
at the dinner table. (One occurrence. Informant: female).

Sources and Annotations: None.

704 (A). Estudia para ser papa y sale camote.
704 (B). Estudió para papa y salió camote.
704 (C). Estudian para papa pero crecen camotes.

Translation or Interpretation: Studies to be potatoe and comes out yam. Studies for pope and turns out sweet potatoe.

Context: A young college boy walked into his home where there were visitors and did not bother to give a greeting. The father shakes his head and says the above proverb, lamenting the lack of manners of the young. (Three occurrences. Informants: two female, one male).

Sources and Annotations: Cerda, p. 307, Estudiar para papa y salir camote. Conde, p. 178, same as A.

705 (A). De los parientes y el sol, entre más lejos mejor.
705 (B). De los parientes y el sol, entre más lejos.
705 (C). Los parientes y el sol, entre más lejos mejor.

Translation or Interpretation: Relatives and the sun, the farther the better.

Context: This was mentioned after a conversation about an intruding mother-in-law. (Three occurrences. Informants: two female, one male).

Sources and Annotations: Cobos, p. 29, same as A; p. 56, Entre los parientes y el sol, entre más lejos mejor; p. 77, same as C; p. 98, Parientes y el sol entre más lejos, mejor. Martinez, p. 91, De los parientes, los jefes y el sol entre más lejos, mejor. Robe, p. 70, same as A. Rodriguez-Marin (1926), p. 118, De los senores y el sol mientras mas lejos mejor. Rubio, p. 142, De los parientes y el sol mientras mas lejos, mejor. Santamaria, p. 413, De los parientes y el sol mientras más lejos, mejor. Sbarbi, p. 757, De los parientes y el sol, cuanto más lejos, mejor. Velasco, p. 54, De los parientes, los jefes, y el sol mientras más lejos, mejor. Yáñez, p. 56, De los padrecitos y el sol, mientras más lejos, mejor.

706 (A). Al mal paso darle prisa.
706 (B). Al mal rato, darle prisa.

Translation or Interpretation: To a bad pace, give haste.

Context: If you are performing something which you do not like to do. Example: for a man washing dishes, he hurries and gets it over with. (Four occurrences. Informants: two female, two male).

Sources and Annotations: Adame, p. 8, same as A; p. 11, same as A. Ballesteros, p. 19, same as A. Conde, p. 32, same as A. Jaramillo, p. 380, El mal paso andarlo pronto. Pérez, p. 118, same as A. Rodriguez-Marin (1926), p. 23, Al mal paso, darse prisa; p. 189, En mal camino, darse prisa. Sbarbi, p. 190, El mal camino andarlo pronto; p. 761, Al mal paso, darse prisa.

707 (A). Déjalos que cordoveen que ya agarrarán su paso.

Translation or Interpretation: Let them buck that in time they will obtain their pace.

Context: Informant tells others this proverb when they try to change other people's minds. (One occurrence. Informant: female).

Sources and Annotations: Yáñez, p. 62, Déjalas que corcoveen, que ya agarrarán el paso.

708 (A). Más vale paso que dure y no trote que canse.
708 (B). Vale más paso que dure y no que recule.
708 (C). Vale más paso que dure y no paso que canse.
708 (D). Más vale paso que llegue que trote que canse.
708 (E). Más vale trote que dure que paso que canse.

Translation or Interpretation: Better pace that lasts and no trot that tires.

Context: None given. (12 occurrences. Informants: six female, six male).

Sources and Annotations: Adame, p. 66, same as A; p. 67, same as A; p. 98, Vale más paso que dure y no trote que canse; p. 99, Vale más paso que dure y no trote que canse. Armas, p. 416, Más vale paso que dure y no que madruge. Cerda, p. 309, A paso que dure. Cobos, p. 80, same as A; p. 120, Vale más paso que dure que no que apresure. Conde, p. 255, Más vale paso que dure y no recule. Gamiz, p. 94, Más vale que dure y no que apresure. Jaramillo, p. 403, Más vale paso que dure, que no que madure; p. 413, Paso que dure y no que madure. Rodriguez-Marin (1930), p. 199, Más vale al paso andar que correr y tropezar; p. 261, Portante que dure, y no trote que sude. Villafuerte, p. 73, Más vale trote que dure que galope que canse.

709 (A). Ya descrubío el pastel.

Translation or Interpretation: Now he discovered the pie.

Context: Meaning that one has discovered what is going on because some one spilled the beans. (One occurrence. Informant: female).

Sources and Annotations: Caballero, p. 486, Descubrir el pastel; p. 989, Se descubrió el pastel. Sbarbi, p. 762, Descubrirse el pastel. Wesley, p. 216, No descubras el pastel.

710 (A). Meter la pata.
710 (B). Metiste la pata.
710 (C). No metas la pata donde no debes.

Translation or Interpretation: Insert the foot.

Context: My grandfather used this when he was telling us that
he almost bought a very good saddle at a very reasonable price
but my grandmother had made a comment about how they had wanted an outrageous price for the same saddle at the store across
the street. The man then realized that it was a more expensive saddle. Grandfather said that my grandmother "metio la
pata."

Sources and Annotations: Armas, p. 308, same as A. Caballero, p. 787, same as A. Gamiz, p. 86, Meter la pata; meter las
cuatro; meter el choclo. Martinez, p. 182, same as A. Santamaria, p. 275, same as A; p. 425, Meter uno su cuchara. Sbarbi, p. 762, Meter uno la pata. Velasco, p. 103, same as A.
Villafuerte, p. 88, same as A.

711 (A). Salir con una pata de gallo.

Translation or Interpretation: Come out with a ridiculous
saying.

Context: Informant said her mother used this proverb on her
daughter. The grandmother asked the little girl to turn off
the water in the sink, and the little girl answered that
there was no key in the room. The grandmother said that, "no
me salgas con una pata de gallo." (One occurrence. Informant: female).

Sources and Annotations: Caballero, p. 588, Eso es salir con
una pata de gallo; p. 979, Salir con su pata de gallo. Sbarbi,
p. 763, same as A.

712 (A). Patas para que son buenas.

Translation or Interpretation: Feet, for what are they good?

Context: My mother was telling my brother to go to the store,
but he wanted to go in the car. She replied with this proverb. (One occurrence. Informant: female).

Sources and Annotations: Armas, p. 329, Patas, para qué los
quiero. Caballero, p. 901, Pies, ¿para qué los quiero?

713 (A). Hay veces que el pato nada y a veces ni agua toma.

Translation or Interpretation: There are times when a duck
swims, and sometimes he does not even drink water.

Context: The meaning of this proverb is that sometimes times are good and you have everything you need to live, like food, money, and health. Then there are other times when things are just not going right and you lack all of the necessities of life. You find yourself at the other extreme, without money, or food, or anything. (One occurrence. Informant: male).

Sources and Annotations: Conde, p. 191, same as A. Martínez, p. 141, Hay veces que el pato nada y veces que ni agua bebe. Yánez, p. 297, Hay veces que nada el pato y otras que ni agua bebe.

714 (A). A volar patos.

Translation or Interpretation: Fly ducks!

Context: An aunt was talking to some visitors and her children were playing in the house when she told them "a volar patos." (One occurrence. Informant: female).

Sources and Annotations: None.

715 (A). Tanto pedo para cagar aguado.

Translation or Interpretation: So much flatulence to defecate soft.

Context: I first heard this from my mother years back. She was trying to tell us that we had made a big thing for nothing. I guess the best translation would be "all that for nothing." (One occurrence. Informant: female).

Sources and Annotations: Conde, p. 384, Tanto pedo para un hollejo.

716 (A). Amigo Pedro, Amigo Juan, pero más amiga la verdad.

Translation or Interpretation: Friend Peter, friend John, but better friend, the truth.

Context: A person can have many friends and out of all, only one is a best friend, the only friend that tells the truth. (One occurrence. Informant: female).

Sources and Annotations: Sbarbi, p. 66, Amigo Pedro, amigo Juan, pero más amigo de la verdad.

717 (A). Lo que se a de pelar que se vaya desgiando.
717 (B). Lo que se vaya a pelar que se vaya remojando.
717 (C). Lo que se a de pelar que se vaya remojando.

Translation or Interpretation: What is to be peeled should be defoliated.

Context: Could be used as a hint or suggestion to a person beginning a complicated project. Or, if afterwards, things have gone array, a "I told you so." (Three occurrences. Informants: female).

Sources and Annotations: Cerda, p. 310, Lo que se ha de pelar, que se vaya remojando. Conde, p. 97, Chile que se ha de pelar que se vaya remojando; p. 238, same as C. Martinez, p. 168, Lo que se ha de pelar, que se vaya remojando; p. 168, same as B. Rubio, p. 300, same as C. Santamaria, p. 438, same as C. Velasco, p. 97, same as B; p. 97, Lo que se ha de pelar que se vaya remojando.

718 (A). No tengo pelos en la lengua.

Translation or Interpretation: I do not have hairs on my tongue.

Context: Minnie uses this proverb to say that you should say what you feel. (One occurrence. Informant: female).

Sources and Annotations: Armas, p. 323, No tener pelos en la lengua. Caballero, p. 855, No tener pelos en la lengua. Conde, p. 299, No tiene pelos en la lengua; p. 415, Yo no tengo pelos en la lengua. Espinosa, A., p. 109, No tiene pelo en la lengua. Rubio, p. 62, same as A.

719 (A). Cuéntale tus penas a quien te las pueda remediar.

Translation or Interpretation: Tell your sorrows to who can remedy them.

Context: Tell your troubles to those who can help. Why tell me? (Four occurrences. Informants: male).

Sources and Annotations: Benavides, p. 89, same as A. Conde, p. 95, Cuenta tu pena al que te entienda. Rodriguez-Marin (1926), p. 42, A quien no te ha de ayudar, no le vayas a llorar.

720 (A). El pendejo trabaja doble.

Translation or Interpretation: The fool works double.

Context: Our uncle has two jobs and both full time. Why? Because he has a mistress with children and he also has his wife. He states that he works to sustain his family, but this is not so. It is because of his mistress and wife. (One occurrence. Informant: female).

Sources and Annotations: Jaramillo, p. 381, El perezoso trabaja doble.

721 (A). Es mejor callado y que te crean un pendejo que hablar y quitar toda duda.

Translation or Interpretation: It is better to be silent and be thought a fool than to speak and remove all doubt.

Context: A person who talks about things he doesn't know, will be thought of as a fool. (Two occurrences. Informants: male).

Sources and Annotations: None.

722 (A). El primer pensamiento es el mejor.

Translation or Interpretation: The first thought is the best.

Context: A. S., who lives in McAllen, Texas and is presently an owner of a produce shed in Pharr, Texas, recalls this proverb about the year 1954. He said that he learned it from his high school baseball coach, who was anglo, but told him it in Spanish. He said that his baseball coach told him while he was getting ready to pitch an important game. He said that his baseball coach would always tell him to pitch the pitch he felt comfortable with and not the one that he thought of as a second choice. He said that he will always remember this because many times it saved him at home, at school, and in life in general. He also repeats this to his family when they are deciding upon something in their lives. I had heard this proverb, and also try to take my first impulse, or thought, for many times it is the correct one. (Three occurrences. Informant: two female, one male).

Sources and Annotations: Benavides, p. 90, same as A. Hudson, p. 121, same as A.

723 (A). Te voy a poner las peras a dos por veinticinco.

Translation or Interpretation: I am going to set (your) pears at 2 for 25.

Context: This proverb is used very often in Mexico, and by people who were born in Mexico and are now living here. It is most often used by the parents directing the son or daughter, meaning that if he or she does not do as told, he or she was going to get it. They were going to get a big whipping. Mrs. R. remembers her mother saying this proverb very often when she was a little girl, and she also recalls other parents directing it to other kids. She says that children were often scared when they would hear it. In most occasions it worked.

236

Now she herself uses it. (One occurrence. Informant: female).

Sources and Annotations: Caballero, p. 908, Poner a uno las
peras a cuatro.

724 (A). Cuando la perra es brava hasta los de casa muerde.

Translation or Interpretation: When the bitch is fierce, she
will even bite the family.

Context: In politics, even when they are friends, they take.
(One occurrence. Informant: male).

Sources and Annotations: Cerda, p. 311, De que la perra es
brava, hasta los de la casa muerde. Conde, p. 92, same as A.
Yañez, p. 69, De que la perra es brava, hasta los de la casa
muerde.

725 (A). Perro ladrador, poco mordedor.

Translation or Interpretation: Barking dog, scanty biter.

Context: B. is a student at Pan American University. She
told me that a dog that barks doesn't bite, meaning that if a
girl says that she wants to fight not to worry, they are just
words, she won't bite. When she was in school back home, she
said that a girl told her that she was going to beat her up.
Bertha got very scared and told her mother, but her mother
told her that the dog that barks doesn't bite. Sure enough,
the next day, when B. asked her "where do you want me to meet
you?" the girl said, very scared, "I was only playing."
(Three occurrences. Informants: one female, one male).

Sources and Annotations: Aranda, p. 16, Gato maullador, pobre
cazador; p. 24, Perro que ladra no muerde. Cerda, p. 312,
Perro que ladra no muerde. Correas, p. 320, Del perro que
muerde y no ladra. Chávez, p. 46, Perro que ladra no muerde.
De Barros, p. 364, Perro ladrador, nunca buen mordedor. Rubio,
p. 96, Perro que ladra no muerde. Sbarbi, p. 788, Perro que
ladra no muerde. Vásquez, p. 89, Perro que ladra no muerde.

726 (A). Perro que da en tragar huevos, aunque le quemes el
horico.

Translation or Interpretation: Dog that (tends) to devouring
eggs, even if you burn its muzzle.

Context: Developing a smoking habit. After you're hooked,
it's very hard to stop. (One occurrence. Informant: male).

Sources and Annotations: Ballesteros, p. 64, Perro que dan de tragar huevos aunque le quemen el hocico. Cerda, p. 312, Perro que da en comer huevos aunque le quemen el hocico. Cobos, p. 99, Perro que da en comer huevos aunque le quemen el hocico. Conde, p. 316, Perro que da en comer huevos aunque le quemen el hocico. Galvan, p. 129, Perro huevero aunque le quemen el hocico; p. 132, Perro huevero aunque le quemen el hocico. Gamiz, p. 94, Perro que da en comer huevos, aunque le quemen el hocico. Paredes, p. 30, El perro que come huevos aunque le quemen el pico. Santamaria, p. 12, Gallina que come huevo, aunque le quemen o le corten el pico; p. 453, Perro que come huevo, si no lo come, lo huele. Sbarbi, p. 788, Perro huevero aunque le quemen el hocico. Villafuerte, p. 182, Perro dañino de huevos aunque le quemen el hocico. Wesley, p. 215, Perro que come huevos sique aunque le queme el pico.

727 (A). <u>Perro</u> que ladra no muerde.

<u>Translation or Interpretation</u>: Dog that barks does not bite.

<u>Context</u>: Possible example would be an individual who talks too much but does not pursue action. (52 occurrences. Informants: 33 female, 17 male, two anonymous).

<u>Sources and Annotations</u>: Adame, p. 79, same as A; p. 80, same as A. Aranda, p. 24, same as A. Armas, p. 419, same as A. Arora, p. 358, Ese es como perro de rancho: ladra pero no muerde. Ballesteros, p. 64, same as A. Cerda, p. 312, same as A. Conde, p. 317, same as A. Chavez, p. 46, same as A. Espinosa, A., p. 109, same as A. Galvan, p. 131, same as A. Glazer, p. 57, same as A. Jaramillo, p. 414, same as A. Lea, p. 237 same as A. Lucero-White, p. 36, same as A. MacArthur, p. 65, same as A. Maldonado, p. 45, Perro que mucho ladra, poco muerde; p. 60, Perro ladrador, nunca buen mordedor. Perez, p. 125, same as A. Robe, p. 71, Ese es como perro de rancho, ladra pero no muerde. Rodríguez-Marín (1926), p. 68, Can que ladra, no muerde; p. 365, same as A. Rubio, p. 96, same as A. Santamaria, p. 453, same as A. Sbarbi, p. 788, same as A; p. 787, Ladreme el perro y no me muerda. Vásquez, p. 89, same as A. Villafuerte, p. 182, same as A. Yáñez, p. 41, same as A; p. 51, same as A.

728 (A). <u>Perro</u> que no sale no encuentra hueso.
728 (B). <u>Perro</u> que no sale no junta hueso.
728 (C). <u>Perro</u> que sale encuentra hueso.

<u>Translation or Interpretation</u>: Dog that does not go out will not find bones.

<u>Context</u>: Informant claims that he hears the above being used whenever he was shy and wouldn't ask girls for dates, or when he just laid around home doing nothing. (Five occurrences. Informants: three female, two male).

Sources and Annotations: Aranda, p. 24, same as A. Cerda, p. 312, same as A. Cobos, p. 99, same as A. Conde, p. 317, Perro que no anda no topa hueso. Chavez, p. 48, same as A. Espinosa, A., p. 109, Perro que no anda no encuentra hueso. Lea, p. 237, same as A. Lucero-White, p. 36, same as A. Rodriguez-Marin (1930), p. 252, Perro que no anda, hueso no tropieza. Rodriguez-Marin (1926), p. 365, Perro que no anda, hueso no halla. Sbarbi, p. 788, same as A.

729 (A). El perro no muerde la mano de comer.

Translation or Interpretation: The dog does not bite the feeding hand.

Context: Old people mention this advice when talking to a potential, or known, abuser of his or her occupation. (One occurrence. Informant: anonymous).

Sources and Annotations: Conde, p. 302, Nunca le muerdas la mano a quien te de de comer.

730 (A). Entre más flaco está el perro, más las pulgas se le cargan.

Translation or Interpretation: The skinnier the dog, the more the fleas load on him.

Context: Everyone always picks on the one who has more necessity. (One occurrence. Informant: female).

Sources and Annotations: Adame, p. 34, same as A; p. 48, same as A. Caballero, p. 97, Al perro flaco todo se le vuelven pulgas. De Barros, p. 102, A perro flaco todo se le vuelven pulgas.

731 (A). Me traiban como el perro en barrio ajeno.
731 (B). Lo agarraron como perro en barrio ajeno.

Translation or Interpretation: They had me like a dog in another's neighborhood.

Context: Used to describe a person that has been verbally beaten or criticized. (Two occurrences. Informants: female).

Sources and Annotations: Conde, p. 44, Anda como perro en barrio ajeno. Galvan, p. 125, Están como perro en barrio ajeno; p. 128, Están como perro en barrio ajeno. Santamaria, p. 453, Como perro en barrio ajeno.

732 (A). Muerto el perro se acaba la rabia.
732 (B). Mata el perro y se acaba la rabia.

Translation or Interpretation: Dead the dog, the rabies ends.

Context: Informant said this proverb to a friend saying that just because he had apologized for an interference he had done it did not mean that it had not happened. This was like, if the dog was dead, there would be no rabies. (Two occurrences. Informants: one female, one dead).

Sources and Annotations: Caballero, p. 800, Muerto el perro se acabo la rabia. Cobos, p. 84, Murió el perro y se acabo la rabia; p. 109, Se murio el perro, se acabó la rabia. Conde, p. 189, Hasta donde duro el perro, duro la rabia. Martinez, p. 186, same as A. Rodriguez-Marin (1926), p. 313, Muerto el perro, se acabo la rabia. Sbarbi, p. 45, Muerto el perro se acabo la rabia; p. 787, Muerto el perro se acabo la rabia. Yáñez, p. 188, same as A.

733 (A). Para cada perro hay su garrote.

Translation or Interpretation: For every dog there is a club.

Context: Used, usually, when a boy or man likes to bully people and then someone beats him. (One occurrence. Informant: male).

Sources and Annotations: None.

734 (A). Todos los perros tienen su día.

Translation or Interpretation: All dogs have their day.

Context: This is an angry man talking about another, who has made him mad. It is equivalent to, "I'll get even with you." (One occurrence. Informant: male).

Sources and Annotations: None.

735 (A). La persona que es mas cabrona es la que ladra más.

Translation or Interpretation: The person who is more of a cuckold is the one who barks more.

Context: None given. (One occurrence. Informant: male).

Sources and Annotations: None.

736 (A). Si no vas a decir algo bueno de una persona mejor no digas nada.

Translation or Interpretation: If you are not going to say something good about a person, better not say anything.

Context: None given. (One occurrence. Informant: female).

Sources and Annotations: None.

737 (A). Hay buenas y malas personas en este mundo.

Translation or Interpretation: There are good and bad persons
in this world.

Context: When I asked my father why there are people who
steal, drink, and kill, he replied with the above proverb.
(One occurrence. Informant: female).

Sources and Annotations: None.

738 (A). El pescado grande se come al chico.
738 (B). El pescado más grande se come al más chico.

Translation or Interpretation: The large fish eats the small
one.

Context: M. tells her kids that a smart person will take advantage of you. (Three occurrences. Informants: one female,
two male).

Sources and Annotations: Caballero, p. 748, Los peces grandes
se comen los chicos. Conde, p. 141, El pez grande se traga al
chico. Correas, p. 108, El pez grande come al chico. Gamiz,
p. 78, El pez grande se come al chico. Jaramillo, p. 381, El
pez grande se come al mas pequeño. Lucero-White, p. 34, Los
peces mayores se tragan a los menores.

739 (A). El pescado por su boca muere.
739 (B). Vas a morir como los pescados, por la boca.

Translation or Interpretation: The fish, because of his
mouth, dies.

Context: Told to a person who talks too much and might get
in trouble because of it.

Sources and Annotations: Adame, p. 31, El pescado por su
boca cae; p. 37, El pescado por su boca cae. Alcalá, p. 91,
Por su boca muere el pez. Caballero, p. 916, Por la boca
muere el pez. Cobos, p. 40, El pescado por la boca muere; p.
100, Por la boca muere el pez. Conde, p. 141, El pez por su
boca muere. Jaramillo, p. 414, Por la boca muere el pez.
Santamaria, p. 340, El pez por la boca muere; p. 454, same
as A.

740 (A). El pescado que se duerme se lo lleva la corriente.

Translation or Interpretation: The fish that falls asleep

is taken by the current.

Context: Telling a person to keep his eyes open and not miss out on an opportunity when it is in front of you. If you keep "falling asleep" you will never accomplish anything. (Eight occurrences. Informants: three female, five male).

Sources and Annotations: Conde, p. 317, Pescado que se duerme se lo lleva la corriente. Yáñez, p. 20, Al pescado que se duerme se lo lleva la corriente.

741 (A). Peso en mano, chivo afuera.

Translation or Interpretation: Peso in hand, goat outside.

Context: There was once a very rich land owner who thought he could outwit his uneducated less prosperous neighbor. It seems that the poor neighbor had come up with a rather large number of sheep by unknown means. The rich landowner thought that he could get his neighbor to sell him the sheep at a very low price. Since the neighbor could not count, he thought he would just tell him "you have, so many sheep so here is the same amount of money for them." Guess who was outwitted? As the rich man approached his neighbor, he told him, "you have fifty sheep, so here are your fifty dollars." The poor, uneducated neighbor told him, "but señor, there are so many sheep, it is too hard to count them right. I know a better way. As you can see, the corral gate is too small to let out more than one sheep at a time, so, as each sheep goes out of the corral, you put a dollar in my hand, that way we will know that no mistake has been made. I would not want you to pay me more money than I have coming." Thus, the saying, "peso en mano, chivo afuera." (Three occurrences. Informants: one female, two male).

Sources and Annotations: Ballesteros, p. 64, same as A. Gamiz, p. 89, same as A. Martinez, p. 82, Chivo brincado, Chivo pagado. Robe, p. 67, same as A. Rodriguez-Marin (1926), p. 101, Chivo fuera, peso duro a la montera.

742 (A). Mi pecho no es bodega.
742 (B). Mi pecho no es bodega de nadie.

Translation or Interpretation: My chest is not a warehouse.

Context: What a person tells me may not stay in my chest, therefore, don't trust me. (Four occurrences. Informants: two female, one male, one anonymous).

Sources and Annotations: None.

743 (A). No se asusten con el <u>petate</u> del muerto.

<u>Translation or Interpretation</u>: Do not be frightened with the sleeping mat of the dead one.

<u>Context</u>: Whenever a person plays dumb and tells you that he knows nothing. (One occurrence. Informant: female).

<u>Sources and Annotations</u>: Cerda, p. 313, Agustarse uno con el petate (sombrero) del muerto.

744 (A). Entre más <u>picante</u>, más constante.

<u>Translation or Interpretation</u>: The spicier, the more constant.

<u>Context</u>: My informant said that this friend of hers always comes to dinner and would never get the message that they didn't want him to eat there everyday. Her mother told her the above phrase. Her food was so good that he couldn't resist to come and eat. (One occurrence. Informant: female).

<u>Sources and Annotations</u>: None.

745 (A). Al que no <u>pide</u> no le dan.

<u>Translation or Interpretation</u>: To the one who does not ask (do not give).

<u>Context</u>: A child was eating a candy when I was also a child. When he had eaten the candy, I told him that I wanted some. He replied with the proverb. (One occurrence. Informant: male).

<u>Sources and Annotations</u>: None.

746 (A). Al <u>pie</u> del cañon.

<u>Translation or Interpretation</u>: At the foot of the cannon.

<u>Context</u>: This saying is a lot like the one about being on the firing line. It means that you have something that you must do, and must not be deterred. This can be used when someone wants you to do something, like go fishing, and because you have to be at work early the next morning, you reply with this saying. (One occurrence. Informant: male).

<u>Sources and Annotations</u>: None.

747 (A). Te doy un <u>pie</u> y agarras pie y mano.

<u>Translation or Interpretation</u>: I give you a foot and you take foot and hand.

Context: When my grandmother was helping my mother in the kitchen, my mother starting noticing that my grandmother was taking over all of the tasks in the kitchen. My mother then said the proverb to her. (One occurrence. Informant: female).

Sources and Annotations: Adame, p. 9, A un villano dale el pie y se toma la mano; p. 14, A un villano dale el pie y se toma la mano. Caballero, p. 730, Les dan el pie y se toma la mano. Espinosa, A., p. 107, Le dan el pie y se toma la mano. Rodriguez-Marin (1926), p. 41, A quien le dan el pie, se toma la mano.

748 (A). Vale más a pie y no a caballo.

Translation or Interpretation: It is better on foot than on horse.

Context: This would mean that it is better to go walking and be safe, than to ride a horse and something to happen. (One occurrence. Informant: female).

Sources and Annotations: None.

749 (A). Piedra que rueda no cría moho.

Translation or Interpretation: Stone that rolls does not create moss.

Context: Informant's mother always used this phrase to refer to her when she was lazying off and gaining weight. She always referred to the rust as being fat. (One occurrence. Informant: female).

Sources and Annotations: Caballero, p. 901, Piedra que rueda no coge musgo. Conde, p. 317, same as A. Covarrubias, p. 809, Piedra movediza, nunca la cubre moho; p. 870, Piedra movidiza, nunca la cubre moho. Espinosa, A., p. 109, Piedra movediza no cria mojo. Espinosa, F., p. 192, Piedra movediza, no le cubre mojo. Gamiz, p. 74, Piedra movediza no crea moho. Jaramillo, p. 414, Piedra movediza no cria lama. Lea, p. 237, Piedra movediza no cria moho. Lucero-White, p. 36, Piedra movediza no cria moho. Robe, p. 70, Piedra que rueda no cria lama. Rodriguez-Marin (1930), p. 252, Piedra que rueda no coge musgo; Piedra movediza no cria moho. Rubio, p. 98, same as A. Sbarbi, p. 797, Piedra movediza nunca la cubre moho.

750 (A). Tira la piedra y esconde la mano.
750 (B). El que tira la piedra esconde la mano.
750 (C). Los que tiran la piedra esconden la mano.
750 (D). No tires la piedra y escondas la mano.

Translation or Interpretation: He throws the stone and hides the hand.

Context: Pete gets a friend of his in trouble at work by accusing him of an act he did not commit. Pete will deny that
he ever said anything against his friend. (Four occurrences.
Informants: Three female, one male).

Sources and Information: Armas, p. 397, Tirar la piedra y
esconder la mano. Caballero, p. 1072, Tirar la piedra y esconder la mano. Conde, p. 388, same as A. Covarrubias, p. 870,
Tirar la piedra y esconder la mano. Chávez, p. 48, same as A.
De Barros, p. 450, Tirar la piedra y esconder la mano. Espinosa, A., p. 111, same as A. Espinosa, F., p. 192, same as A.
Gamiz. Jaramillo, p. 426, Tirar la piedra y esconder la mano.
Maldonado, p. 26, Echa la piedra y esconder la mano. Martinez,
p. 264, same as A. Rodriguez-Marin (1930), p. 148, Hecho villano, tirar la piedra y esconder la mano; p. 160, La caridad
es la piedra filosofal. Sbarbi, p. 797, Tirar la piedra y
esconder la mano. Yáñez, p. 9, Tirar la piedra y esconder la
mano; p. 53, Avientan la piedra y esconde la mano.

751 (A).   Calla y coje piedras. Si de alguien te quieres
            vengar, has de callar, aunque la injuria más segura
            es olvidarla que vengarla.

Translation or Interpretation: Be quiet and gather stones.
If of someone you revenge, you should be quiet, although the
injury most surely will be forgotten than avenged.

Context: It is better to forgive and forget than to get into
larger problems.

Sources and Annotations: Cobos, p. 68, La mejor venganza es
olvidar la injuria; p. 99, Perdonar mejor que vengar. Conde,
p. 379, Si te has de vengar, te has de callar. Lucero-White,
p. 36, Olvidar la injuria es la mejor venganza. Rodriguez-
Marin (1930), p. 338, Yo que callo, piedras apano. Rodriguez-
Marin (1926), p. 394, Quien calla, piedras apanas, y tiempo
vendra en que las esparza.

752 (A).   Las piedras rodando se encuentran.
752 (C).   Rodando, las piedras se encuentran.

Translation or Interpretation: Rolling stones will meet each
other.

Context: Once my parents and I were outside a parking lot
waiting for a sister. Close by were a couple who had not seen
each other for a long time, and looked happy, seeing each other again. Then, my father said to us, "las piedras rodando
se encuentran." (Seven occurrences. Informants: five female, two male).

Sources and Annotations: Ballesteros, p. 9, same as A. Cobos,
p. 71, same as A; p. 106, same as A. Conde, p. 224, same as A.

245

Espinosa, A., p. 107, same as A. Robe, p. 71, Andando la piedra se encuentran. Rubio, p. 287, same as A. Vásquez, p. 89,
same as A.

753 (A).   Dormir a _pierna_ suelta.

Translation or Interpretation: To sleep with loose leg.

Context: My mother used this proverb when telling my grandmother that my father never hears anything at night, and is
never bothered by anything, since he, "duerma a pierna suelta."
(One occurrence. Informant: female).

Sources and Annotations: Armas, p. 250, same as A; p. 350,
Roncar a pierna suelta. Caballero, p. 134, A pierna suelta. p.
516, same as A. Conde, p. 120, Durmiendo a pierna suelta.
Covarrubias, p. 484, Dormir a pierna tendida; p. 870, Dormir
a pierna tendida es con descuido.

754 (A).   No les busques tres _pies_ al gato porque le hallas
           cuatro.
754 (B).   No le busques _patas_ al gato.
754 (C).   No le busques tres _pies_ al gato.
754 (D).   No le busques tres _pies_ al gato sabiendo que tiene
           cuatro.
754 (E).   No le busques tres _pies_ al gato porque le encuentras
           cuatro.

Translation or Interpretation: Do not look for three feet on
a cat because you will find four.

Context: This _dicho_, or proverb, is used to poke fun at people who consistently read between the lines and, as a result,
think they have uncovered facts which are contrary to the
truth. (13 occurrences. Informants: seven female, six male).

Sources and Annotations: Alcala, p. 297, Buscar tres o cinco
pies al gato. Armas, p. 227, Busques tres pies al gato. Balle
steros, p. 33, same as C. Benavides, p. 89, same as A. Cobos,
p. 45, El que le busca tres pies al gato le halla cuatro; p.
92, same as D. Espinosa, A., p. 107, Le busca un pie al gato
y le halla cuatro. Galvan, p. 125, Buscarle tres patas al
gato; p. 128, Buscarle tres patas al gato. Glazer, p. 43, same
as C. Jaramillo, p. 369, Buscarle tres pies al gato. MacArthur, p. 19, Le andas buscando cinco pies al gato. Maldonado,
p. 94, Buscais cinco pies al gato, y no tiene mas de cuatro;
no que cinco son con el rabo. Perez, p. 124, No le busques
tres patas al gato porque tiene cuatro. Rubio, p. 68, Buscarle
tres pies al gato sabiendo que tiene cuatro. Yanez, p. 243,
Buscarle tres pies al gato.

755 (A). No puedes soplar y comer pinole al mismo tiempo.

Translation or Interpretation: You cannot blow and eat cereal meal at the same time.

Context: When an individual is trying to do two things at the same time and he has time only for one. Example: A wife needs to do the cooking and wants to go shopping too. (One occurrence. Informant: male).

Sources and Annotations: Cerda, p. 315, No se puede silbar y comer pinole. Cobos, p. 83, Miel en la boca y guarda la bolsa. Conde, p. 297, No se puede chiflar y comer pinole. Gamiz, p. 75, No se puede chiflar y beber agua. Rubio, p. 57, No se puede soplar y comer pinole. Yáñez, p. 354, No se puede soplar y comer pinole.

756 (A). Tan igual es el pinto como el colorado.

Translation or Interpretation: So much the same is the paint-ed one as the red one.

Context: Meaning that two people are the same no matter what color, because some people will say, "I can't do it the same as Mrs. Smith because she's white and I'm brown--Mexican." (One occurrence. Informant: female).

Sources and Annotations: Conde, p. 384, Tanto tienes tanto vales, nada tienes nada vales. Yáñez, p. 160, La yunta de Trujillos: Tan malo el pinto como el amarillo; p. 199, Tan peor el pinto como el amarillo.

757 (A). Es un piojo resucitado.

Translation or Interpretation: He is a resucitated louse.

Context: They say it to a person who has always been poor, but when he has money he acts as if he has always had it. (One occurrence. Informant: female).

Sources and Annotations: Espinosa, A., p. 104, Dios no libre del piojo resucitado. Martinez, p. 225, Piojo resucitado. Rodriguez-Marin (1930), p. 115, El piojo resucitado, ¡Pega cada bocado..! Rodriguez-Marin (1926), p. 500, Un piojo resu-citado, ¡Como pica el condenado. Santamaria, p. 483, Piojo resucitado. Sbarbi, p. 801, Ser uno un piojo resucitado. Velasco, p. 132, Piojo resucitado.

758 (A). Pisa bien y no resbales.

Translation or Interpretation: Step well and do not slip.

Context: A girl who keeps her two feet on the ground will likely not get pregnant. (Two occurrences. Informants: one female, one male).

Sources and Annotations: None.

759 (A). El placer no comunicado no da cumplida alegría ni es bien logrado.

Translation or Interpretation: The pleasure not communicated does not give accomplished joy, not is it well attained.

Context: You need to express your feelings to be understood by the people who are around you. (One occurrence. Informant: female).

Sources and Annotations: Rodriguez-Marin (1926), p. 367, Placer no comunicado no es bien logrado.

760 (A). De la mano a la boca se pierde la sopa.
760 (B). Del plato a la boca se cae la sopa.
760 (C). Del plato a la boca aveces se cae la sopa.
760 (D). Del plato a la boca se pierde la sopa.

Translation or Interpretation: From the hand to the mouth the soup is lost.

Context: There's many a slip between the cup and the lip. (Nine occurrences. Informants: four female, three male, two anonymous).

Sources and Annotations: Adame, p. 23, same as C; p. 26, same as C. Armas, p. 411, same as B. Ballesteros, p. 23, Del plato a la boca a veces se cae la sopa. Cobos, p. 29, same as A. Conde, p. 108, same as B. De Barros, p. 168, Del plato a la boca se enfría la sopa. Jaramillo, p. 376, same as D. Lucero-White, p. 33, same as A. MacArthur, p. 35, same as D. Rodriguez-Marin (1926), p. 113, De la mano a la boca no se pierde la sopa; p. 118, same as D.

761 (A). No soy plato de segunda mesa.
761 (B). Yo no soy plato segunda mesa.

Translation or Interpretation: I am not plate of second table.

Context: One of our friends was invited to a Senior Prom which she was anxious to (attend). The boy made the mistake of saying that he had invited so and so but that she couldn't go. Our friend reproached him and told him that she was not second choice, and declined to go to the prom. (Four occurrences. Informants: three female, one male).

Sources and Annotations: Caballero, p. 839, No me gusta ser
plato de segunda mesa. Conde, p. 175, Es plato de segunda
mesa; p. 415, same as B. Martinez, p. 225, Plato de segunda
mesa. Rubio, p. 99, Plato de segunda mesa, ni en la otra vida
menos es ésta. Velasco, p. 132, Plato de segunda mesa.

762 (A). Parece que no quiebra un plato.

Translation or Interpretation: He looks as if he could not
break a plate.

Context: None given. (One occurrence. Informant: male).

Sources and Annotations: Caballero, p. 804, Cualquiera diría
que no rompe plato; p. 880, same as A. Conde, p. 314, Parece
que no quiebra un plato todos los tiene mochos. Yáñez, p. 68,
Parece que no quiebra un plato y es capaz de acabar con lo
cerra.

763 (A). No es igual comer, a tirarse con los platos.

Translation or Interpretation: It is not the same to eat as
to throw the plates at each other.

Context: Mr. Martinez told me a saying last week and recalls
when he was married, but now that he is divorced, he realizes
that it is hard to do everything around the house. He says
that his mother kept saying this, because now, whenever he
needs anything done for him, she always says "No es igual comer que tirarse con los platos, ¿Verdad hijo?" (Two occurrences. Informants: one female, one male).

Sources and Annotations: Cobos, p. 88, No es lo mismo ver
comer que tirarse con los platos. Conde, p. 282, No es lo
mismo comer, que tirarse con los platos. Martinez, p. 194, No
es lo mismo comer que tirarse con los platos. Rodriguez-Marin
(1926), p. 330, No es lo mismo comer que tirarse los platos.
Santamaria, p. 383, No es lo mismo comer o ver comer, que
tirarse con los platos. Sbarbi, p. 805, No es lo mismo comer
que tirarse con los platos. Velasco, p. 111, No es lo mismo
comer que tirarse con los platos.

764 (A). Pobre del pobre que al cielo no va, lo fregaron
         aquí y lo friegan allá.
764 (B). El que al cielo no va, lo friegan aquí y lo friegan
         allá.

Translation or Interpretation: Poor of the poor who to heaven does not go, they annoy him here and they annoy him there.

Context: My father-in-law said that he remembers hearing
this proverb from his older brother, Melitón, when he was

249

about twenty-eight years old. Circa 1947. He lived with his family in Matamoros, Mexico. He and his brother Melitón has to work very hard to earn a living for the family. They were paid very low wages, and worked at odd jobs here and there. Melitón used to say that the bosses paid very low wages and took advantage of the poor worker. He used to say that the poor suffer and are treated bad here on earth. The poor man dies and if he does not go to heaven, he also gets the shaft in hell. (Three occurrences. Informants: one female, two male).

Sources and Annotations: Conde, p. 318, same as A. Gamiz, p. 90, Pobre del pueblo que al cielo no va...lo muelen aqui y lo muelen alla. Jaramillo, p. 384, El que es bobo al cielo no va: lo friegan aquí y lo friegan alla. Martinez, p. 226, same as A. Pérez, p. 125, Pobre del pobre solo que al cielo no va. Vásquez, p. 89, same as A.

765 (A). Más vale _ponerse_ una vez colorado que cien descolorido.

Translation or Interpretation: Better to turn red one time than pale one hundred times.

Context: When someone asks you for money and you don't say no, and the person you loaned the money to doesn't pay. You have to be reminding him a lot of times to pay your money, because you didn't say no in the first place. (One occurrence. Informant: male).

Sources and Annotations: Adame, p. 98, Vale más una vez ponerse colorado, y no cien veces descolorido; p. 100, Vale más una vez ponerse colorado, y no cien veces descolorido. Armas, p. 416, same as A. Caballero, p. 775, Más vale ponerse una vez colorado, que ciento descolorido. Conde, p. 255, Same as A. Jaramillo, p. 402, Más vale una vez colorado que cien descolorido. Rodriguez-Marin (1926), p. 298, Más vale ponerse una vez colorado que ciento amarillo o descolorido. Santamaria, p. 380, Más vale una vez colorado que ciento descolorido. Yanez, p. 280, same as A.

766 (A). La _práctica_ hace el maestro.

Translation or Interpretation: Practice makes the master.

Context: Professional football player. He will practice his skill until he becomes good at it. (One occurrence. Informant: female).

Sources and Annotations: Ballesteros, p. 29, same as A. Cobos, p. 69, same as A. Espinosa, F., p. 111, La esperiencia Jaramillo, p. 398, same as A. Rodriguez-Marin (1926), p. 253, same as A; p. 381, Practicar hace maestro, que no leer en el cuaderno.

767 (A). Hasta la pregunta es necia.

Translation or Interpretation: Even the question is foolish.

Context: A person asks a question whose answer is common knowledge. (One occurrence. Informant: male).

Sources and Annotations: None.

768 (A). Nunca preguntes lo que no te importa.
768 (B). Nunca preguntes lo que no te interesa.
768 (C). No preguntes lo que no te importa.

Translation or Interpretation: Never ask what does not concern you.

Context: My father said he would use this proverb when other people wouldn't mind their own business. (Three occurrences. Informants: one female, two male).

Sources and Annotations: Cerda, p. 318, same as A. Rubio, p. 67, same as A.

769 (A). Vale más prevenir que lamentar.
769 (B). Vale más prevenir que no tratar de remediar.

Translation or Interpretation: Better to prevent than lament.

Context: It's best you do things right the first time and not have to worry about it never getting done or of it ending up wrong. (Two occurrences. Informants: one female, one male).

Sources and Annotations: Ballesteros, p. 27, Es mejor prevenir que lamentar. Conde, p. 173, Es mejor evitar que lamentar; p. 403, Vale más prever que lamentar. De Barros, p. 278, Más vale prever que lamentar. Jaramillo, p. 388, Es mejor prevenir que curar. Rodriguez-Marin (1926), p. 298, same as A. Sbarbi, p. 820, Más vale prevenir que lamentar.

770 (A). El prometer no empobrece, el dar es el que aniquila.

Translation or Interpretation: To promise does not impoverish, the giving is what annihilates.

Context: If you are a member of a club or organization and you are always volunteering to do everything, that doesn't mean you are going to do it. (One occurrence. Informant: male).

Sources and Annotations: Adame, p. 32, same as A; p. 38, same as A. California Spanish Proverbs and Adages, same as A. Cerda, p. 318, same as A. Conde, p. 141, same as A. Gamiz, p. 79, same as A. Rodriguez-Marin (1930), p. 240, Ofrecer no empobrece; p. 259, Por ofrecer nadie llego a empobrece. Rodriguez-Marin (1926), p. 165, El ofrecer no empobrece; p. 375, El prometer, nadie llego a empobrecer.

771 (A). Donde una puerta se cierra, otra se abre.
771 (B). Con una puerta se cierra, otra se abre.
771 (C). Cuando una puerta se cierra, mil se abren.
771 (D). Cuando la última puerta se cierra las demás se abren.
771 (E). Cuando una puerta se cierra, dos mil se abren.

Translation or Interpretation: Where one door is closed, another opens.

Context: When something drastic happens and you feel that it's the end of the world, one should not give up, but rather, believe that another door will eventually open and make things even better for one. (Six occurrences. Informants: female).

Sources and Annotations: Adame, p. 17, Cuando una puerta se cierra, otra se abre; p. 21, Cuando una puerta se cierra, otra se abre. Aranda, p. 7, same as E. Caballero, p. 414, Cuando una puerta se cierra, otra se abre. Cobos, p. 26, Cuando una puerta se cierra, cien se abren. Covarrubias, p. 886, same as A. De Barros, p. 157, Cuando una puerta se cierra, otra se abre; p. 182, same as A. Espinosa, F., p. 199, same as A. Galvan, p. 126, Cuando una puerta se cierra, otra se abre; p. 133, Cuando una puerta se cierra, otra se abre. Jaramillo, p. 371, Cuando una puerta se cierra ciento se abren. Maldonado, p. 54, same as A. Martinez, p. 75, Cuando una puerta se cierra, dos mil se atrancan. Rodriguez-Marin (1926), p. 96, Cuando se cierra una puerta, se abren cincuenta; p. 97, Cuando una puerta se cierra, ciento se abren; p. 469, Si se te cierra una puerta, otra hallarás abierta; p. 472, Si una puerta se cierra, ciento se abren. Sbarbi, p. 828, Cuando una puerta se cierra, ciento se abren.

772 (A). En la puerta de mi casa tengo una mata de arróz, no
          tienes para cigarros y quieres andar con dos.
772 (B). En la puerta de mi casa tengo una mata de arroz, no
          tiene para cigarros y quiere tener de dos.

Translation or Interpretation: At the door of my house I have a rice plant, you do not have for cigarettes and you want to court two.

Context: This dicho is often used in reference to a man who likes courting more than one woman. It may also be used when

a girl has found out her boyfriend is dating another girl be-
sides her. (Two occurrences. Informants: female).

Sources and Annotations: None.

773 (A). Es puro de noche y de día es cigarro.

Translation or Interpretation: He is cigar by night and by
day he is cigarette.

Context: It is used to describe a person who is guilty of
adultry. (One occurrence. Informant: female).

Sources and Annotations: Martinez, p. 231, Se me hace que
eres puro puro y al amanecer cigarro.

774 (A). Querer es poder.

Translation or Interpretation: To will is power.

Context: If one has a desire to accomplish something in life,
chances are that that individual will succeed. (Six occurrences. Informants: two female, four male).

Sources and Annotations: Adame, p. 83, same as A. Aranda, p.
25, same as A. Ballesteros, p. 14, same as A. Caballero, p.
994, same as A. Cobos, p. 50, El que quierre, puede; p. 103,
same as A. Conde, p. 330, same as A. De Barros, p. 271, Mas
hace el querer que el poder; p. 271, Mas vale el que quiere
que no el que puede. Espinosa, A., p. 101, same as A. Galvan,
p. 132, same as A; p. 133, same as A. Rodriguez-Marin (1930),
p. 264, Querer y poder no es todo uno; p. 287, Quien quiere,
puede. Rodriguez-Marin (1926), p. 387, same as A. Santamaria,
p. 544, same as A. Sbarbi, p. 836, same as A.

775 (A). Quien ama a quien no te ama, responde a quien no te
        llama, andarás carrera vana.

Translation or Interpretation: Whoever loves one who does not
love you answers to who does not call, you will follow a course
in vain.

Context: If a person loves a person who doesn't speak, or
even, know her, she will waste their time just by dreaming the
impossible. (One occurrence. Informant: male).

Sources and Annotations: Conde, p. 38, Ama a quien te ama, y
andarás carrera vana. Sbarbi, p. 63, Ama a quien no te ama,
responde a quien no te llama, y andarás carrera vana.

776 (A). Quien guarda su secreto, excusa mucho mal. Guarda
el secreto en tu seno y no lo metas en alguen más.
Secreto de uno, secreto es. Secreto de dos, secreto
de Dios. Secreto de tres de todos es.

Translation or Interpretation: He who guards his secret, excuses much wrong. Guard the secret in your chest and do not
put it in another's. Secret of one, a secret it is. Secret of
two, secret of God. Secret of three, of all it is.

Context: If you tell your secret to another person, that person will soon tell another and another and everybody will know
your secret. (One occurrence. Informant: female).

Sources and Annotations: Rodriguez-Marin (1930), p. 300,
Secreto no es lo que saben tres.)

777 (A). Quien hoy llora mañana canta.

Translation or Interpretation: Who today cries, tomorrow
sings.

Context: Informant heard his mother say this when he was upset about a neighbor child who would not let him play ball.
(One occurrence. Informant: male).

Sources and Annotations: Rodriguez-Marin (1926), p. 408,
Quien hoy llora, mañana rie.

778 (A). Quien mal dice, peor oye.

Translation or Interpretation: Who tells wrong, worse hears.

Context: My grandmother used this when her neighbor, the
town gossip, came to the house to visit. The neighbor overheard my grandparents arguing. When the neighbor left, grandmother said the neighbor would make the incident a lot bigger
when she retold it. Sure enough, she did. (One occurrence.
Informant: female).

Sources and Annotations: Rodriguez-Marin (1930), p. 278, Quien
más desea, pobre es por rico que sea. Rodriguez-Marin (1926),
p. 406, Quien habla mal, oye peor - o que oiga peor.

779 (A). Quien no anda a prisa llega tarde a misa.

Translation or Interpretation: Whoever does not walk in haste
arrives late to mass.

Context: My mother used this proverb on a friend who always
complained of not finding a job, yet, he slept til noon every-

day. (One occurrence. Informant: female).

Sources and Annotations: Conde, p. 147, same as A.

780 (A). Quien no cae, no se levanta.

Translation or Interpretation: He who does not fall down, does not get up.

Context: "At one time or another something is going to hap-pen to you," my informant said. "You have to go through life having your downfalls, but you're always going to get up. You can't get up without falling down first." He said he did not remember where he first heard this saying, but he understood it to be a popular proverb. (One occurrence. Informant: male).

Sources and Annotations: Sbarbi, p. 181, same as A.

781 (A). Quien se quema con sopa a la otra vez la sopla.

Translation or Interpretation: Who burns himself with soup will blow on it next time.

Context: My informant claims that his mother told him this proverb once, when he burned his tongue, while tasting the food being cooked on the stove. (One occurrence. Informant: male).

Sources and Annotations: Rodriguez-Marin (1926), p. 436, Quien una vez se quemo con la sopa a otra vez, sopla.

782 (A). Quien tiene dinero tiene compañeros.

Translation or Interpretation: He who has money has friends.

Context: None given. (One occurrence. Informant: male).

Sources and Annotations: Conde, p. 151, El que tiene dinero tiene buen compañero. De Barros, p. 405, same as A. Rodríguez-Marin (1930), p. 272, Quien dinero no tiene, tanpoco amigos ni parients; p. 283, Quien no tiene dineros no tiene compa-ñeros.

783 (A). A quien dices tu secreto, das tu libertad y estás
　　　　　sujeto.

Translation or Interpretation: To whom you tell your secret, you give your freedom and are liable.

Context: If you tell somebody what you did, you would be always his friend because you may think that that person might
tell your secrets. (One occurrence. Informant: female).

Sources and Annotations: Correas, p. 20, same as A. De Barros, p. 104, same as A. Rodriguez-Marin (1930), p. 302, Si
al amigo tu secreto dices, cogido te tiene por las narices.

784 (A). Cada quien sabe donde le aprieta el zapato.

Translation or Interpretation: Everyone knows where the shoe
cramps.

Context: Everyone knows his worries and sorrows. (One occurrence. Informant: female).

Sources and Annotations: De Barros, p. 127, Cada uno sabe
donde le aprieta el zapato. MacArthur, p. 20, Tú sabes donde te
aprieta el zapato. Molera, p. 67, Cada uno sabe donde le aprieta el zapato.

785 (A). Cada quien tiene lo que granjea.

Translation or Interpretation: Everyone has what they earn.

Context: I may be very fond of my mother, this, I take her
everywhere and try to give her everything. I can give as much
of a son's love to her to show that I need her, but my brother
can be the opposite. (One occurrence. Informant: female).

Sources and Annotations: None.

786 (A). Hallarás quien te dé menos quien te ruege.

Translation or Interpretation: You will find who will give
you, but not who will beg you.

Context: The informant told me that her husband once invited
her to go out and eat. Then she told him that she was too
tired. So, her husband said, "hallarás quien te de, menos quien
te ruege," and her husband went out by himself. She has never
turned him down since then. (Three occurrences. Informant:
female).

Sources and Annotations: Conde, p. 191, Hay quien te de, pero
no quien te ruegue; p. 385, Tendras quien te dé, pero no quien
te ruegue. Martinez, p. 134, Habra quien te dé, pero no quien
dé ruegue; p. 261, Tendras quien te dé, pero no quien te ruegue.

787 (A). ¿Lo bailado quien te lo quita?

Translation or Interpretation: The danced, who will remove it?

Context: Informant said this to me when my father was getting after me for going out without his permission. She told me, "don't worry, you already did it." (Two occurrences. Informants: one female, one not stated).

Sources and Annotations: Jaramillo, p. 399, Lo bailado, quien me lo quita? Martinez, p. 240, ¿Quien me quita lo bailado?

788 (A). No preguntes quien se murió, nomas sigue la carrosa.

Translation or Interpretation: Do not ask who died, just follow the hearse.

Context: Don't make waves. You just follow the crowd and you'll find out what is happening. (Two occurrences. Informants: male).

Sources and Annotations: Ballesteros, p. 53, No preguntes quien es el muerto, nomás sigue la carroza.

789 (A). Quien a solas se conseja, a solas se desconseja.

Translation or Interpretation: Who to themselves counsel, to themselves will uncounsel.

Context: If a person is counseling himself on what is wrong and what is right, he will think things the best way he thinks is good or bad. (One occurrence. Informant: female).

Sources and Annotations: Rodriguez-Marin (1930), p. 270, Quien consigo se aconseja, si mal; p. 289, Quien solo se aconseja, solo se meja. Rodriguez-Marin (1926), o. 392, Quien a solas se aconseja, a solas se remesa -- o se desconseja. Sbarbi, p. 31, same as A.

790 (A). Quien busca, halla.
790 (B). Quien busca, encuentra.
790 (C). El que busca encuentra.

Translation or Interpretation: Whoever seeks, finds.

Context: When I was looking for my tennis racket, but not really hard enough, my mother found it and she told me the proverb. (Seven occurrences. Informants: Four female, two male, one unstated.

Sources and Annotations: Adame, p. 32, same as B; p. 39, same as B. Caballero, p. 543, El que busca halla. Cobos, p. 104, same as A. De Barros, p. 390, same as A. Espinosa, A., p. 105, El que busca halla; Lea, p. 234, El que busca halla. Lucero-

White, p. 34, El que busca, halla. Rodriguez-Marin (1926), p. 394, same as A. Rubio, p. 73, Once se busca se jalla. Sbarbi, p. 168, same as A.

791 (A). Quien canta, sus males espanta.

Translation or Interpretation: He who sings drives his worries away.

Context: If you are worrying about something, it is sometimes better to sing and your worries are forgotten for a while. (One occurrence. Informant: female).

Sources and Annotations: Armas, p. 412, El que canta, su mal espanta. Campa, p. 64, Quien canta su mal espanta. Conde, p. 142, El que canta, males espanta. Covarrubias, p. 289, same as A. De Barros, p. 391, same as A. Espinosa, F., p. 69, same as A. Galván, p. 127, same as A. Jaramillo, p. 381, El que canta, sus penas espanta. Maldonado, p. 60, same as A. Rodriguez-Marin (1926), p. 395, Quien canta, su mal -- o sus males -- espanta; p. 426, Quien ríe y canta sus males espanta. Sbarbi, p. 199, same as A.

792 (A). Quien come y condesa, dos veces pone la mesa.

Translation or Interpretation: A penny saved is a penny earned.

Context: I first heard this proverb from my mother when I told her I wanted to buy a new car. She felt that I did not need one at the time, and responded with the proverb. (One occurrence. Informant: female).

Sources and Annotations: Covarrubias, p. 347, same as A. De Barros, p. 187, El que come y deja, dos veces pone la mesa; p. 391, same as A. Espinosa, F., p. 83, same as A. Rodriguez-Marin (1926), p. 396, Quien come y condesa -- oy deja --, dos veces pone mesa.

793 (A). Quien mucho duerme poco aprende.
793 (B). El que mucho duerme poco aprende.
793 (C). El que tanto duerme poco aprende.

Translation or Interpretation: Whoever sleeps much learns little.

Context: Attentiveness and alertness are essential for learning. (Eight occurrences. Informants: Four female, three male, one unstated).

Sources and Annotations: Aranda, p. 26, same as A. Cobos, p. 46, same as B; p. 104, Quien duerme mucho, poco aprende,

Conde, p. 343, same as A. De Barros, p. 399, same as A. Lucero-White, p. 36, same as A. Maldonado, p. 46, same as A. Rodriguez-Marin (1926), p. 413, Quien mucho duerme, nada aprende.

794 (A). Quien todo lo quiere, todo lo pierde.

Translation or Interpretation: Who everything wants, everything loses.

Context: Some people who wish for a lot sometimes lose it because they might spend it for something that is not worth anything. (One occurrence. Informant: female).

Sources and Annotations: Cobos, p. 52, El que todo lo quiere, todo lo pierde; p. 106, same as A. Jaramillo, p. 385, El que todo lo quiere, todo lo pierde. Lea, p. 237, same as A. Lucero-White, p. 36, same as A. Perez, p. 125, same as A. Rubio, p. 130, Quien todo quiere todo pierde. Sbarbi, p. 836, same as A.

795 (A). ¿A quien le dan pan que llore?
795 (B). ¿A quien le dan pan que no llore?
795 (C). No le den pan que llore.

Translation or Interpretation: Who do they give bread to who cries?

Context: My informant said that this proverb means that if everything is going the way you want, are you going to complain? My informant first heard this proverb from her grandfather when she was in her teens. Her grandfather had come down Victoria, Texas for a visit, and informant was commenting to her grandfather about a certain relative who had everything going his way and seemed to be very content. My informant's grandfather then used this proverb to describe the individual. (Eight occurrences. Informants: five female, two male, one unstated).

Sources and Annotations: Adame, p. 9, same as A; p. 13, same as A. California Spanish Proverbs and Adages, same as A. Cobos, p. 15, same as A. Conde, p. 49, same as A. Espinosa, A., p. 102, A quien le dan pan que no coma? Martinez, p. 35, same as A. Santamaria, p. 395, same as A.

796 (A). A quien le pique que se rasque.
796 (B). Si te pica ráscate.

Translation or Interpretation: Whom it itches, let him scratch himself.

Context: This probably another version of, "If the shoe fits.." Two occurrences. Informants: one female, one male).

Sources and Annotations: Galván, p. 124, Al que le de comezón que se rasque; p. 126, Al que le de comezón que se rasque. p. 133, Al que le de comezón que se rasque. Jaramillo, p. 366, Al que le pique que se rasque. Rodriguez-Marin (1930), p. 291, Quien tiene sarna, la rasca. Rodriguez-Marin (1926), p. 41, same as A. Santamaria, p. 461, same as A.

797 (A). Cada quien con su cada cual.

Translation or Interpretation: Everyone with his every which.

Context: When we criticize others and somebody reprimands us. (One occurrence. Informant: female).

Sources and Annotations: Cobos, p. 19, same as A. Conde, p. 70, same as A. Covarrubias, p. 730, Cada qual, case con su igual. Espinosa, F., p. 65, Cada cual con su cada cual. Martinez, p. 53, same as A. Rubio, p. 76, same as A. Velasco, p. 30, same as A.

798 (A). Cada quien rasquensen con sus uñas.

Translation or Interpretation: Everyone scratch with their own nails.

Context: The item implies that everyone looks out for himself. The informant stated that the preacher related the item to the congregation during his sermon. The point being that people do not do enough for other people, but instead feed their own selfishness. (One occurrence. Informant: female).

Sources and Annotations: Ballesteros, p. 21, Cada quien se rasca con sus uñas. Cobos, p. 19, same as A. Conde, p. 70, Cada quien que se rasque con sus uñas. Martinez, p. 243, Rascarse con sus propias uñas. Rubio, p. 77, Cada quien se rasca con sus uñas. Santamaria, p. 14, same as A. Velasco, p. 142, Rascarse con sus propias uñas.

799 (A). Cada quien tiene su manera de abajarse de su burro.

Translation or Interpretation: Everyone has his manner of getting off his donkey.

Context: This is said when someone is trying to tell you to do something in a certain way and you want to do it your own way. (One occurrence. Informant: female).

Sources and Annotations: Jaramillo, p. 372, Cada uno tiene su modito de matar pulgas. Rodriguez-Marin (1930), p. 49, Cada uno tiene su manera de pajear. Santamaria, p. 113, Cada uno tiene su modo de apearse; p. 530, Cada quien tiene su modo de matar pulgas. Villafuerte, p. 136, Cada uno tiene su manera de apiarse.

800 (A). Dime con quien andas y te diré quien eres.
800 (B). Dime con quien andas y te digo quien eres.
800 (C). Dime con quien te juntas y te digo quien eres.
800 (D). Dime con quien te juntas y te diré quien eres.
800 (E). Dime a quien prefieres y te diré quien eres.
800 (F). Dime con quien hablas y te diré quien eres.

Translation or Interpretation: Tell me with who you walk and I will tell you who you are.

Context: Many times people can tell what type of person we are just by looking at our friends and acquaintances. (91 occurrences. Informants: 62 female, 24 male, five not stated).

Sources and Annotations: Adame, p. 24, same as A; p. 28, same as A. Aranda, p. 9, same as A. Armas, p. 411, same as A. Ballesteros, p. 3, same as A. Benavides, p. 90, same as A. caballero, p. 503, Dime con quien andas. California Spanish Proverbs and Adages, p. 121, Dime con quien andas y te diré quien eres. Cobos, p. 32, same as A. Conde, p. 113, same as A. Chávez, p. 46, same as A. De Barros, p. 174, same as A. Espinosa, A., p. 104, Dime con quien andas y yo te dire quien eres. Galván, p. 128, same as A; p. 133, same as A. Glazer, p. 48, same as A. Jaramillo, p. 377, same as A. Lea, p. 234, same as A. Lucero-White, p. 33, same as A. MacArthur, p. 25, same as A. Perez, p. 120, same as A. Rodriguez-Marin (1930), p. 89, same as A; Dime con quien andas y decirte he lo que hablas; Dime con quien te vas y te dire con quien volveras; Dime con quien tratas y te dire tus mañas; Dime con quien vas y decirte he lo que haras; Dime con quien vienes y te dire que mañas tienes. Rodriguez-Marin (1926), p. 131, Dime con quien te a-companas y te dire tus mañas; p. 132, Dime de que te alabas y te dire lo que te falta. Rubio, p. 149, same as A. Sbarbi, p. 77, Dime conquien andas, decirte he quien eres. Vásquez, p. 88, same as A.

801 (A). Quieren dado y empujado.

Translation or Interpretation: They want it given and pushed.

Context: A person wants something given but then want it with-out asking for it. In a way wants the other person to beg him to take it. (One occurrence. Informant: female).

Sources and Annotations: Conde, p. 99, Dado, rogado y arrem-pujado; p. 239, Lo quiere dado, rogado y arrempujado. Martinez, p. 83, Dado, rogado, puesto en la puerta y arrempujado. Velasco, p. 49, Dado, rogado, puesto en la puerta y arrempujado.

802 (A). Bendita sea la rama que del tronco sale.

Translation or Interpretation: Blessed be the branch that from the trunk springs.

Context: This is one proverb which is frequently heard from parents or grandparents when their children, or grandchildren, have accomplished things throughout their lives. In other words, parents brag about their children resembling them in their accomplishments. This proverb was often proclaimed to my grandmother because of her hard working abilities and her most generous nature. (Two occurrences. Informants: female).

Sources and Annotations: Sbarbi, p. 841, Bien haya la rama que al tronco sale.

803 (A). Nunca por las ramas bajes, camina siempre hacia el tronco.

Translation or Interpretation: Never through the branches descend, travel always towards the trunk.

Context: This proverb is used to tell somebody that he should go to the head, or the root, whenever something is needed, instead of going to those not in power. (One occurrence. Informant: female).

Sources and Annotations: None.

804 (A). Si visitas no hagas rancho.

Translation or Interpretation: If you visit don't make ranch.

Context: My informant said that her mother would always tell her this proverb whenever she would ask permission to go play with her neighbor. The proverb means that it's all right to go visit somebody, but don't stay too long. (One informant: female).

Sources and Annotations: None.

805 (A). Tengo malos ratos pero no malos gustos.

Translation or Interpretation: I have bad times but not bad tastes.

Context: In a conversation between two girls, one is telling the other what a great guy the new classmate is, and the other girl does not feel the same way. She will tell her this proverb. (One occurrence. Informant: female).

Sources and Annotations: Martinez, p. 262, same as A.

806 (A). El remedio y el trapito y úntamele tantito.

Translation or Interpretation: The remedy and the little rand, and anoint it a little bit.

Context: Be nice to him and butter him up. (One occurrence. Informant: female).

Sources and Annotations: None.

807 (A). No te revientes reata que es el último tirón.
807 (B). Hay reata, no te revientes que es el ultimo tirón.

Translation or Interpretation: Do not break rope that it is the last tug.

Context: My informant told me that he and a friend were going on a long trip and were having trouble with their car. They had already gone fifty miles and needed ten more miles to go. His friend then used the proverb above. (Three occurrences. Informants: one female, two male).

Sources and Annotations: Ballesteros, p. 43, Ay correa no te aflojes que es el ultimo tiron. Cerda, p. 320, same as A. Conde, p. 58, Ay reata no te revientes que es el ultimo jalon. Martinez, p. 43, Ay reata no te revientes que es el ultimo jalon. Santamaria, p. 19, Ay reata no te revientes. Velasco, p. 24, Ay reata no te revientes que es el ultimo jalon.

808 (A). Un resbalón de lengua es peor que el de los pies.

Translation or Interpretation: A slip of the tongue is worse than a slip of the feet.

Context: If a person talks too much, he may say something which will get him in trouble. (One occurrence. Informant: female).

Sources and Annotations: Aranda, p. 30, same as A.

809 (A). El respeto al derecho ajeno es la paz.

Translation or Interpretation: Respect of another's right is peace.

Context: John has respect for other people's rights and feelings. Consequently, there is peace and harmony with those he interacts with. (Six occurrences. Informants: five female, one male).

Sources and Annotations: Ballesteros, p. 6, same as A. Conde, p. 152, same as A. Velasco, p. 68, El respeto al derecho ajeno es la conservación de la dentadura.

810 (A). El _rey_ va a donde puede, no a donde quiere.

Translation or Interpretation: The king goes where he can, not where he wants.

Context: A small person, or a boy, goes where their parents take him, not where he wants to go. (One occurrence. Informant: female).

Sources and Annotations: None.

811 (A). Hablando del _rey_ de Roma, mira quien se asoma.
811 (B). Hablando del _rey_ de Roma, pronto se asoma.
811 (C). Hablando del _rey_ de Roma, San Pedro se asoma.
811 (D). Hablando del _rey_ de Roma y él que se asoma.
811 (E). Hablando del _rey_ de Roma y las narices asoma.
811 (F). Hablando del _rey_ de Roma en la puerta se asoma.
811 (G). Hablando del _rey_ de Roma, y aquí está.

Translation or Interpretation: Speaking of the king of Rome, look who appears.

Context: When a person is talking about someone and that person suddenly comes in. (14 occurrences. Informants: nine female, four male, one not stated).

Sources and Annotations: Adame, p. 32, Hablando del Rey de Roma y en eso se asoma; p. 33, Hablando del Rey de Roma y en eso se asoma. Aranda, p. 16, Hablando del Rey de Roma, el a la puerta se asoma. Ballesteros, p. 50, same as B. Benavidez, p. 89, same as A. Caballero, p. 336, Como el ruin de Roma, que en cuanto se le mienta asoma; p. 561, En hablando del ruin de Roma; En nombrando al ruin de Roma. Cerda, p. 320, same as B. Cobos, p. 55, En nombrando al rey de Roma y por la puerta se asoma; p. 60, Hablando del Rey de Roma y el a la puerta se asoma. Conde, p. 187, same as D. Chavez, p. 49, Hablando del Rey de Roma cuando se asoma. Gamiz, p. 92, Hablando de Rey de Roma, pronto se asoma. Glazer, p. 50, same as A. Jaramillo, p. 393, same as D. Pérez, p. 122, Hablando de Rey de Roma y pronto la cabeza asoma; Hablando del diablo pronto la cabeza asoma.

812 (A). Del _rico_ no apesta nada.

Translation or Interpretation: Of the rich, nothing stinks.

Context: When applying for a loan, use cologne. (One occurrence. Informant: male).

Sources and Annotations: Adame, p. 23, same as A.

813 (A).   En el <u>rico</u> es alegría y en el pobre borrachera.

<u>Translation or Interpretation</u>:   In the rich it is gaity, and in the poor, drunkeness.

<u>Context</u>:   Those that are poor will always remain the same, so enjoy the drunken life of the poor.   Status will never change. (One occurrence.   Informant: female).

<u>Sources and Annotations</u>:   Conde, p. 159, En el pobre es borrachera y en el rico es alegría. Villafuerte, p. 306, same as A.

814 (A).   Ese es <u>rico</u> que está bien con Dios.

<u>Translation or Interpretation</u>:   He is a rich one who is well with God.

<u>Context</u>:   My informant speaks of a certain family who were very poor, yet very religious.   This family seemed to always be cheery and happy, even when they only had the basic essentials to stay alive.   (One occurrence.   Informant: female).

<u>Sources and Annotations</u>:   Correas, p. 69, Aquél es rico que está bien con Dios; o que esta en gracia de Dios. Sbarbi, p. 858, same as A.

815 (A).   <u>Ricos</u> han caído, cuanto más este pobre que no tiene nada.

<u>Translation or Interpretation</u>:   Rich ones have fallen, more so this one who has nothing.

<u>Context</u>:   One day he heard this proverb from his grandmother. (One occurrence.   Informant: male).

<u>Sources and Annotations</u>:   Velasco, p. 84, Hemos visto caer iglesias cuanto más ese jacal.

816 (A).   Aquéllos son <u>ricos</u> que tienen amigos.

<u>Translation or Interpretation</u>:   Those are rich ones that have friends.   Those who have friends are rich.

<u>Context</u>:   I heard my mother use this proverb on my younger sister.   She is very shy and does not like to make friends very easily.   (One occurrence.   Informant: female).

<u>Sources and Annotations</u>:   Correas, p. 69, Aquél es rico que tiene amigos; o aquél es noble y rico que tiene amigos; same as A.   Sbarbi, p. 68, same as A.

817 (A). Le dan <u>ride</u> y quiere manejar.

<u>Translation or Interpretation</u>: They give him a ride and he wants to drive.

<u>Context</u>: This is used when you do something for someone and they expect more of you, and they tell you they expect more. (25 occurrences. Informants: 15 female, nine male, one not stated).

<u>Sources and Annotations</u>: Glazer, p. 58, Pides "ride" y quieres manejar.

818 (A). Si te <u>ríes</u> mucho sales llorando.

<u>Translation or Interpretation</u>: If you laugh much you come out crying.

<u>Context</u>: My informant first heard this saying from her mother when she was a little girl. At that time, she and her little sister were laughing and laughing about something or other when her mom said it. They disregarded her warning, thinking it was a silly superstition, and continued joking and laughing with each other. Later, over some petty thing, my informant does not recall, she and her sister got into an argument which led to a fight and ended up crying. It was then that they realized that what their mother had told them had come true. She remembers that, for a time after that, until she grew up and knew better, she and her sister actually believed this superstition and abided by it. (One occurrence. Informant: female).

<u>Sources and Annotations</u>: Rodríguez-Marín (1926), p. 490, Tras mucho reír, mucho llorar suele venir.

819 (A). Cuando el <u>río</u> suena, es que agua lleva.
819 (B). Si el <u>río</u> suena, es que agua trae.

<u>Translation or Interpretation</u>: When the river sounds, it is that it carries water.

<u>Context</u>: When a river is noisy, it insinuates that people are talking about some individual, or certain thing. It is because it carries water (which means) that much talking is done by the people and maybe there is something true about it. In some cases, people have been known to talk and gossip so much about a certain person, or thing, that certainly something is true about what they are talking. My informant told me that people like to talk and say many things about other people. Sometimes it may have a little truth in what they are talking, but sometimes they just talk to pass time. (Two occurrences. Informants: female).

Sources and Annotations: Caballero, p. 413, Cuando el río
suena agua lleva. Sbarbi, p. 860, Cuando el río suena, agua
o piedra, lleva.

820 (A). Al río revuelto, ganancia de pescadores.

Translation or Interpretation: Stirred river, gain of fisher-
men.

Context: When we were younger, we worked picking melons and
one day, early in the morning in the fields, it was a great
day to pick melons--they were nice and big. My uncle said
this saying. (Two occurrences. Informants: one male, one
unstated.

Sources and Annotations: Adame, p. 34, En río revuelto, ganancia de pescadores; p. 48, same as B. Armas, p. 331, pes-
caren río revuelto. Ballesteros, p. 1, same as A. Cobos, p.
10, Agua revuelta ganancia de pescadores; p. 106, Río revuelto, ganancia de pescadores. Conde, p. 52, same as A. Covarrubias, p. 120, A río buelto ganancia de pescadores; p. 242, A
río buelto ganancia de pescadores. Espinosa, A., p. 106, En
agua revuelta ganancia de pescadores. Gamiz, p. 81, same as
A. Jaramillo, p. 364, same as A; p. 420, Río revuelto, ganancia de pescadores. Lea, p. 237, Río revuelto ganancia de pes-
cador. Lucero-White, p. 36, Río revuelto, ganancia de pesca-
dor. Robe, p. 69, same as A. Sbarbi, p. 859, A río revuelto,
o vuelto, ganancia de pescadores.

821 (A). Ropa limpia no necesita jabón.

Translation or Interpretation: Clean clothes do not need
soap.

Context: The proverb may be used to mean that if you believe
you are not doing anything wrong, then there is no need for
you to feel ashamed. (Four occurrences. Informants: one
female, two male, one not stated).

Sources and Annotations: Cerda, p. 321, same as A. Cobos, p.
70, La ropa limpia no necesita jabón. Conde, p. 359, same as
A.

822 (A). El ruin y el mesquino andan dos veces el camino.

Translation or Interpretation: The wicked and the evil walk
the road two times.

Context: None given. (One occurrence. Informant: female).

Sources and Annotations: None.

823 (A). Vale más rodear que rodar.
823 (B). Vale más rodear que caer.

Translation or Interpretation: It is better to go around than to roll.

Context: Informant says that he was driving his truck full of grain. There was a bridge and also a route he could have taken around the bridge that seemed like it was falling apart. Instead, he took the short cut--the bridge--and it broke, causing him to lose his grain. A man who was with him told him the above. (Two occurrences. Informants: male).

Sources and Annotations: Armas, p. 416, Más vale rodear que rodar. Cobos, p. 81, Mas vale rodear que no rodar. Conde, p. 255, Más vale rodear que rodar; p. 403, same as A. Espinosa, A., p. 102, same as A. Gamiz, p. 93, Mucho mejor es rodear y no exponerse a rodar. Jaramillo, p. 403, Más vale voltios que rodar. Rodriguez-Marin (1930), p. 203, Más vale rodear que atascar; p. 203, Mas vale rodear que tropezar.

824 (A). Preguntando se llega a Roma.

Translation or Interpretation: Asking, one gets to Rome.

Context: When another is having trouble finding, or looking for something, she always asks for help. She is not afraid or timid. (One occurrence. Informant: female).

Sources and Annotations: Alcala, p. 505, Quien pregunta a Roma. Cobos, p. 101, same as A. De Barros, p. 383, Preguntando se va a Roma. Jaramillo, p. 414, Preguntando se va a Roma. Santamaria, p. 42, same as A.

825 (A). A ver si como roncas duermes.
825 (B). A ver si como roncan duermen o nomás les gusta
          hablar.

Translation or Interpretation: Let us see if you sleep like you snore.

Context: She talks of how she wants to get her Master's (Degree), and perhaps step into an administrative position someday. Her friends heard her wanting to do this for years. She has now, finally, accomplished what she bragged about for so long. (Three occurrences. Informants: two female, one male).

Sources and Annotations: Adame, p. 14, same as A. Ballesteros, p. 43, A ver si como roncan duerme. Galván, p. 124, A ver si como roncan duermen; p. 133, A ver si como roncan duermen. Martínez, p. 41, A ver si como roncan duermen. Robe, p. 66, A ver si así como roncas, duermes. Santamaria, p. 43, A ver si como roncan, duermen; p. 256, A ver si como roncan duermen. Velasco, p. 23, A ver si como roncan duermen.

826 (A). No hay rosa sin espina.

Translation or Interpretation: There is not a rose without a thorn.

Context: This is when you cannot get something worthwhile without sacrificing for it. You have to work for what you want. (Four occurrences. Informants: three female, one unstated).

Sources and Annotations: Aranda, p. 22, same as A. Cobos, p. 92, same as A. Conde, p. 291, No hay rosas sin espinas. Lea, p. 238, No hay rosa sin espinas. Lucero-White, p. 36, No hay rosa sin espinas. Rodriguez-Marin (1926), p. 325, Ni rosa sin espinas, ni tahur sin monina; p. 339, same as A. Sbarbi, p. 866, No hay rosa sin espinas.

827 (A). Nunca falta un roto para un descosido.
827 (B). Para cada roto hay un descosido.

Translation or Interpretation: There never lacks one torn for one ripped.

Context: One time, there was an older lady who got married after everyone thought she never would. She had few qualities, and the bridegroom was seen to have even less. At the wedding, everyone commented on the truth of this dicho. (Three occurrences. Informants: two male, one unstated).

Sources and Annotations: Adame, p. 70, same as A; p. 77, same as A. Aranda, p. 22, same as A. Armas, p. 418, same as A. Ballesteros, p. 33, same as A. California Spanish Proverbs and Adages, same as A. Cobos, p. 89, No falta un roto para descosido. Conde, p. 301, same as A. Espinosa, A., p. 108, No falta un roto para un descosido, ni aguja con que coserlo. Gamiz, p. 76, No falta un roto para un descosido. Martinez, p. 194, Nunca falta un roto para un descosido; p. 209, Nunca falta un roto para un descosido ni una media sucia para un pie podrido. Rodriguez-Marin (1926), p. 362, Para un roto hay siempre un descosido. Sbarbi, p. 867, same as A. Velasco, p. 111, same as A.

828 (A). Mucho ruido y pocas nueces.

Translation or Interpretation: Much noise and few nuts.

Context: My friend told the above proverb to a lady when they were conversing at work after lunch. (One occurrence. Informant: female).

Sources and Annotations: Aranda, p. 15, Es más el ruido que las nueces. Caballero, p. 251, Cascar y no nueces. Cobos, p. 57, Es mas el ruido que las nueces; p. 83, same as A. Cobarrubias, p. 832, Más es el ruido que las nuezes. De Barros, p. 271, Más es el ruido que las neces. Espinosa, A., p. 108, same as A. Espinosa, F., p. 212, Más es el ruido que las nuezes. Gamiz, p. 81, Es mas el ruido que las nueces. Maldonado, p. 58, Más es el ruido que las nueces. Paredes, p. 32, same as A. Robe, p. 68, Es mas el ruido que las nueces. Rodriguez-Marin (1930), p. 254, Pocas veces es menos el ruido que las nueces. Rodriguez-Marin (1926), p. 17, A las veces, se hace un pan como unas nueces; p. 291, Más es el ruido a veces que las nueces.

829 (A). No les busques ruido al chicharron.
829 (B). No hay que buscarle ruido al chicharron.
829 (C). No les busques al chicharron porque siempre hace ruido.

Translation or Interpretation: Do not look for noise in the fried scrap.

Context: Informant uses this proverb, meaning don't ask for trouble. (Three occurrences. Informants: one female, two male).

Sources and Annotations: Cerda, p. 322, Buscarle el ruido al chicharrón. Conde, p. 292, same as A. Martinez, p. 49, Buscarle ruido al chicharrón. Robe, p. 69, Andar buscándole ruido al chicharrón. Velasco, p. 28, Buscarle ruido al chicharrón; p. 110, No buscarle ruido al chicharrón.

830 (A). Dicen que no hay sábado sin sol ni viejito sin amor.

Translation or Interpretation: They say there is no Saturday without sun, nor old man without love.

Context: None given. (One occurrence. Informant: female).

Sources and Annotations: De Barros, p. 318, Ni sábado sin sol, ni moza sin amor, mi viejo sin dolor, ni puta sin arrebol. Maldonado, p. 59, Ni sabado sin sol, ni mosa sin amor, ni viejo sin dolor. Sbarbi, p. 872, No hay sábado sin sol, ni mocita, o moza, sin amor, ni vieja sin arrebol, o sin dolor.

831 (A). Saber es poder.

Translation or Interpretation: To know is power.

Context: As a child was told that if she learned, or became educated, she would have better opportunities. (Two occurrences. Informants: one female, one male).

Sources and Annotations: Ballesteros, p. 15, same as A. Cobos, p. 107, same as A. Espinosa, A., p. 102, same as A. Rodriguez-Marin (1926), p. 445, same as A. Sbarbi, p. 874, same as A.

832 (A). Mejor es saber mucho y hablar poco que saber poco y hablar mucho.

Translation or Interpretation: It is better to know much and speak little than to know little and speak much.

Context: An example concerned a friend of my informant's who loved to argue even when she knew nothing of the subject being discussed. (One occurrence. Informant: female).

Sources and Annotations: None.

833 (A). Cuanto sabes no dirás, cuanto ves no juzgarás si quieres vivir en paz.

Translation or Interpretation: As much as you know don't say, as much as you see don't judge if you want to live in peace. (One occurrence. Informant: male).

Context: Many times somebody will start spreading rumors, and someone else will just come up and say this so that all of us can hear it. In essence, they were trying to tell us not to spread rumors. He did not remember where he first heard the proverb, but he indicated it was one he has heard and repeated often, when the situation called for it. The proverb's popularity, he said, may be partly due to the three-line rhyme-- "dirás, juzgarás, and paz." (One occurrence. Informant: male).

Sources and Annotations: Maldonado, p. 53, same as A.

834 (A). Bien sabe el sabio que no sabe, el necio piensa que sabe.

Translation or Interpretation: Well knows the wise man that he does not know, the fool thinks he knows.

Context: The wise man knows the limits of his knowledge. He knows that he does not know everything. What he knows, he does not make a point of telling, so my informant said. The fool, or the one with the big mouth, maintains that he knows something when you know just how little he really knows. "I only know that I know nothing," he quipped. (One occurrence. Informant: male).

Sources and Annotations: Rodriguez-Marin (1930), p. 117, El sabio cree que no sabe y el necio piensa que sabe. Rodriguez-Marin (1926), p. 57, same as A; p. 445, Sabe el sabio que no sabe, y el necio piensa que sabe.

835 (A). Un sabio piensa lo que dice, un sonzo dice lo que piensa.

Translation or Interpretation: A wise man thinks what he says, a fool says what he thinks.

Context: None given. (One occurrence. Informant: female).

Sources and Annotations: Rodriguez-Marin (1926), p. 500, Unos saben lo que hacen, y otros hacen lo que saben.

836 (A). Si te queda el saco, póntelo.
836 (B). Si te queda el zapato, póntelo.
836 (C). Al que le quede el saco, que se lo ponga.
836 (D). Si te cae el saco, pontelo.
836 (E). Si le viene el saco, póngaselo.
836 (F). Si no te cae el saco no te lo pongas.

Translation or Interpretation: If the coat fits, put it on.

Context: None given. (19 occurrences. Informants: 14 female, three male, two not stated).

Sources and Annotations: Adame, p. 86, Si te queda el chaleco póntelo; p. 88, Si te queda el chaleco póntelo. Armas, p. 408, Al que le venga el guante que se lo plante. Ballesteros, p. 20, same as C. Espinosa, A., p. 106, El que le zapato que se lo ponga. Gamiz, p. 92, Al que le venga el saco que se lo ponga. Glazer, p. 44, Al que le caiga el saco que se lo ponga. Jaramillo, p. 362, Al que le caiga guante que se lo chante. Robe, p. 69, same as E. Rodriguez-Marin (1930), p. 30, Al quien le venga el guante que se lo chante. Santamaria, p. 54, Al que le venga el saco, o el guante que se lo ponga, o que se lo plante. Yáñez, p. 53, same as A.

837 (A). Más vale salud que dinero.

Translation or Interpretation: Health is better than money.

Context: My informant told me of a friend of hers who is very wealthy but is also too depressed to enjoy her money. (One occurrence. Informant: female).

Sources and Annotations: None.

838 (A). Según San Andrés, el que parece tonto, lo es.
838 (B). Come dice San Andrés, el que es cara de burro.

Translation or Interpretation: According to Saint Andrew, he who looks like a fool, is.

Context: Once, about three weeks ago, my brothers and I were talking bad about the Hidalgo County District Attorney, Mr. Oscar B. McInnis. We were discussing about how come a very distinguished person, who knows and practices law, could have gone in this kind of problem just for a bitch. My brothers did not know Mr. McInnis, but when one of them saw his picture in the newspaper, he told me this proverb. The proverb just means that when you see somebody who looks like a dummy is, because he is one. Do not speculate. (Two occurrences. Informants: male).

Sources and Annotations: Martinez, p. 280, Ya lo dijo San Andres: el que tiene cara de pendejo, lo es.

839 (A). Cuando San Juan baje el dedo.

Translation or Interpretation: When Saint John lowers his finger.

Context: This proverb is used as a joke or a humerous way of getting someone to do something quick. For example, someone may ask, "when is he going to arrive?" The reply, "No llega hasta que San Juan baje el dedo." He won't arrive until St. John lowers his finger. (One occurrence. Informant: female).

Sources and Annotations: Cerda, p. 322, same as A. Jaramillo, p. 395, Hasta que San Juan agache el dedo. Robe, p. 72, same as A. Sbarbi, p. 883, Hasta que San Juan baje el dedo. Yáñez, p. 56, same as A.

840 (A). ¿Qué culpa tiene San Juan que San Pedro esté pelón?

Translation or Interpretation: What fault does Saint John have that Saint Peter is bald?

Context: My informant told me that this saying (was told to him constantly by his father), especially when he was in a

273

bad mood. He remembers hearing this saying since he was a
little boy. He remembers his father telling him that it
wasn't everyone's fault that one person made him angry and be
mad at the world. (One occurrence. Informant: male).

Sources and Annotations: None.

841 (A). Sancas secas y fundío gordo.

Translation or Interpretation: Dry legs and big butt.

Context: The informant often remarks this when she passes in
front of a full length mirror and sees herself. (One occurrence. Informant: female).

Sources and Annotations: None.

842 (A). Sangre de venado, que se vaya por un lado. Sangre
de chivito, que se vaya derechito.

Translation or Interpretation: Blood of deer, may it go by
the side. Blood of kid, may it go straight.

Context: When she worked in the fields and a storm was coming, the people who wanted to work would say the first line,
and the lazy people would say the second. (One occurrence.
Informant: female).

Sources and Annotations: Cerda, p. 322, ¡Sangre de venado,
todo lo que digas se irá por un lado! Cobos, p. 108, ¡Sangre
de venado, todo lo que digas se irá para un lado! Galván, p.
130, Sangre de venado; p. 133, Sangre de venado que se valla
por un lado sangre de un perrito que se vaya derechito; p.
134, Sangre de venado, que por un lado; p. 127, Sangre de
perrito que se vaya derechito.

843 (A). La sangre es más gruesa que agua.

Translation or Interpretation: Blood is thicker than water.

Context: I remember when I was a very young man my brother
got into a fight with another boy in the neighborhood. I in-
tervened in the fight and soon the fight was over. When my
mother got wind of what had happened, she really gave us a
good spanking. My uncle smiled and said, "hija, la sangre es
más gruesa que agua." (One occurrence. Informant: male).

Sources and Annotations: Ballesteros, p. 8, La sangre es más
gruesa que el agua.

844 (A). A buen <u>santo</u> te encomiendas.

<u>Translation or Interpretation</u>: To a good saint entrust your-self.

<u>Context</u>: One day a friend of mine invited me to the movies, but depended on me to pay for her. It turned out I was out of money myself. (Two occurrences. Informants: one female, one male).

<u>Sources and Annotations</u>: Cerda, p. 323, same as A. Galván, p. 124, A buen santo te encomiendas; p. 133, A buen santo te en-comiendas. Martínez, p. 12, same as A. Robe, p. 68, same as A. Rubio, p. 5, same as A. Sbarbi, p. 894, Ecomendarse a buen santo.

845 (A). A cada <u>santo</u> se le llega su día.
845 (B). A cada <u>santo</u> en su capillita se le llega su día.

<u>Translation or Interpretation</u>: To each saint his day comes.

<u>Context</u>: The student who told me this proverb heard it from her mother whenever someone would make her mad, or upset. This proverb is said when persons are upset by others. The meaning of this proverb is that everything done unto you will return to the person, and it works visa-versa. That is why people should not talk about other people because, you never know when it will happen to you. (Three occurrences. Infor-mants: two female, one unstated).

<u>Sources and Annotations</u>: Adame, p. 9, A cada santo se le llega su función. Aranda, p. 1, A cada santo se le llega su función. Cerda, p. 323, A cada santo se le llega su función. Chávez, p. 47, A cada santo se le llega su función. Cobos, p. 9, A cada santo se le llega su función. Galván, p. 124, same as A; p. 127, same as A. Lea, p. 233, A cada santo se le llega su función. Lucero-White, p. 33, A cada Santo se le llega la función. MacArthur, p. 18, same as A. Robe, p. 65, A cada santo se le llega su función.

846 (A). Cada <u>santo</u> siente su pena.

<u>Translation or Interpretation</u>: Each saint feels his grief.

<u>Context</u>: Sometimes we do things which are bad, but we do not get caught. However, our conscience does not let us forget it. (One occurrence. Informant: female).

<u>Sources and Annotations</u>: None.

847 (A). Ni tanto que queme el <u>santo</u>, ni tanto que no lo
          alumbre.
847 (B). No tanto que queme el <u>santo</u>, ni tanto que quede
          oscuro.

<u>Translation or Interpretation</u>: Not so much to burn the saint,
not so little as not to illuminate.

<u>Context</u>: Be moderate in whatever you attempt. (Two occur-
rences. Informants: one female, one male).

<u>Sources and Annotations</u>: Adame, p. 69, same as A; p. 72, same
as A. Cerda, p. 323, Ni tanto que queme el santo, ni tan poco
que no lo alumbre. Gamiz, p. 77, same as A. Jaramillo, p, 407,
same as A. Rodriguez-Marin (1930), p. 222, Ni tanto que no se
gante, ni tan poco que no baste. Villafuerte, p. 121, Ni cerca
que te quemes, ni lejos que te enfríes.

848 (A). Rogar al <u>santo</u> hasta pasar el tranco, pasado el
          tranco y <u>olvida</u> el santo.

<u>Translation or Interpretation</u>: Beg the saint until passing
the threshold, passing the threshold forget the saint.

<u>Context</u>: If a person is in trouble he prays for help and
passing the trouble he forgets that he had prayed. (One occurrence. Informant: female).

<u>Sources and Annotations</u>: Rodríguez-Marín (1930), p. 249,
Pasado el santo hacéis la fiesta. Rodríguez-Marín (1926), p.
101, Charco pasado, santo olvidado; p. 442, Pío pasado, santo
olvidado. Sbarbi, p. 895, Rogar al santo hasta pasar el tranco.

849 (A). Come <u>santos</u> y caga diablos.

<u>Translation or Interpretation</u>: Eat saints and shit devils.

<u>Context</u>: A person who practices his faith, yet does evil
things. (One occurrence. Informant: not stated).

<u>Sources and Annotations</u>: Martinez, p. 60, same as A.

850 (A). Mejor vistiendo <u>santos</u> que desvistiendo borrachos.

<u>Translation or Interpretation</u>: Better dressing saints than
undressing drunkards.

<u>Context</u>: I first heard this proverb three months ago when
my sister became engaged. My mother, my sisters, and this
friend of mine were discussing the plan for my sister's wedd-

ing at my house. My friend asked my older sister when she
planned to get married. My sister told her she did not wish
to, because of the way most marriages turned out now a days.
My mother said it is right to think that way -- es mejor pensar así porque es mejor vistiendo santos que desvestir borrachos. The meaning of this is that when one is single, one is
supposedly considered a "virgin." A virgin's duty is supposedly to dress saints. However, when one is married one's
duty is to care for one's husband, and that includes undressing him when he comes home drunk. (One occurrence. Informant: female).

Sources and Annotations: Ballesteros, p. 27, Es mejor vestir
santos que desvestir borrachos. Jaramillo, p. 403, Más vale
vestir santos que desvestir borrachos; p. 419, Quedarse para
vestir santos. MacArthur, p. 18, Se quedó para vestir santos.
Sbarbi, p. 896, Quedarse para vestir santos.

851 (A). Para que te vales de santos habiendo tan lindo Dios.
851 (B). Para que te vales de santos habiendo tan gran Dios.
851 (C). Para que pierdes tiempo en santos habiendo tan gran
        Dios.
851 (D). Para que te fías de santo habiendo un Dios tan bueno.
851 (E). Para que te vales de santos habiendo tan buen Dios.

Translation or Interpretation: Why patronize saints when
there's such a fine God.

Context: When you need the services of a mechanic you don't
go to the plumber and vice versa. You go to the experts.
(Six occurrences. Informants: three female, two male, one
not stated).

Sources and Annotations: Ballesteros, p. 41, Para que piensas
en santos habiendo tan lindo Dios? Cobos, p. 98, ¿Para qué
pedirle a los santos habiendo tan lindo Dios. Yáñez, p. 314,
Que te andas valiendo de ángeles habiendo tan lindo Dios.

852 (A). Según el sapo, la pedrada.

Translation or Interpretation: According to the toad, the
blow from a stone.

Context: If a person goes to buy a pair of shoes, which are
not priced, the seller might price the shoe according to the
buyer's status. (Two occurrences. Informants: one female,
one male).

Sources and Annotations: Armas, p. 185, Alba es sapita, pero
graciosa; p. 232, Como sea el sapo, así es la pedrada; p. 420,
Según el sapo asi es la pedrada. Rubio, p. 144, Según el sapo
as es la pedrada.

853 (A).   Secreto entre dos no es secreto.

Translation or Interpretation: Secret among two is not a secret.

Context: If you want to keep a secret, keep it between yourself and God only.

Sources and Annotations: None.

854 (A).   Sedacito nuevo donde te pondré, sedacito viejo donde
           te arumbaré.

Translation or Interpretation: New (sieve) where shall I put you, old (sieve) where shall I put you away.

Context: My informant told me that her daughter had just gotten a little puppy. He used to bathe him and sleep with him, but after a while, she just forgot about him, and wouldn't even bathe him anymore. (One occurrence. Informant: female).

Sources and Annotations: Martinez, p. 147, Jarrito nuevo, ¿dónde te pondré? Rodríguez-Marin (1930), p. 52, Cedacito nuevo, tres dias en estaca, y después tirado por el suelo. Velasco, p. 88, Jarrito nuevo, ¿dónde te pondré?

855 (A).   Cinco sentidos tenemos, cinco sentidos perdemos.
           Todos los cinco perdemos cuando nos enamoramos.

Translation or Interpretation: Five senses we have, five senses we lose. All five we lose when we fall in love.

Context: One of my cousins was in love, so everybody kept telling her this, telling her that she had lost all her five senses. (Two occurrences. Informants: female).

Sources and Annotations: None.

856 (A).   Hay que ser listo como serpientes, pero dócil como
           palomas.

Translation or Interpretation: One must be clever like a serpent, but docil like doves.

Context: When I was a child I used to ask my mother how I could go to school and avoid getting into fights. Therefore, she said this. (One occurrence. Informant: male).

Sources and Annotations: None.

857 (A). Lo que <u>siembras</u> eso es lo que cosechas.
857 (B). Lo que <u>siembras</u> tienes.
857 (C). Lo que <u>siembras</u> eso levantas.
857 (D). Lo que <u>siembras</u> es lo que levantas.
857 (E). Lo que <u>siembras</u> levantas.
857 (F). Lo que <u>siembras</u> recogerás.

<u>Translation or Interpretation</u>: What you sow is what you harvest.

<u>Context</u>: Someone trying to tell another that the way he treats people is the way he will be treated. (Seven occurrences. Informants: five female, two male).

<u>Sources and Annotations</u>: Adame, p. 57, Lo que se siembra, es lo que se levanta; p. 65, Lo que se siembra, es lo que se levanta. Ballesteros, p. 41, Lo que siembras levantas. Cobos, p. 75, same as F. Gamiz, p. 89, Lo que siembras, cosecharás. Lucero-White, p. 33, Como siembras, segarás. Rodriguez-Marin (1930), p. 185, Lo que se siembra, se siega; p. 279, Quien mal siembra, mal siega. Rodriguez-Marin (1926), p. 117, De lo que siembra se coge; p. 274, Lo que siembras cogerás.

858 (A). Cuando el <u>sol</u> sale, para todos sale.
858 (B). El <u>sol</u> para todos nace.

<u>Translation or Interpretation</u>: When the sun comes out it comes out for all.

<u>Context</u>: Used to point out that the sun will shine equally on all people. (Three occurrences. Informants: two female, one male).

<u>Sources and Annotations</u>: Caballero, p. 414, Cuando sale el sol sale para todos. Cobos, p. 25, same as A. De Barros, p. 153, same as A. Jaramillo, p. 386, El sol sale para todos. Martinez, p. 113, El sol sale para todos. Rodriguez-Marin (1926), p. 361, Para todos sale el sol. Sbarbi, p. 914, Para todos sale el sol. Velasco, p. 68, El sol sale para todos.

859 (A). Ni da <u>sol</u>, ni sombra.

<u>Translation or Interpretation</u>: He does not give sun nor shade.

<u>Context</u>: A young lady gets married and finds out her husband is always nagging. (One occurrence. Informant: female).

<u>Sources and Annotations</u>: Caballero, p. 822, No dejarle a sol ni a sombra.

860 (A). No quieras tapar el <u>sol</u> con un dedo.
860 (B). No puedes tapar el <u>sol</u> con un dedo.
860 (C). No se puede tapar el <u>sol</u> con un dedo.

<u>Translation or Interpretation</u>: Do not try to cover the sun with one finger.

<u>Context</u>: Informant's niece got pregnant and was sent to another city. Her aunt says she is studying up there. (Three occurrences. Informants: female).

<u>Sources and Annotations</u>: Adame, p. 83, Quieres tapar el sol, con un dedo; p. 84, Quieres tapar el sol, con un dedo. Aranda, p. 23, No me tapes el sol con la mano. Armas, p. 345, Quierer tapar el sol con un dedo. Espinosa, A., p. 109, No se tapa el sol con la mano.

861 (A). <u>Sombra</u> no se hizo en una hora.

<u>Translation or Interpretation</u>: Shade was not made in an hour.

<u>Context</u>: A guy fixing his car to use it that evening. He cannot get it fixed by evening. The guy gets all upset about it, and his father says, "sombra no se hizo en una hora." (One occurrence. Informant: male).

<u>Sources and Annotations</u>: Adame, p. 85, Roma no se hizo en un día. Jaramillo, p. 408, No se puede repicar y andar en la procesión. Rodriguez-Marin (1926), p. 344, No se hizo Roma en un dia; No se hizo Sevilla en un solo día.

862 (A). Saludando con <u>sombrero</u> ajeno.

<u>Translation or Interpretation</u>: Greeting with another's hat.

<u>Context</u>: Whenever someone else takes credit for giving you something that really isn't yours. (Two occurrences. Informants: female).

<u>Sources and Annotations</u>: Adame, p. 52, Haciendo caravana con sombrero ajeno; p. 53, Haciendo caravana con sombrero ajeno. Armas, p. 300, Lucir con sombrero ajeno; p. 359, Saludar con sombrero ajeno. Cerda, p. 324, Haciendo caravana con sombrero ajeno. Cobos, p. 61, Hacer caravana con sombrero ajeno. Gamiz, p. 84, Saludar con sombrero ajeno. Martinez, p. 134, Hacer carevana con sombrero ajeno. Velasco, p. 80, Hacer caravana con sombrero ajeno.

863 (A). Vale mas un <u>sonso</u> que dos.

Translation or Interpretation: It is better one fool than two.

Context: My mother would use this when my brother and I were trying to make each other mad, by arguing about something dumb. She would tell whoever was making sense in his argument to stop it, and then she would tell us this saying. (One occurrence. Informant: female).

Sources and Annotations: None.

864 (A). El <u>sordo</u> no oye pero compone.
864 (B). No oye pero compone.
864 (C). El que no oye compone.

Translation or Interpretation: The deaf one does not hear but he composes.

Context: Whenever you make something up that you think you heard but was not actually what was said, the other person would quote the proverb. (41 occurrences. Informants: 27 female, 13 male, one unstated).

Sources and Annotations: Adame, p. 33, same as A; p. 46, same as A. Ballesteros, p. 49, same as A. Cerda, p. 324, same as A. Cobos, p. 52, same as A. Gamiz, p. 94, same as A. Glazer, p. 59, same as A. Martinez, p. 113, same as A. Robe, p. 69, same as A.

865 (A). <u>Soy</u> pobre pero honrado.

Translation or Interpretation: I am poor but honorable.

Context: A person can be poor and very well respected, while a rich person who has cheated other people to get what he wanted, is disliked by the community. (One occurrence. Informant: female).

Sources and Annotations: Galván, p. 127, El ser pobre no es deshonra. Lucero-White, p. 35, Más vale el pobre honrado que el rico malvado.

866 (A). Lo que logramos sin el <u>sudor</u> de nuestro trabajo lo damos sin que nos pese.

Translation or Interpretation: What we obtain without the sweat of our work we give away without regret.

Context: A friend of mine sold a lot that had been given as a wedding gift by his father. He readily spent the money, and soon, he was as he had been before selling the property. His

father, absolutely disgusted and offended, said, "what we acquire without sweat we give away without regret." The young
man had sold the lot for much less than it was actually worth.
(One occurrence. Informant: male).

Sources and Annotations: None.

867 (A). Las suegras ni de azúcar son buenas.

Translation or Interpretation: Mothers-in-law, even made of
sugar are not good.

Context: Used when complaining about your mother-in-law. (One
occurrence. Informant: female).

Sources and Annotations: De Barros, p. 441, Suegra, ni de
azúcar buena; nuera ni de pasta ni de cera. Rubio, p. 288, Las
suegras ni de barro son buenas. Sbarbi, p. 921, Suegra ni aun
de azucar es buena.

868 (A). La suerte no es para quien la busca, sino para quien
        la encuentra.

Translation or Interpretation: Luck is not for those who look
for it, but for those who find it.

Context: My informant tells me of a friend she knew who came
over from Mexico with nothing but his intelligence. He began
working at a packing shed, saved his pennies, and soon bought
his own shed. (One occurrence. Informant: female).

Sources and Annotations: Sbarbi, p. 923, La suerte no es para
quien la busca.

869 (A). La suerte de la fea la bonita la desea.
869 (B). La gracia de la fea, la bonita la desea.

Translation or Interpretation: The luck of the ugly one, the
pretty one desire.

Context: Sometimes a not very pretty girl may have real good
luck with boys, and the beautiful girl may not. The pretty
one may wish for the not so pretty one's luck. (Six occurrences. Informants: female).

Sources and Annotations: Adame, p. 57, same as A; p. 61, same
as A. Cobos, p. 71, same as A. De Barros, p. 441, same as A.
Espinosa, A., p. 101, same as A. Galvan, p. 127, La suerte de
la fea, la hermosa la desea; p. 128, La suerte de la fea, la
hermosa la desea; p. 129, La suerte de la fea, la hermosa la
desea; p. 130, La suerte de la fea, la hermosa la desea. Jara-

millo, p. 398, same as A. Rodriguez-Marin (1926), p. 239, La
fortuna de la fea la bonita la desea.

870 (A). Hay que sufrir para merecer.
870 (B). El que sufre aprende a merecer.

Translation or Interpretation: One must suffer to deserve.

Context: A person, like my aunt, suffers because her mother
is very ill, and she takes care of her. But soon she will be
repaid by God. (Two occurrences. Informants: female).

Sources and Annotations: Adame, p. 52, same as A; p. 54, same
as A. Gamiz, p. 78, Sufrir para merecer. Rodriguez-Marin, p.
242, O te confiesas, o te condenas; p. 282, Quien no padece,
no merece.

871 (A).   Una tamalera no puede ver a otra.

Translation or Interpretation: One tamal maker cannot stand
to see another.

Context: There were two ladies who owned two restaurants,
individually owned by each lady, and they both tried to drag
the customers off the street into their own restaurant. They
would say "my restaurant is so much better than my neighbor's."
(One occurrence. Informant: male).

Sources and Annotations: Martinez, p. 270, Una tamalera siente que otra se le ponga enfrente. Velasco, p. 160, Una tamalera no quiere que otra se le ponga enfrente.

872 (A). Tarde que temprano.

Translation or Interpretation: Late than early.

Context: A neighbor needed help and was refused, and he said,
"all right, sooner or later you will need some help." (One
occurrence. Informant: female).

Sources and Annotations: Cobos, p. 75, Lo que se ha de hacer
tarde que se haga temprano. Sbarbi, p. 932, Tarde que temprano, enfermo o sano, hemos de caer en invierno, en primavera,
en otoño o en verano.

873 (A). Es más caliente la tarde que la mañana.

Translation or Interpretation: The afternoon is hotter than
the morning.

Context: A married couple thinks they are having problems in the beginning, but they will have more later on. (Three occurrences. Informants: two female, one not stated).

Sources and Annotations: None.

874 (A). Dicen que son más frescas las tardes que las mañanas.

Translation or Interpretation: They say that the afternoons are cooler than the mornings.

Context: None given. (One occurrence. Informant: female).

Sources and Annotations: Robe, p. 63, Son más frescas las tardes que las mañanas.

875 (A). Aquí se quebro una taza, cada quien para su casa.

Translation or Interpretation: A cup broke here, everyone to their home.

Context: A cup is not broken literally, but the proverb may be spoken to give someone the idea that it is time for them to leave. (Four occurrences. Informants: three female, one male).

Sources and Annotations: Conde, p. 52, same as A. Espinosa, A., p. 100, En el medio de la casa- se quebro una taza! Cada va-a mundo para su casa. Martinez, p. 36, Aquí se rompió una taza, cada quien para su casa.

876 (A). Cuando el tecolote canta el indio muere, esto no es cierto pero sucede.

Translation or Interpretation: When the owl sings the Indian dies, this is not true, but it happens.

Context: I learned this Mexican proverb while I was at my Spanish class in Mexico. I was thirteen years old and I was attending secondary school in Mexico. My Spanish teacher told us one day that he was going to explain some of the most popular Mexican proverbs, so he did. The proverb means that there are a vast number of superstitions when it says: "When the owl sings a person dies." Later, on the next line, it refers to a warning to the persons who do not believe in these superstitions, when it says: "This is not true, but it happens." This, obviously, means that whether a person believes or not, in superstitions, they still happen. (One occurrence. Informant: male).

Sources and Annotations: Armas, p. 196, No le hagas caso a eso; esta tecolote; p. 410, Cuando el tecolote canta, el indio

muere. Conde, p. 91, same as A. Gamiz, p. 88, Si el tecolote
canto, el indio muere, ello no es cierto, pero sucede. Martinez, p. 74, Cuando el tecolote canta el indio muere; no es
cierto pero sucede. Rubio, p. 161, Si el tecolote canta el
indio muere; esto no es cierto pero sucede. Velasco, p. 44,
Cuando el tecolote canta el indio muere; ello no es cierto,
pero sucede.

877 (A). Todavía ves la tempestad y no te **hincas**.

Translation or Interpretation: Still, you see the storm and
you do not kneel.

Context: When a person is in trouble and he keeps getting
into more trouble. (Two occurrences. Informants: male).

Sources and Annotations: Cerda, p. 326, same as A. Cobos, p.
115, Todavia ven la tempestad, y no se hincan. Conde, p. 177,
Estas oyendo los truenos y no te hincas. Galvan, p. 129, Ven
la tempestad y no se hincan; p. 134, Ven la tempestad y no se
hincan. Martinez, p. 275, Ves el temblor y no te hincas.
Velasco, p. 74, Estas mirando la procesion y no te hincas.

878 (A). El buen tendedor con pocas orquillas tiende.

Translation or Interpretation: The person who is good at hanging clothes to dry, with a few clothes pins hangs his wash.

Context: A very efficient person does not need many expla-
nations in carrying out her job. (One occurrence. Informant:
female).

Sources and Annotations: Espinosa, A., p. 109, Para buen en
tendedor pocas palabras. Lucero-White, p. 33, A buen entendedor pocas palabras.

879 (A). El peor testigo es el que fue tu amigo.

Translation or Interpretation: The worst witness is the one
who was your friend.

Context: When there are two very close friends and each knows
everyone of their secrets, and their good and bad things they
have made, or done, in their lives. If they get in a fight,
the person who had been his best friend could be the worse
witness if he speaks. (One occurrence. Informant: female).

Sources and Annotations: Correas, p. 107, same as A.

880 (A). Si quieres estar bien servido, sírvete a <u>ti</u> mismo.

<u>Translation or Interpretation</u>: If you want to be well served, serve yourself.

<u>Context</u>: A young man was used to having his meal served to him perfectly all the time. He was complaining once about not being served well by his mother. She served him out of love she said, then, "serve yourself how you want." (One occurrence. Informant: female).

<u>Sources and Annotations</u>: Espinosa, A., p. 102, Si quieres ser bien servido sírvete a ti mismo.

881 (A). Al mal <u>tiempo</u> buena cara.

<u>Translation or Interpretation</u>: To the bad time, a good face.

<u>Context</u>: Even on a very hard day or in bad days, always have a smile on your face. (Seven occurrences. Informants: six female, one not stated).

<u>Sources and Annotations</u>: Adame, p. 8, Al mal tiempo dale buena cara; p. 11, Al mal tiempo dale buena cara. Armas, p. 407, same as A. Cobos, p. 13, A mal tiempo, buena cara. Conde, p. 32, same as A. De Barros, p. 93, same as A. Galvan, p. 124, Al mal tiempo buena cara; p. 125, Al mal tiempo buena cara, p. 130, Al mal tiempo buena cara; p. 134, A mal tiempo buena cara. MacArthur, p. 1, same as A. Rodriguez-Marin (1926), p. 23, same as A.

882 (A). Dar <u>tiempo</u> al <u>tiempo</u>.

<u>Translation or Interpretation</u>: Give time to time.

<u>Context</u>: We should not be so rushed always. Wait and see what will happen next. (One occurrence. Informant: male).

<u>Sources and Annotations</u>: Caballero, p. 446, same as A. Conde, p. 100, Dar tiempo al tiempo es buen advertimiento; p. 191, Hay que darle tiempo al tiempo. Rodriguez-Marin (1926), p. 104, Dar tiempo al tiempo es buen advertimiento. Sbarbi, p. 941, same as A. Yañez, p. 311, Dando tiempo al tiempo.

883 (A). El <u>tiempo</u> es oro.

<u>Translation or Interpretation</u>: Time is gold.

<u>Context</u>: I was once just taking it easy doing nothing when a friend of mine told me not to waste my time and do something worthwhile. She told me that time was gold. (One occurrence. Informant: female).

Sources and Annotations: Adame, p. 33, same as A; p. 46, same as A. Ballesteros, p. 27, same as A. Cobos, p. 53, same as A. Gamiz, p. 75, El tiempo es dinero. Jaramillo, p. 386, same as A. MacArthur, p. 36, same as A. Rodriguez-Marin (1926), p. 172, same as A. Sbarbi, p. 942, El tiempo es dinero, u oro.

884 (A). El tiempo no aprovechado es tesoro mal gastado.

Translation or Interpretation: Time not benefited from is a treasure badly spent.

Context: A person who was supposed to be studying was going to the movies instead. When graduation came around, he wasn't there to attend the ceremonies. (One occurrence. Informant: male).

Sources and Annotations: Rodriguez-Marin (1926), p. 483, Tiempo ido, nunca más venido; Tiempo ido, para siempre perdido; Tiempo ido, tiempo perdido; Tiempo mal gastado, nunca recobrado.

885 (A). El tiempo perdido, los santos lo lloran.

Translation or Interpretation: Lost time, the saints will cry for.

Context: Mary took advantage of time. She didn't wait until the last minute to study for her exam. As a result, she did well on the examination. (One occurrence. Informant: female).

Sources and Annotations: Cerda, p. 327, same as A. Cobos, p. 53, El tiempo perdido, los angeles lo lloran; p. 115, Tiempo perdido los santos lo lloran. Conde, p. 153, same as A. Gamiz, p. 75, El tiempo perdido hasta los santos lo lloran. Lea, p. 238, same as A. Lucero-White, p. 36, Tiempo perdido los santos lo lloran. MacArthur, p. 15, same as A.

886 (A). Hay más tiempo que vida.

Translation or Interpretation: There is more time than life.

Context: Most people today are always in some form of a rush, but a person does and time goes on. (Five occurrences. Informants: male).

Sources and Annotations: Benavides, p. 89, same as A. Conde, p. 190, same as A.

887 (A). Piensa, que el tiempo no se recupera jamás.

Translation or Interpretation: Think, that lost time is never recovered.

Context: Procrastinating about a chore. (One occurrence. Informant: female).

Sources and Annotations: Rodriguez-Marin (1930), p. 118, El tiempo perdido, para siempre es ido; p. 318, Tiempo paraso, jamas tornado. Rodriguez-Marin (1926), p. 173, El tiempo que una vez se pierde nunca mas vuelve; p. 483, Tiempo perdido, para siempre ido.

888 (A). Vale más llegar a tiempo que no ser invitado.

Translation or Interpretation: It is better to get there in time than not to be invited.

Context: When a person isn't invited and he jokes, or teases a guy who gets to a play just in time. (One occurrence. Informant: male).

Sources and Annotations: Armas, p. 306, Más vale llegar a tiempo que ser convidado; p. 416, Más vale llegar a tiempo que ser convidado. Cobos, p. 57, Es lo mismo llegar a tiempo que ser convidado; p. 80, Más vale llegar a tiempo que ser convidado; p. 120, Vale más llegar a tiempo que ser convidado. Conde, p. 254, Más vale llegar a tiempo que ser convidado. Espinosa, A., p. 111, Vale más llegar a tiempo que ser convidado. Gamiz, p. 94, Vale más llegar a tiempo que ser invitado. Jaramillo, p. 403, Más vale llegar a tiempo que estar convidado, MacArthur, p. 12, Más vale llegar a tiempo, que ser invitado. Martinez, p. 176, same as A. Velasco-Valdez, p. 100, Más vale llegar a tiempo que ser convidado. Villafuerte, p. 382, Vale más llegar a tiempo que ser invitado.

889 (A). La tienda abierta y el dependiente dormido.

Translation or Interpretation: The store is open and the attendant is asleep.

Context: Many times I have heard it mentioned when someone's zipper is noticeably down. (One occurrence. Informant: not stated).

Sources and Annotations: None.

890 (A). Entre más tiene más gasta.

Translation or Interpretation: The more he has the more he spends.

Context: Informant told me that she has a neighbor who is earning his money somewhat illegally, and each time gets more and more involved. He is always buying things they do not need. (Two occurrences. Informants: one female, one not stated).

Sources and Annotations: None.

891 (A). Entre más **tienes** más quieres.
891 (B). Entre más **tiene** uno más quiere.
891 (C). El que más **tiene** más quiere.

Translation or Interpretation: The more you have the more you want.

Context: Informant told me her husband always uses this expression when she starts saying that she wants something, especially if he just got paid. (Four occurrences. Informants: three female, one male).

Sources and Annotations: Ballesteros, p. 7, same as A. Conde, p. 95, Cuanto más tienes, más quieres; p. 146, same as C. Galvan, p. 126, Cuando más se tiene, mas se quiere; p. 133, Quien más tiene más quiere. Lea, p. 235, El que más tiene más quiere; p. 235, same as C. Lucero-White, p. 34, same as C. Rodriguez-Marin (1926), p. 89, Cuando el hombre mas tiene, más quiere; p. 413, Quien mucho tiene, más quiere.

892 (A). A la **tierra** que fueras has lo que vieras.
892 (B). A la **tierra** que fueras has como vieras.
892 (C). A la **tierra** que fueras has como vieras y en la tuya como pudieras.

Translation or Interpretation: To the land you go, do what you see.

Context: What my father has said is, in order to live in peace one must do as the rest of the people. In other words, if in Rome do as the Romans. (Four occurrences. Informants: two female, two male).

Sources and Annotations: Adame, p. 8, same as A; p. 10, same as A. Armas, p. 407, same as A. Cerda, p. 327, same as A. Cobos, p. 10, A donde fueras, has lo que vieres. Conde, p. 22, A donde quiera que fueras, has lo que vieres; p. 28, same as A. Chávez, p. 44, A la tierra que fueras, hace lo que veras. Espinosa, A., p. 98, same as A. Jaramillo, p. 361, same as A. Rodriguez-Marin (1926), p. 7, A donde fueras has como vieres; p. 91, Cuando fueres a la boda, deja puesta tu olla; p. 187, En la tierra do vivieres, has como vivieres; p. 505, Ve donde vas, y como vieres, así has, y como sonaren, así bailarás.

893 (A).   En tierra de ciegos el turto es rey.
893 (B).   El tuerto es rey en el país de los ciegos.
893 (C).   En el país de los ciegos el tuerto es rey.
893 (D).   En la casa de los ciegos el tuerto es rey.

Translation or Interpretation: In the land of the blind, the
one-eyed is king.

Context: In a world of conformity it is the individual, the
one who sets out from the rest, who is usually seen as the
leader of a group. (11 occurrences. Informants: six female,
four male, one not stated).

Sources and Annotations: Adame, p. 34, same as A; p. 47, same
as A. Aranda, p. 15, same as A. Ballesteros, p. 6, same as A.
Benavides, p. 89, same as A. Campa, p. 63, En la tierra del
ciego el tuerto es rey. Cobos, p. 55, En la tierra del ciego
el tuerto es rey. Conde, p. 163, same as A. Correas, p. 126,
same as A. Espinosa, A., p. 106, En la tierra del ciego el
tuerto es rey. Galvan, p. 128, same as A; p. 134, En la tierra
del ciego el tuerto es rey. Gamiz, p. 82, En la tierra de los
ciegos el tuerto es rey. Jaramillo, p. 387, same as C. Lea,
p. 235, En el reino de los tuertos el ciego es rey. Lucero-
White, p. 34, En el reino de los ciegos el tuerto es rey.
Rodriguez-Marin (1926), p. 187, En la tierra de los ciegos,
es feliz el tuerto; p. 194, same as A. Sbarbi, p. 947, same
as A.

894 (A).   Siembra uno en tan mala tierra que ni la semilla
           levanta.

Translation or Interpretation: One plants in such bad soil
that not even the seed is harvested.

Context: Roberto first heard this proverb one time, when they
were working in the melons about ten years ago. There had
been a big drought in Starr County, and the farmers had plant-
ed, but the crop produced very little, and the people would
say: "Siembra uno en tan mala tierra que ni la semilla levanta." This means that sometimes you plant in such a bad
soil that you won't make a profit. My informant heard this
usually among farmers who do not make a profit. Some people
also use this proverb when something goes wrong. (One occurrence. Informant: male).

Sources and Annotations: Ballesteros, p. 26, El que siembra
en tepetate, ni la semilla levanta. Caballero, p. 996, Sembrar en mala tierra. Cerda, p. 238, El que siembra en tierra
ajena, ni la semilla levanta. Cobos, p. 51, El que siembra

en tierra ajena, hasta la semilla pierde. Conde, p. 150, El
que siembra en tepetate, ni la semilla levanta. Rodriguez-
Marin (1930), p. 274, Quien en ruin tierra siembra, tiene mala
cosecha. Sbarbi, p. 947, Sembrar en mala tierra.

895 (A). Todo es según el color del cristal con que se mira.
895 (C). Todo puede ser verdad como todo puede ser mentira,
          depende con el cristal que lo miras.

Translation or Interpretation: Everything is according to the
color of the glass with which one sees.

Context: This proverb means everything, or anything can be
true or it can be a lie. It depends on how one sees it. Your
point of view. For example, I can see something as the truth,
while on the other hand, you can see it as a lie, depending on
how you look at it. (Two occurrences. Informants: one female, one male).

Sources and Annotations: Adame, p. 34, En este mundo traidor
ni todo es verdad ni todo es mentira. Todo es de acuerdo con
el cristal que se mira; p. 47, En este mundo traidor ni todo
es verdad ni todo es mentira. Todo es de acuerdo con el cristal que se mira. Armas, p. 249, Depende del cristal con que
se mire. Caballero, p. 1076, same as A. Conde, p. 390, same as
A. Gamiz, p. 82, Todo depende del color del cristal con que
se mira. Jaramillo, p. 425, same as A.

896 (A). Todo por servir se acaba.
896 (B). Por servir se acaba.

Translation or Interpretation: Everything, for serving, fin-
ishes itself.

Context: When my mother's refrigerator broke down my dad told
her this saying. (Three occurrences. Informants: one female,
two male).

Sources and Annotations: Adame, p. 91, same as A; p. 93, same
as A. Ballesteros, p. 16, same as A. Conde, p. 390, same as
A. Rubio, p. 196, same as A.

897 (A). Todo se paga en esta vida.

Translation or Interpretation: Everything will be paid for in
this life.

Context: One of my friends' boyfriend would be real mean to
her. After some time they broke up. I then told my friend
this proverb pertaining to her ex-boyfriend. Now he wants

her back and he's the one who is suffering now. (One occurrence. Informant: female).

<u>Sources and Annotations</u>: Rubio, p. 196, Todo se paga en este mundo.

898 (A). A <u>todo</u> le tiras y a nada le das.
898 (B). A <u>todo</u> le tiras y a nada le pegas.

<u>Translation or Interpretation</u>: You shoot at everything and hit nothing.

<u>Context</u>: A friend of hers wants to become a nurse, a beautician, and a good wife and mother, all at once, so she applied this proverb to her. (Four occurrences. Informants: three female, one male).

<u>Sources and Annotations</u>: Cerda, p. 328, A todo le tira y a nada le da. Conde, p. 54, A todo le tira y a nada le da. Chavez, p. 49, A todo le tira y a nada le pega. Galvan, p. 124, A todo le tira y a nada le da. Wesley, p. 216, A todo le tira y a nada le da.

899 (A). No <u>todo</u> lo que brilla es oro.
899 (B). No <u>todo</u> lo que relumbra es oro.
899 (C). No es oro <u>todo</u> lo que reluce.

<u>Translation or Interpretation</u>: Not all that glitters is gold.

<u>Context</u>: This proverb reminds me of a girl who thought this boy she was dating was rich because he had a nice car and fancy clothes. It turns out his sisters were the ones that paid for everything. (15 occurrences. Informants: 11 female, three male, one not stated).

<u>Sources and Annotations</u>: Adame, p. 70, same as A; p. 77, same as A. Aranda, p. 23, same as B. Armas, p. 321, No ser oro todo lo que reluce; p. 417, same as C. Ballesteros, p. 33, same as A. Caballero, p. 828, same as C. Cobos, p. 88, same as C; p. 94, same as B. Conde, p. 299, same as B. Covarrubias, p. 841, same as C; p. 902, same as C. Espinosa, A., p. 108, same as B. Espinosa, F., p. 173, same as C. Galvan, p. 131, same as C; p. 133, same as C. Gamiz, p. 75, same as A. Jaramillo, p. 409, same as A. Lucero-White, p. 36, same as C. Maldonado, p. 59, No es todo oro lo que reluce. Rubio, p. 64, same as B. Yanez, p. 237, No todo lo que reluce es oro.

900 (A). Todos tenemos cola que nos pisen.

Translation or Interpretation: We all have a tail to be stepped on.

Context: No one is perfect. (One occurrence. Informant: female).

Sources and Annotations: Adame, p. 91, same as A; p. 94, same as A.

901 (A). Donde todos salen llorando no puedo yo ir a cantar.

Translation or Interpretation: Where everyone comes out crying, I cannot go to sing.

Context: If there is a funeral and everybody is crying, a person cannot go in, especially singing. (One occurrence. Informant: female).

Sources and Annotations: Conde, p. 274, Ni a reír donde lloran, ni a llorar donde ríen.

902 (A). En donde bailan y tocan, todos se embocan.

Translation or Interpretation: Where there is dancing and music everyone crams in.

Context: At a wedding reception a lot of people went uninvited, especially young people. The mother of the bride said the above to some of my friends. (Three occurrences. Informants: two female, one male).

Sources and Annotations: Cobos, p. 33, same as A. Conde, p. 116, same as A. Robe, p. 65, Donde bailan y tocan, todos embocan.

903 (A). Tolandrones para los preguntones.

Translation or Interpretation: Bruises for the inquisitive.

Context: This proverb was learned by my mother when she was growing up, circa 1940, in Mercedes, Texas. My mother says she remembers hearing it told to her and her brother and sisters from her mother and her mother's mother. The proverb is used in situations where one does not want someone to know what one has. My mother used the following: Por ejemplo, le preguntas a tu papá ¿Qué traes ahí? o ¿Qué es eso? Y el te dice, "tolondrones para los preguntones." (For example, you ask your dad, "what do you have there?" or "what is that?"

He may answer you, "bruises for the inquisitive." (one occurrence. Informant: female).

Sources and Annotations: Armas, p. 226, Botones para los preguntones. Conde, p. 331, ¿Qué son? son tolondrones para preguntones. Martinez, p. 265, Tones pa' los preguntones.

904 (A). Tonto, tonto, pero no tanto.

Translation or Interpretation: Stupid, stupid, but not so
much.

Context: Her husband was going out on her. She thought she
had him where she wanted, but apparently not. This proverb
reminded her of her thinking he was naive about women, but not
after all. (One occurrence. Informant: female).

Sources and Annotations: Sbarbi, p. 955, Aunque tonto no
tonto.

905 (A). Cualquier tonto gana dinero pero no cualquiera lo
            sabe ahorrar.
905 (B). Cualquier pendejo puede hacer dinero, pero no cual-
            quiera lo sabe cuidar.
905 (C). Cualquiera gana dinero, pero no cualquiera lo cuida.

Translation or Interpretation: Any fool can earn money but
not anyone knows how to save it.

Context: My boyfriend earns more money per week than I do,
but yet, he spends it faster than I do. I can stretch five
dollars a week when he can't even stretch twenty dollars.
(Five occurrences. Informants: one female, three male, one
not stated).

Sources and Annotations: None.

906 (A). Se hace tonto para comer a puños.
906 (B). Me hago sonsito para comer a puños.

Translation or Interpretation: He pretends to be stupid to
eat by handfuls.

Context: Informant informed me of times when she and her sisters used to try to avoid doing housework and would fake illness. (Five occurrences. Informants: four female, one male).

Sources and Annotations: Cobos, p. 62, Hazte el tonto y come
con las dos manos. Espinosa, A., p. 120, Se hace tonto pa'
amasarla mejor.

907 (A). A lo colorado se le va el <u>toro</u>.

<u>Translation or Interpretation</u>: To the red the bull charges.
The bull charges the red.

<u>Context</u>: This is more bar-room laughter jokes. The man tells
his friends of how he saw "a lo colorado se le fue el toro."
(One occurrence. Informant: not stated).

<u>Sources and Annotations</u>: None.

908 (A). Para los <u>toros</u> del Jaral, los caballos de allí mismo.

<u>Translation or Interpretation</u>: For the bulls from Jaral,
horses from the same place.

<u>Context</u>: Used in reference to a mean or strong person who
could be matched by a person with his same background. (Four
occurrences. Informants: two female, one male, one unstated).

<u>Sources and Annotations</u>: Ballesteros, p. 64, Pa' los toros
del Jaral, los caballos de alla mismo. Conde, p. 308, Para
cada uno no hay como el suyo. Gamiz, p. 80, same as A. Martinez, p. 216, Pa los toros de Jaral, los caballos de alla mismo. Rubio, p. 80, Pa los toros del Jaral los caballos de alla
mismo. Santamaria, p. 205, same as A. Velasco, p. 127, Pa los
toros de Jaral los caballos de alla mismo. Yañez, p. 199, Pa
los toros del Tecuan los caballos de allá mismo.

909 (A). Las <u>torres</u> más altas han caído contimas esta que no
          está.
909 (B). La <u>torre</u> más alta se ha caído que no te caigas tú.
909 (C). <u>Torres</u> muy altas se ven arrastradas por el suelo.
909 (D). Las <u>torres</u> más altas se caen, imagínate las que
          están empesando.
909 (E). Si ricos han caido, contimas este pobre que no tiene
          nada.

<u>Translation or Interpretation</u>: Taller towers have fallen,
morse so, this one which is not.

<u>Context</u>: My mother said this proverb to my brother, who was
about to move to his new home. Both my brother and his wife
were spending quite a bit of money buying things for the house.
My brother told my mother how much he had made at work and
that everything seemed to be going all right. He said he sort
of showing off, and mom told him this proverb. She said that
it is better not to brag, because you are never sure what is
expected ahead in your life. She was happy to know that they
were managing well, but she did not want him to brag about it.
I was there and what she said is true. Things like that should
be kept within yourself. It is not good to brag. (Seven oc-

currences. Informants: four female, two male, one not stated).

Sources and Annotations: Conde, p. 392, Torres más altas ha
visto caer. De Barros, p. 453, Torres más altas cayeron.
Velasco, p. 84, Hemos visto caer iglesias cuantimas ese jacal.

910 (A). Anda buscando trabajo rogándole a Dios no encontrarlo.

Translation or Interpretation: He/she is looking for work
begging God not to find any.

Context: People who are lazy and do not want to work almost
always say they are going to find employment, but never seem
to have any luck in obtaining a job. (Two occurrences. Informants: female).

Sources and Annotations: Conde, p. 65, Buscar trabajo rogando
a Dios no hallar. Espinosa, A., p. 99, Buscando trabajo y rogando a Dios no hallarlo; p. 120, Buscando trabajo y rogando
a Dios no hallarlo. Martinez, p. 49, Buscar trabajo rogando a
Dios no encontrarlo. Rubio, p. 69, Buscar trabajo rogando a
Dios no hallar. Velasco, p. 28, Buscar trabajo rogando a Dios
no encontrarlo.

911 (A). Tiene dos trabajos, de enojarse y conformarse.

Translation or Interpretation: He has two jobs, to get angry
and to (be content).

Context: My informant's friend had a neighbor who was always
getting mad with her husband. Her husband took things very
cool. My informant told her this proverb. (One occurrence.
Informant: female).

Sources and Annotations: Conde, p. 385, Tendrás doble trabajo
--enojarte y conformarte. Rodriguez-Marin (1926), p. 428,
Quien se enoja, dos trabajos toma: uno en enojarse y otro en
desenojarse. Yáñez, p. 35, Yo soy el unico causante y tendre
doble trabajo: enojarme y desenojarme al reconocer que soy
menso.

912 (A). Me lleva el tren.

Translation or Interpretation: The train takes me.

Context: A person uses it when he is at a point where he feels
disgusted. (One occurrence. Informant: female).

Sources and Annotations: Cerda, p. 330, Llevárselo a uno el
tren. Conde, p. 260, same as A. Martinez, p. 181, same as A.
Santamaria, p. 216, Llevárselo a uno el tren. Velasco, p. 102,
same as A; p. 147, se lo lleva el tren.

913 (A). Acá tropezando, allá cayendo, vamos viviendo.

Translation or Interpretation: Here tripping, there falling,
we go living.

Context: Don Erasmo says he often uses this whenever somebody
is feeling sorry for himself because something has gone wrong.
(One occurrence. Informant: male).

Sources and Annotations: Rodriguez-Marin (1930), p. 324, Tropezando y cayendo, vamos viviendo; p. 327, Unas veces tropezando y otras cayendo, vamos viviendo.

914 (A). Tú vas y no volverás.

Translation or Interpretation: You go and will not return.

Context: This is a story of two brothers, they were Juan and
Pedro. Juan, for being the most intelligent to keep himself
alive, decided to take his dog along to review his life alone.
He never went hungry. He would always ask for food for the
dog, and he ate it all. That was the life of Juan. Pedro was
a little crazy. He decided to take the door from their old
house to sleep on it. Pedro also decided to go away to make
his own life. He took a dirt road and he kept saying, "you
will go, but will not return. You will go but will not return." Until suddenly it was getting dark and he was getting
sleepy. Suddenly he saw a large shade tree surrounded by
footprints of men. Anyway, he was so tired that he decided to
stay. He climbed the tree with the door, not leaving he behind. Suddenly, some bandits arrived and went under the tree.
Pedro sees a lantern, and sees them dividing some money among
themselves. Pedro had to urinate. Pedro could sustain it no
longer, so he urinated on one of the bandits. Pedro felt like
doing no. 2, and it fell right on the same bandit. The bandit
got scared when (shit) fell on him and he said, "this is not
bird's (shit)." Suddenly, the door moved from the top of the
tree and the bandits ran from fright, forgetting the money.
Seeing that the bandits ran, Pedro did not take a moment or
two to get to the money, and forgot all about the door. That's
why he said, "You will go but, will not return." He, then,
did not need the door any longer because he was rich. (One occurrence. Informant: female).

Sources and Annotations: Sbarbi, p. 971, Cuando tu vas, yo
vuelvo.

915 (A). <u>Tú</u> y las carabinas de Ambrosio son la misma cosa.

<u>Translation or Interpretation</u>: You and the rifles of Ambrose are the same thing.

<u>Context</u>: When you want something done correctly and someone volunteers for the job, the person who wants that particular thing done correctly has very little faith in the person that volunteers. (One occurrence. Informant: female).

<u>Sources and Annotations</u>: Caballero, p. 234, Carabinas de Ambriosio; p. 342, Como las carabinas de Ambrosio; p. 1014, Ser una cosa lo mismo que la carabina de Ambrosio. Espinosa, A., p. 106, Es como la carabina de Ambriosio en el mejor tiempo fanta.

916 (A). Para cuando <u>tú</u> vas yo vengo.

<u>Translation or Interpretation</u>: By the time you're going, I'm already coming.

<u>Context</u>: She says she is constantly telling her daughter to do things, and by the time she gets to them, she has already done it for her. She says this proverb to her. (Four occurrences. Informants: two female, two male).

<u>Sources and Annotations</u>: Conde, p. 310, Para cuando tú te vas yo ya vengo, si es que allá no me entretengo. Martinez, p. 75, Cuando tu te vas yo ya vengo. Sbarbi, p. 971, Cuando tú vas; yo vuelvo.

917 (A). Más vale <u>tuerto</u> que ciego.

<u>Translation or Interpretation</u>: Better one-eyed than blind.

<u>Context</u>: None given. (One occurrence. Informant: female).

<u>Sources and Annotations</u>: Maldonado, p. 44, same as A. Sbarbi, p. 971, same as A.

918 (A). Me he de comer esta <u>tuna</u> aunque me espine la mano.

<u>Translation or Interpretation</u>: I shall eat this prickly pear even if I prick my hand.

<u>Context</u>: Usually said among the men. When a man sees a good looking woman and he definitely likes her. He will do anything and everything to accomplish his goal. Which is probably to marry her, if they make it. (Five occurrences. Informants: male).

Sources and Annotations: Adame, p. 66, Me he de comer esa
tuna, aunque me espine la mano; p. 68, Me he de comer esa
tuna, aunque me espine la mano. Ballesteros, p. 52, same as A.
Cerda, p. 330, same as A. Conde, p. 258, same as A. Velasco,
p. 102, Me he de comer esa tuna, aunque me espine la mano.

919 (A). Los últimos serán los primeros.

Translation or Interpretation: The last shall be the first.

Context: My grandfather told me this when I was a child and
wanted to be the first in the line to break the piñata at a
birthday party. I was around five or six years old. (One
occurrence. Informant: female).

Sources and Annotations: Conde, p. 242, same as A. Jaramillo,
p. 401, same as A. Rodriguez-Marin (1926), p. 280, same as A.
Sbarbi, p. 973, Los últimos son los primeros.

920 (A). Sacar las uñas.

Translation or Interpretation: Draw the fingernail.

Context: Informant was told this proverb by her mother. They
were talking about the neighbor who seemed always very nice
and friendly, until the day they happened to park the car in
front of the neighbor's house. The neighbor came over and
told them to find someplace else to park the car, in a very
rude manner. When the neighbor left, the mother said, "ya
sacó las uñas." (One occurrence. Informant: female).

Sources and Annotations: Sbarbi, p. 975, Sacar uno las uñas.

921 (A). Cada uno habla como uno es.

Translation or Interpretation: Everyone talks the way he is.

Context: "When you say something," he said, "you relate to
people what kind of person you are." Once in a while you hear
someone say something and right away you'll know he doesn't
know what he's talking about. That gives him away. "If you
speak," he said, "be sure of what you say," My informant said
he heard this many times while growing up in the Rio Grande
Valley, but he could not remember who first told him. (One
occurrence. Informant: male).

Sources and Annotations: Maldonado, p. 97, same as A. Sbarbi,
p. 974, Cada uno habla como quien es.

922 (A). Cada uno para sí y Dios para todos.

Translation or Interpretation: Everyone for himself and God for everyone.

Context: You will take care of yourself, and God will pass judgment on others. (One occurrence. Informant: female).

Sources and Annotations: Lea, p. 233, same as A. Lucero-White, p. 33, samd as A. Rodriguez-Marin (1926), p. 66, Cada uno por si, y Dios por todos.

923 (A). Da y ten y uno hara bien.
923 (B). Da y ten y harás bien.

Translation or Interpretation: Give and have and one will do well.

Context: In church, almost the same principle is taught. (Two occurrences. Informants: one male, one not stated).

Sources and Annotations: Cobos, p. 27, same as B. Conde, p. 101, Da y ten y harás bien. Pérez, p. 119, Da y ten y háras bien.

924 (A). Dejar a uno es oscuras.

Translation or Interpretation: To leave one in darkness.

Context: Our neighbor had been telling us about a novela (soap opera) on television, sometime back called "Dulcemente María." She was going to tell us the ending when the phone rang and she went to answer it. My mother then told me that "nos dejo en oscuras." (One occurrence. Informant: female).

Sources and Annotations: Caballero, p. 463, Dejar a obscuras a uno.

925 (A). Lo que uno no puede ver en su casa lo ha de tener.
925 (B). Lo que uno no puede ver, donde quiere lo ha de tener.

Translation or Interpretation: What one cannot stand to see, in their house it shall be.

Context: If you can't stand a child that is always meddling in your conversation and you have a relative that does just that same thing. (Four occurrences. Informants: three female, one male).

Sources and Annotations: Cobos, p. 74, Lo que en la calle no puedas ver, en tu casa lo has de tener. Conde, p. 239, same as A. Martinez, p. 166, Lo que más se odia en la casa se tiene.

926 (A). Pegársele a uno las sábanas.

Translation or Interpretation: To have the bed sheets stick
to oneself.

Context: Informant was told this by her mother. Informant
wanted to be the first one to show her father the present she
had made for him on Christmas Eve. Her sister beat her to it
and showed it to her father. She started crying and her mother said, "vez, si no se te hubieran pegado las sabanas no es-
tuvieras llorando." (One occurrence. Informant: female).

Sources and Annotations: Armas, p. 330, Pegarse las sábanas.
Caballero, p. 994, Se le han pegado las sábanas. Covarrubias,
p. 930, Pegársele las sábanas. Santamaria, p. 436, Pegársele
a uno las cobijas o el petate; p. 456, Pegársele a uno el
petate.

927 (A). Uno es el que carga la lana y otro es el que corre
          la fama.

Translation or Interpretation: One carries the wool -- money
-- and the other gets the fame.

Context: A boss may receive all the credit for doing a certain task, while in reality, his assistant did all the work
and never received the credit. (One occurrence. Informant:
male).

Sources and Annotations: Adame, p. 95, Unos tienen la fama, y
otros cargan la lana; p. 97, Unos tienen la fama, y otros cargan la lana. Conde, p. 401, Unos tienen la fama y otros lavan
la lana. De Barros, p. 463, Unos tienen la fama y otros car-
dan la lana. Espinosa, A., p. 102, Unos son los de la fama y
otros cargan la lana. Gamiz, p. 83, Unos son los de la fama y
otros son los que lavan la lana. Martinez, p. 271, Unos son
los de la fama y otros cargan la lana. Rodriguez-Marin (1926),
p. 499, Unos cargan la lana y otros tienen la fama. Santamaria,
p. 263, Mayo tiene la fama y Junio lava la lana. Velasco, p.
161, Unos son los de la fama y otros los que cargan la lana.

928 (A). Cada uno en su casa y Dios en la de todos.

Translation or Interpretation: Everyone in their house, and
God in all of them.

Context: This proverb refers to those people or situations
in which we should mind his or her business. In other words,
we should not be trying to solve other people's affairs.
(Four occurrences. Informants: three female, one male).

Sources and Annotations: Caballero, p. 213, same as A. Cobos,
p. 20, Cada uno en su casa y Dios en la de todos. Conde, p.

70, same as A. De Barros, p. 127, same as A. Jaramillo, p. 369, Cada uno en su casa y Dios en la de todos. Maldonado, p. 97, Cada uno en su casa y Dios en la de todos que es padre poderoso. Paredes, p. 30, Cada quien en su casa y Dios en la de todos. Sbarbi, p. 217, same as A.

929 (A). Cada uno habla de la feria según como le vaya en ella.

Translation or Interpretation: Each one talks about the fair depending on how it went for him.

Context: My brother used to brag about how much money he used to earn in Michigan, but this experience was short lived. (Two occurrences. Informants: one female, one male).

Sources and Annotations: Caballero, p. 213, Cada cual habla de la feria según le va en ella. Cobos, p. 20, Cada uno habla de la feria asegun le va enella. Conde, p. 70, same as A. Covarrubias, p. 351, Cada uno cuenta de la feria, como le va en ella; p. 589, Cada uno dice de la feria como le va en ella. De Barros, p. 126, Cada uno dice de la feria como le va en ella. Espinosa, F., p. 112, Cada uno dize de la feria como le va en ella. Gamiz, p. 78, Cada quien habla de la feria según le va en ella. Jaramillo, p. 369, Cada uno habla de la feria según como le va en ella. Lea, p. 233, Cada uno cuenta de la feria según lo que ve en ella. Lucero-White, p. 33, Cada uno cuenta de la feria según lo que ve en ella. Maldonado, p. 25, Cada uno dice de la feria como le va en ella. Martinez, p. 53, Cada quien habla de la villa según le va en ella. Rodriguez-Marin (1926), p. 65, Cada uno habla de la feria según le va en ella.

930 (A). Para uno que madruga otro que no duerme.
930 (B). Para uno que madruga may otro que no se acuesta.
930 (C). Para uno que madruga hay otro que va en la noche.

Translation or Interpretation: For one that gets up early, another who doesn't sleep.

Context: When one had to take his product to market he would try to get as little rest as possible and leave to the market as early as possible. Another individual would probably not sleep and be at the market as early as possible. (Seven occurrences. Informants: three female, four male).

Sources and Annotations: Ballesteros, p. 34, same as B. Cobos, p. 98, Para un madrugador, otro que no duerme. Martinez, p. 219, Para uno que madruga hay otro que se desuela. Rodriguez-Marin (1930), p. 248, Para un madrugador, uno que no se acostó. Velasco, p. 129, Para uno que madruga hay otro que se desvela. Yañez, p. 279, Para uno que madruga otro que no se acuesta.

931 (A). Unos corren la liebre y otros sin correr la alcanzan.
931 (B). Uno correó la liebre y otro sin correrla la alcanza.

Translation or Interpretation: Some run the hare, and others,
without running, overtake it.

Context: My two cousins were talking about their girlfriends,
and one was saying that he got his girlfriend by having to
chase her, while the other girl came to the other cousin, and
one of them said, "uno corrio la liebre y otro sin correr la
alcanzo." (Two occurrences. Informants: one female, one
male).

Sources and Annotations: Cobos, p. 118, Uno corre la liebre
y otro es el que alcanza. Conde, p. 410, Unos corren la liebre
y otros la alcanzan. Espinosa, A., p. 113, Unos son los que
corren la liebre...Gamiz, p. 83, Uno corre la liebre y otro
la alcanza. Lucero-White, p. 36, Unos corren la liebre y otros
la alcanzan. Wesley, p. 217, Unos corren a la liebre y otros
sin correr la alcanzan. Yanez, p. 279, same as A.

932 (A). Unos nacen con estrellas y otros nacen estrellados.

Translation or Interpretation: Some are born with stars,
and others are born smashed.

Context: Some people are born lucky and don't have to work
hard to get what they want, but there are some people who
work very hard and don't get what they want. (Seven occurrences. Informants: five female, one male, one unstated).

Sources and Annotations: Adame, p. 95, same as A; p. 96,
same as A. Caballero, p. 1105, same as A. Conde, p. 401,
same as A. Jaramillo, p. 428, same as A. Rodriguez-Marin
(1930), p. 329, Unos nacen con estrella, y otros sin ella.
Rodriguez-Marin (1926), p. 500, same as A.

933 (A). Unos nacemos de pies y otros de cabeza.

Translation or Interpretation: Some of us are born standing,
and others head first.

Context: A girl was talking about how she wished for something, and another replied with this proverb. (One occurrence. Informant: female).

Sources and Annotations: Caballero, p. 806, Nacer de cabeza;
Nacer de pie. Espinosa, A., p. 111, Unos nacen de pies y
otros de cabeza.

934 (A). Te pescamos en las <u>uvas</u>.

<u>Translation or Interpretation</u>: We caught you in the grapes.

<u>Context</u>: Informant told me it happened that she went out and then saw her boyfriend with another girl. Then her sister told him, "te pescamos en las uvas." He had lied to her. (One occurrence. Informant: female).

<u>Sources and Annotations</u>: None.

935 (A). Ya ni me <u>va</u> ni me viene.

<u>Translation or Interpretation</u>: Now it neither goes nor comes for me.

<u>Context</u>: My informant first heard this proverb from his mother. My informant said that his mother would always say the proverb whenever she heard of a rumor about her that wasn't true. Also, when somebody would give her a choice of where to go, meaning that it made no difference to her where she went. (One occurrence. Informant: male).

<u>Sources and Annotations</u>: Caballero, p. 813, Ni me va ni me viene. Conde, p. 174, Eso no me va ni me viene.

936 (A). Poco a poco se <u>va</u> lejos.

<u>Translation or Interpretation</u>: Little by little one goes far.

<u>Context</u>: While working in the fields one day we were very tired and the rows, being half a mile long, seemed impossible to finish. We told my father we probably would not finish and he said we would. He then stated the proverb. (One occurrence. Informant: female).

<u>Sources and Annotations</u>: Ballesteros, p. 34, same as A. Caballero, p. 913, Poquito a poco se va lejos. Cobos, p. 100, Poco a poco se anda lejos. Espinosa, A., p. 109, Poco a poco se anda lejos. Espinosa, F., p. 45, Andando y andando van a lexos. Galván, p. 130, same as A; p. 132, same as A. Rodriguez-Marin (1930), p. 25, Andando, andando van a lejos. Rubio, p. 100, Poco a poco se anda lejos.

937 (A). Más <u>vale</u> poco y bien ganado que mucho y enlodado.

<u>Translation or Interpretation</u>: It is better to have little and well gained than much and soiled.

Context: The informant heard it from her mother when she was young and they were talking of what they had and did not have. (One occurrence. Informant: female).

Sources and Annotations: Cobos, p. 120, Vale más poco y bien ganado que mucho y enzoquetado. Conde, p. 259, Mejor poco y bien arado, que mucho y mucho aranado. Espinosa, F., p. 194, Más vale poco y bueno que mucho y malo. Rodriguez-Marin (1926), p. 298, Mas vale poco y bien ganado que mucho y allegado.

938 (A). Lo que mucho vale, mucho cuesta.

Translation or Interpretation: What is worth much, costs much.

Context: My informant tells me of a girl who loved a boy very much. The boy's job took him to another part of the country, and she decided, after much thought, to go with him. (Three occurrences. Informants: female).

Sources and Annotations: Cobos, p. 74, same as A. Conde, p. 237, same as A. Rodriguez-Marin (1926), p. 271, same as A.

939 (A). Más vale pobre que solo.

Translation or Interpretation: It is better poor than alone.

Context: Sometimes people who are very well off act very snobbish and do not have very many friends. (One occurrence. Informant: female).

Sources and Annotations: Paredes, p. 32, same as A. Perez, p. 123, same as A.

940 (A). Más vale solo que mal acompañado.
940 (B). Mejor solo que mal acompañado.
940 (C). Más vale andar solo que mal acompañado.
940 (D). Más vale estar solo que mal acompañado.
940 (E). Es mejor andar solo que mal acompañado.
940 (F). Es mejor estar solo que mal acompañado.

Translation or Interpretation: It is better alone than in bad company.

Context: My friend was a divorcee. She met this guy, so they decided to live together for a while. This guy was something else. He would get drunk, beat her up, and then beat up her kids. One day we were talking and I told her this proverb. (33 occurrences. Informants: 25 female, seven male, one not stated).

Sources and Annotations: Adame, p. 98, same as A; p. 100, same as A. Armas, p. 416, same as A. Ballesteros, p. 30, Más vale ir solo que mal acompaniado. Benavides, p. 90, same as A. Caballero, p. 775, Más vale ir solo que mal acompañado. Cobos, p. 81, same as A; p. 121, Vale más solo que mal acompañado. Conde, p. 404, Vale más solo que mal acompañado. Galvan, p. 128, same as E; p. 130, same as E. Glazer, p. 60, same as A. Jaramillo, p. 403, same as A. Lucero-White, p. 35, same as A. Perez, p. 123, same as A. Rodriguez-Marin (1926), p. 503, Vale más solo que mal acompañado. Vasquez, p. 89, same as A.

941 (A). Más vale tarde que nunca.
941 (B). Es mejor tarde que nunca.
941 (C). Más vale llegar tarde que no llegar nunca.
941 (D). Más vale llegar tarde que nunca.
941 (E). Vale más tarde que nunca.
941 (F). Vale más tarde y no nunca.

Translation or Interpretation: It is better late than never.

Context: I used this proverb whenever I'm late for school, or work. I drive fast and then I think about this proverb and slow down. I'd rather be late than never get there at all. (34 occurrences. Informants: 25 female, eight male, one not stated).

Sources and Annotations: Armas, p. 416, same as A. Ballesteros, p. 31, same as A. Benavides, p. 89, same as D. Cobos, p. 81, same as A. Conde, p. 255, same as A. Correas, p. 541, same as A. De Barros, p. 343, same as A. Espinosa, A., p. 111, same as E. Espinosa, F., p. 224, same as A. Galvan, p. 131, same as A; p. 134, same as A. Gamiz, p. 90, same as A. Glazer, p. 59, same as E. MacArthur, p. 26, same as E. Maldonado, p. 58, same as A. Pérez, p. 123, same as A. Sbarbi, p. 979, same as A.

942 (A). El valiente vive mientras el cobarde quiere.
942 (B). El valiente muere cuando el cobarde quiere.
942 (C). El valiente vive hasta que el cobarde quiere.

Translation or Interpretation: The brave one lives while the coward wants.

Context: One of my sons was very small and everyone picked on him. A year later he became stronger, then the people who used to pick on him wouldn't anymore. (Six occurrences. Informants: two female, three male, one not stated).

Sources and Annotations: Adame, p. 33, El valiente dura mientras el cobarde llega; p. 46, El valiente dura mientras el cobarde llega. Ballesteros, p. 27, same as C. Conde, p. 154, same as C. Martinez, p. 114, El valiente existe hasta que el cobarde quiere. Rodriguez-Marin (1930), p. 335, Vive el valiente mientras el cobarde quiere. Rubio, p. 208, same as A. Yanez, p. 104, same as A.

943 (A). Con la vara que mides será medido.

Translation or Interpretation: With the rod that you measure you will be measured.

Context: Mrs. Gomes gave two examples to explain the proverb: "If you insult someone, God will judge you by that," and "the way you treat others they will treat you the same." She believes in this proverb and believes it applies to everyone. (Eight occurrences. Informants: four female, four male).

Sources and Annotations: Adame, p. 16, same as A; p. 20, same as A. Aranda, p. 6, same as A. Ballesteros, p. 21, Con la vara que tu mides, te mediran. Conde, p. 83, same as A. Espinosa, A., p. 103, same as A. Galvan, p. 126, same as A; p. 134, same as A. Gamiz, p. 77, same as A. Jaramillo, p. 371, same as A. Robe, p. 66, Con la vara que midas seras tambien medido. Rodriguez-Marin (1926), p. 81, same as A. Vasquez, p. 90, same as A. Yáñez, p. 172, same as A.

944 (A). No te ahoges en un vaso de agua.
944 (B). No te ahoges en tu vaso de agua.

Translation or Interpretation: Don't drown in a glass of water.

Context: This proverb can be used effectively with any situation in which a person is over reacting. (Five occurrences. Informants: two female, three male).

Sources and Annotations: Caballero, p. 69, Ahogarse en una gota de agua. Conde, p. 290, No hay que ahogarse en un vaso de agua. Covarrubias, p. 58, Ahogarse en poca agua. Espinosa, A., p. 110, Se ahogan en un charro de agua. Jaramillo, p. 365, Ahogarse en un vaso de agua. Rodriguez-Marin (1926), p. 338, No hay que ahogarse en poca agua como Juan de Porras. Santamaria, p. 55, Ahogarse en poca agua, en un vaso de agua. Sbarbi, p. 39, Ahogarse en poca agua; p. 42, No hay que ahogarse en poca agua, como Juan de Porras.

945 (A). Quien tiene buen <u>vecino</u> tiene buen amigo.

<u>Translation or Interpretation</u>: He who has a good neighbor has a good friend.

<u>Context</u>: When you go out of town you have a person who will watch your house more closely. (One occurrence. Informant: female).

<u>Sources and Annotations</u>: Ballesteros, p. 35, same as A.

946 (A). Vale más un <u>vecino</u> cercano que un hermano lejano.

<u>Translation or Interpretation</u>: It is better to have a neighbor who is near than a brother who is far.

<u>Context</u>: You can rely on, and trust, a neighbor more than a relative. (One occurrence. Informant: female).

<u>Sources and Annotations</u>: Cerdą, p. 331, Vale más el cercano es el pariente más lejano.

947 (A). No necesito <u>vejigas</u> para nadar.

<u>Translation or Interpretation</u>: I do not need balloons to swim.

<u>Context</u>: A person who can stand on her own without the assistance of anyone. Very independent. (One occurrence. Informant: female).

<u>Sources and Annotations</u>: Martinez, p. 201, same as A. Santamaria, p. 45, No necesitar uno de guajes para nadar; p. 257, No necesitar mates para nadar. Velasco, p. 117, No necesito guajes para nadar.

948 (A). Poco <u>veneno</u> no mata.

<u>Translation or Interpretation</u>: A little poison won't kill.

<u>Context</u>: We were eating <u>menudo</u> once and were running low on corn tortillas. When my one year old son threw the last tortilla on the floor, I immediately picked it up. (Four occurrences. Informants: one female, three male).

<u>Sources and Annotations</u>: Adame, p. 79, same as A; p. 82, same as A. Aranda, p. 30, Un poquito de veneno no mata. Caballero, p. 905, same as A. Cobos, p. 100, Poco venevo no mata pero ataranta. Conde, p. 319, Poco veneno no mata, y lo que no mata engorda. Martinez, p. 226, Poco veneno no mata ni mucho si no es activo. Robe, p. 68, Poquito veneno no mata. Rodriguez-Marin (1926), p. 369, Poco veneno no daña o mata. Sbarbi, p. 968, same as A.

949 (A). Y no <u>vengo</u> a ver si puedo sino porque puedo vengo.

Translation or Interpretation: And I don't come to see if I can, it is because I can that I come.

Context: This is a macho proverb. It relates to instances. It can relate to a man that is going to fight or do a task, etc. (One occurrence. Informant: male).

Sources and Annotations:. Conde, p. 300, same as A. Galván, p. 132, same as A. Martínez, p. 209, same as A; p. 284, same as A. Velasco, p. 122, same as A.

950 (A). Como te <u>veo</u> me vi, como me ves te verás.
950 (B). Como te <u>ves</u> me vi, como me <u>veo</u> te has de ver.
950 (C). Asi como tu te ves me <u>veo</u>, y así como me ves te ven.

Translation or Interpretation: How I see you I was seen, How you see me you will be seen.

Context: My informant told me that her grandmother had said that this little girl was looking at her strangely because she was old looking, so she told the girl the above phrase. (Six occurrences. Informants: female).

Sources and Annotations: Conde, p. 80, same as A. Gamiz, p. 89, same as A. Rodriguez-Marin (1926), p. 77, Como eres fui, como soy te verás.

951 (A). <u>Ver</u> es creer.
951 (B). <u>Ver</u> para creer.

Translation or Interpretation: To see is to believe.

Context: When my "lazy" cousin told me he was finally going to look for a job I told him that seeing was believing. (Two occurrences. Informants: female).

Sources and Annotations: Alcala, p. 643, same as B. Balles-teros, p. 17, same as B. Cobos, p. 122, same as A. Conde, p. 406, Ver para creer, como Santo Tomás. Covarrubias, p. 1000, Ver y creer. Espinosa, F., p. 241, Ver y creer. Galvan, p. 126, same as A; p. 134, same as A. Jaramillo, p. 428, Ver para creer y para no errar, tocar. Rodriguez-Marin (1930), p. 245, Para creer, no hay cosa como ver. Rodriguez-Marin (1926), p. 301, Más vale ver que creer; p. 449, Santo Tomas, ver y creer, y nada mas; Santo Tome, ver y creer. Sbarbi, p. 989, Más vale ver que creer.

952 (A). La <u>verdad</u>, aunque severa, es amiga verdadera.

Translation or Interpretation: The truth, although it hurts, is a true friend.

Context: A new friend of mine at college wore her dresses very short. She had very skinny legs, and did not look very nice in her short dresses. Our landlady told me I should mention it to her, and then said the proverb. I couldn't tell my friend. (One occurrence. Informant: female).

Sources and Annotations: Cobos, p. 71, same as A.

953 (A). La verdad no peca pero incomoda.
953 (B). La verdad no peca pero desincomoda.

Translation or Interpretation: The truth doesn't sin, but it does inconvenience.

Context: One time, a friend was telling me about something my boyfriend had done. I told her I did not believe her, and became somewhat upset. She then said, "la verdad no mata pero incomoda. (Eight occurrences. Informants: seven female, one not stated).

Sources and Annotations: Adame, p. 57, same as A; p. 62, same as A. Ballesteros, p. 9, same as A. Cerda, p. 332, same as A. Cobos, p. 71, same as A. Galvan, p. 129, La verdad no mata pero incomoda. MacArthur, p. 35, El que dice la verdad no peca, pero incomoda. Robe, p. 60, same as A. Rodriguez-Marin (1926), p. 107, Decir verdad no es pecado, pero cae en desagrado. Santamaria, p. 257, same as A.

954 (A). Lo que es verdad, coraje dá.

Translation or Interpretation: What is true, anger gives.

Context: For as long as I can remember, this phrase has been in my memory very clearly. During my early adolescence, I would hear it regularly, especially from my mother. This phrase is usually said when an argument is occurring. Perhaps a person is honestly accusing the other of lying, cheating, or not doing what he is supposed to. In defense, the other person will object of the accusation in anger. At this moment, the phrase is very effective when it comes to reasoning. The accusing person supports himself by telling the other person that "lo que es verdad, coraje da." However, a person, in defense, can also use this phrase. If he uses false accusations on his opponent to arouse his anger, he can use this phrase to support himself. This phrase is mind bending. There is both good reasoning and good poetry in it. (One occurrence. Informant: female).

Verdad / Verdades

Sources and Annotations: Glazer, p. 60, Cuando no es verdad, ni coraje da.

955 (A). Lo que es verdad no es chisme.

Translation or Interpretation: What is truth is not gossip.

Context: A person who has the facts isn't merely gossiping. (Two occurrences. Informants: one female, one not stated).

Sources and Annotations: None.

956 (A). Sino es verdad ni coraje da.
956 (B). Lo que no es verdad ni coraje da.
956 (C). Cuando no es verdad ni coraje da.
956 (D). No siendo verdad ni coraje da.

Translation or Interpretation: If it is not true it doesn't cause anger.

Context: Whenever accused of something which you haven't done, usually gets you angry, and the other person concludes that you are being accused for something you did do. Our sister always says the above to us when we are accused of something which we didn't do and we get angry. (12 occurrences. Informants: nine female, three male).

Sources and Annotations: Glazer, p. 60, same as B.

957 (A). Al decir las verdades se pierden las amistades.

Translation or Interpretation: Upon telling the truth friendships are lost.

Context: When you tell a friend the truth he, or she, will get mad, or hurt, and your friendship won't be the same. (One occurrence. Informant: female).

Sources and Annotations: Aranda, p. 1, same as A. Sbarbi, p. 990, Con la verdad se arisola la amistad.

958 (A). Las verdades las trae el tiempo, la justicia, Dios.

Translation or Interpretation: Time brings the truths, and God brings justice.

Context: None given. (One occurrence. Informant: female).

Sources and Annotations: Sbarbi, p. 992, Para verdades, el tiempo, y para justicia, Dios.

959 (A). No saber lo que es la <u>verguenza</u>.

<u>Translation or Interpretation</u>: Not to know what shame is.

<u>Context</u>: Informant heard her mother use this proverb when her young sister came home very late, and then lied about it. The mother found out and told her, "no sabes lo que es la verguenza." (One occurrence. Informant: female).

<u>Sources and Annotations</u>: None.

960 (A). Lo que no <u>ves</u> no duele.

<u>Translation or Interpretation</u>: What you don't see won't hurt.

<u>Context</u>: This, my brother told me when I told him not to be fooling around so much. (One occurrence. Informant: male).

<u>Sources and Annotations</u>: None.

961 (A). La primera <u>vez</u> que me engañes la culpa es tuya, la otra es mía.

<u>Translation or Interpretation</u>: The first time that you fool me, the fault is yours, the next, it is mine.

<u>Context</u>: When a person lies to you for the first time it is not your fault because you take his word. But the next time it is your fault, because you already know that you can't take his word. (One occurrence. Informant: male).

<u>Sources and Annotations</u>: None.

962 (A). La primera <u>vez</u> es muchachada, la segunda vez es sin-verguenzada.

<u>Translation or Interpretation</u>: The first time it is youthfulness, the second time it is shamelessness.

<u>Context</u>: When young people start using drugs, or say, for example, a young girl starts having sex, they get pregnant the first time. According to them, they did not know they would get pregnant; the second time they do it is because they like it. (One occurrence. Informant: female).

<u>Sources and Annotations</u>: Espinosa, A., p. 111, Unos son sin-verguenceros y otros sinverguenzos son.

963 (A). Una <u>vez</u> nos lleva el coyote, dos veces no.

Translation or Interpretation: You don't make the same mistake twice. One time the coyote may take us, but not twice.

Context: In his job he made a mistake, but he wasn't about to make the same mistake twice. (One occurrence. Informant: male).

Sources and Annotations: Rubio, p. 205, Una vez llevaría el coyote, no dos.

964 (A). No cantes victoria aunque en el estribo estés, que muchos en el estribo suben y suelen quedarce a pie.

Translation or Interpretation: Don't sing victory although on the stirrup you are, for many on the stirrip climb and end up on foot.

Context: This proverb has two meanings: Don't count your chickens before they hatch; Even though you are at the top, don't take it for granted; you will not always be on the top. (Two occurrences. Informants: female).

Sources and Annotations: None.

965 (A). Come y bebe, la vida es breve.

Translation or Interpretation: Eat and drink, life is short.

Context: Eat, drink, and be merry, for tomorrow you die. (One occurrence. Informant: female).

Sources and Annotations: None.

966 (A). Date buena vida, temerás más la caída. A gran salto, gran quebranto.

Translation or Interpretation: Give yourself good life, and you will lose everything if the police catch you.

Context: If you get into hard business and gain much money, you will lose everything if the police catch you. (One occurrence. Informant: female).

Sources and Annotations: Sbarbi, p. 998, Date buena vida, temeras más la caída.

967 (A). Hacer la vida pesada.

Translation or Interpretation: To make life heavy. To make life miserable.

Context: My informant's brother would give the family a hard time. He was a misfit. (One occurrence. Informant: female).

Sources and Annotations: Aranda, p. 16, same as A.

968 (A). Entre más viejo más pendejo.
968 (B). Mientras más viejo, más pendejo.
968 (C). Entre más grande más pendejo.

Translation or Interpretation: While getting older, more of a fool. The older, the more of a fool.

Context: If a son is a gambler, and time after time he loses money, this person's father may say, "you never will learn to stop gambling even if you always lose. The older you get, the dumber you are." (Five occurrences. Informants: one female, four male).

Sources and Annotations: Cobos, p. 56, same as A. Martinez, p. 118, same as A.

969 (A). Dime de donde vienes y te diré a donde vas.

Translation or Interpretation: Tell me where you came from, and I will tell you where you are going.

Context: A person telling another that what he does, or his actions, will determine what kind of person he is. (One occurrence. Informant: not stated).

Sources and Annotations: None.

970 (A). Viejo el viento y todavia sopla.
970 (B). Más viejo esta el aire y todavía sopla.
970 (C). Dicen que el amor es viejo, viejo el viento y todavia sopla.

Translation or Interpretation: Old is the wind and it still blows.

Context: Whenever an elderly person confronts someone who tells them that they can't do something because they are too old, they retort with this dicho. (Six occurrences. Informants: four female, two male).

Sources and Annotations: None.

971 (A). Si en viernes te ríes, en un sábado lloras.

Translation or Interpretation: If on Friday you laugh, on Saturday you cry.

Context: I heard this on a Friday. It was used when my in-formant's sister was laughing with much more gusto than the rest of the group. Since I heard this I have asked several, longtime Valley residents if they are familiar with the pro-verb. Everyone I spoke with has heard it. It apparently has no underlying meaning. It may be used by anyone on a Friday, to anyone who is laughing. Although, most of the group is laughing, it is usually directed to the loudest laughter. It is generally considered to be a humorous comment in itself. (One occurrence. Informant: female).

Sources and Annotations: None.

972 (A). Saca la viga de tu ojo antes que saques la de tu hermano.

Translation or Interpretation: Remove the beam from your eye before removing the one from your brother.

Context: It is applicable to many situations where the elder brother is to sacrifice personally for his brother. It is to hurt him before his brother. An honorable type of idea. (One occurrence. Informant: not stated).

Sources and Annotations: Espinosa, A., p. 111, Ven un popote en el ojo ajeno y no ven una viga en el suyo. Gamiz, p. 77, Ver la paja en ojo ajeno y no la viga en el nuestro. Rodri-guez-Marin (1930), p. 236, No tesaques un ojo por sacar los dos a otro. Rodriguez-Marin (1926), p. 347, No ves la viga que hay en tu ojo y ves la paja en el otro; p. 505, Vemos la paja en el ojo ajeno y no vemos la viga en el nuestro.

973 (A). La virtud del joven es el fuerza, del viejo la ex-periencia.

Translation or Interpretation: The virtue of youth is strength, of age, it is experience.

Context: Young people depend on vitality, and the old on experience. (One occurrence. Informant: female).

Sources and Annotations: Adame, p. 57, same as A.

974 (A). Vísteme despacio que de prisa ando.

Translation or Interpretation: Dress me slow that I am in a hurry.

Context: A man told his wife this in order to get to work on time. (Two occurrences. Informants: one male, one not stated).

Sources and Annotations: Adame, p. 24, Despacio que de prisa vamos; p. 28, Despacio que de prisa vamos. Caballero, p. 491, Despacio que estoy de prisa. Cobos, p. 122, Visteme despacio que tengo prisa. Conde, p. 110, Despacio que vas de prisa. Jaramillo, p. 428, same as A. Rodriguez-Marin (1926), p. 509, same as A.

975 (A). Viuda fea pero platuda será siempre hermosa viuda.

Translation or Interpretation: Ugly widow, but with much silver, will always be a beautiful widow.

Context: This proverb was told to me when I was about ten years old. A friend of the family got married with a woman who was twice his age. I was very curious about this, so I decided to ask about this, then he told me this proverb. This proverb means, to the young man, that even if a woman looks old and ugly, and if she is lonely and with money, it does not matter how ugly or old she might be; as long as she has money she will always be pretty. (One occurrence. Informant: male).

Sources and Annotations: Conde, p. 408, same as A. Martinez, p. 276, Viuda y fea, pero platuda, es siempre una hermosa viuda.

976 (A). Vive y deja vivir.

Translation or Interpretation: Live and let live.

Context: Informant always says this when someone comes to her talking about others. (Two occurrences. Informants: female).

Sources and Annotations: None.

977 (A). Como se vive se muere.

Translation or Interpretation: How one lives, one dies.

Context: A friend of mine who liked easy women and booze, was killed in an automobile accident. He had been drinking. (One occurrence. Informant: male).

Sources and Annotations: Conde, p. 80, same as A. Espinosa, F., p. 104, Es onbre de dure cervicis. Rodriguez-Marin (1926), p. 78, same as A; p. 87, Cual la vida, tal la muerte; p. 437, Quien vive bien, muere bien, quien mal vive, mal muere; p. 487, Tal vida, tal muerte. Sbarbi, p. 1016, same as A.

978 (A). Si quieres <u>vivir</u> sano, acuéstate y levántate temprano.

Translation or Interpretation: If you want to live healthy,
go to bed, and rise early.

Context: My informant's mother would tell her this before
she would go to bed at night. (One occurrence. Informant:
female).

Sources and Annotations: Rodriguez-Marin (1930), p. 6, Acostarse temprano y levantarse temprano siempre es sano. Rodriguez-Marin (1926), p. 468, same as A.

979 (A). Al más <u>vivo</u> se le van los pies.

Translation or Interpretation: To the smartest one, his feet
will go on him. The smartest one loses his footing.

Context: Said to a person who is upset over making a mistake.
It is meant to make the person feel better. My grandmother
always said this to us as we were growing up. She used to
say this to me when I was learning how to cook and bake. (One
occurrence. Informant: female).

Sources and Annotations: Robe, p. 63, same as A.

980 (A). El más <u>vivo</u> vive del más pendejo.
980 (B). Me voy y lo dejo, para que el más <u>vivo</u> viva del más
pendejo.

Translation or Interpretation: The wiser one lives of the
most foolish.

Context: A rich farmer took advantage of the poor farm workers by only paying them a dollar fifty ($1.50) an hour. (Six
occurrences. Informants: five female, one male).

Sources and Annotations: Ballesteros, p. 2, Del tonto vive
el vivo. Martinez, p. 155, La mitad viva vive de la mitad pen-
deja. Vasquez, p. 90, El vivo vive del pendejo. Yáñez, p. 69,
Los vivos viven de los tarugos y estos nomás de su trabajo.

981 (A). <u>Yerba</u> mala nunca muere.
981 (B). <u>Yerba</u> mala no muere.
981 (C). <u>Cosa</u> mala nunca muere.

Translation or Interpretation: Bad weed never dies.

Context: Delfina says this is used when someone who is good
for the world passes away. It makes you wonder about all the
bad people who are better off dead. But bad people are like

bad weed; you don't get rid of it. Delfina has learned it at
home when she was growing up. She uses it a lot herself. It
can also be used jokingly to make someone who is sick feel
better, or to cheer them up. Sometimes, Delfina said, when
her husband is worried about his health, she will say this to
him. This causes him to laugh and say, "so that's what you
think of me?" (Six occurrences. Informants: five female,
one not stated).

Sources and Annotations: Adame, p. 16, same as C; p. 20, same
as C. Ballesteros, p. 37, same as A. Cobos, p. 24, same as C.
Conde, p. 193, Hierba mala nunca muere. De Barros, p. 147,
same as C; p. 262, Mala cosa nunca muere. Galvan, p. 126, same
as C; p. 129, La mala yerba nunca muere; p. 131S, same as A.
p. 135, La mala yerba nunca muere. Gamiz, p. 91, Cosa mala
nunca muere, si muere ni falta hace. Jaramillo, p. 402, mala
yerba no muere. Martinez, p. 283, Yerba mala nunca muere y si
muere no hace falta. Robe, p. 68, Yerba mala nunca muere y si
muere no hace falta. Rubio, p. 105, Cosa mala nunca muere y si
muere ni falta hace. Santamaria, p. 405, same as C. Sbarbi, p.
1020, same as A. Villafuerte, p. 209, same as C. Yanez, p. 206,
Cosa mala nunca muere y si muere no hace falta.

982 (A). Ahora es cuando _yerbabuena_, hay que darle sabor al
caldo.
982 (B). Ahora es cuando chile verde, les has de dar sabor al
caldo.

Translation or Interpretation: Now is when mint should give
the broth flavor.

Context: Now it's your turn to speak. (Two occurrences. Informants: one female, one male).

Sources and Annotations: Conde, p. 24, same as A. Martinez,
p. 19, same as A. Paredes, p. 29, Ahora, es cuando, yerbabuena,
le has de dar sabor al caldo. Pérez, p. 118, Ahora, es cuando,
yerbabuena, le has de dar sabor al caldo. Velasco, p. 13,
Ahora, es cuando, yerbabuena, le has de dar sabor al caldo.

983 (A). _Yo_ soy quien soy y no me parezco a nadie.

Translation or Interpretation: I am who I am, and I don't look
like anyone.

Context: A friend was talking to my cousin when, suddenly,
she replied, "You're just like the rest of them." My cousin
said, "yo soy quien soy y no me parezco a nadie." (Two occurrences. Informants: one female, one male).

Sources and Annotations: Conde, p. 415, same as A. Martinez,
p. 284, same as A. Velasco, p. 170, same as A.

984 (A). Yo visto el mono para que otra lo baile.

Translation or Interpretation: I dress the monkey so that another may dance with it.

Context: It means that the wife will wash, cook, and iron for her husband, while he goes out without her and has fun with other girls. My sister does funny things. When her husband and she are going out, she irons his clothes and everything, but if he is going out by himself, she will not iron his clothes. I once asked her why, and she told me this proverb. (One occurrence. Informant: female).

Sources and Annotations: Adame, p. 95, Unos visten al mono pa que otros lo bailen; p. 97, Unos visten al mono pa que otros lo bailen. Conde, p. 408, Viste al mona pa'que otra la baile. Martinez, p. 16, Adornar el chango pa'que otro lo baile. Santa-maria, p. 293, Vestir la mona para que otro la baile.

985 (A). Si te aprieta el zapato quitátelo y si no, póntelo.

Translation or Interpretation: If the shoe is tight on you take it off, if not, put it on.

Context: I have an uncle who never made up his mind on what he wanted to be when he grew up. Right now he is thirty-seven years old and not doing anything. (One occurrence. Informant: female).

Sources and Annotations: Galván, p. 124, Al que le queda el zapato que se lo ponga. Pérez, p. 119, Al que le apriete el zapato que se lo afloje.

986 (A). La zorra nunca se ve la cola.
986 (B). La zorra nunca se mira la cola.
986 (C). La zorra nunca se ve la cola ni el zorillo su fun-dillo.
986 (D). La zorra nunca se mira la cola ni el zorrillo su fundillo.
986 (E). La zorra nunca se ve la cola aunque la traiga en rastra.

Translation or Interpretation: The fox never sees its own tail.

Context: Never pass judgement on others before looking at yourself to find out if you are not guilty of exactly the same thing. (29 occurrences. Informants: 16 female, 13 male).

Sources and Annotations: Adame, p. 57, La zorra no se ve la cola; p. 62, La zorra no se ve la cola. Ballesteros, p. 63, same as A. Cerda, p. 335, La zorra nunca se ve su cola. Cobos, p. 72, same as B; p. 94, No se ve la cola la zorra pero si la ajena. Conde, p. 227, same as A. Gamiz, p. 83, La zorra nunca se ve su cola. Glazer, p. 60, same as B. Sbarbi, p. 1027, La zorra por la cola.

Appendixes

Tabular Summary Data

1. INFORMANTS' COUNTRY OF BIRTH

Mexico	750	21.5%
United States	2,153	61.8%
Not Stated	568	16.3%
Other	14	.4%
	3,485	

2. LANGUAGES SPOKEN BY INFORMANT

English/Spanish	2,269	65.1%
Spanish	1,054	30.2%
English	57	1.6%
Not Stated	71	2.5%
Other	34	1.1%
	3,485	

3. INFORMANTS' ETHNIC GROUP

Mexican American	2,155	62 %
Mexican	924	27 %
Spanish	119	3 %
Not Stated	103	3 %
Other	184	5 %
	3,485	

4. INFORMANTS' SEX

Female	2,265	65 %
Male	1,043	30 %
Not Stated	177	5 %
	3,485	

Appendix

5. INFORMANTS' AGE

	Female	Male	Not Stated
0-10		1	
11-20	228 (6.5%)	85 (2.4%)	1
21-30	554 (15.9%)	314 (9.0%)	28 (.8%)
31-40	324 (9.3%)	133 (3.5%)	23 (.7%)
41-50	392 (11.2%)	101 (2.9%)	3 (.1%)
51-60	261 (7.5%)	176 (5.1%)	
61-70	241 (6.9%)	82 (2.4%)	2 (.1%)
71-80	61 (1.8%)	55 (1.6%)	5 (.1%)
81-90	11 (0.3%)	9 (0.3%)	
91-100	3 (0.1%)	3 (0.1%)	
Not Stated	90 (5.5%)	84 (2.4%)	115 (3.3%)

6. INFORMANT HEARD PROVERB FROM

Mother	529	24.0%
Father	325	14.8%
Friend	541	24.6%
Parents	203	9.2%
Spouse	62	2.8%
Grandmother	110	5.0%
Grandfather	59	2.7%
Relative	265	12.0%
In-laws	16	.7%
Others	93	4.2%
Not Stated	1,282	36.7%
	3,485	

7. INFORMANTS' OCCUPATION

Agriculturalists	2	Builder	1
Aide	8	Bus driver	1
Air condition mechanic	1	Businessman	20
Air traffic controller	1	Career planner	1
Ambulance attendant	1	Carpenter	24
Attorney	2	Case evaluator	2
Auto parts	11	Cashier	6
Baby sitter	6	Chemist	1
Bank employee	1	Cleaners	12
Bank examiner	1	Clerk	31
Barber	1	Clerk typist	9
Bartender	3	Coach	1
Beer distributor	1	Commissioner	1
Beautician	12	Computer technician	1
Body man	1	Concrete finisher	2
Body shopman	1	Contractor	2
Bookkeeper	15	Construction worker	11
Boxer	1	Cook	25

Cosmetologist	1	Nurse	3
Counselor	17	Nutrition aide	27
County foreman	1	Optical Assistant	2
Crew loader	1	P A instructor	1
Criminal investigator	1	Painter	3
Custodian	13	Pemex	7
Custom broker	2	Petroleos Mexicanos	6
Dental assistant	2	Pharmacist	5
Department manager	5	Plant helper	1
Deputy director	4	Postman	1
Diagnostician	2	Printer	2
Dietician	6	Probation Officer	3
Director	5	Professor	3
Director of Housing	2	Programmer	1
Director of S E R M	1	Plumber	1
Disabled	17	Ranger	23
Domestic	28	Receptionist	1
DPS trooper	1	Recreation	1
Drafting	1	Retired	47
Electrical serviceman	1	Respiratory therapist	3
Engineer	2	Sales clerk	4
Factory worker	4	Salesperson	65
Farmer	23	Sergeant	1
Foreman	1	School principal	18
Gas station worker	1	School supervisor	15
Grant writer (USA)	1	Seamstress	13
Hairdresser	13	Secretary	173
Health clinic administrator	2	Self-employed	21
Health worker	1	Shop foreman	1
Heavy equipment operator	6	Social worker	25
Homemaker	34	Sorter	1
Housekeeper	2	Speech therapist	1
Housewife	987	Stock clerk	13
Inspector	1	Storekeeper	1
Insurance clerk	1	Student	880
Insurance representative	3	Sugar mill	1
Janitor	1	Tailor	2
Laborer	134	Tax assessor	2
Lab technician	3	Tax clerk	10
Library aide	4	Tax collector	14
Library clerk	1	Teacher	141
Liquor control	1	Teacher's aide	41
L V N	1	Teacher consultant	1
Machine operator	13	Teacher substitute	1
Maid	3	Technician	10
Manager	14	Texas Parks and Wildlife	9
Man power	2	Truck driver	19
Meat cutter	1	Typist	1
Mechanic	14	Unemployed	30
Medical doctor	5	U S D A worker	2
Merchant	1	Utility man	5
Minister	10	Veteran recruiter	7
Moore Paint Company	2	Veterinarian	1
Navy	1	Vice President of bank	1
Notary public	1	Vocational instructor	12
Nurse's aide	7	Water plant operator	3

Appendix

Waiter	1	Y S D director	24
Welder	3	Yardman	4
Welfare worker	4	Not Stated	124
			3,485

8. INFORMANTS' OCCUPATION BY TYPES OF WORK

Professional	236	6.8%
Managerial	103	2.9%
Clerical	267	7.7%
Sales	110	3.1%
Crafts persons	208	6.0%
Operative	124	3.6%
Service workers	198	5.7%
Private Households	100	2.9%
Housewives	987	28.3%
Students	880	25.3%
Not Stated	157	4.5%
Self-employed	21	0.6%
Unemployed	30	0.8%
Retired	64	1.8%

9. APPROXIMATE DATE INFORMANT FIRST HEARD PROVERB

1902	1	1937	9
1906	4	1938	4
1910	2	1939	26
1911	5	1940	78
1912	3	1941	13
1913	2	1942	8
1914	3	1943	18
1916	4	1944	13
1917	1	1945	45
1918	2	1946	23
1919	15	1947	7
1920	8	1948	23
1921	2	1949	47
1922	2	1950	148
1923	7	1951	26
1924	4	1952	13
1925	7	1953	8
1926	6	1954	22
1927	2	1955	23
1928	2	1956	23
1929	9	1957	26
1930	55	1958	24
1931	37	1959	77
1932	4	1960	134
1933	10	1961	31
1934	19	1962	22
1935	15	1963	17
1936	20	1964	44

1965	44	1974	67
1966	24	1975	61
1967	28	1976	89
1968	43	1977	78
1969	83	1978	91
1970	142	1979	101
1971	41	1980	2
1972	48	1981	1
1973	48	Not Stated	1,300
			3,485

10. PLACE COLLECTED

Alamo	46	Lozano	4
Aunt's House	1	Lull	1
Bovina	1	Lyford	8
Bowling Alley	1	Mathis	7
Brownsville	3	McAllen	480
Car	1	Mercedes	126
Corpus Christi	37	Mexico	120
Crystal City	1	Mission	234
Daughter's house	3	Monte Alto	30
Delmita	8	Montgomery Wards	1
Donna	66	Mother's house	6
Eagle Pass	3	Movies	1
Edcouch	5	Office	4
Edinburg	637	Oklahoma	1
El Sauz	26	Peñitas	2
Elsa	22	Pharr	335
Escobares	30	Port Isabel	2
Falcon Heights	13	Premont	1
Falfurrias	4	Progreso	1
Friends	1	Puerto Rico	1
Grandfather's house	3	Raymondville	26
Grandmother's house	1	Restaurant	3
Harlingen	192	Rio Grande City	98
Havana	2	Rio Hondo	3
Hebbronville	2	Roma	117
Hidalgo	5	San Antonio	5
Home of informant	36	San Benito	52
Houston	2	San Isidro	16
In the Valley	30	San Juan	58
Jacksonville, NC	1	San Manuel	2
La Casita	1	Santa Rosa	1
La Feria	24	Sebastian	1
La Grulla	47	Sinton	1
La Joya	5	Southeast Asia	1
Laredo	2	Sullivan	15
Linn	1	Uncle's House	2
Los Angeles, CA	1	United States	10
Los Arrieros	1	Weslaco	184
Los Fresnos	1	Work	74
Los Saenz	7	Not Stated	178
			3,485

327

Proverb Collection Form

The Proverb:

Translation of the Proverb in English: (As best possible
with explanation)

An example (CASO) of the use of the Proverb from actual
life:

INFORMANT: LANGUAGE SPOKEN:

NAME & AGE: PLACE COLLECTED:

SEX: DATE COLLECTED:

OCCUPATION: DATE INFORMANT FIRST
                                HEARD THE PROVERB:
ETHNIC GROUP:

COUNTRY OF BIRTH:

ADDRESS & PHONE NO. OF INFORMANT:

                                Student's Name:

                                Address & Phone:

Indexes

A. Spanish Version

B. English Version

Ability, 933
Absolution, 189
Abuse, 680
Abuser, 738, 739
Abusive, 818
Accompanied, 940
Acquaintance, 694, 787, 985
Act, 471
Actions, 652, 653
Advancing, 78
Advice, 192-195
After, 71
Afternoon, 650, 873, 874
Ahead, 103
Aid, 73, 109, 111, 266
Alert, 795
Alike, 439
All, 895-902
Alone, 371
Anglo, 451
Angry, 5, 13, 108, 339, 560,
 528, 840, 935
Anglo, 451
Animal, 47
Another, 15
Annoyance, 723
Annihilates, 770
Ant, 496, 676
Appealing, 574
Appear, 811
Appearance, 50-51, 920
Apples, 574
Apprentice, 54

Ardor, 63
Are, 800
Around, 823
Arrange, 490
Arriving, 547, 548, 824
Asking, 39, 319, 745, 768, 903
Atmospheric, 390
Attending, 768
Authentic, 229
Back, 401
Bad, 561
Badly, 560
Balloons, 947
Barber, 77
Bark, 725, 727, 735
Battle, 90
Be, 405-406
Beak, 656
Beam, 972
Beard, 77-78
Beast, 526-527
Beautiful, 612
Bed, 146
Before, 427
Beg, 467, 745, 780
Beggar, 532, 533
Believing, 169, 895
Bell, 137
Belly, 701-703
Bend, 279
Benefited, 884
Better, 151, 937-941
Bird, 686-700

Index

February, 411
Feeling, 662, 753
Females, 426
Field, 696
Fierce, 724
Fighting, 24, 343, 344, 499
Fill, 702-703
Find, 790
Finger, 46, 235-236
Finish, 254
Fire, 499, 544
First, 39, 319
Fish, 738-740
Floats, 79
Flour, 469
Flower, 416, 575
Flower pot, 416
Fly, 596-597, 714
Following, 788
Food, 182
Fool, 720-721, 746-748, 754
Forcing, 118
Foreign, 15, 127, 298-299
Forest, 594
Forgetting, 33, 42, 75, 363
Forgiveness, 189
Foresee, 769, 785
Fortune, 35, 932
Fourth, 666
Fox, 986
Fraud, 72
Fried, 829
Friends, 21-25, 175, 284,
    295, 302, 574, 681, 716,
    782, 945
Friendship, 14, 26-28, 144,
    208, 957
Friday, 971
Fright, 743
Fruit, 418
Future, 341, 777
Faity, 813
Generous, 267, 271-273, 930
Genius, 440
Given, 231-232, 237, 783
Giving, 80, 233, 237, 319
Glad, 702
Glass, 944
Glitters, 535, 899
Goat, 124-125
God, 202, 263-268, 320, 344,
    337-338, 414, 694, 814, 910
Godchild, 14
Goes, 395, 935-936
Going, 696
Gold, 883, 899

Good, 96-97, 202-203, 652, 712
Gossip, 778, 955
Gourds, 453
Grace, 450
Grapes, 934
Greed, 568
Green, 163
Grey hair, 138-139
Ground, 65
Guard, 159
Guatemala, 454
Gutter, 309
Habit, 204, 457, 726
Hairs, 718
Hand, 567-570
Handle, 185, 208
Happy, 665
Harvest, 345
Has, 890
Hat, 862
Having, 427, 891
He, 284-388
Head, 121-123
Health, 837
Hearing, 300, 337, 342, 778,
    864
Hearse, 788
Heart, 196-197
Heaven, 682
Heifer, 81
Here, 74, 419
Hidden, 164
Hindering, 73
Hills, 163
Hoe, 74
Hold, 340
Hole, 605
Honor, 598, 865
Hoping, 307, 403-404
Horse, 112-120
Hot, 227
House, 150-155
Human beings, 68
Hunger, 315, 373, 466-468, 667
Hunter, 157
Hurrying, 290, 706, 779
Hurt, 599, 960
I, 365, 865, 949, 983-984
Ice, 473
Ignorant, 636-637
Impede, 148
Impostor, 743
Impoverish, 770
Impulsion, 501
Incline, 196
Incommodious, 953

Index

About the Compiler

MARK GLAZER is Head of the Rio Grande Folklore Archive, and Professor of Anthropology and Associate Dean, College of Arts and Sciences, Pan American University. His earlier books include *High Points in Anthropology, Studies in Turkish Folklore,* and *Flour From Another Sack.* He has contributed widely to various scholarly journals.